D1368502

Studies in International Economics and Institutions

Hans-Jürgen Vosgerau (Ed.)

New Institutional Arrangements for the World Economy

With 26 Figures

Springer-Verlag
Berlin Heidelberg New York
London Paris Tokyo

Professor Dr. Hans-Jürgen Vosgerau
Universität Konstanz
Sonderforschungsbereich 178
Postfach 55 60
D-7750 Konstanz, FRG

ISBN 3-540-50480-X Springer-Verlag Berlin Heidelberg New York Tokyo
ISBN 0-387-50480-X Springer-Verlag New York Heidelberg Berlin Tokyo

Printing: Weihert-Druck GmbH, Darmstadt
Bookbinding: T. Gansert GmbH, Weinheim-Sulzbach
2142/7130-543210

Introduction to the Series

"Studies in International Economics and Institutions"

Many international economic problems arise from inadequate relations between economic transactions across national borders and the institutional framework within which they take place. To analyse the dynamic interdependencies between international transactions of various kinds and different international institutions is the aim of the Sonderforschungsbereich 178 "Internationalisierung der Wirtschaft" at the University of Konstanz, Germany, which has been supported by the Deutsche Forschungsgemeinschaft since 1986.

The present series is planned to include publications devoted to the analysis of topics outlined above. It is not restricted to results of the Sonderforschungsbereich 178. It will include monographs, conference proceedings and other collections from the areas of international economics - theoretical, empirical and applied. In particular, contributions to international public choice and international new-institutional economics are welcome. The series will also cover studies in international law, applying the emerging "law and economics" results to international economic problems.

The series is edited by the "Sprecher des Sonderforschungsbereichs 178" in cooperation with members of the Sonderforschungsbereich. An advisory board of consulting editors is being formed. At present it consists of John S. Chipman (Minneapolis, Minnesota, USA), Elhanan Helpman (Tel Aviv, Israel), Ronald W. Jones (Rochester, New York, USA) and Murray C. Kemp (Kensington, New South Wales, Australia).

TABLE OF CONTENTS

Introduction

New Institutional Arrangements for the World Economy

Hans-Jürgen Vosgerau, Konstanz

I.   The Problem

During the first days of July 1987 the newly established Sonderforschungsbereich 178 "Internationalisierung der Wirtschaft" held its first symposium in
Konstanz/Bodensee. "New Institutional Arrangements for the World Economy" were
discussed by a group of economists and lawyers working in the fields of international trade, international monetary economics, international finance, international
public choice, and international economic law. Cooperation between these areas of
research is an important condition for attaining the long-term aim of the
Sonderforschungsbereich, viz. analysis of the complex interdependencies between
international economic transactions of various kinds and international economy-
related institutions in a broad sense. The nature of these interdependencies seems to
be crucial for the world economy's further development. A better understanding of
their characteristics will be helpful for the solution of most imminent international
economic problems.

Four problem areas were especially addressed during the conference, each consisting of three or four contributions. The revised papers are presented in this
volume, each followed by a comment of the invited discussant, or by a summary of
the discussion. The last contribution is meant as a summary conclusion and has no
comment.

The four problem areas discussed were: (1) Exchange rate stabilization and economic policy coordination, (2) International financial markets and their regulation,
(3) Protectionism and the Uruguay GATT-round, and (4) The institutional framework for international production.

Studies in International Economics and Institutions
Vosgerau (Ed.) New Institutional Arrangements for the World Economy
© Springer-Verlag Berlin Heidelberg 1989

II.   An Overview of the Papers

(1) Exchange Rate Stabilization and Economic Policy Coordination

In the introductory paper Thomas *Willett* pleads for national reforms with the aim of adapting macroeconomic policies better to the needs of international stabilization. Sebastian *Edwards* presents an empirically founded analysis of the effect of floating exchange rates on the economic development of third world countries which he classifies as essentially negative. Manfred *Wegner* finally investigates reasons for the success - not anticipated by many observers - of the European Monetary System, which under the dominant influence of the Deutsche Bundesbank brought about a high degree of currency stability in Europe.

(2) International Financial Markets and their Regulation

National regulations still play an important rôle for financial markets. Kenneth *Scott* reports on the American system of bank regulations, a report which is extended to other countries by Karl *Kreuzer* in his comment. Recent financial innovations, which are analyzed by David *Folkerts-Landau*, are largely reactions to such regulations; their effects in various countries therefore differ depending on the national framework. One example of those innovations are debt-equity swaps conceived as a vehicle to transform problematic bank credits into direct investments mainly in South-American countries: Günter *Franke* presents a highly critical analysis of this subject. Finally, international financial services are related to bank regulations by Anthony *Saunders* and Ingo *Walter*.

(3) Protectionism and the New GATT-Round

International transactions of services play an important rôle in the Uruguay round. Herbert *Grubel* addresses the subject and denies the need for a new international institution, a GATT for services. His arguments are first, that services do not fundamentally differ from commodities and second, that the existing GATT mechanism is not suitable for efficient liberalization. Very critical comments on the real efficiency of present GATT rules were also offered by Arye *Hillman* and Michael *Finger*. Following the initial success of several tariff reductions, GATT since a decade or so increasingly suffers from the influence of pressure groups. Both authors demonstrate for the US how import-competing industries, by using legal possibilities, are able to avoid the need to adjust.

(4) The Institutional Framework for International Production

The organization of production involving several countries has undergone important changes during the last two decades in many sectors. Horst *Siebert* analyzes for the extraction of natural resources the transition from highly hierarchical organizations to complex systems of contracts binding together a variety of otherwise independent actors. Multinational enterprises on the other hand can gainfully exploit learning effects associated with production in various plants, if they efficiently coordinate those effects between their plant locations: this is demonstrated and analyzed by Eirik *Furubotn*. - International rules for the behaviour of international business are only timidly emerging and are still very weak. Nevertheless, Christian *Kirchner* argues that the "Restrictive Business Practices Code", an example of international soft law, has some effects on the behaviour of international actors in the field. - The volume is concluded by Carsten-Thomas *Ebenroth*'s analysis of the tensions between competing national jurisdictions and the processes of internationalization. Differences between national laws can be exploited by internationally active agents, forcing legislators to react, to adapt or to contemplate "New Institutional Arrangements for the World Economy".

III. Some Highlights of the Discussion

Every paper was followed by a lively discussion, which was introduced by an invited comment. Some arguments came up repeatedly, which suggests that they touched fundamental problems. Only these recurrent themes shall be briefly reported.

(1) The most important of these basic questions seemed to be the *relation between national and international institutions*. Again and again, the argument was advanced that in order to improve free international exchanges national obstacles should be removed, national institutions should be reformed. This applies to trade barriers as well as to inadequate monetary policies. The argument corresponds to a highly sceptical attitude vis-à-vis international organizations: GATT regarding commodity trade and the followers of Bretton Woods institutions regarding monetary matters.

Perhaps under hegemonial conditions international institutions could be satisfying: British rule until the First World War or American dominance after the Second. But meanwhile the economic weights have changed: the EEC has strengthened Europe, Japan and the Pacific Basin have emerged as a third centre, so the relative position of the US has weakened. Future developments in the USSR, in China and elsewhere may further modify this process of decentralization or at least regionalization. The task of coordination has become increasingly complex, and it remains controversial whether it can better be accomplished by organized international and supranational institutions or by competition between independent national institutions.

(2) A special aspect of the relations between national and international institutions concerns the effects of international influences upon national economic policy, notably the possibility of lobbies and *particular interest groups* to attain selfish aims: national authorities may use GATT-rules as a justification for denying protection to powerful industries. Unpopular stabilization measures may be sold to a reluctant short-sighted public by referring to relevant conditions imposed by the International Monetary Fund. International institutions in these cases fulfil the functions of a kind of precommitment by relatively weak national governments whose internal authority is thereby strengthened.

(3) When economic conditions are changing, existing institutions may become inadequate. The question then arises, in which way institutions should be adapted or *new* institutions *created*. There were many advocates of the opinion that institutional arrangements should be left free to develop as the needs in the markets demand it, and that their performance and thus their adequacy should be tested by competition. With respect to recent financial innovations this thesis seems to be

plausible. Although some regulating authorities are hesitating, competition for profitable banking and other financial activities forces them to accept a high degree of laissez-faire.

(4) Nevertheless there remains the question, within which *broader framework* institutional change should occur, the question of the constitutional characteristics of such framework. The answer evidently presupposes a theoretical justification for the decision to regulate some transactions, to deregulate others, nationally as well as internationally. In the last analysis external effects will play a crucial rôle here, because external effects of various kinds and the public goods characteristics of certain objects of transactions are the ultimate reasons for the existence of institutional rules which go beyond those familiar from competitive markets.

(5) The more actual present-day-problems were discussed, the easier explicative and normative aspects of the analysis got mixed up. Not only for methodological reasons, but also in the interest of mutual understanding it seems important to clearly distinguish different *levels of analysis*.

The economic explication of existing national and international institutions is on one level, the proposal to change a specific institution is on another. The latter has to take into account all the available knowledge of the consequences of such reforms and has to formulate a clear picture of the aims of any reform. These points were particularly emphasized by Eirik Furubotn, one of the pioneers of modern institutional economics.

(6) The critique of existing international economic institutions was sometimes very harsh during the conference. At the same time, many participants stressed the fact that after the Second World War there was a relatively high degree of success in coping with the problems of the world economy. Indeed, nobody could really imagine what would have happened without GATT or IMF. The assertion that a specific institution would need reform is in reality of limited value only, if the problem of political acceptance and realization is not solved. In this field there remain huge tasks for public choice, legal and economic analysis, some of which the Konstanzer Sonderforschungsbereich will address during the coming years.

IV.   Acknowledgements

Papers and comments included in this volume were revised by the authors. For efficient help with the editing tasks I am grateful to Christian Conrad. Hertha Kopp did a marvellous job typing and arranging diverse manuscripts and various floppy disks in their present form. The financial basis was provided by the Deutsche Forschungsgemeinschaft. Sincere thanks are extended to all of these.

I. Exchange Rate Stabilization

A Public Choice Analysis of Strategies
for Restoring International Economic Stability

Thomas D. Willett

I.   Introduction

By almost any measure the world economy over the past decade and a half has been disappointing. Thus the current concerns with the possible need for major reforms in our international institutional arrangements are quite understandable. However, it is argued in this paper that proposals for such reforms frequently are seriously defective because their authors have failed to consider adequately the types of political considerations emphasized in public choice analysis.

The analysis will focus on international monetary issues both because of their importance in their own right and because it has frequently been argued that deficiencies in the operation of the international monetary system have been a major cause of the increasing strains being faced by the international trade system. While one may still argue about the exact magnitude of the disruptive effects which international monetary instability has had on international trade and its contribution to the rise of protectionist pressures and the international debt crisis, that these effects have been important is certainly beyond serious question.[1]

---

[1]   As John Chipman notes in his comments on this paper I have not attempted to define international monetary instability explicitly. This is because there is no good single measure of instability. Even limiting the question to exchange rate instability, a number of statistical measures have been used. For example, different calculations have been presented based on such considerations as bilateral versus multilateral and real versus nominal exchange rates with several different measures being commonly used for both real and multilateral exchange rates. Furthermore, ex post measures of exchange rate volatility are not always good measures of ex ante uncertainty and instability, especially where official exchange market intervention and controls are prevalent. For recent discussions of the effects of exchange rate instability on international trade and protectionist pressures see Bergsten and Williamson (1983), Dornbusch and Frenkel (1987), Feigenbaum and Willett (1985), IMF (1984a), McCulloch (1987), and Willett (1986).

Studies in International Economics and Institutions
Vosgerau (Ed.) New Institutional Arrangements for the World Economy
© Springer-Verlag Berlin Heidelberg 1989

What is at issue is the cause(s) of international monetary instability and what can be done to reduce this instability. These, of course, have been widely debated topics in recent years.[2] Two fundamentally opposing views have come to dominate these discussions. One is that the observed exchange rate volatility and international monetary instability has been due primarily not to defects of the current floating exchange rate system itself, but rather to underlying instabilities. From this perspective what is needed is better national economic policies and improved luck with respect to external shocks such as the OPEC disruptions. With more stable underlying conditions floating rates will provide a reasonably stable international monetary environment. Furthermore, in the absence of more stable underlying conditions floating rates provide an essential shock absorber which, while not reducing the international transmission of instability as much as many advocates had initially anticipated, still is the most effective damage control mechanism available.

At the other extreme is the view that defects in the operation of our flexible rate system itself have been a substantial contributor to the observed international monetary instability. Therefore, major international monetary reform is essential. We may distinguish two (not mutually exclusive) variants of this view. One focuses on perceived technical inefficiencies in the operation of flexible exchange rates. Destabilizing speculation and international currency substitution are the most frequently emphasized causes. The second variant goes beyond technical economic considerations and sees the loss of financial discipline generated by the breakdown of the Bretton Woods system as a major cause of recent instability. Both variants point to the need for new international agreements on exchange rates in order to restore stability. Some advocate the need to return all the way to fixed exchange rates while others would settle for or prefer a somewhat more flexible system of

---

2   For examples of recent assessments see Aliber (1987), Arndt, Sweeney and Willett (1985), Bigman and Taya (1983), Bilson and Marston (1984), Dreyer, Haberler, and Willett (1982), IMF (1984b, and 1984c), Frankel (1987), and von Furstenberg (1983).

target zones for exchange rates.[3] Both groups, however, see direct agreements to impose greater exchange rate stability (fixity) as essential to, rather than as following from, the creation of greater domestic monetary stability in the major industrial countries.

I shall argue that neither of the two major contending points of view offers a fully satisfactory basis for generating global monetary stability. In my judgment the available empirical evidence more strongly supports the first view with respect to the causes of exchange rate instability, but this leaves open the question of how we can hope to generate more stable underlying conditions. It will be argued that we have little basis for optimism that substantial improvements in domestic economic policy making and international policy coordination will come about naturally. Thus, there is a need for fundamental institutional reforms to reduce macroeconomic instability.[4] However, while possibly useful for some particular countries, internationally-oriented reforms in the exchange rate system are unlikely to provide effective or efficient forms of discipline for most industrial countries. Consequently, I conclude that while efforts to improve the operation of our international monetary institutions are well worthwhile, the surest way to create greater international monetary stability over the long run is for the major industrial countries to adopt domestic institutional reforms to limit the range of fluctuations of their monetary and fiscal policies.

---

[3] For recent discussions and critical analysis of the major variants of the target zone approach, see Cooper (1986b), Dornbusch (1986), Frenkel and Goldstein (1986), and Williamson (1986, and 1987). One of the most forceful recent advocates of a return to fixed rates with coordinated monetary policies among the major industrial countries has been Ronald McKinnon (1982, 1984, and 1985). Advocates of target zones and a return to fixed rates differ considerably in their views on the effectiveness of sterilized intervention in the foreign-exchange market, i.e., official intervention which does not influence the domestic money supply. On this issue see the discussion and references in Kenen (1987).

[4] While the need to adopt domestic reforms to provide monetary discipline has long been a part of Milton Friedman's advocacy of flexible exchange rates, such considerations have frequently been ignored by advocates of flexible rates. For an important recent exception see Genberg and Swoboda (1987) and for earlier discussions of the views of the German council of Economic Experts who advocated such an approach see Gutowski (1977, and 1978).

II. Issues Raised by the Public Choice Perspective

While it has become common for economists to distinguish between positive and normative economic analysis, we really need to divide discussions of economic policy issues into three major categories. One is the selection or determination of policy objectives. It is this aspect which is normally considered to distinguish normative from positive economic analysis. The second category concerns analysis of the best technical means of achieving these policy objectives. For example, will an interest rate or a money growth rule provide a more stable growth in aggregate demand? This is standard positive economic analysis. According to the standard optimal economic policy framework which has been widely used by economists this two-stage breakdown gives us the basic elements of policy analysis.[5] There has been considerable difference of opinion expressed about the relative importance of positive versus normative considerations as causes of differences in economists' policy recommendations and the extent to which individuals' normative views tend to influence their positive analysis, but traditionally most policy analysis has been limited to this range of considerations.[5]

The public choice or political economy approach introduces a third important set of considerations - the role of the operation of the policy process in aggregating the preferences of individuals into the decision making process on public policy

---

[5] Some of this controversy over the role of differences in values or objectives can be clarified by distinguishing between the signs attached to different considerations in individuals' utility functions, for example, is inflation perceived as a good or bad, and the tradeoffs among various goods. Even when there is relatively little disagreement about the former, there can still be considerable disagreement about the latter. Thus, in my experience, differences in the weights attached to objectives have been an important source of policy disagreements. For contrasting views of the importance of differences in objectives versus positive technical analysis in international monetary debates see Cohen (1977) and Cooper (1975).

issues.[6] This question, in turn, has both positive and normative aspects - how does any particular set of institutional arrangements actually operate and what norms for aggregation are viewed as desirable.

Failure to clearly distinguish among these different facets of policy analysis has often generated unnecessary confusion in discussions of issues such as whether it was desirable or undesirable for international monetary arrangements to influence domestic monetary policy. Those advocating such influence tended to describe it as balance of payments discipline, while those who wish to avoid such influence have tended to refer to the need to remove balance of payments constraints over domestic policies.[7] Such issues cannot be discussed productively within the traditional two-stage optimal economic policy framework because discipline is neither an ultimate policy objective nor a positive policy strategy.

Underlying differences on this issue were often unstated or little analyzed views on how political processes operated. Those who saw a need for international monetary arrangements to provide domestic financial discipline implicitly or explicitly, viewed domestic policy making processes as operating in ways which generated serious biases toward the overexpansion of aggregate demand and consequent inflation. While often asserted as a self-evident proposition, this is, in fact, far from the case. Once one recognizes the public choice distinctions between the desirability of particular policy outcomes and the desirability of particular decision-making processes, then observing that inflation is greater than one's own personal preference

---

[6]   In Willett (1983) I attempt to contrast optimal policy and political economy approaches to analyzing international monetary issues. In this paper I use public choice and political economy approaches in a broad sense to include the main variants of non-Marxist approaches to political economy. For more detailed characterizations of the public choice approach to international economic issues, see Frey (1984, and 1985), Tollison and Willett (1982), Vaubel (1986), and Willett (1980). For examples of authors who stress the need to take a political economy perspective but who would probably not identify themselves with the public choice school, see Cooper (1975), Cohen (1977) and Odell (1982). On the differences between the traditional theory of economic policy and constitutional political economy approaches, see also the discussion by Buchanan (1987).

[7]   For recent discussions of and reference to the discipline debate see Cooper (1986a) and Willett and Mullen (1982).

is not a sound basis for attempting to impose constraints on the operation of the policy process.

Of course even ignoring issues of operationality, there is no universally-accepted criterion for how preferences should be aggregated. For example, because of the possibility of rational ignorance emphasized in public choice analysis, the widely-used median-voter criteria may yield results quite different from those of the informed median-voter model.[8] (It is, in fact, this difference that drives the pioneering political business cycle model of Nordhaus [1975]). Furthermore, even if uniformly good information is held by all decision makers, one may wish to take differences in intensities of preference into account.[9] Despite such disagreements about what norms should be used, few I suspect, would favor the criterion that one particular economist's preferences should serve as the appropriate social norm. Thus, it behooves those advocating the adoption or continuation of institutional arrangements which would constrain the operation of the policy process to present arguments not just that recent policy outcomes have been bad, but that this has been due to a significant degree to problems with the way in which the policy process operates.

My own studies of the operation of the influences on macro economic policy making in the industrial countries in the post-war period and my reading of the available literature on this subject have convinced me that there are serious biases at work which do tend to contribute to the generation of macro economic insta-bility and inflation.[10] In my own view, it is the differences in the short run and longer run relationships among inflation, interest rates, and output combined with

---

[8]   On the implications of different public choice models for macroeconmic pressures see Willett and Banaian (forthcoming).

[9]   See, for example, the discussion and references in Mueller, Tollison, and Willett (1976).

[10]   See Willett (forthcoming). For other recent analysis and references to the literature on political influences on macroeconmic policies see Buchanan and Wagner (1977), Hibbs (1987), Hibbs and Fassbender (1981), Hirsch and Goldthorpe (1978), Frey and Schneider (1985), and Toma and Toma (1986). For a collection of studies which generally argue (unconvincingly in my judgment) against the view that there have been significant biases, see Lindberg and Maier (1985).

the shortness of the effective time horizon which tends to dominate government decision making in these areas which are the primary causes of this bias. Unless they are perfectly anticipated, expansionary policies will have most of their favorable effects on output and interest rates in the short run with most of the undesirable effects on inflation coming later. Conversely with contractionary policies, the costs in terms of higher interest rates and unemployment tend to come first while the benefits of reduced inflation tend to develop more slowly. Their concerns with short-term employment, output, and interest rate effects give governments incentives both to initiate and validate disturbances to a greater degree than is desirable from a longer run perspective.

The recent ability of both President Reagan and Prime Minister Thatcher to follow sustained anti-inflation policies without being thrown out of office by the voters suggests that there are limits to the tolerance for inflation in the industrial countries. In my judgment these policy experiences are not sufficient basis for confidence that enough learning behavior has occurred to eliminate the recurrence of serious inflationary biases in the future. It must be acknowledged, however, that there is far from a consensus about the relative importance of the causes of such biases and many Keynesians and rational expectations economists and political liberals sharply dispute that there has been a significant systematic bias at all. While accepting that it is not a view which all reasonable people would accept at the present time, the remainder of this paper will be based on the assumption that it is desirable to attempt to impose a greater degree of discipline over monetary and fiscal policy making in the major industrial countries.

III.   Evaluating Strategies for Creating Monetary Discipline:
        International Versus Domestic Approaches

It is interesting to note that even some leading Keynesian-oriented economists such as John Williamson now believe that we need institutional reform to promote greater discipline over macro economic policies. Williamson (1986) has, in fact, presented as a major aspect of his advocacy of a system of internationally-agreed target zones for exchange rates among the major industrial countries its hoped-for effects on discipline.[11]

As James Buchanan (1983) has suggested, it is useful to separate discussions of the need for major institutional reforms to exert greater discipline from the analysis of particular proposals. Concentration on the latter by advocates of reform runs the danger of undermining efforts to develop a consensus on the need for reform. On the other hand, I believe that it would be a mistake to delay substantive evaluation of alternative proposals until a consensus on the need for major reform had developed. For one thing, particular proposals may become hot on the agenda of official policy discussions and thus force a need for short-term policy analysis. The current official interest by a number of countries in systems of target zones for exchange rates is an example.

A second point is that while some may become convinced that there are, in fact, serious difficulties with the current largely discretionary monetary systems they see even greater problems with the best known types of proposals for reform. In my own case, despite my belief that there are substantial difficulties with our current system, I doubt that I would vote for a return to a gold standard if that were the only alternative. The increased variability of velocity in the United States and other major countries in recent years has lead some prominent monetarists to abandon their support for simple Friedman-type monetary rules (see, for example, Laidler [1981]), and certainly has not helped convert more Keynesian-oriented economists to this approach. Thus, there is an important need to investigate the possibilities of developing a broader set of possible institutional reforms than have been prominent in previous discussions of reform. Following Buchanan's warning, however, we should be careful to make clear the purpose of each particular discussion.

In judging specific proposals, it is important to attempt to clearly distinguish between two different aspects of effectiveness. One is the desirability of the out-

---

[11] Perhaps in part in response to the criticisms of this analysis by Branson (1986), Cooper (1986b), and Dornbusch (1986), Williamson (1987) appears to have modified somewhat his optmism that exchange rate targets would substantially constrain national fiscal policies. For additional discussion of possible effects of the international monetary system on fiscal discipline see Laidler (1987).

comes generated by the rules of the reform. Thus, for example, requiring a steady growth in the monetary base would do little to promote stability if there is tremendous volatility in the money multiplier and velocity. On this aspect of the question, traditional economic analysis is of tremendous importance. We know, for example, from the literature on the theory of optimal currency areas and open economy macro that the effects of fixed versus flexible exchange rates on a country's macroeconomic stability will be heavily influenced both by the structure and openness of the economy in question and by the types of disturbances that it faces.[12] In a world with no economic and financial disturbances, any type of monetary rule would work equally well. Particular narrow rules are based on assumptions about the relative stability of some types of relationships relative to others. For example, stability in the aggregate demand and supply of gold and constancy of real exchange rates combined with instability in national demand for money functions would imply that a gold standard would yield a stable growth of aggregate demand while a national monetary rule would not. On the other hand, stability in national demands for money combined with variability in equilibrium real exchange rates would cause a simple money supply rule to generate a stable growth in aggregate demand while a rule based on maintaining fixed exchange rates would be destabilizing.

The second aspect of effectiveness is enforceability - how much effect on desired actual behavior the proposed reform is likely to have. Analysis of this dimension should include consideration of the incentives created for actors to pay attention to the dictates of the reform and the extent to which behavior can be altered to circumvent the intentions of the reform. Thus, for example, a reform which merely passed a sense of the legislature condemning inflation and unemployment would be unlikely to substantially effect behavior over the longer run. Likewise, a reform which mandated a balanced budget or a fixed rate of monetary growth would be unlikely to be very effective if there were little discouragement to taking financing

---

[12]   See, for example, the contributions in Arndt, Sweeney, and Willett (1985), Bhandari (1985) and Bilson and Marston (1984). For recent non-technical discussions of these issues see Cooper (1986) and Willett (1985).

off the monetary authorities.[13] And even a strong form of the gold standard would do little if it were abandoned every time there were a crisis.

Likewise, when Ronald McKinnon (1982, 1984, and 1985) presents his proposal for fixed exchange rates and monetary coordination for Germany, Japan, and the United States, he invariably gives illustrations of how his system would work in terms of disturbances such as international currency substitution for which most economic models suggest fixed exchange rates would be part of the optimal discretionary economic policy response. The problem is that the available empirical research suggests overwhelmingly that these are not the only major types of disturbances with which the system must cope. Indeed, for the United States the most recent research suggests that these disturbances do not appear to have been very important quantitatively, much less dominant.[14]

The available empirical evidence similarly fails to support the view that destabilizing speculation has been a major cause of the observed volatility of exchange rates among the major countries.[15] It is true that empirical exchange-rate models have been found to have little short-term predictive power and a number of studies have found evidence suggesting that the foreign exchange markets do not behave with ideal speculative efficiency. Although the evidence is mixed, it is quite possible that bandwagon effects or speculative bubbles (the preferred terminology of rational expectations modelers), may at times push particular exchange rates too high or too low, but the general course of most major exchange-rate movements can be quite plausibly explained in terms of underlying economic and financial developments. This is certainly true of the fall of the dollar under President Carter and the subsequent rise under President Reagan. Thus, in my judg-

---

[13] For a fascinating discussion of how state governments have gotten around prohibitions on deficit financing see Bennett and DiLorenzo (1984).

[14] For analysis and references to this empirical literature see Arndt, Sweeney and Willett (1985), McKinnon (1984), Willett (1985), and Willett et al. (forthcoming).

[15] For recent analysis of speculation and exchange rate behavior see the contributions and references in Arndt, Sweeney, and Willett (1985), Bhandari and Putnam (1983), Bigman and Taya (1983), Bilson and Marston (1984), Frankel and Froot (1987), Frenkel (1983), Jones and Kenen (1985), and Kansas City Federal Reserve Bank (1985).

ment, neither of the two rationales - the avoidance of speculative excesses nor of optimal policy responses to disturbances - presents a strong case for a return to a generalized system of fixed exchange rates among the major industrial countries.

Consider, for example, the case of the strong dollar caused by the huge U.S. budget deficits. The maintenance of fixed exchange rates would have forced a massive substantial monetary expansion in the United States and a huge contraction abroad. Neither would have been desirable. More likely, they probably would have generated the widespread adoption of capital controls and/or the abandonment of the fixed-rate system.

Of course, one can paint a more desirable scenario, as has John Williamson (1986), in which the pressures of the exchange rate against its target level would force a reduction in the U.S. budget deficit. There is little basis for expecting that exchange rate reforms would induce such behavior, however. In the first place, it would be technically undesirable even if politically feasible to construct a rule for fiscal policy based on exchange-rate movements. Not only are exchange-rate movements influenced by many other considerations, but even the direction of the relationships between budget deficits and exchange rates or balance-of-payments pressures is not the same across the major industrial countries, nor is it always the same for each country over time. On technical grounds, the best that could be hoped for would be the type of rule that requires domestic macropolicy adjustments in the direction of restoring payments equilibrium. In the absence of domestic institutional reforms, the same types of political pressures which generated the budget deficit in the first place would dictate that typically most of the required adjustments would fall on monetary policy.

Furthermore, in the absence of explicit agreements on money supply behavior over and above exchange-rate obligations, there is a substantial likelihood that for large economies the effects of payments imbalances on domestic money supplies would be largely sterilized.[16] There is still a rather widespread belief spurred by the escalation of world-wide inflation in the 1970s that the Bretton Woods pegged rate

---

[16] On the substantial degree of sterilization by the industrial countries under the Bretton Woods system see the analysis and references in Darby, et al. (1983) and Laney and Willett (1982).

system did provide some "nominal anchor for the world monetary system" (Barro, 1982, p. 185). Systematic empirical research, however, finds no restraining influences at all of U.S. gold losses or payments deficits on the behavior of the U.S. money supply in the post-war period.[17] Furthermore, as several authors have argued (see Rogoff, 1985; Vaubel, 1987; and Willett and Mullen, 1982), in the absence of separate provisions for monetary control, the short-run pegging of exchange rates can increase the incentives for politically-motivated overexpansion of the economy.

If, in fact, a fixed exchange-rate system can only be assured of providing effective financial discipline if it is coupled with additional agreements on monetary behavior, then one must ask shouldn't priority be given to adopting such agreements on monetary restraint directly.

IV.   Taking a Constraint Instead of Policy Rule Approach

In a world in which there are many different types of disturbances, it is not possible to develop a relatively simple policy rule which will closely approximate optimal discretionary policy responses. Where the demand for money and equilibrium real exchange rates are both highly variable, neither fixed exchange rates nor fixed national money supply growth rules will work well. In such a world how can we impose desirable against excessive inflationary tendencies induced by political considerations without at the same time frequently forcing the monetary authorities to take destabilizing policy actions?

The basic answer lies in shifting emphasis from attempting to impose a particular policy rule to eliminate discretion and instead focusing on the design of a system of constraints which would limit the ability of governments to maintain a sustained

---

[17]   See Darby (1983) and Briggs, et al. (forthcoming).

bias over time.[18] In this latter approach, the monetary constraint system would be defined in terms of outcome variables such as the price level or average rate of growth of nominal income. As long as the outcomes remained within the average values established by the constraint, the authorities would have freedom to follow discretionary policies as they saw fit.

If outcomes violated the constraints then direct limits on the rate of growth of a monetary variable such as the base would be imposed until outcomes were brought back within the constraints. Within this framework, exchange rate developments might often give useful signals to the monetary authorities without forcing automatic adjustments. If the outcome variables trended increasingly close to one of the boundaries of the constraint set, however, then the authorities would have increasing incentives to lean harder against this trend if they want to maintain their scope for future discretion. In this way the existence of the constraint set could exert a continuous but non-rigid influence on the behavior of the monetary authorities.

This general approach leaves open such important issues as the best ways to define outcome and control variables and the stringency of the constraints. In the spirit of Buchanan's plea to not let details stand in the way of developing a basic consensus, I shall omit further discussion here of my own favorite particulars for the specifics of such proposals, especially as my views on these are available elsewhere.

An important advantage of the national constraint approach is that it offers a far better basis for working out compromises among different schools of economic thought than do the traditional approaches. For example, Keynesians and monetarists can debate over the width of the constraints and perhaps stand a fair chance of ultimately reaching a compromise acceptable to a substantial majority, a feature particularly important for constitutional type reforms. By contrast, how would one go about trying to split the difference between economists wanting a fixed exchange rate and those wanting a fixed specific money supply growth rate?

---

[18] For recent examples of different possible types of domestically-oriented constraint systems see Christ (1983), Leijonhufvud (1984), Mayer and Willett (forthcoming), Niehans (1978) and Weintraub (1983). I have offered a proposal of my own in Willett (1986).

Such a domestically based monetary reform would undoubtedly be more difficult to achieve than would the adoption of an exchange rate rule. It would also be likely to be much more durable, however. The experience of the European Monetary System with pegged exchange rates in the last few years has shown the exchange rate oriented approach to have more scope for exerting discipline than I would have anticipated, but it has proved to be far from a durable constitutional type reform.[19] For smaller, more open economies there would be no reason to preclude EMS-type exchange rate arrangements as a complement to the domestic based approach advocated here, but this or other exchange-rate based approaches such as the target zone approach cannot form the basis for a durable general system of discipline for large countries.[20] Without the adoption of sustained disciplined macroeconomic policies by the United States, the achievement of a satisfactory degree of international monetary stability is impossible.

The desirability of adopting national limitations on the size of budget deficits is perhaps even clearer. In this case I suspect that direct limitation on the permissible size of deficits combined with a provision for some degree of overrides by a high majority vote may be the best form of constraint system to adopt, but there are numerous considerations involved which require both careful technical economic and political economy analysis.[21]

V.   Concluding Remarks

Exchange rate-oriented reforms may have merits for some particular countries, but the most productive emphasis for debate on institutional reforms for the major

---

[19] On the recent experience with the EMS see Ungerer, Evans, and Nyberg (1983) and Wegner (1985). For a critical evaluation of the initial political motivations for the EMS see Vaubel (1986).

[20] As is emphasized in the theory of optimal currency areas (see, for example, Tower and Willett [1976] and Willett [1985]), the case for a fixed exchange rate becomes stronger, ceteris paribus, the smaller and more open is the economy in question.

[21] For recent analysis and references to the literature on proposals for budget limitations, see Buchanan, Rowley and Tollison (1987).

industrial countries should focus on domestically-oriented reforms to limit the allowable range of variability in national monetary and fiscal policies. The same type of public choice analysis which leads me to advocate this approach would also force me to predict that there is not a high probability of this strategy being adopted.[22] I am convinced that it is important to attempt to focus attention on the harder to achieve, but potentially highly-productive types of reforms, rather than simply concentrating on short-term strategies of greater exchange-rate and international policy coordination.

One of the most productive outlets for international cooperation over the next few years might be the mutual exploration of such monetary and fiscal issues by national governments and the staffs of the major international organizations such as the IMF and OECD. There are, of course, a number of non-trivial international financial issues such as the handling of the developing country debt crisis, which require the attention of international officials. There may be scope for improving our international trade institutions, for example, through the strengthening of the GATT despite settlement mechanisms and continuation of the economic summits should prove helpful in maintaining the resolve of our political leaders to fight the most blatant of domestic protectionist pressures. Likewise, continued efforts to strengthen the IMF's international surveillance process may be well worthwhile. Still, in the area of macroeconomics and exchange rate policy, I believe that a coordinated attack on the issues of designing and implementing national constraint systems to limit the variability of monetary and fiscal policies would contribute much more toward improving international monetary stability than would the continued discussion of short run fine tuning that has tended to dominate international discussions in the past. Indeed, within a widely adopted system of national constraints, the stabilized expectations which should be generated could substantially increase the scope for effective short-run discretionary international policy coordination.

---

[22] For an interesting discussion of the conditions under which new monetary constitutions have been adopted historically, see Bernholz (1987).

References

Aliber, Robert Z. (ed.), (1987), *The Reconstruction of International Monetary Arrangements,* St. Martin's Press, New York, N.Y.

Amacher, Ryan, Robert D. Tollison and Thomas D. Willet (eds.), (1976), *Economic Approaches to Public Policy*, Cornell University Press, Ithaca, N.Y.

Arndt, Sven, Richard J. Sweeney and Thomas D. Willett (1985), *Exchange Rates, Trade, and the U.S. Economy*, Ballinger Press for the American Enterprise Institute for Public Policy Research, Cambridge, MA.

Barro, Robert (1982), "United States Inflation and the Choice of Monetary Standard", in Hall, Robert (ed.), *Inflation, Causes and Effects*, University of Chicago Press, Chicago, Il., p. 105.

Bennett, James T. and Thomas J. DiLorenzo, (1984), "Political Entrepreneurships and Reform of the Rent Seeking Society", in Collander, David C. (ed.), *Neo Classical Political Economy*, Ballinger Press, Cambridge, MA., pp. 217-228.

Bergsten, C. Fred and John Williamson (1983), "Exchange Rates and Trade Policy", in Cline, William R. (ed.), *Trade Policy in the 1980s*, MIT Press for the Institute for International Economics, Cambridge, MA.

Bernholz, Peter (1987), "The Implementation and Maintenance of a Monetary Constitution", in Dorn, James A. and Anna J. Schwartz, *The Search for Stable Money*, University of Chicago Press, Chicago, Il., pp. 83-118.

Bhandari, Jagdeep S. (ed.), (1987), *Exchange Rate Management Under Uncertainty*, MIT Press, Cambridge, MA.

Bhandari, Jagdeep S. and Bluford Putnam (eds.), (1983), *Economic Interdependence and Flexible Exchange Rates*, MIT Press, Cambridge, MA.

Bigman, D. and T. Taya (eds.), (1983), *Exchange Rate and Trade Instability: Causes, Consequences, and Remedies*, Ballinger Press, Cambridge, MA.

Bilson, J. and R. Marston (eds.), (1984), *Exchange Rate Theory and Practice*, University of Chicago Press, Chicago, Il.

Branson, William H. (1986), "The Limits of Monetary Coordination as Exchange Rate Policy", *Brookings Papers on Economic Activity* 1, pp. 175-194.

Briggs, John, D.B. Christenson, Pamela Martin and Thomas D. Willett, "The Decline of Gold as a Source of Monetary Discipline", in Willett, Thomas D., forthcoming.

Buchanan, James M. (Spring 1983),"Rules vs. Discretion in Monetary Policy: Comment", *CATO Journal* 3, pp. 143-145.

Buchanan, James M. (1987), "Comment: Constitutional Strategy and the Monetary Regime", in Dorn, James A. and Anna J. Schwartz, *The Search for Stable Money*, University of Chicago Press, Chicago, Il., pp. 119-128.

Buchanan, James M. and Richard E. Wagner (1977), *Democracy in Deficit: The Political Legacy of Lord Keynes*, Academic Press, New York, N.Y.

Buchanan, James M., Charles K. Rowley and Robert D. Tollison (eds.), (1987), *Deficits*, Basil Blackwell, Oxford.

Campbell, Colin D. and William K. Dougan (eds.), (1986), *Alternative Monetary Regimes*, The Johns Hopkins University Press, Baltimore, MD.

Christ, Carl (Spring 1983), "Rules vs. Discretion in Monetary Policy", *CATO Journal* 3, pp. 121-141.

Cohen, Benjamin J. (1977), *Organizing the World's Money: The Political Economy of International Monetary Relations*, Basic Books, New York, N.Y.

Cooper, Richard N. (1975), "Prolegomena to the Choice of an International Monetary System", in Bergsten, C.F. and Lawrence Krause (eds.), *World Politics and International Economics* The Brookings Institute, Washington, D.C.

Cooper, Richard N. (1986a), "A Monetary System Based on Fixed Exchange Rates", in Campbell and Dougan, pp. 85-109.

Cooper, Richard N. (1986b), "Dealing With the Trade Deficit in a Floating Rate System", *Brookings Papers on Economic Activity* 1, pp. 195-207.

Darby, Michael (1983), "The United States as an Exogeneous Source of World Inflation Under the Bretton Woods System", in Darby, Michael, et al. (eds.), *The International Transmission of Inflation*, National Bureau of Economic Research, University of Chicago Press, Chicago, Il., pp. 478-490.

Darby, Michael, A.E. Gandolfi Lothian, A.J. Schwartz and A.C. Stockman (eds.), (1983), *The International Transmission of Inflation*, National Bureau of Economic Research, University of Chicago Press, Chicago, Il.

Dorn, James A. and Anna Schwartz (eds.), (1987), *The Search for Stable Money*, University of Chicago Press, Chicago, Il.

Dornbusch, Rudiger (1986), "Flexible Exchange Rates and Excess Capital Mobility", *Brookings Papers on Economic Activity*, 1, pp. 209-226.

Dornbusch, Rudiger and Jeffrey S. Frenkel (1987), "Macroeconomics and Protection", in Stern, Robert M., *U.S. Trade Policies in a Changing World Economy*, MIT Press, Cambridge, MA., pp. 77-130.

Dreyer, Jacob, Gottfried Haberler and Thomas D. Willett (eds.), (1982), *The International Monetary System*, American Enterprise Institute for Public Policy Research, Cambridge, MA.

Federal Reserve Bank of Kansas City (1985), *The U.S. Dollar - Recent Developments, Outlook, and Policy Options*, Federal Reserve Bank, Kansas City, MO.

Feigenbaum, Susan and Thomas D. Willett, (1985), "Domestic versus International Influences on Protectionist Pressure in the United States", in Arndt, Sven W., Richard J. Sweeney and Thomas D. Willett (eds.), *Exchange Rates, Trade, and the U.S. Economy*, American Enterprise Institute for Public Policy Research, Washington, D.C.

Frankel, Jacob A. (ed.), (1983), *Exchange Rates and International Macroeconomics*, University of Chicago Press, Chicago, Il.

Frankel, Jacob A. and Morris Goldstein (1986), "A Guide to Target Zones", International Monetary Fund *Staff Papers* 33, No. 4 (December), pp. 633-673.

Frankel, Jacob A. (1987), "The International Monetary System: Should it be Reformed?" *American Economic Review* 77, No. 2 (May), pp. 205-210.

Frenkel, Jeffrey A. and K.A. Froot (1987), "Using Survey Data to Test Standard Propositions Regarding Exchange Rate Expectations", *American Economic Review*, (March), pp. 133-153.

Frenkel, Jeffrey A. and Richard Meese (1987), "Are Exchange Rates Excessively Variable?" National Bureau of Economic Research Working Paper (April).

Frey, Bruno S. (1984a), *International Political Economics*, Basil Blackwell, Oxford.

Frey, Bruno S., (1984b), "The Public Choice View of International Political Economy", *International Organization* 38 , pp. 199-223.

Frey, Bruno S., and Friedrich Schneider (1985), "On the Modelling of Politico-economic Interdependence", *European Journal of Political Research* 3, No. 4, pp. 339-360.

Furstenberg, George M. von (ed.),(1983), *International Money and Credit: The Policy Roles*, International Monetary Fund, Washington, D.C.

Genberg, Hans and Alexander K. Swoboda (1987), "Fixed Exchange Rates, Flexible Exchange Rates, or the Middle of the Road: A Reexamination of the Arguments in View of Recent Experience", in Aliber, Robert Z., *The Reconstruction of International Monetary Arrangements*, St. Martin's Press, New York, N.Y., pp. 92-116.

Grubel, Herbert G. (1987), "The Evolving International Monetary System: Past Plans and Optimality", in Aliber, Robert Z., *The Reconstruction of International Monetary Arrangements*, St. Martin's Press, New York, N.Y., pp. 1-20.

Gutowski, Armin (1978), "International Guidelines and Principles for National Financial and Exchange Rate Policies: Discussion", in Dreyer, Jacob, Gottfried Haberler and Thomas D. Willett, *Exchange Rate Flexibility*, American Enterprise Institute for Public Policy Research, Washington, D.C., pp. 197-200.

Gutowski, Armin, "Commentary", in Katz, Samuel I. (1979), *U.S.-European Monetary Relations*, American Enterprise Institute for Public Policy Research, Washington, D.C., pp. 70-74.

Hibbs, Douglas A., Jr. (1987), *The Political Economy of Industrial Democracies*, Harvard University Press, Cambridge, MA.

Hibbs, Douglas A., Jr.(1981), and Heino Fassbender, *Contemporary Political Economy*, North Holland, Amsterdam, pp. 231-248.

Hirsch, Fred, and John Goldthorpe (eds.), (1978), *The Political Economy of Inflation*, Harvard University Press, Cambridge, MA.

International Monetary Fund (1984a),"Exchange Rate Volatility and World Trade", Occasional Paper No. 28 (July), International Monetary Fund, Washington, D.C.

International Monetary Fund (1984b), "Issues in the Assessment of the Exchange Rates of Industrial Countries", Occasional Paper No. 29 (July), International Monetary Fund, Washington, D.C.

International Monetary Fund (1984c), "The Exchange Rate System: Lessons of the Past and Options for the Future", Occasional Paper No. 30 (July), International Monetary Fund, Washington, D.C.

Jones, Ronald W., and Peter B. Kenen, (eds.), (1985), *Handbook of International Economics*, Vol. 2, North-Holland, Amsterdam.

Kenen, Peter B. (1987), "Exchange Rate Management: What Role for Intervention?" *American Economic Review* No. 2 (May), pp. 194-199.

Laidler, David (1981), "Monetarism: An Interpretation", *Economic Journal* 91 (March), pp. 1-29.

Laidler, David (1987), "International Monetary Institutions and Deficits", in Buchanan, Rowley, and Tollison, pp. 338-357.

Laney, Leroy R., and Thomas D. Willett (1982), "The International Liquidity Explosion and Worldwide Inflation: The Evidence from Sterilization Coefficient Estimates", *Journal of International Money and Finance* (August), pp. 141-152.

Leijonhufvud, Axel (1984), "Constitutional Constraints on the Monetary Powers of Government", in McKenzie, Richard B. (ed.), *Constitutional Economics: Containing the Economic Powers of Government*, Lexington Books, Lexington, MA., pp. 95-107.

Lindberg, Leon N. and Charles S. Maier (1985), *The Politics of Inflation and Economic Stagnation*, The Brookings Institution, Washington, D.C.

McCulloch, Rachel (1987), "Unexpected Real Consequences of Floating Exchange Rates", in Aliber, Robert Z., *The Reconstruction of International Monetary Arrangements*, St. Martin's Press, New York, N.Y. , pp. 21-45.

McKinnon, Ronald I. (1982), "Currency Substitution and Instability in the World Dollar Standard", *American Economic Review* (June), pp. 320-333.

McKinnon, Ronald I. (1984), *An International Standard for Monetary Stabilization*, Institute for International Economics, Washington, D.C.

McKinnon, Ronald I. (Fall 1985), "The Dollar Exchange Rate as a Leading Indicator for American Monetary Policy", *Academic Conference Volume*, San Francisco Federal Reserve Bank, pp. 161-206.

McKinnon, Ronald I., Christopher Radcliffe, K.-Y. Tan, Arthur Warga and Thomas D. Willett (1984), "International Influences on the U.S. Economy: Summary of an Exchange", *American Economic Review* (December), pp. 1132-1134.

Magee, Stephen P. and Leslie Young (1987), "Endogeneous Protection in the United States, 1980-1984", in Robert M. Stern, *U.S. Trade Policies in a Changing World Economy*, MIT Press, Cambridge, MA., pp. 145-195.

Mayer, Thomas and Thomas Willett, "Evaluating Proposals for Fundamental Monetary Reform", in Willett (forthcoming).

Mueller, Dennis C., Robert D. Tollison, and Thomas D. Willett (1986), "Solving the Intensity Problem in Representative Democracy", in Amacher, Ryan C., Robert D. Tollison and Thomas D. Willett, (eds.), *The Economic Approach to Public Policy*, Cornell University Press, Ithaca, N.Y., pp. 444-473.

Niehans, Jurg, (1978), *The Theory of Money*, The Johns Hopkins University Press, Baltimore, MD.

Nordhaus, William (1975), "The Political Business Cycle", *Review of Economic Studies* 42, No. 2 (April), pp. 169-190.

Odell, John (1982), *U.S. International Monetary Policy*, Princeton University Press, Princeton, N.J.

Rogoff, K. (1985), "Can International Monetary Policy Cooperation be Counterproductive?" *Journal of International Economics* 18, pp. 199-217.

Tollison, Robert D., and Thomas D. Willett (1982), "Power, Politics, and Prosperity: Alternative Views of Economic Interdependence", in Finger, Michael J. and Thomas D. Willett (eds.), "The Internationalization of the World Economy", *The Annals* (March).

Toma, Eugenia F. and Mark Toma (1986), *Central Bankers, Bureaucratic Incentives, and Monetary Policy*, Martinus Nijhoff Publishers, Dordrecht, The Netherlands.

Tower, Edward and Thomas D. Willett (1976), *The Theory of Optimum Currency Areas and Exchange Rate Flexibility*, Special Papers in International Economics, Princeton University, Department of Economics, Princeton, N.J.

Ungerer, Horst, Owen Evans and Peter Nyberg (1983), "The European Monetary System: The Experience, 1979-82", Occasional Paper No. 19 (May), International Monetary Fund, Washington, D.C.

Vaubel, Roland (1986), "A Public Choice Approach to International Organization", *Public Choice* 51, pp. 39-57.

Wegner, Manfred (1985), "External Adjustment in a World of Floating", in Tsoukalis, Loukas (ed.), *The Political Economy of International Money*, Sage Publications, London, pp. 103-135.

Weintraub, Robert E. (Spring 1983), "What Type of Monetary Rule?", *CATO Journal* 3, pp. 171-84.

Williamson, John (1986), "Target Zones and the Management of the Dollar", *Brookings Papers on Economic Activity* 1, pp. 165-174.

Williamson, John (1987), "Exchange Rate Management: The Role of Target Zones", *American Economic Review* 77, No. 2 (May), pp. 200-204.

Willett, Thomas D. (1980), "Some Aspects of the Public Choice Approach to International Economic Relations", Working Paper (January), Claremont Graduate School, The Claremont Center for Economic Policy Studies, Claremont, CA.

Willett, Thomas D. (1983), "Functioning of the Current International Financial Systems", in Furstenberg, George von (ed.), *International Money and Credit*, International Monetary Fund, Washington, D.C.

Willett, Thomas D. (Fall 1985a), "The Dollar Exchange Rate as a Leading Indicator for American Monetary Policy: Comment", Academic Conference, San Francisco Federal Reserve Bank, pp. 207-214.

Willett, Thomas D. (1985b), "Macroeconomic Policy Coordination Issues Under Flexible Exchange Rates", *ORDO* 35, pp. 137-149.

Willett, Thomas D. (1986), "Exchange-Rate Volatility, International Trade, and Resource Allocation: A Perspective on Recent Research", *Journal of International Money and Finance* Supplement (March).

Willett, Thomas D. (1987), "A New Monetary Constitution", in Dorn and Schwartz, pp. 145-160.

Willett, Thomas D. (forthcoming), *Political Business Cycles*, Pacific Institute for Public Policy Research, San Francisco, CA.

Willett, Thomas D. and John E. Mullen (1982), "The Effects of Alternative International Monetary Systems on Macroeconomic Discipline and the Political Business Cycle", in *Political Economy of International and Domestic Monetary Relations*, Iowa State University Press, Ames, IA, pp. 143-159.

Willett, Thomas D., and King Banaian, "Models of the Political Process and Their Implications for Stagflation: A Public Choice Perspective", in Willett (forthcoming).

Willett, Thomas D., et al. (1987), "Currency Substitution, U.S. Money Demand, and International Interdependence", in *Contemporary Policy Issues*, V (July), pp. 76-82.

COMMENTS

John S. Chipman

When I agreed to be a discussant of this paper, I had only the title in front of me, which referred to "international *economic* stability". However, the text of the paper is concerned with international *monetary* stability. This term, however, is not defined in the paper. Surely if we are to discuss it we must have a way of ident-ifying it and measuring it from observable data -of being able to say that the amount of it has increased or decreased since last year - unless indeed it is one of those phenomena once described by Fritz Machlup as being like a pretty girl: I can't define the concept but I know one when I see one.

One possibility would be to define monetary instability by exchange-rate volatility. But then the question of whether there is more monetary stability under fixed than under flexible exchange rates would be tautological. It seems clear to me that any reasonable definition of monetary stability must involve real rather than nominal variables; for if monetary instability means that only nominal variables change, why should anybody but economists be worried about it? We come back then to the notion of economic welfare. Even if we are to take a "public-choice" approach to this phenomenon, a precise definition of the phenomenon itself seems to require value judgments and interpersonal comparisons which are inherent in any index which balances the welfares of different individuals.

When one looks at instances that seem to exemplify undesirable features of the international mechanism of adjustment, they include cases of changes in income distribution across classes at a given time and changes in income distribution over time. In fact, any capital movement from one country to another entails such dis-tributional consequences. A capital movement or unilateral transfer from country A to country B requires a reallocation of resources out of nontradables to tradables in country A and from tradables to nontradables in country B. Factors used relatively

Studies in International Economics and Institutions
Vosgerau (Ed.) New Institutional Arrangements for the World Economy
© Springer-Verlag Berlin Heidelberg 1989

intensively in the tradables sectors in country B will, in general, suffer a fall in real earnings as they have to move to the nontradables or service sectors; if they are relatively influential (as in the case of labor in democratic countries), they will press for protectionist measures. In country A it is factors used relatively intensively in the nontradables sectors that will appeal to their government for relief. One has to balance the losses of these factors against the gains of the factors intensive in the nontradables sectors in country B and in the tradables sectors in country A. If the gains in utility are equal to the losses, and if utility functions are concave and the social-welfare function linear, there is a net social loss in both countries. Actually, there is a net gain in country B and a net loss in country A, but one cannot ignore the political pressures of the losers in either country. If the transfer is a loan that is eventually at least partially repaid, there is a reverse welfare movement in the future. If the loan was not socially productive, there is certainly a net loss over time.

It seems fair to say that most of the recent examples of so-called "international monetary instability" fall into this category. (Some economists, notably Ronald McKinnon, have stressed the role of currency substitution; but it is difficult to know whether such substitution would have occurred in the absence of the large-scale capital movements that have taken place.) The Brazilians, Argentines, and Mexicans borrowed heavily in the 1970s on the false assumption of ever-rising oil prices, and are now repaying at least part of their debts. Even taking account of the partial forgiveness of their debts, in retrospect their discounted welfare is probably less than it would have been had more rational policies of intertemporal resource allocation been pursued. And it is hard for me to believe that the erroneous expectations concerning future oil prices were a consequence of a regime of floating rather than fixed exchange rates.

Except for the OPEC shocks themselves, it is difficult to think of a single case of "international monetary stability" that has not found its source in a ubiquitous phenomenon: public-sector deficits. Public borrowing for nonproductive uses was at the root of the British balance-of-payments crises during the Bretton-Woods era and of the crisis that ended Bretton Woods: Lyndon Johnson's covert deficits to finance the Vietnam war. The source of the most recent problems has surely been Ronald Reagan's deficits. As Professor Willett points out, advocates of a fixed-exchange rate regime have not adequately considered how it would have coped with these massive deficits.

Seventy years ago, Frank Taussig pointed out that a gold standard and a flexible-exchange-rate regime would produce exactly the same real changes in response to capital movements. Under a gold standard, nominal prices of nontradables would rise in the receiving country and fall in the paying country; under floating, the receiving country's currency would appreciate relative to that of the paying country. In both cases, the relative prices of tradables and nontradables would change in the same way. And as Friedman pointed out, under flexible exchange rates, a change in just one price would essentially do the trick, and it would also circumvent downward inflexibility in nominal prices in the paying country.

There appear to be two problems: (1) what type of regime can best withstand shocks, and (2) what type of regime can best prevent the shocks to begin with? Usually only question (1) is posed, but I think that question (2) is still more relevant. For it seems that the greatest source of shocks is national governments themselves. The problem is: how can national governments be forced to balance their budgets? Putting the question another way: is not the real problem not that of devising better *international* institutions, but that of devising better *national* ones? This is the message that I get from reading Professor Willett's paper.

Controls over international capital movements are certainly not the correct remedy. There is no more justification for *inter*temporal autarky than there is for *intra*temporal autarky.

Optimal international allocation of resources is as important across time as across commodities. But the one type of intertemporal allocation of resources that cannot be justified by this type of argument is government borrowing to finance consumption or military expenditures; the way to control these types of unproductive capital movements is to enforce balancing of national budgets. Could a supranational monetary authority accomplish this, more or less as a national monetary authority enforces such discipline on state governments in the U.S.? I do not know the answer to this question.

Implications of Alternative International Exchange Rate Arrangements for the Developing Countries

Sebastian Edwards*

I.   Introduction

Contrary to what was expected by the proponents of freely fluctuating exchange rates, the abandonment of the Bretton Woods system in the early 1970s has not resulted in a more stable international economic environment. In fact, in the recent years the degree of volatility of some of the key variables has increased substantially with respect to the 1950s and 1960s. As a result of this a number of economists, both in academia and in policy circles, have recently argued that the international economic system is ripe for a new reform. Most of these reform proposals call for institutions that would result in a more active nominal exchange rate management by the U.S. and the key OECD countries (i.e. the establishment of a target zone for the dollar) or even in a return to the gold standard.[1]

Most of the recent discussion on institutional reforms of the international monetary system has concentrated on the effects of this type of action on a handful of large countries. This has also been the case with the recent theoretical literature on the subject. For example, many of the new papers on the effects of policy coordination have used strategic behavior analyses where two players - usually the U.S. and the rest of the OECD - decide whether to cooperate or not in policy matters. A number of these studies have shown that under a number of circumstances cooperative solutions dominate noncooperative ones. Although interesting and relevant, this approach concentrates exclusively on the large players, tending to ignore the effects of different policies and of alternative international institutional arrangements on

---

*   David Gould provided able research assistance.

[1]   See, for example, Williamson (1983) and McKinnon (1984). Frankel and Meese (1987) have recently addressed the issue of whether industrial countries' exchange rates have been excessively volatile.

Studies in International Economics and Institutions
Vosgerau (Ed.) New Institutional Arrangements for the World Economy
© Springer-Verlag Berlin Heidelberg 1989

the smaller countries.[2] However, there are a number of channels through which greater instability in the large countries can affect the destinies of the smaller nations. One such channel, which is the focus of this paper, is exchange rate variability in the U.S. and OECD.

In theory, a high degree of instability in these large countries' currencies can spill over in a number of ways to the smaller countries. It is even possible that an unstable international environment will be more harmful to the LDCs than to the large countries themselves.[3]

The purpose of this paper is to analyze real exchange rate behavior in a selected group of developing countries, both during the last few years of the Bretton Woods era and during the floating rates period. We first discuss how the current floating exchange rates regime has reduced the smaller countries' ability to pursue a stable exchange rate policy. In the empirical part of the paper we analyze whether the increase in real exchange rate instability experienced by the industrial nations has also taken place in the developing countries after the abandonment of Bretton Woods (on real exchange rate [RER] instability in the industrialized nations see Table 1). In analyzing real exchange rate behavior in the LDCs we look both at the official foreign exchange market and at the black or parallel market for foreign exchange. We also provide preliminary empirical results on the effects of RER instability on growth, investment and exports in the developing countries. This is an important issue with a number of policy ramifications. Indeed, to the extent that higher RER variability has negatively impacted growth and exports, there are reasons to implement policies, both at the country and at the international levels, towards reducing this variability, and producing a more stable international environment.

---

[2]   On policy coordination see the essays in Buiter and Marston (1986). On a historical analysis of policy coordination using the strategic behavior approach see Eichengreen (1985). See Darby (1986) for a critical view on this literature.

[3]   Helleiner (1981) discusses some of these issues. Edwards (1987) contains an empirical analysis on the causes of exchange rate instability in the developing nations.

The paper is organized in the following form: Section I is the introduction. Section II discusses issues related to the sources of real exchange rate instability in the developing nations. A distinction is made between bilateral and multilateral or effective real exchange rates, and the role of volatility in the industrial nations as a source of exchange rate instability in the developing countries is discussed. This section also touches briefly on the distinction between equilibrium and disequilibrium real exchange rates.

Table 1

Real Exchange Rate Instability in Industrial Countries:
1964 - 1983*

	1964-83	1964-70	1974-83
United States	1.62	0.62	2.17
United Kingdom	2.45	1.43	3.20
France	1.76	1.22	2.14
FR Germany	1.89	1.37	1.95
Japan	2.54	0.90	3.72
Canada	1.75	0.56	1.71
Italy	2.35	1.91	2.55

* Index of instability constructed by the IMF as quarter-to-quarter changes in real effective exchange rate relative to trend.

Source: IMF (1984).

In Section III the historical behavior of real exchange rates in a group of 23 developing nations is empirically analyzed. A number of variability measures are presented and discussed. In Section IV we analyze the role of a prevalent institution in the developing countries: black (or parallel) markets for foreign exchange. Bilateral real exchange rate indexes are constructed using data on quotations on black markets. The extent of instability of black market RERs is then investigated. Section V deals with the real effects of RER variability using cross section data for

23 developing countries. This empirical investigation distinguishes three periods: 1965-1971, corresponding to the last years of the Bretton Woods system, and 1972-85 and 1978-85, two subperiods corresponding to the floating systems. Regression results that try to capture the effects of real exchange rate instability on output growth, exports growth and investment are presented for the three periods. Section VI contains some concluding remarks, including a discussion on some of the other channels through which international instability affects the LDCs. Also, some of the policy ramifications of the empirical results presented in the paper are further discussed.

II.   Sources of Real Exchange Rate Variability Under Alternative International Exchange Rate Arrangements

II.1   Defining "the" Real Exchange Rate

Currently, a number of alternative definitions of "the" real exchange rate are used in the literature. Although most writers define the real exchange rate as a relative price, there are some disagreements on which relative price should be called "the" real exchange rate (see Edwards, forthcoming, for a detailed analysis on the subject). While some authors define it in the tradition of the Purchasing Power Parity (PPP) theory as the nominal exchange rate (E) times the ratio of foreign to domestic price indexes, others define the real exchange rate as the (domestic) relative price of tradable to nontradable goods (Dornbusch, 1980).

When faced with the practical decision of constructing time series of real exchange rate indexes for the developing countries analysts are confronted with significantly fewer options than those suggested by more theoretical discussions. In fact, the construction of actual indexes is surrounded by a number of problems, ranging from finding proxies for the analytical constructs to deciding which price indexes to use, and so on. Given the particularly severe data constraint encountered in the majority of the developing countries, measured RER indexes invariably take the following form:

$$RER = \frac{E \ P*}{P} \tag{1}$$

where E is either the bilateral or the effective (i.e. multilateral) nominal exchange rate, P* is some foreign price index and P is a domestic price index. To the extent that the analyst requires periodicity and reliability the choices of P* and P are limited to CPIs and WPIs (or its components).

II.2   Exchange Rate Regimes, Domestic Exchange Rate Policies and Sources of Real Exchange Rate Variability

Movements in actual RERs are the result of either changes in nominal exchange rates or of movements in price indexes. Naturally, the relative importance of these two sources of RER variability will be different under alternative exchange rate regimes. In a generalized and strict fixed international exchange rate arrangement, nominal exchange rate movements are ruled out by definition. Changes in relative prices become the sole source of RER movements. In less rigid fixed exchange rate regimes, such as the Bretton Woods system, nominal exchange rates are sometimes adjusted - for example, when there is a "fundamental disequilibrium" - but movements in relative price indexes remain as the major source of RER variability.

Things are very different in a free exchange rate regime. In this case, nominal exchange rate movements become dominant. Moreover, since nominal exchange rates behave like asset prices, they tend to be much more volatile than goods prices (Frenkel, 1981, Edwards 1983). In this case nominal exchange rate movements become the overwhelming dominant source of short-run RER volatility. In fact, Katseli (1984) has shown that most of the recent increase in RER instability in the industrial countries can be explained by the highly volatile nominal exchange rates (see also IMF, 1984).

Whether in a particular small country nominal exchange rate movements or relative price changes are the dominant source of RER volatility will depend both on the nominal exchange rate policy followed by that country, *and* on the international exchange rate system. For example, in an international floating exchange system, as the one currently in effect, a small country that decides to follow a fixed exchange rate policy, pegging its currency value to that of its major trade partner cannot avoid (effective) nominal exchange rate instability. In fact, under a floating international exchange rate system it is substantially more difficult for a small developing nation to adopt a stable nominal exchange rate policy.

This can be easily seen by looking at the sources of variability of nominal *effective* exchange rates under alternative *international* exchange rate systems. The index of the nominal effective exchange rate (NEER) is equal to:

$$\text{NEER} = \sum_{i=1}^{k} \alpha_i \, E_i \qquad (2)$$

where the α_i's are weights ($\Sigma \, \alpha_i = 1$) and the E_i are indexes of bilateral nominal exchange rates between the country in question and its k principal trade partners. Assume that the U.S. is this small country's most important trade partner, and, thus the first term in the sum in equation (2). The NEER index, then, can be written as

$$\text{NEER} = \alpha_{US} \, E_{US} + \sum_{i=2} \alpha_i \, E_i \qquad (3)$$

However, by triangular arbitrage it is possible to write the country's bilateral nominal rate with respect to country j (E_j) as its nominal rate with respect to the US (E_{US}), times the bilateral rate between the US and country j $(E_{US,j})$:

$$E_j = E_{US} \, E_{US,j} \qquad (4)$$

Consequently, the nominal effective exchange rate can be written as

$$\text{NEER} = E_{US} \{ \alpha_{US} + \sum_{i=2} \alpha_i \, E_{US,i} \} \quad , \qquad (5)$$

where the $E_{US,i}$ are bilateral indexes of the nominal exchange rate between the US dollar and country i's currency (for i=1,...,k).

From equation (2) it is apparent that movement in this country's nominal effective exchange rate will depend both on its nominal exchange rate policy with respect to the U.S. dollar, as well as on the *international exchange rate system* (captured by the $E_{US,j}$'s). Under a generalized fixed rates regime, as the Bretton Woods system, by choosing a fixed rate with respect to the U.S. (or other major currency) this country can stabilize its nominal effective exchange rate. This is because in this case both E_{US} and the $E_{US,j}$ will be fixed. However, under a floating international regime, if the authorities in this small country peg their currency to the U.S. dollar they will, by definition, float against all other advanced currencies. Even if E_{US} is fixed, NEER will move. In this case percentage changes in the NEER will be equal to:[4]

$$\text{dlog (NEER)} = \gamma \sum_{i=2} \delta_i \text{dlog } E_{US,i} \tag{6}$$

where $\gamma = (\sum_{i=2} \alpha_i E_{US,i})/(\alpha_{US} + \sum \alpha_i E_{US,i})$, and $\delta_i = (\alpha_i E_{US,i})/(\sum_{i=2} \alpha_i E_{US,i})$. Thus, even if a small country pegs its nominal rate to the U.S. (i.e., dlog E_{US} = 0), it cannot avoid changes in its NEER, as long as the U.S. dollar fluctuates against the other currencies.

In terms of variability, the variance of the log of the NEER will be equal to:

$$V(\log \text{ NEER}) = V(\log E_{US}) + V (\log \psi) + 2 \text{ cov}(\log E_{US}, \log \psi) \tag{7}$$

where $\psi = \{ \alpha_{US} + \sum_{i=2} \alpha^i E_{US,i}\}$. Under fully fixed nominal rates, V (log NEER) = $V(\log E_{US})$ = $V(\log E_{US,j})$ = 0. This is because *all* nominal exchange rates are fixed. However, under a floating international monetary system, fixing to the U.S. dollar will not eliminate NEER fluctuations. In this case, V(log NEER)> 0.

In theory, under the current floating exchange rate regime a small developing country can still pursue a stable exchange rate policy by periodically (daily?) adjusting its parity with respect to the U.S. dollar, in a way such that the NEER remains constant. In this case the rule for adjusting the dollar exchange rate is given by:

---

[4]   since it is assumed that this country has pegged its nominal rate with respect to the U.S. dollar, dlog E_{US} = 0.

$$\text{dlog}\left[E_{US}\right]_t = -\gamma \sum_{i=2} \delta_i \, \text{dlog} \left[E_{US,i}\right]_t \qquad\qquad (8)$$

II.3   Variability, Uncertainty and Equilibrium Real Exchange Rates

Although increased volatility and heightened uncertainty regarding real exchange rate changes are welfare reducing,[5] it is incorrect to think that all movements in RERs are harmful. Indeed, many times RER changes represent "equilibrium movements", justified by changes in the "fundamental" determinants of the equilibrium RERs. For example, a worsening in a country's terms of trade is a real shock that will result in an *equilibrium* change - in this case devaluation - of the real exchange rate. Likewise, changes in taxes on trade and on the degree of exchange controls will also introduce important changes in the equilibrium REER. Being able to distinguish equilibrium from disequilibrium movements in RERs has in fact become a major challenge for macroeconomic analysts.

The equilibrium RER can be defined as the relative price of tradables to non-tradables that, for given (equilibrium or sustainable) values of other relevant variables such as trade taxes, international prices, capital and aid flows, and technology, results in the simultaneous attainment of *internal* and *external* equilibrium. In this context, *internal equilibrium* is defined as meaning that the nontradable goods market clears in the current period, and is expected to be in equilibrium in future periods. *External equilibrium*, on the other hand, is attained when the current account balance in the present period, and the expected current account balances in future periods, satisfy the intertemporal budget constraint that states that the discounted value of the current account balances has to be equal to zero. In other words, external equilibrium means that the current account balances (current and future) are compatible with long run sustainable capital flows.

A number of important implications follow from this definition of the equilibrium real exchange rate (ERER). First, the ERER is not an immutable number. When

---

[5]   See, for example, the discussion in Willett (1986).

there are changes in any of the other variables that affect the country's internal and external equilibria, there will also be changes in the equilibrium real exchange rate. For example, the RER "required" to attain equilibrium will not be the same with a very low world price of the country's main export, than with a very high price of that good. In a sense, then, the ERER is itself a function of a number of variables including import tariffs, export taxes, real interest rates, capital controls and so on. These immediate determinants of the ERER are the so-called *real exchange rate fundamentals*. Second, there is not "one" equilibrium real exchange rate, but rather a path of equilibrium RERs through time. Third, the path of ERER will not only be affected by the current values of the fundamental determinants, but also by the expected future evolution of these variables. To the extent that there are possibilities for intertemporal substitution of consumption via foreign borrowing and lending, and in production via investment, expected future events - such as an expected future change in the international terms of trade, for example - will have an effect on the current value and complete time path of the ERER.

Although the equilibrium real exchange rate is a function of real variables only, the actual real exchange rate responds both to real and monetary variables. The existence of an equilibrium value of the real exchange rate does not mean that the actual real rate has to be *permanently* equal to this equilibrium value. In fact, the actual RER will normally exhibit short run departures from its equilibrium value. Short run and even medium run deviations that are typically not very large and that stem from short term frictions and adjustment costs can be quite common. However, there are other types of deviations that can become persistent through time, generating major and sustained differentials between actual and equilibrium real exchange rates, or real exchange rate *misalignments*. A very important question is whether the extent and magnitude of deviations of actual RERs from their equilibrium values depend on the international exchange rate arrangements. Unfortunately, this is a question that cannot be answered satisfactorily - at least not for a large number of countries - given our current ability (or *in*ability, should we say) to compute the equilibrium path of RERs. At the present time we should be content with analyzing the effects and consequences of RER volatility.

III. Real and Nominal Exchange Rate Variability
in Selected Developing Countries: 1965-1985

In this section we analyze the evolution of the degree of variability of a series of exchange rate measures for 23 developing nations. The analysis deals with both nominal and real exchange rates and distinguishes between the Bretton Woods era and the current floating rate regime.

III.1 Official Nominal Exchange Rates and RER Variability
in 23 Developing Countries

Series of real bilateral (with respect to the U.S. dollar) and real effective exchange rates were constructed and analyzed for 23 developing countries. In the construction of the indexes of the real effective exchange rate the following equation was used:

$$\text{REER}_{jt} = \frac{\sum_{i=1}^{k} \alpha_i E_{it} P^*_{it}}{P_{jt}} \qquad (9)$$

where REER_{jt} is the index of the effective real rate in period t for country j; E_{it} is an *index* of the nominal rate between country i and country j in period t: $i = 1,...,k$ refers to the k partner countries used in the construction of the REER index: α_i is the weight corresponding to partner i in the computation of MRER_i; P^*_{it} is the price *index* of the i partner in period t; and p_{jt} is the price index of the home country period t. An increase in the value of this index of REER reflects real depreciation, whereas a decline implies real appreciation in the domestic country. Two indexes of REERs were constructed. The first index - which can be considered as a proxy for the relative price of tradables - used the partner countries' WPIs as the P^*_{it}'s and the home country CPI as P_{jt}. For notation purposes this index was called REER.

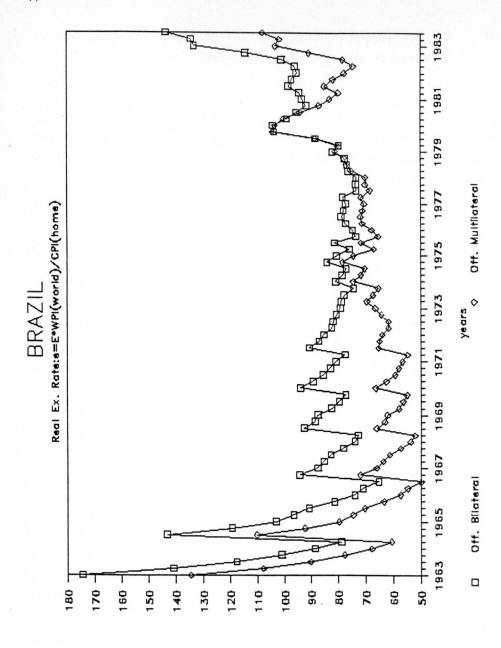

BRAZIL

Real Ex. Rate:e=E*WPI(world)/CPI(home)

years

□ Off. Bilateral ◇ Off. Multilateral

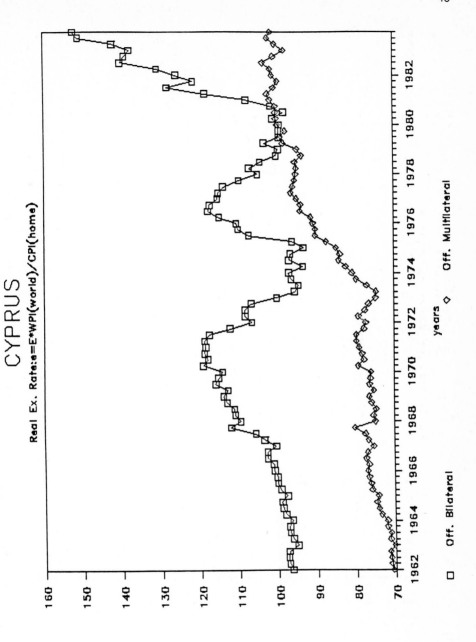

CYPRUS

Real Ex. Rate:e=E*WPI(world)/CPI(home)

□ Off. Bilateral   ◇ Off. Multilateral

years

45

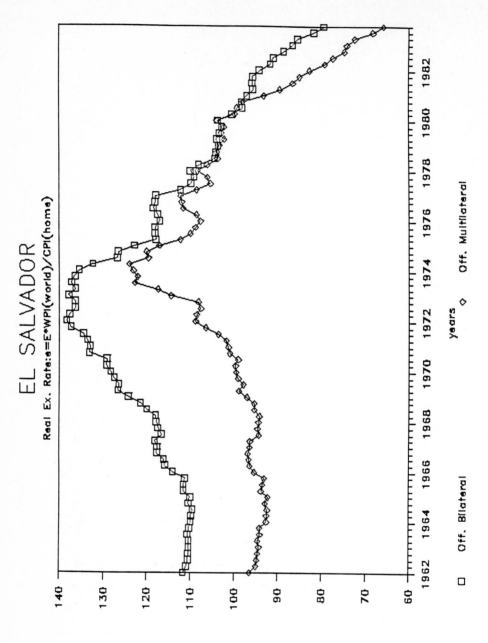

EL SALVADOR

Real Ex. Rate:e=E*WPI(world)/CPI(home)

years

□ Off. Bilateral   ◇ Off. Multilateral

47

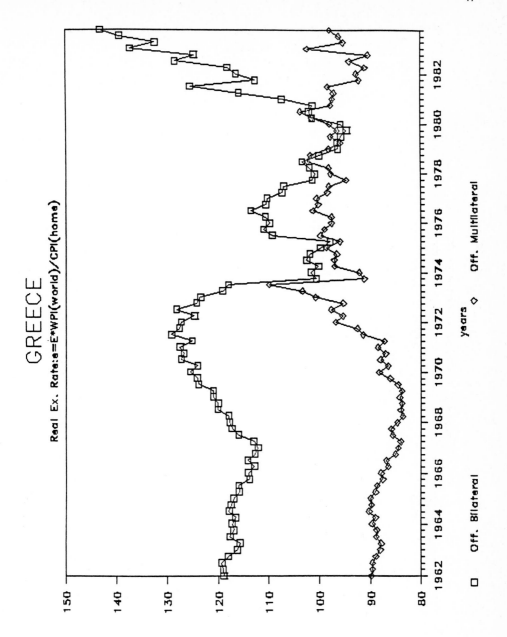

GREECE

Real Ex. Rate:e=E*WPI(world)/CPI(home)

□ Off. Bilateral   years ◇ Off. Multilateral

48

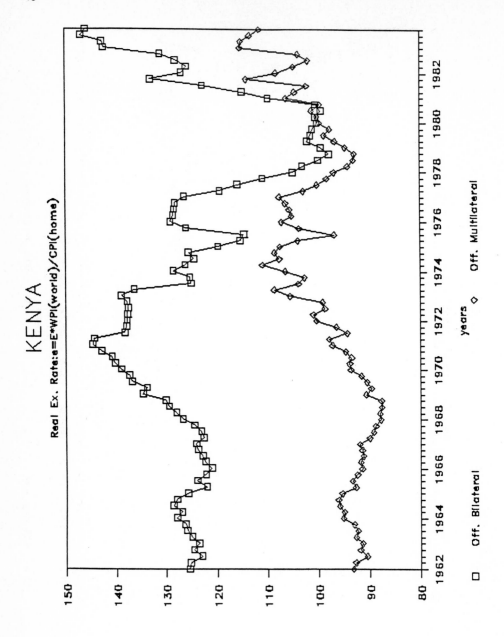

KENYA

Real Ex. Rate:e=E*WPI(world)/CPI(home)

years

□   Off. Bilateral   ◇   Off. Multilateral

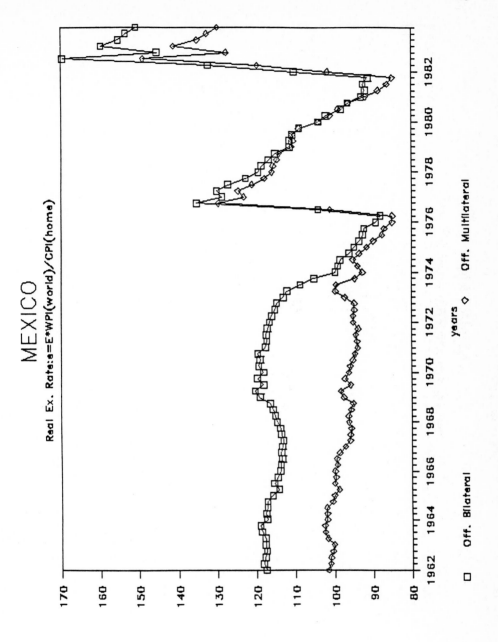

MEXICO

Real Ex. Rate:a=E*WPI(world)/CPI(home)

□   Off. Bilateral   ◇   Off. Multilateral

years

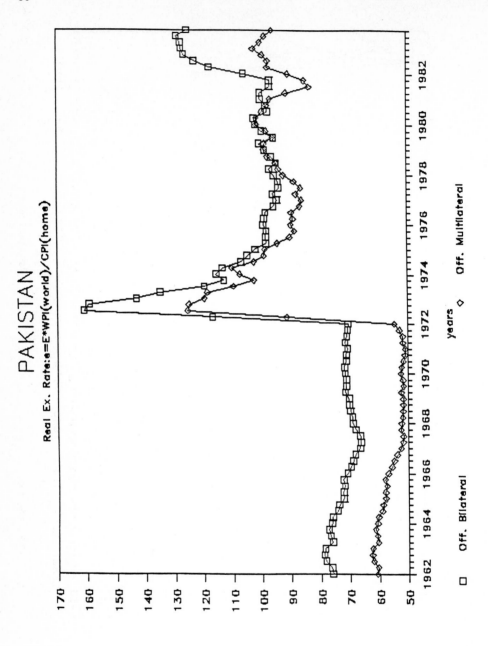

PAKISTAN

Real Ex. Rate:e=E*WPI(world)/CPI(home)

□ Off. Bilateral   ◇ Off. Multilateral

years

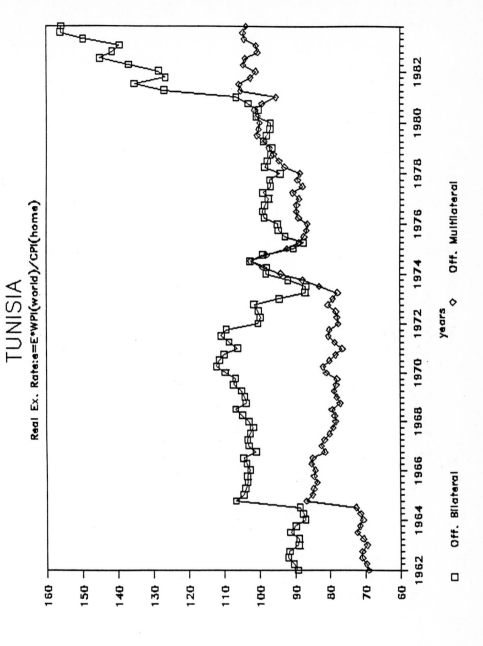

TUNISIA

Real Ex. Rate:e=E*WPI(world)/CPI(home)

□   Off. Bilateral   years   ◇   Off. Multilateral

52

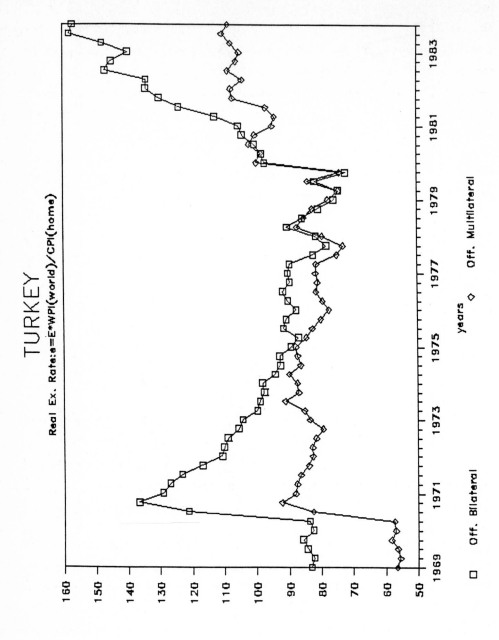

TURKEY

Real Ex. Rate:e=E*WPI(world)/CPI(home)

□ Off. Bilateral   years   ◇ Off. Multilateral

The second index - which is related to the more traditional PPP measure - was used for both partners' and the domestic country consumer price indexes. In the construction of both indexes the following procedure was followed: (1) The weights (α's) were trade weights constructed using data from the International Monetary Fund *Directions of Trade*. (2) In both cases the ten larger trade partners in 1975 were used for the construction of the real exchange rate indexes.

Two indexes of bilateral real exchange rates with respect to the U.S. were also constructed. These indexes were defined as:

$$RER = \frac{E \ WPI^{US}}{CPI} , \qquad (10)$$

and,

$$BRER2 = \frac{E \ CPI^{US}}{CPI} , \qquad (11)$$

where E is the bilateral (official) nominal exchange rate with respect to the U.S. dollar; CPI^{US} and WPI^{US} are the consumer and wholesale price indexes; and CPI is, as before, the domestic country CPI. RER, then, is the bilateral counterpart of MRER1. On the other hand, BRER2 uses both the domestic country and the U.S. CPIs and has historically been the most popular RER index in policy analyses.

Figures 1 through 10 show the behavior of the real effective exchange rate index REER and the bilateral index RER for a "representative" group of 10 of these 23 developing countries. As may be seen, for most countries both indexes tended to move in the same direction throughout most of the period; this is particularly the case for 1960 through 1971. After that year, when the major currencies abandoned the fixed parties in many countries, the multilateral and bilateral indexes started to exhibit some difference in behavior. This is especially the case during the 1980s where in many countries the bilateral and effective real exchange rate indexes even moved in opposite directions. This reflects the fact that in most of these countries the national nominal exchange rate policies have traditionally been pursued using the U.S. dollar as the reference currency; between 1980 and 1985, however, as the U.S. dollar appreciated dramatically against the other major currencies, so did the currencies of many of these developing countries. As a result for this period in most countries the index of the real multilateral rate is below the index of the bilateral rate.

In order to formally compare the behavior of the four alternative indexes of the real exchange rate constructed using official data, coefficients of correlations between the multilateral and the bilateral real exchange rate indexes were computed. A number of regularities emerged from this analysis. First, in most countries the two alternative definitions of the bilateral real exchange rate index moved closely together during this period. In 17 out of the 23 countries considered, the coefficient of correlation between the two bilateral indexes was above 0.9 and in all of them it exceeded 0.8. Second, the two indexes of trade weighted real effective exchange rates also moved closely together. In 20 out of the 23 countries the coefficient of correlation exceeded 0.9. And third, the behavior of the bilateral and multilateral RER indexes have been quite different in many of these countries. In 16 cases the coefficient of correlation between MRER and BRER was below 0.6 and in two countries it was even negative.

The real exchange rate indexes depicted in Figures 1 through 10, as well as those for the other countries, have two interesting characteristics. First, they show that in most countries the real exchange rate has been fairly variable. Second, in spite of the observed variability, in many of these countries it appears that these indexes have not had significant trends during the whole long period under consideration. For the shorter, more recent periods of time, however, in a number of cases negative trends can be detected.

Tables 2 and 3 contain data on coefficients of variation of the real effective exchange rate REER and the bilateral exchange rate RER for four different time periods for the 23 LDCs considered in this study. The first time period, 1965-1971, corresponds to the Bretton Woods system. The second and third periods correspond to the current floating rates system: 1972-1985 includes every year since the abandonment of Bretton Woods.

Table 2

Coefficient of Variation of Real Effective Exchange Rate

Index for 23 Developing Countries

	(1) 1965-1971	(2) 1972-1985	(3) 1978-1985	(4) 1965-1985
Brazil	14.43	18.22	15.01	20.72
Colombia	9.23	10.73	6.49	11.78
Cyprus	2.06	9.46	2.56	12.03
El Salvador	3.47	18.44	1.75	15.06
Ethiopia	2.61	15.71	7.87	13.09
Greece	2.70	3.68	3.64	6.68
India	10.13	12.11	3.06	17.93
Israel	11.68	13.19	7.56	14.13
Kenya	3.10	5.51	6.76	103.77
Korea	4.87	6.64	4.12	8.88
Malaysia	3.02	7.91	7.88	7.72
Malta	6.54	9.35	6.11	16.36
Mauritius	4.48	5.47	5.21	7.99
Pakistan	4.35	11.37	4.65	27.06
Philippines	14.79	6.32	7.71	14.97
Singapore	3.45	7.42	5.70	6.43
South Africa	3.19	7.94	8.65	10.37
Sri Lanka	7.11	40.37	6.57	53.88
Thailand	3.16	6.15	8.12	8.22
Tunisia	3.32	9.22	4.49	10.88
Turkey	21.96	13.69	13.09	17.21
Yugoslavia	18.86	12.23	14.00	14.91
Zambia	9.41	6.89	7.48	8.22

Source: See text.

Table 3

Coefficient of Variation of Bilateral Real Exchange Rate
Index for 23 Developing Countries

	(1) 1965-1971	(2) 1972-1985	(3) 1978-1985	(4) 1965-1985
Brazil	13.71	22.49	21.50	21.40
Colombia	9.61	9.72	5.11	10.10
Cyprus	3.76	15.61	15.36	14.19
El Salvador	3.51	17.02	13.69	13.82
Ethiopia	2.62	14.23	4.94	13.29
Greece	1.75	11.97	14.59	9.78
India	10.75	11.96	5.69	14.90
Israel	13.16	13.35	6.33	13.40
Kenya	3.13	10.18	13.25	8.39
Korea	3.93	7.21	6.91	7.46
Malaysia	3.64	6.84	4.86	6.06
Malta	8.48	11.29	9.47	14.44
Mauritius	6.54	10.77	14.04	9.89
Pakistan	3.71	13.29	10.41	25.44
Philippines	15.19	7.89	9.90	12.60
Singapore	3.91	7.08	2.79	7.76
South Africa	1.79	9.53	10.66	8.45
Sri Lanka	7.78	40.02	3.39	53.20
Thailand	2.94	3.25	3.99	3.13
Tunisia	1.97	20.11	18.37	17.66
Turkey	20.19	23.90	25.33	23.77
Yugoslavia	18.88	22.99	28.00	21.54
Zambia	7.18	11.75	15.02	10.42

Source: See text.

The third period, 1978-1985, on the other hand, concentrates on the last 8 years of the floating system, where the new institutional setting was already well in place. The fourth column in these tables includes the complete period 1965-1985. The data in Tables 2 and 3 are quite revealing, showing that there has indeed been a substantial increase in the degree of real exchange rate instability in most of these countries after the abandonment of the Bretton Woods system. For example, Table 2 shows that the coefficient of variation of REER has been higher in the post Bretton Woods era (1972-1985) in 19 of the 23 countries. Notice, however, that in the more recent period (1978-1985) there has been somewhat of a decline in the degree of REER variability. Still, in 13 out of the 23 cases it is higher than during the six final years of the Bretton Woods era. The data on bilateral RER variability in Table 3 shows an even clearer increase in instability. In 22 out of the 23 countries the CV is higher in the 1972-1985 period than during 1965-1971. In 17 of these countries this index of instability was higher during 1978-1985 than during 1965-1971.

The use of the coefficient of variation as a measure of the real exchange rate variability presupposes that these REERs have had a stationary mean. This, in fact, is a realistic assumption. Edwards and Ng (1985c) have found that in most LDCs there are not significant REER trends over the longer run. Different authors, however, have used different measures of variability. Stockman (1983) used the variance; the IMF (1984) used period-to-period changes; Katseli (1984) and Melvin and Berstein used standard deviations; and DeGrauwe, Janssens and Lilianert (1984) used mean absolute changes. Williamson (1983) also used coefficients of variation to compute nominal exchange rate variability. In the present investigation, in order to check whether the regularities detected in Tables 2 and 3 were influenced by the specific variability index used, other indicators of instability were also constructed. For example, when data on the standard deviation of the *detrended* log of the REER were analyzed, the findings in Tables 2 and 3 were strongly confirmed: after the abandonment of the Bretton Woods system the extent of real exchange rate instability increased substantially in the developing countries. In the next section we look at nominal exchange rate instability and the sources of RER variability in a number of these countries.

III.2 Nominal Exchange Rate Changes and Sources of Real Exchange Rate Instability

Table 4 contains data on the variance of the rate of change of the nominal real effective exchange rate (V(dlog NEER) and on the rate of international inflation (V(dlog P*)) faced by these 23 countries during the three periods under consideration.[6] Two main results emerge from this table. First, in the great majority of these countries - in 11 out of the 16 cases for which there are complete data - the variance of changes in the nominal *effective* exchange rate has increased substantially after the abandonment of the Bretton Woods system. Second, in almost every country the variance of nominal exchange rate movements surpasses that of international inflation during every period under analysis.

Between 1965 and 1971, seven out of the 23 countries had a strict official fixed exchange rate with respect to the U.S. dollar - Greece, Yugoslavia, El Salvador, Pakistan, Thailand, Kenya, Zambia. Between 1972 and 1984, on the other hand, only one of these countries, El Salvador, still had a fixed exchange rate with respect to the U.S. dollar. Although this doesn't indicate, by any means, causality, it is fairly suggestive of the difficulties encountered by most countries during the turbulent floating rates period to maintain a stable nominal exchange rate policy with respect to their major trade partner.

---

[6] This rate of international inflation is the rate of change of the international price index used in the construction of the REERs indexes. It is calculated as a weighted average of the WPJs of each country's ten most important trade partners.

Table 4

Variability of Nominal Effective Exchange Rates

and Foreign Price Index

Country	Variance d log NEER			Variance d log P*		
	1965-71	1972-85	1978-85	1965-71	1972-85	1978-85
Greece	0.000061	0.0012380	0.0013187	0.00017535	0.0007060	0.0004814
Malta	0.000086	.	.	0.00007329	0.0003604	0.0002167
Turkey	0.009836	0.0080481	0.0109155	0.00056312	0.0032325	0.0031733
Yugosl.	0.006893	0.0040986	0.0047132	0.00160748	0.0012110	0.0010724
S. Africa	0.00126	0.0017454	0.0017488	0.00004520	0.0002895	0.0002326
Brazil	0.001764	0.0082608	0.0077734	0.00057846	0.0053131	0.0038124
Colombia	0.003275	0.0003630	0.0003259	0.00055993	0.0004997	0.0002340
El Salv.	0.000016	0.0002807	0.0003297	0.00009248	0.0003775	0.0002769
Cyprus	0.000148	0.0000978	0.0000868	0.00083140	0.0001371	0.0000919
Israel	n.a.	0.0124743	0.0136216	0.00030685	0.0053418	0.0023807
Sri Lanka	0.000715	0.0070968	0.0052601	0.00020247	0.0004572	0.0003589
India	.	0.0022641	0.0003578	0.00068693	0.0009137	0.0007551
Korea	0.010710	0.0037008	0.0016755	0.00023953	0.0005760	0.0003577
Malaysia	.	0.0002316	0.0003162	0.00011317	0.0001657	0.0001703
Pakistan	0.043851	.	.	0.00013212	0.0008509	0.0006037
Philipp.	0.003968	0.0021897	0.0035979	0.00039977	0.0004347	0.0002577
Singapore	0.000015	0.0002911	0.0001833	0.00010856	0.0003030	0.0001848
Thailand	0.000082	0.0009186	0.0011190	0.00009056	0.0001771	0.0001647
Ethiopia	0.000021	0.0006656	0.0008170	0.00069957	0.0013081	0.0006413
Kenya	.	0.0007593	0.0010388	0.00027780	0.0004447	0.0003425
Mauritius	0.009003	.	.	0.00024388	0.0007448	0.0011043
Tunisia	0.000033	0.0003150	0.0002736	0.00032423	0.0006683	0.0002859
Zambia	0.000081	0.0028155	0.0026826	0.00030254	0.0007467	0.0008624

Source: See text.

In Table 5 we present exchange rate variability data for three countries that maintained, throughout the period, a fixed official nominal exchange rate with respect to the U.S. dollar. Naturally, the variance of the bilateral rate of devaluation is zero for both subperiods. What is quite impressive, however, is the very dramatic (to put it mildly) jump in the variance of the rate of devaluation of the nominal effective exchange rate. Again, this clearly indicates the important changes suffered by the developing countries after the abandonment of the Bretton Woods regime.

Table 5

Nominal Exchange Rate Variability in Countries
with a Fixed Rate with Respect to the U.S. Dollar*

	1965-1971		*1972-1984*	
	Variance d log E_{US}	Variance d log NEER	Variance d log E_{US}	Variance d log NEER
Dominican Republic	0.0	4×10^{-6}	0.0	0.026
El Salvador	0.0	16×10^{-6}	0.0	0.0003
Guatemala	0.0	16×10^{-6}	0.0	0.0003

* These variances have been computed using quarterly data on the bilateral and effective nominal exchange rates.

IV.   Black Markets and Real Exchange Rates Variability

The RER indexes used in the analysis of Section II were constructed using data on official nominal exchange rates. However, in many developing countries, at different points in time, there have been quite extensive parallel (or black) markets for foreign exchange. The coverage and importance of these parallel market varies from country to country and period to period. In some cases these are quite thin, and are mainly used by those nationals that want to spend their vacation abroad and are only allowed a limited quota of foreign exchange at the official rates. In other cases, the coverage of the parallel market is very generalized, and the parallel market exchange rate is the relevant marginal rate for most transactions. The degree of legality of these parallel markets also varies from case to case. While in some cases they are quasi-legal and accepted by the authorities as a minor nuisance, in others they are strongly repressed, with the authorities severely persecuting those that engage in black market transactions.

By the very nature of these markets - illegal or quasi-illegal - it is not possible to have accurate data on volume of transactions and on their relative importance. However, there are fairly reliable data on parallel market quotations and parallel market premia. Generally speaking the premium will become higher as exchange controls become more pervasive and generalized, and as fewer and fewer transactions are allowed through the official market. Moreover, under conditions of generalized exchange controls and rationing the RER indexes computed using official rates will become almost completely useless.

In this study data on parallel market quotations were collected for 20 out of the 23 countries considered in Section II. These quotations refer to the nominal exchange rate with respect to the U.S. dollar. The data collected were used to construct series on parallel market premia and on parallel market bilateral (with respect to the U.S.) real exchange rate indexes. Figures 11 through 20 depict the behavior of the parallel market premium for our group of 10 "representative" countries. As can be seen the premia have varied significantly across countries and periods. The case of Pakistan is particularly interesting, showing how the premium can not only become extremely acute, but also exhibit dramatic jumps.

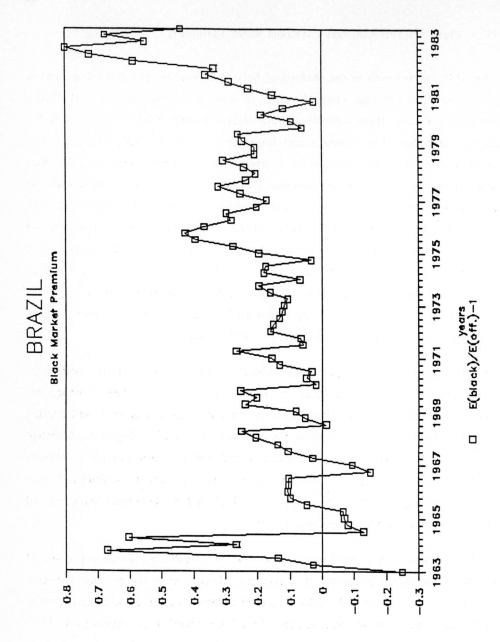

BRAZIL

Black Market Premium

□   E(black)/E(off.)−1

years

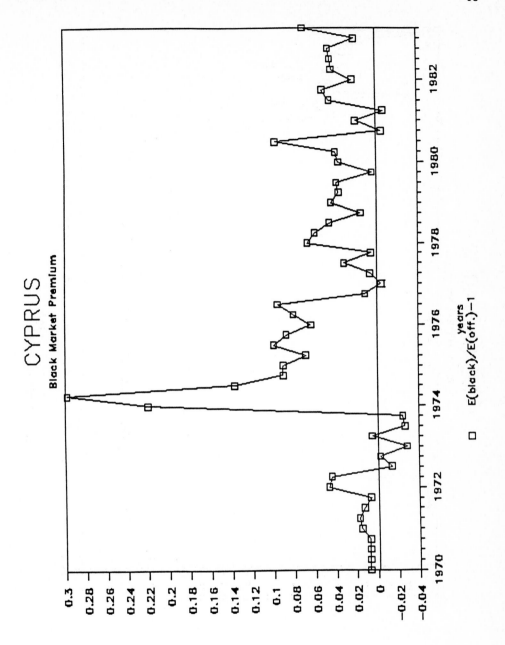

CYPRUS

Black Market Premium

□   E(black)/E(off.)−1

years

64

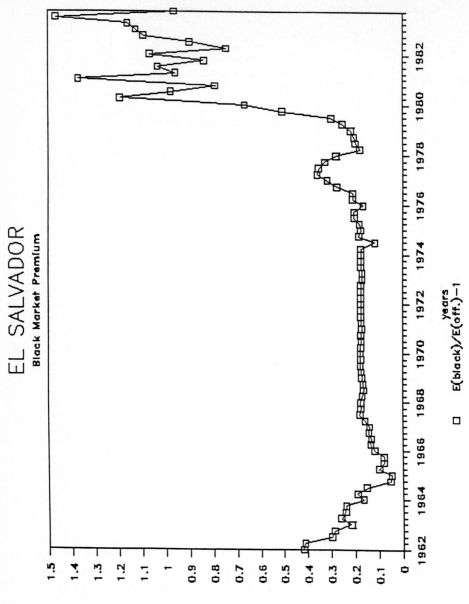

EL SALVADOR

Black Market Premium

□   E(black)/E(off.)−1

years

GREECE

Black Market Premium

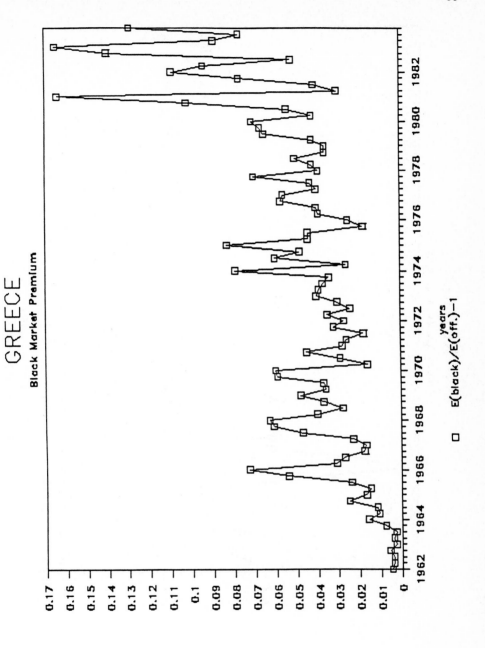

□   E(black)/E(off.)−1

years

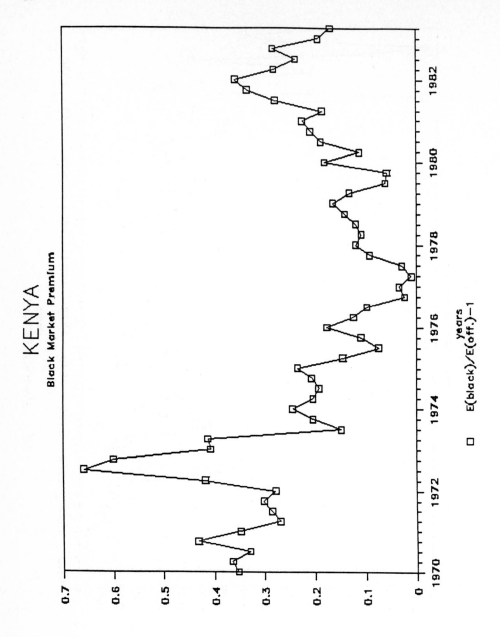

KENYA

Black Market Premium

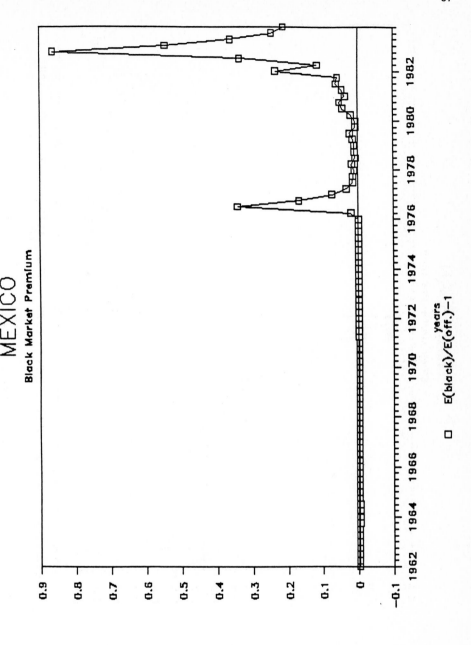

MEXICO

Black Market Premium

□ E(black)/E(off.)−1

years

68

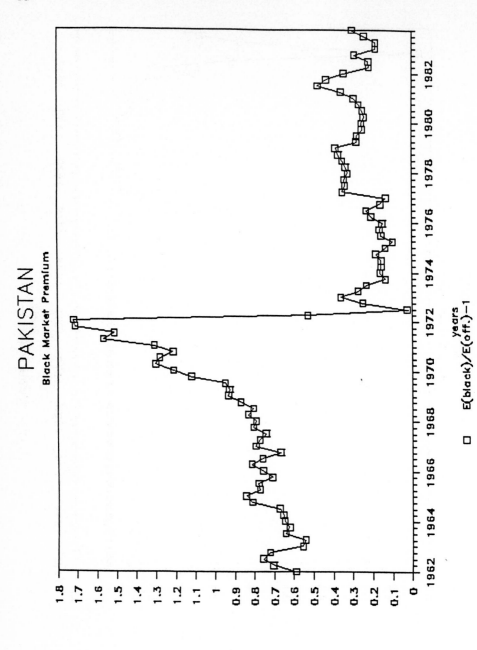

PAKISTAN

Black Market Premium

□   E(black)/E(off.)−1

years

PHILIPPINES

Black Market Premium

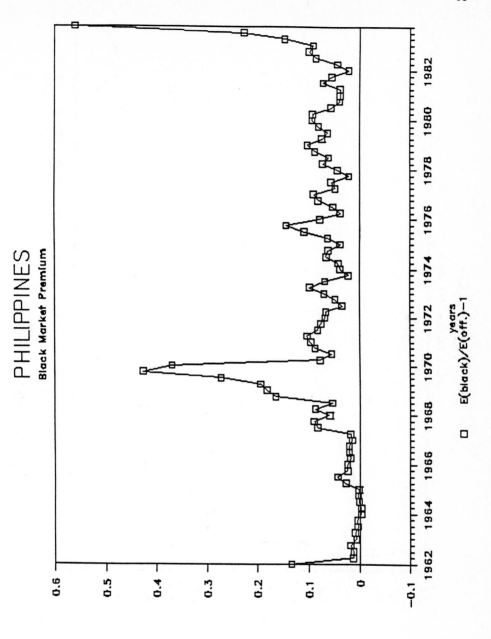

□   E(black)/E(off.)−1

TUNISIA

Black Market Premium

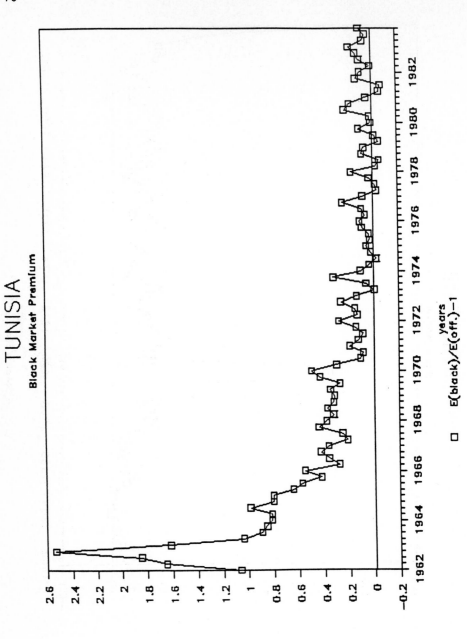

□   E(black)/E(off.)-1

years

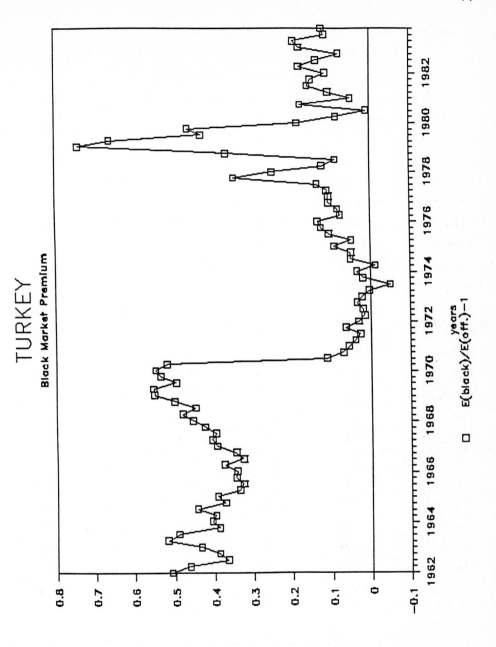

TURKEY

Black Market Premium

Table 6
Basic Statistical Properties of Black Market Premium*
(Quarterly Data: 1965 - 1983)

	Mean	St. Dev.	C.V.	Max.	Min.
Brazil	19.35	17.53	90.62	79.95	-15.00
Colombia	13.47	16.29	120.99	87.40	-1.27
Cyprus	4.23	5.63	133.24	29.79	-2.82
El Salvador	26.62	36.04	98.40	146.66	4.66
Ethiopia	56.15	43.24	77.01	175.84	1.77
Greece	5.08	3.14	61.95	16.43	1.49
India	34.40	26.07	75.80	124.00	6.10
Israel	16.12	18.13	112.33	72.27	-10.66
Kenya	22.12	13.62	61.59	65.89	1.11
Korea	9.76	11.31	11.95	60.70	-5.23
Malaysia	0.71	0.99	138.93	3.61	-1.40
Pakistan	54.52	42.28	77.55	171.95	2.58
Philippines	8.70	8.96	102.95	55.85	0.17
Singapore	0.28	0.67	237.97	2.59	-0.80
South Africa	11.97	10.01	83.61	49.88	-19.73
Sri Lanka	89.80	58.96	65.65	220.25	1.70
Thailand	0.09	1.85	187.90	6.37	-5.19
Tunisia	17.37	18.02	103.74	80.31	-7.14
Turkey	21.98	19.13	87.02	74.12	-4.82
Yugoslavia	8.40	7.07	84.15	26.02	-6.41
Zambia	93.19	50.54	54.23	201.66	29.08

Source: Based on raw data obtained from various issues of *Pick's Currency Year-book.*

* In some countries the time period is slightly shorter, due to data limitations.

As is discussed in Edwards (forthcoming) in a vast number of cases the parallel market premium increases very rapidly in the period immediately preceding a (major) nominal devaluation, and falls quite drastically immediately following the devaluation. This was indeed the case in Pakistan in 1972. Table 6 contains a summary of some of the premia's most important statistical properties for 21 out of the 23 developing countries considered in this study.

There is no reason why the parallel market RER index (PMRER) should move closely with an index constructed using the official nominal exchange rates. In fact, there are a number of circumstances under which, in a country with pegged nominal *official* rates, these two RER indexes will tend to move in opposite directions. This will be the case, for example, when there is a massive domestic credit creation under generalized exchange controls and active parallel markets. In this case, the higher growth of domestic credit will tend to generate an appreciation of the official RER index - via a higher price of nontradables - and a devaluation of the parallel market RER - through a jump in the nominal black market rate that exceeds the increase in the price level. Table 7 contains coefficients of correlation between the parallel market and official RER bilateral indexes. The parallel market index was constructed as:

$$PMRER1_t = (PM)_t \, \frac{WPI^{US}}{CPI}$$

where $(PM)_t$ is an index of the parallel market bilateral rate with respect to the U.S. dollar, WPI^{US} is the U.S. wholesale price index and CPI is the domestic country consumer price index. PMRER1 then is the bilateral parallel index equivalent to the bilateral RER in Section III. The coefficients of correlation in Table 7 clearly captures the fact that the parallel and official RER index indeed behave very differently. In fact in 10 out of the 21 cases the coefficient turned out to be negative. This shows that in a number of cases it can be misleading to concentrate our analysis only on RER indexes constructed using official exchange rate data.

Table 7

Coefficient of Correlation of Bilateral Real Exchange Rate Indexes
Constructed Using Official and Parallel Nominal Exchange Rates

	Coefficient of Correlation
Brazil	0.642
Colombia	0.337
Cyprus	0.124
El Salvador	0.434
Ethiopia	0.312
Greece	-0.436
Guatemala	-
Guyana	-
Honduras	-
India	-0.215
Israel	0.317
Kenya	0.217
Korea	-0.142
Malaysia	-0.053
Malta	-
Mauritius	-
Pakistan	-0.007
Philippines	0.620
Singapore	0.875
South Africa	0.326
Sri Lanka	-0.044
Thailand	-0.419
Tunisia	-0.688
Turkey	-0.347
Yugoslavia	0.477
Zambia	-0.091

Source: See text.

V.   Real Exchange Rate Volatility and Economic Performance

From a theoretical perspective it has been well established that real exchange rate disequilibrium and heightened uncertainty regarding RER behavior will have negative effects on economic performance (Willett, 1986). Empirically, however, there has been more difficulty finding evidence that supports these theoretical insights. According to the IMF (1984), for example, there is insufficient evidence linking increased real exchange rate instability to less active international trade. To quote the Fund (1984, page 36):

> The large majority of empirical studies on the impact of exchange rate variability on the volume of international trade are unable to establish a systematic significant link between measured exchange rate variability and the volume of international trade, whether on an aggregate or on a bilateral basis.

In its own empirical investigation the Fund found no empirical evidence of a relationship between exchange rate instability and bilateral trade flows for 7 industrial nations. Cavallo and Cotani (1985), however, were able to find some evidence on a negative relation between RER variability and economic performance. Their analysis looked only at bilateral rates and concentrated on official nominal exchange rates. We have seen above, however, that not only effective and bilateral rates behave in a significantly different way, but also that black market and official rates many times move in opposite directions.

In this section we report some regression results on the relation between real exchange rate instability and economic performance using cross section data for our 23 developing nations. The data were broken into two periods: 1965 - 1971 corresponding to the last six years of the Bretton Woods System, and 1978 - 1985 corresponding to the most recent period with an international floating exchange rate system. The analysis dealt with four different measures of economic performance: (1) average rate of growth of real GDP over each of the two periods considered; (2) average rate of growth of real GDP per capita; (3) average rate of growth of real export; and (4) average investment-output ratio. The regressions were estimated both in levels as well as in logs. The equations actually estimated were:

$$X_n = \alpha + \beta \ \delta_n + \Sigma j_i \ Z_{ni} + \omega_n \tag{12}$$

and,

$$\log X_n = \alpha' + \beta' \log \delta_n + \Sigma j_i \log Z_{ni} + \varepsilon_n \tag{13}$$

where the following notation has been used:

$X_n =$ performance variable (average growth of GDP; average growth of GDP per capita; average growth of exports; and average investment ratio) for country n.

$\delta_n =$ coefficient of variation of the real exchange rate index for country n. Three indexes were considered: bilateral; effective and black market.

$Z_{in} =$ other relevant variables.

$\varepsilon_n, \omega_n =$ error terms, assumed to have the usual properties.

Depending on the left hand side variable different Z_{in}'s were included. In the two output growth equations, two Z_{in}'s (i.e. "other" variables) were incorporated to the regressions: investment-output ratio and variability (coefficient of variation) of the international terms of trade. The investment variable was incorporated as a way to capture the effects of capital accumulation in explaining cross country growth differentials. Its coefficient is expected to be positive. The terms of trade variability was added in an effort to incorporate other sources of external instability faced by these nations, and its sign is expected to be negative. In the growth of exports equations the variability index of the terms of trade was the only Z_{in} included; its sign is expected to be negative. Finally, in the investment ratio equation no additional variables (Z_{in}'s) were incorporated.

Our interest is to find out whether greater real exchange rate instability has indeed been associated to some kind of "poorer" economic performance. In terms of equations (12) and (13) we are interested in testing whether coefficients ß and ß' are significantly negative, or if, as suggested by the IMF, there has been no relation between exchange rate instability and economic performance. The output growth equations performed better when they were estimated in levels. The exports and investment equations, on the other hand, generated better fits when estimated in logs. For the sake of saving space we only report these better results. Other estimates, including those obtained when nonlinear terms were added, are available from the author on request.

Tables 8 through 12 contain the regression results obtained when "official" RER indexes were used in the computation of the RER variability measure. A number of interesting results emerge from these tables. In particular, there seems to be a definite difference in the way these variables have interacted during the Bretton Woods and the floating rates periods. Although, given the average cross country nature of the analysis, it is not possible to compute traditional F-statistics to test for homogeneity, the results are quite strong in indicating a structural break between the two periods. While real exchange rate instability played no role in the Bretton Woods era, they help explain cross country differentials in economic performance during the more recent period. Moreover, during the more recent floating rates era there is a quite clear negative relation between real exchange rate instability and those of our real exchange rate measures.

Table 8

Cross Country Regressions: Average Growth of Real GDP and
Real Exchange Rate Variability, 1965-1971 and 1978-1985 (OLS)

Period	Constant	Variability of RER Bilateral	Variability of RER Effective	Investment Ratio	Variability T of T	R^2
65-71	1.716 (0.600)	-0.091 (-0.747)	-	0.303 (2.436)	-0.068 (-0.457)	0.306
65-71	1.460 (0.519	-	-0.086 (-0.681)	0.310 (2.428)	-0.056 (-0.383)	0.302
78-85	1.898 (1.036)	-0.185 (-3.044)	-	0.194 (3.261)	-0.043 (-0.895)	0.579
78-85	2.244 (1.120)	-	-0.279 (2.500)	0.157 (-0.300)	-0.016	0.532

Numbers in parentheses are t-statistics.

Table 9

Cross Country Regressions: Average Growth of

Real GDP Per Capital and Real Exchange Rate Variability:

1965-1971 and 1978-1985 (OLS)

Period	Constant	Variability of RER Bilateral	Variability of RER Effective	Investment Ratio	Variability T of T	R^2
65-71	-2.044 (-0.739)	-	-0.157 (-1.262)	0.432 (3.447)	-0.143 (-0.988)	0.486
65-71	-1.738 (-0.593	-0.136 (-1.120)	-	0.415 (3.377)	-0.157 (-0.517)	0.476
78-85	-1.160 (-0.593)	-	-0.250 (-2.143)	0.207 (3.377)	-0.0027 (-0.517)	0.606
78-85	-1.137 (-0.691)	-0.182 (-3.327)	-	0.239 (4.492)	-0.062 (-1.140)	0.699

Numbers in parentheses are t-statistics.

Table 10

Cross Country Results: Investment Ratio and Real Exchange Rate Variability:

1965-1971 and 1978-1986 (OLS)*

Period	Constant	log of RER Variability Bilateral	log of RER Variability Effective	R^2
65-71	2.886 (64.113)	0.038 (0.626)	-	0.013
65-71	2.839 (24.464	-	0.033 (0.507)	0.009
72-85	3.203 (39.849)	-0.158 (-2.092)	-	0.127
72-85	3.472 (16.940)	-	-0.173 (-2.048)	0.123

* The dependent variable is the log of the gross investment to GDP Ratio.

Table 11

Cross Country Regressions: Export Growth and

RER Variability:

1965-1971 and 1978-1985 (OLS)*

Period	Constant	*log of Variability* Bilateral RER	*Effective* REER	*log of Variability* T of T	R^2
65-71	2.067	-	-0.121	-0.664	0.147
	(1.715)		(0.296)	(-1.487)	
65-71	2.644	-0.333	-	-0.145	0.195
	(6.488)	(-1.615)	-	(-0.953)	
78-85	1.353	0.326	-	0.099	0.067
	(2.928)	(0.898)		(0.205)	
78-85	0.917	-	0.286	0.019	0.054
	(1.207)		(0.789)	(0.093)	

*   The dependent variable is the log of the average rate of growth of real exports.

Numbers in parentheses are t-statistics.

Tables 8 and 9 contain the regression results for the average rate of growth of real GDP and real GDP per capita. The results are quite satisfactory, especially for the floating rates era. The R^2s indicate that a fairly significant fraction of the variability of average rates of growth across countries can be explained by these equations. Not surprisingly, the investment ratio is positively related to the average rates of growth. Those countries that accumulate capital more rapidly have generally grown at a faster average rate. This result holds both for the Bretton Woods period as well as for the floating rates period. Notice, however, that there is a marked difference in the magnitude of the coefficients. For the more recent era the point estimates are almost one half of those obtained for the Bretton Woods period. As noted, the coefficients of the RER variability indexes are quite different across periods. The results do provide quite strong support to the hypothesis that, during the floating rates period, higher real exchange rate instability has been associated to poorer economic performance. It is interesting to note that both in tables 8 and 9 the coefficients of the index of instability for the real effective rate are higher than those of the index of instability for the real bilateral rate. In all equations the index of instability of external terms of trade turned out to be nonsignificantly different from zero.

How can we account for the differences in the results for the Bretton Woods and floating rates period? A possible explanation lays on the different nature of real exchange rate instability in both periods. During the old institutional arrangements real exchange rate movements were much more predictable, since by design wide daily fluctuations in third parties' bilateral rates were not an important source of nominal real exchange rates instability.

Table 10 presents the regression results for the investment equation. A double log specification was used. In many ways these results are similar to those on real output growth, indicating that during the floating rates period there has been a pretty strong negative relation between the degree of real exchange rate instability and investment. Notice, however, that these equations only explain a very low percentage of the cross country variation of investment ratios. Finally, table 11 contains the results for the export growth equations. Interestingly enough, these results are in line with those of the IMF, indicating that there is no significant connection between RER instability and exports performance. However, a word of caution related to measurement is needed here. The exports growth data used in these regressions refer to exports in real U.S. dollars, and have been computed as the rate of growth of exports in U.S. dollars deflated by the U.S. WPI. There is, then, a potential valuation problem that may be responsible for the fact that the coefficients of the variability indexes are nonsignificant.

The reports mentioned above were obtained using indexes of instability of RER which were constructed using official data on nominal exchange rates. However, as was shown in Section IV above, in the developing countries many times there are significant departures of the black market rate from the official rates. For this reason performance equations using instability of black market rates were also estimated. The following result was obtained for the floating rates period and for the rate of growth of real GDP.

$$\text{Growth Real GDP} = \underset{(1.812)}{2.507} - \underset{(-3.445)}{0.190} \text{ Variability BMRER}$$

$$+ \underset{(2.939)}{0.166} \text{ Investment Ratio} - \underset{(-0.910)}{0.004} \text{ Variability T of T}$$

$$R^2 = 0.646$$

This result supports our previous findings, indicating that higher real exchange rate instability has been clearly associated with poorer economic performance (i.e. real growth) during the Bretton Woods period. The interesting thing here is that since we are dealing with black market instability, this measure is clearly dependent on the policies followed by the government. In order to further analyze these issues regressions including both official RER instability and variability of the black market RER were estimated. This allows us to have some idea of how, with other things given, each of these sources of instability has affected economic performance:

$$\text{Growth Real GDP} = \underset{(1.767)}{3.208} - \underset{(-1.427)}{0.711} \text{ Variability BMRER}$$

$$+ \underset{(2.767)}{0.153} \text{ Investment Ratio} - \underset{(0.176)}{0.009} \text{ Variability T of T}$$

$$- \underset{(-2.239)}{0.138} \text{ Variability BMRER}$$

$$R^2 = 0.694$$

VI. Concluding Remarks

The evidence presented in this paper shows that in the developing countries, as well as in the DCs, real exchange rate instability has greatly increased after the abandonment of the Bretton Woods regime. Moreover, the cross country regression analysis indicates that, at least during the recent floating rates era, there has been a strong negative relation between higher real exchange rate instability and economic performance, measured by real growth of GDP and real growth of GDP per capita.

The increase in real exchange rate instability in the developing nations has, in a large part, been the result of the higher degree of variability of third (developed) parties. In fact, it is argued in the paper that the abandonment of the international monetary system based on fixed exchange rates has greatly reduced the (practical) ability of the developing nations to engage in stable nominal exchange rate policies, generating in this way higher RER variability and poorer economic performance. It would seem, then, that an important (indirect) effect of a reform of the international monetary institutions geared at reducing exchange rate fluctuations would help the poorer nations reduce the extent of instability to which their RERs are now subject.

References

Barro, R.J. (1983), Real Determinants of the Real Exchange Rates, unpublished paper (November).

Brecher, R. (1974), Minimum Wages and the Pure Theory of International Trade, *Quarterly Journal of Economics*.

Cavallo, D., and J. Cotani (1985), Real Exchange Rates in LDCs, Unpublished Manuscript, World Bank.

Darby, M. (1983), International Economic Policy Co-ordination and Transmissions: A Review. *Oxford Economic Papers*, 38 (November).

Cooper, R. (1971), Exchange Rate Devaluation in Developing Countries, *Princeton Essays on International Finance*.

De Grauwe, P., M. Janssens and H. Lelianert (1984), Real Exchange Rate Variability During 1920-26 and 1973-82, Unpublished Manuscript.

De Grauwe, P., and M. Rosiers (1984), Real Exchange Rate Variability and Monetary Disturbances, Unpublished Manuscript.

Diaz-Alejandro, C. (1986), *Exchange Rate Devaluation in a Semi-Industrialized Economy: Argentina 1955-1961*, MIT Press.

Dornbusch, R. (1974), Tariffs and Nontraded Goods, *Journal of International Economics* (May), pp. 117-185.

Dornbusch, R. (1976), The Theory of Flexible Exchange Regimes and Macroeconomic Policy, *Scandinavian Journal of Economics*, 78 (May), pp. 255-257.

Dornbusch, R. (1980), *Open Economy Macroeconmics*, Basic Books, New York.

Dornbusch, R. (1983), Remarks on the Southern Cone, *IMF Staff Papers* (March).

Dornbusch, R. (undated), Panel Discussion on Opening of the Economy.

Dornbusch, R. (1986a), Special Exchange Rates for Capital Account Transactions, *World Bank Economic Review* (September).

Dornbusch, R. (1986b), Special Exchange Rates for Commercial Transactions, in Edwards, S. and L. Ahamed (eds.), *Economic Adjustment and Exchange Tastes in Developing Countries*, University of Chicago Press.

Edwards, S. (1983), Floating Exchange Rates, Expectations and New Information, *Journal of Monetary Economics* (May).

Edwards, S. (1984), The Order of Liberalization of the External Sector, *Princeton Essays on International Finance*, No. 156.

Edwards, S. (1985a), Stabilization and Liberalization: An Evaluation of the Years of Chile's Experiment with Free Market Policies, 1973-1983, *Economic Development and Cultural Change* (January).

Edwards, S. (1985b), Money, the Rate of Devaluation and Interest Rates in a Semi-Open Economy, *Journal of Money, Credit and Banking* (February).

Edwards, S. and F. Ng (1985c), Trends in Real Exchange Rate Behavior in Selected Developing Countries, CPD Working Paper, The World Bank.

Edwards, S. (1986a), Tariffs, Terms of Trade and Real Exchange Rates in Inter-temporal Models of the Current Account, Working Paper, Dept. of Economics, UCLA.

Edwards, S. (1986b), Are Devaluations Contractionary?, *Review of Economics and Statistics* (August).

Edwards, S. (1986c), Exchange Rate Misalignment in Developing Countries: Analytical Issues and Empirical Evidence, CPO Working Paper, The World Bank.

Edwards, S. (1986d), Economic Liberalization and the Real Exchange Rate in Developing Countries, paper presented at the Carlos-Diaz-Alejandro Memorial Conference, Helsinki (August).

Edwards, S. and S. van Wijnbergen (1986), The Welfare Effects of Trade and Capital Market Liberalization, *International Economic Review* (February).

Edwards, S. (forthcoming), *Real Exchange Rates, Devaluation and Adjustment*, MIT Press.

Edwards, S. and A. Cox Edwards (1987), *Monetarism and Liberalization: The Chilean Experiment*, Ballinger.

Eichengreen, B. (1985), International Policy Coordination in Historical Perspective: A View from the Interwar Years, in W. Buiter and R. Marston (eds.), *International Economic Policy Coordination,* Cambridge University Press.

Frankel, J. and R. Meese (1987), Are Exchange Rates Excessively Volatile?, Working Paper, University of California, Berkeley.

Frenkel, J. (1981), Flexible Exchange Rates, Prices and the Role of News: Lessons from the 1970's, *Journal of Political Economy* 89, pp. 665-705.

Harberger, A. (1986a), Economic Adjustment and the Real Exchange Rate, in Edwards, S. and L. Ahamed (eds.), *Economic Adjustment and Exchange Rates in Developing Countries*, University of Chicago Press.

Harberger, A. (1986b), A Primer on the Chilean Economy, in Choksi and D. Papageorgiuous, *Economic Liberalization in Developing Countries*, Blackwell, Oxford.

Helleiner, G., (1981) *The Impact of the Exchange Rate System on the Developing Countries*, Report prepared for the Group of Twenty-Four.

Horn, S., R. Horn and D. Duncan (1975), Estimating Heteroscedastic Variances in Linear Models, *Journal of the American Statistical Association* (June), pp. 380-385.

International Monetary Fund (1984), *Exchange Rate Volatility and World Trade*, Washington, D.C. (July).

Katseli, L. (1985), Real Exchange Rates in the 1970's, in J. Bilson and R. Marston (eds.), *Exchange Rate Theory and Practice*, University of Chicago Press.

Lizondo, J.S. (1986), Exchange Rate Reunification, paper presented at Econometric Society Meetings, Cordoba, Argentina.

McKinnon, R. (1984), *International Standard for Monetary Stabilization*, MIT Press, Cambridge, MA.

Melvin, M. and D. Bernstein (1984), Trade Concentrations, Openness and the Impact of Real Factors on Deviations from Purchasing Power Parity, *Journal of International Money and Finance* (December), pp. 369-376.

Stockman, A. (1983), Real Exchange Rates und Alternative Nominal Exchange Rate Systems, *Journal of International Money and Finance* (April).

Willett, T. (1986), Exchange Rate Volatility, International Trade, and Resource Allocation: A Perspective on Recent Research, *Journal of International Money and Finance* (March), pp. 101-112.

Williamson, J. (1983), *The Exchange Rate System*, Institute of International Economics, Washington D.C.

COMMENTS

Peter Bernholz

Sebastian Edwards has presented an interesting and convincing empirical study. It gives strong support to the hypothesis that real exchange rate instability has greatly increased for developing countries after the end of the Bretton Woods regime. Moreover, strong evidence is provided that this greater variability of real exchange rates has had a sizable negative impact on average real growth and on average real per capita growth in these countries. The influence on investment ratios turns out to be much weaker, whereas no such influence seems to exist on the growth of exports. The latter result is in accordance with earlier research, notably a study of the International Monetary Fund.

Looking at the estimated equation (V, last paragraph), it is interesting to note that the impact of the variability of the official real exchange rate on the growth of real gross domestic product is much greater than that of the variability of the black market real exchange rate, but that only the latter turns out to be significant. I do not find an explanation for this fact in the paper and wonder whether Sebastian Edwards could give us some additional information.

The author states that the "increase in real exchange rate instability in the developing nations has, in a large part, been the result of the higher degree of variability of third (developed) parties" (in VI, 2nd paragraph). Though it can be scarcely doubted that the change to flexible exchange rates increased real exchange rate instability, and Edwards gives some definitional support to this (in II.2), I cannot see empirical support in his paper for the assertion that the instability has "*in a large part*" been a consequence of this factor. From Tables 2 and 3 we see only that the Coefficient of Variation has increased after 1971 for all but 4 or 1 out of 23 cases respectively for the Real Effective and for the Real Bilateral Exchange Rate. If we consider the period from 1978-85, however, for the Real Effective

Studies in International Economics and Institutions
Vosgerau (Ed.) New Institutional Arrangements for the World Economy
© Springer-Verlag Berlin Heidelberg 1989

Exchange Rate, then the Coefficient of Variation has only increased in 13 out of the 23 cases, whereas this is true for 17 cases for the Bilateral Real Exchange Rate. But the latter should not be influenced by real exchange rate variability among the U.S. dollar and the currencies of third countries, at least not according to the definitional arguments made (in II.2). Thus the latter figure should be smaller than the former, which is not the case.

It is interesting, moreover, to observe the vast differences of the Coefficients of Variation in Tables 2 and 3 for different countries, and the strong differences of their changes after the abolishing of the Bretton Woods System. This seems to suggest that other factors than the change of the exchange rate regime have been more important for increased volatility. One factor which comes to mind in this regard are the strongly increased and substantially different levels and volatilities of the rates of inflation. It has been shown elsewhere (Bernholz 1982; Bernholz, Heri and Gaertner 1985) that we have good empirical and theoretical support for the hypothesis of an influence of these factors on real exchange rates.

The point just mentioned should be of particular relevance for developing countries. If such a country inflates its money supply more than its main trading partners, then an undervaluation of its currency should result, according to this theory. The undervaluation, however, implies a positive feedback on domestic inflation because of higher import prices and a stimulation of exports. Because of political reasons many governments seem to react to this development with exchange controls and an effort to stabilize official exchange rates. But with higher rates of inflation this will, in time, lead to an overvaluation of the currency, in a period where only undervalued rates would clear exchange markets. Consequently, a substantial balance of payments deficit develops which implies stricter exchange controls and, after some time, enforces a strong devaluation often leading back to undervalued equilibrium exchange rates. It is obvious that, if this description of political-economic relationships is correct, we can point to an important domestic cause of real exchange rate instability.

Let us turn next to some other critical remarks. In V (paragraph 1), Edwards points out that "from a theoretical perspective it has been well established that real exchange rate disequilibrium and heightened uncertainty regarding RER (real exchange rate) will have negative effects on economic performance". But when we look at his empirical work, it appears that the effect of exchange rate disequilibrium has not been tested. For only the coefficient of variation of the real exchange rate and not the divergence of its level from purchasing power parity have been used as independent variables in the empirical estimations. This is somewhat surprising, especially since some effort is extended on defining an equilibrium real exchange rate (in II.3). I do not know whether this omission is related to the fact that no formal definition of this equilibrium real exchange rate (composed of weighted real exchange rates?) has (or can?) be given, so that Edwards does not propose a measure of divergence of the actual from the equilibrium real exchange rate. But why should purchasing power parity not be taken as a long-term equilibrium concept? So that the divergence of actual real exchange rates from purchasing power parity could be used?

The equilibrium real exchange rate, as defined verbally by the author, has some additional problems. Is it dynamically stable, i.e., are there economic forces driving the actual real exchange rate towards it? It is not clear that Edwards thinks this to be the case (in II.3, last paragraph). But what forces are then responsible for letting the actual real exchange rate deviate persistently from the equilibrium real rate?

Another question which I would like to ask concerns the selection criterion of the 23 countries considered in the empirical study. Why is it that countries like Argentina, Chile, Mexico and Peru are missing? It would also be interesting to know which official exchange rates have been used in cases of countries with multiple rates.

I conclude with a point concerning exchange rate policies. Let us assume that it is true that the volatility of the U.S. dollar vis-à-vis the currencies of third countries has been a major source of the strong variability of real exchange rates of developing countries. Whey then could these countries stabilize their real exchange rates better by pegging nominal exchange rates not to the U.S. dollar but to weighted baskets of the currencies of their main trading partners? It seems that such a policy has been followed quite successfully by countries like Norway, Sweden and Finland, and I do not see why developing countries could not follow the same recipe.

References

Bernholz, Peter (1982), Flexible Exchange Rates in Historical Perspective, *Princeton Studies in International Finance*, vol. 49, Princeton University, International Finance Section, Dept. of Economics.

Bernholz, Peter; Gaertner, Manfred; and Heri, Erwin (1985), Historical Experiences with Flexible Exchange Rates, *Journal of International Economics*, vol. 19, pp. 21-45.

The European Monetary System:
A Regional Bretton Woods or an Institutional Innovation?*

Manfred Wegner

I.   Introduction

The breakdown of the Bretton Woods regime and the shift to floating exchange rates in 1973 was a response to changing circumstances and policy behaviour due to real shocks and inflationary pressures. Experience with flexible exchange rates reveals a number of weaknesses for which the new system cannot be blamed entirely - and there is a growing clamour for exchange rate stability and even for a more systemic reform of the existing international monetary regime.

The on-going debate about the relative strengths or weaknesses of alternative exchange rate regimes has provided valuable theoretical insights. But the gulf between the different positions is wide (Crockett and Goldstein, 1987) and the empirical evidence for the various arguments is still insufficient for giving clear-cut answers. The European Monetary System (EMS) is one of the rare real world "experiments" and a showpiece presenting some lessons on how alternatives to the present regime might function. The EMS, once called a "theoretical impossibility", has become an accepted and successful institutional monetary arrangement.

The main and immediate objective of the EMS was to create "closer monetary co-operation leading to a zone of monetary stability" by "pursuing policies conducive to greater stability at home and abroad" (Bremen Declaration, July 6 and 7, 1978). The move towards a more stable system was triggered by the attempt to protect the European countries against the vagaries of the declining U.S. dollar and to increase the cohesion of the European currencies in the face of growing external uncertain-

---

*   I gratefully acknowledge the helpful comments and suggestions from Daniel Hardy and the constructive criticism of the participants of the Symposium.

Studies in International Economics and Institutions
Vosgerau (Ed.) New Institutional Arrangements for the World Economy
© Springer-Verlag Berlin Heidelberg 1989

ties and instabilities. The initiative in creating the EMS was also based on a fundamental political reason: to relaunch the process of European political and economic integration which had been eroded by the economic turbulences and shocks of the 1970s.

In general, the establishment of the EMS, which came into operation in March 1979, was not hailed in Europe. Many economists and market operators remained deeply sceptical about the desirability and the viability of the project. The EMS was seen, at the end of the 1970s, by most academic economists as an "at best superfluous and at worst dangerous initiative" (Thygesen 1981). They feared that a quasi-fixed system would undermine national efforts to pursue target-constrained monetary policies; introduce large real exchange rate distortions because of insufficient nominal corrections; lead to macro-economic inconsistencies due to the unsolved problem of "who should adjust to whom"; and reduce the discipline of inflation-prone countries by the availability of generous credit facilities. Economic fundamentalists did not believe in the disciplinary forces of the system and refused the gradual development towards monetary unification or the transfer of decision-making powers to an European institution. In the early 1980s it was sometimes argued that the EMS survived for the "wrong reasons" and only because of the strong U.S. dollar associated with a weak deutsche mark.

The opponents in Germany feared a loss of monetary control and the risks of higher inflation. In weaker and more inflation-prone countries it was argued that the burden of adjustment would produce a deflationary bias for them. The Italian government decided to join the EMS only after having been allowed to use much wider fluctuation margins than the other participants. Ireland insisted on the provision that large subsidized loans for selected infrastructure projects be made available to less prosperous member states of the EC. The British government could not be convinced to join the exchange rate mechanism and remains outside even today. Only France and the Benelux countries entered the new arrangements without reservations.

The relative success of the EMS has surprised most observers. The system has survived many unexpected shocks and policy changes, has adopted to the protracted swings of the dollar, but failed to be developed towards the planned institutional phase. Most initial sceptics and opponents, such as the Bundesbank, agree now that the EMS was much more beneficial than anticipated and that the critical contentions were not justified. The British industrial and banking establishment now favours an entry into the exchange rate system. The discussion and pressures to improve the functioning of the EMS and the role of the ECU continue.

Why is it that the EMS has been able to silence the former anxieties? What have been the most important features and indicators of the relative success of the EMS? How far has the system contributed to the improved policy performance and stability of its participants? What are the new institutional arrangements and mechanisms which brought about the greater exchange rate stability and a closer policy convergence among the member countries? Does the system need institutional improvements to defend the achievements of the past eight years and to reap the potentials of higher economic welfare?

This paper addresses a number of issues in assessing the performance of the EMS since its inception in 1979. The first part describes the new institutional arrangements in the EMS in comparison to the Bretton Woods regime and the functioning of the system at work with its mixture of institutional procedures and unwritten rules in managing the monetary cooperation within the EMS. The second section examines the performance of the exchange rate mechanism in improving the nominal and real stability of exchange rates, as well as the convergence and policy cooperation among the member countries. The final chapter concludes with a discussion of some recent proposals for exchange rate and policy coordination.

II. New Institutional Arrangements: Rules and Discretion

The EMS is based on

- a grid of stable but adjustable exchange rates,

- the mutual obligations of the participating central banks to defend the agreed bilateral central rates within a narrow range of ± 2.5% (or ± 6% for Italy) and

- a commitment to enhance the convergence of economic policies and of economic performance towards greater stability.

For the superficial observer the EMS may look like the old Bretton Woods system decorated with some formal innovations. But the EMS is more than a simple replica of the former system and has developed into an exchange rate system *sui generis*.

Broadly speaking, the existing mechanisms and the functioning of the system consists of the following components (van Ypersele and Koeune, 1984):

- an exchange rate and intervention mechanism based on the maintenance of bilateral parities and on strict intervention rules;

- the automatic very short-term credit facilities and medium-term financial assistance (and other Community loans) which support the credibility of the intervention commitments and have been greatly expanded over the former "snake" arrangements:

- the divergence indicator and

- the composite monetary unit: ECU (the European Currency Unit) being regarded as the centre of the EMS.

What makes the functioning of the EMS differ from the Bretton Woods regime cannot be defined only in form of written provisions. It includes also the adoption of flexible and unwritten rules in managing the system to react to changing policy problems.

The essential new institutional aspects of the EMS have been:

- the ECU and the divergence indicator,

- the collective decision-making in adjusting bilateral parities, and

- the ensuing progress in economic policy coordination.

Official ECU and Divergence Indicator: Disappointed Hopes

The ECU is a composite monetary unit or basket serving several functions (official instrument of settlement between the EMS member central banks, reserve asset, numéraire for determining the central rates) which are not explored further here. Also, the unexpected expansion of the private ECU is not discussed.

It is worthwhile to note that the initial plans for the EMS were based on much more radical innovations than realized in the later agreement. The initial proposals for the exchange rate mechanism had been based on the ECU (basket) system and the obligation to act and to intervene in response to the divergence indicator. The strong opponents of an ECU basket system, including the Bundesbank, feared that the orientation of national monetary policies towards an average norm would not favour greater stability but induce inflationary reactions. After intense discussions the traditional parity grid solution (with bilateral intervention limits) was finally agreed upon.

The official ECU has not acquired the central role as a means of settlement and reserve asset which had originally been intended. But there is one function which makes this unit of account different from the SDR or the "snake" arrangements: the ECU denominates the obligatory interventions and credit operations, thus taking up the notion of Community burden-sharing of the exchange risks for both the creditor and debtor central banks. In all former arrangements the exchange rate risks were exclusively carried by the debtor country. In the EMS, the value in national currency of the debts and claims - created in the intervention mechanism to defend the bilateral margins - is influenced by the behaviour of all currencies in the basket and thus by the financial and monetary policies of all EMS countries.

In the negotiating stage and early years of the EMS, the divergence indicator was seen as the most original and major institutional innovation of the new regime. The divergent indicator was initially planned to function as an objective indicator or trigger for consultations and adjustments by measuring the deviation of each EMS currency from the Community average represented by the ECU. The final agreement (Resolution of the European Council of December 5, 1978) stated that the crossing by a member currency of its threshold of divergence (75% of the maximum spread of divergence from all other currencies) would "result in a presumption that the authorities concerned would correct the situation by adequate measures, namely

- diversified interventions,
- measures of domestic monetary policy (such as interest rates),
- changes in central rates, and
- other measures of economic policy".

In practice, the divergence indicator became a supplementary device, functioning as an early warning system in the first years of the EMS. The divergence indicator has played a much smaller role than was originally envisaged partly because of the widespread recourse to intramarginal interventions and partly because of distortions due to the inclusion of the pound sterling and the application of wider margins for the Italian lira.

Exchange Rate Realignments: Rules and Procedures

Under the Bretton Woods agreement the condition for exchange rate adjustment was given only if a country had to correct a "fundamental disequilibrium". Although this requirement had the purpose of limiting the number of exchange rate changes, the problem turned out to be that there were too few adjustments in the Bretton Woods system. Parity changes were essentially based on unilateral decisions and ratified by the IMF in a formal way except for adjustments within a 20% band of the parity (where the approval of the Fund was necessary) (Dam, 1982). The weak institutional framework of the IMF and the excess rigidity of exchange rates in a period of growing macro-economic divergence contributed finally to the breakdown of the Bretton Woods system.

The experience with parity changes in the EMS has been quite different. There have been 11 currency realignments over the eight years of the EMS. Parity changes in the EMS are "subject to mutual consent" and have become, in practice, a truly collective decision within a multilateral framework.

The EMS is no rigid fixed-rate system nor has it led to a crawling peg system as some observers concluded after the small adjustments in the first years. It would be wrong to give equal importance to all of the numerous parity adjustments. Table 1 provides a rough idea about the magnitude and frequency of the eleven realignments of EMS central rates which have taken place over the eight years since the system was launched in March 1979. They are of a mixed variety:

- in three cases only *one* individual currency was involved (DKr, lira and £Ir) in a unilateral devaluation;

- on two occasions the central rates of *two* currencies had been corrected simultaneously (DM and DKr, BF and DKr);

- in July 1985 the lira devalued whereas all other currencies revalued, and in January 1987 *three currencies* (DM, f., and BF) revalued together vis-à-vis all other countries;

- in several years (1979, 1981, 1982 and 1986), two consecutive parity adjustments had taken place, mostly within an interval of some months;

- in four cases (1981, 1982, 1983 and 1986) comprehensive and multilateral adjustments occurred accompanied by changes in the monetary and policy stance.

The collective and bargaining character of realignments in the EMS evolved only gradually. The first three parity changes in 1979 and 1981 still followed the pattern of the Bretton Woods and "snake" arrangements. The devaluation of the Danish krone (5%) in 1979 and of the lira (6%) in early 1981 had been the result of informal (telephone) procedures and of unilateral decisions by the interested countries. Since then, EMS realignments moved away from unilateral decisions and towards the discretionary collective management of exchange rates and monetary policies.

Since the fifth realignment (February 1982) parity changes were based on joint decision-making and have all been more comprehensive adjustments involving most and sometimes all participants in the EMS (except the unilateral devaluation of the Irish pound in 1986). The actual result of the realignment bargaining process rarely met the initial requests of the countries. For example, in February 1982 the EMS countries refused the request for a 12% devaluation of the Belgian franc and for a 7% devaluation of the Danish krone and granted much smaller adjustments of 8.5% and 3% respectively. Also in April 1986, the French government brought down the demanded devaluation, after hard bargaining and play-acting, from 8% to 5.8% against the deutsche mark.

Table 1:

Adjustments of Central Rates in the EMS (in %)

	Date of central rate change	DM	f.	BF/LF	FF.	Lit	DKr	£Ir	Largest bilateral change (%)	Period between 2 realignments (months)
1.	24. 9. 1979	+2					-3		5	-
2.	30.11. 1979						-5		5	2
3.	22. 3. 1981					-6			6	16
4.	5.10. 1981	+5.5	+5.5		-3	-3			8.5	6
5.	22. 2. 1982			-8.5			-3		8.5	5
6.	14. 6. 1982	+4.25	+4.25		-5.75	-2.75			10	4
7.	21. 3. 1983	+5.5	+3.5	+1.5	-2.5	-2.5	+2.5	-3.5	9	9
8.	22. 7. 1985	+2	+2	+2	+2	-6	+2	+2	8	28
9.	6. 4. 1986	+3	+3	+1	-3		+1		6	8
10.	4. 8. 1986							-8	8	4
11.	12. 1. 1987	+3	+3	+2					3	5
	Cumulative changes[1] vis-à-vis - other EMS-countries	37	16	-9	-19	-26	-13	-13		
	- 19 industrial countries	24	15	-10	-19	-26	-12	-14		

[1] In terms of effective (double export weighted) nominal exchange rates since the beginning of 1979.

Source: EC-Commission.

The collective exchange rate management has been put to the test several times in the two years since 1981 as the result of the abrupt policy changes in France and the growing divergence between France and Germany. The size and frequency of central rate adjustments increased significantly in this turbulent period. The multilateral realignments in 1981, 1982 and 1983 have all been in the 8 to 10% range for several bilateral rates, especially for the FF and the DM. Then the years from 1983 to 1985 became the calmest period in the eight years history of the EMS without central rate changes for 28 months.

Realignment *procedures* now follow a well established routine: one or two members request a meeting of the Monetary Committee which was set up in 1958 and is composed of high officials from finance ministries, central banks and the EC-Commission. The Monetary Committee discusses the overall monetary and exchange rate situation of the countries which are diverging most or the individual country which suffers from acute exchange rate pressures. This advisory institution prepares possible options. The session is followed (the next day) by a meeting of the Ministers of Finance and Economics and of the Central Bank Governors of the EMS (including those of the UK, Greece, Spain and Portugal) which work out a compromise including also the outline for monetary and budgetary policy measures. The final new central rates are fixed by the Finance Ministers in their function as the EC Council of Ministers. The unanimity rule for deciding parity changes leads sometimes to very serious arguments and tensions between the participants. The exchange rate and policy package must be acceptable to all partners and credible for the exchange and financial markets. Once there was the grave threat that France would leave the system in order to realize her ambitious expansive programme started after the 1981 presidential elections. The dangerous divergence in the thrust of French and German macro-economic policy was solved by the economic U-turn of French policies towards a policy of rigour. This policy alignment was linked to the exchange rate adjustment.

Criteria for Exchange Rate Policies and the Role of Objective Indicators

Adjustments of central rates appear sometimes spectacular but they are not necessarily the most important events in the process of managing a more stable exchange rate system. The permanent job of managing the EMS is in the hands of the participating central banks. They have steered the system through frequent periods of exchange market strains (Ungerer et al., 1983, 1986). In many cases monetary authorities fought against exchange market pressures with substantial interventions, mostly "intramarginal" interventions before reaching the obligatory intervention limits, and with the help of interest rate changes or other short-term monetary policies.

The EMS provides almost unlimited and mostly unconditional credit facilities for the financing of interventions, which again is different from the Bretton Woods system. Intervention and other temporary actions to defend the mutually agreed central rates within the fluctuation band are only efficient and credible when the disciplinary constraints of the system move the price and cost trends towards more convergence and stability.

The common reason for exchange rate adjustments has been the appearance of inflation differentials between the member countries. Often exchange rate changes became inevitable when political changes due to elections were combined with a lack of commitment to reducing the existing cost and price differentials between the EMS currencies and to redressing external imbalance. The efficient management of the EMS has to find an optimum path between the desire to use fixed exchange rates as means of forcing the convergence of cost and price trends by appropriate monetary cooperation and the need to use flexible responses to defuse speculative capital movements and to adjust to real disturbances.

Exchange rate realignments, interventions and macro-economic policy cooperation are all part of an interactive process of implementing rules and discretionary decisions. The intervention rules are necessary to manage the exchange rate mechanism. They have to be supplemented by discretionary policy-making to support the macro-economic adjustment and to respond to unexpected contingencies. The smooth functioning of the EMS is based on a pragmatic balance between rules and discretionary decisions. This approach is inevitable as long as a convincing theory of exchange rate determination is lacking and the uncertainty and disagreements about the impacts of individual policies and their interaction exist.

The permanent surveillance of exchange rate markets and of relevant policy variables is part of the cooperative framework of the EMS. The use of *objective indicators* for monitoring the performance of individual countries and assessing the consistency of economic policies has a long history in the European Community. In the EMS, the divergence indicator did not play the prophylactic role as an early warning device or in guiding policy reactions which was originally expected. Its main fault - besides technical deficiencies - was perhaps to be concerned exclusively with exchange rate movements. More comprehensive and objective indicators were necessary to advise policy makers on whether national currencies are out of line with economic fundamentals (over- or undervalued) and whether this imbalance should be left to resolve itself by the usual automatic reserve flow mechanism and domestic monetary conditions or whether it should be remedied by a parity change. A set of objective indicators was designed by the Commission's services to help to monitor the performance of exchange rates and economic policies by the Monetary Committee. They center around the following main economic aggregates:

- the external disequilibrium (the current account in % of GDP);

- the (net) reserves (enabling a country to pay for its imports);

- the price or cost competitiveness (several real effective exchange rate indices);

- the external indebtedness and the real interest rates (as measure for the strength or weakness of a pegged currency);

- several instruments (money supply, public finance), economic performance indicators (employment, wages, investment) and global economic objectives (prices, real GDP).

The updating and exchange of these data is supplemented by regular and systematic country examinations within the Monetary Committee which meets monthly. The sharing of information and its collective interpretation is a necessary condition for understanding how the monetary policy of each participant works, what the policy reaction functions are and what ramifications policy actions have for other countries. The use of objective indicators can be interpreted as an attempt to "depoliticize" the realignment process and to find a solution to the old issue, familiar from the Bretton Woods system, "who adjusts to whom?". The use of indicators of economic performance, economic policy and intermediate variables (see Crocket and Goldstein, 1987) can provide a useful framework for policy-making but is not sufficient to determine an optimum and consistent policy mix for all participants which distributes equitably the adjustment costs. A more formalized and stringent system of objective indicators would probably be objected to by the major countries which fear a loss of their national sovereignty.

But the regular monitoring and interpretation of exchange rate and macro-economic indicators are more than useful background information. They form the necessary framework for the collective learning process which is essential to successful policy coordination. The institutionalized cooperation in the EMS has been able to balance the flexible use of rules (concerning central rates, interventions, credit facilities, etc.) and of discretion. Discretionary decisions are necessary in handling complex events, external shocks and contingencies which cannot be recognized in advance and settled by clearly defined rules (Kindleberger 1986).

III. Exchange Rate Stability and Policy Convergence within the EMS

The attempt to appraise the EMS since its inception in 1979 involves a number of difficult issues. They range from more technical ones, such as the reduction of exchange rate variability and inflation rates, to the degree of convergence of economic policies and the improvement of economic welfare resulting from the working of the new system. Although there is a growing literature on the theoretical features of the EMS and its empirical performance, final conclusions about the costs and benefits of the EMS are premature.

The most-used method in recent empirical research in assessing the performance of the EMS is to compare the developments in the EMS countries during the last seven or eight years with those prior to the inception of the EMS - mostly for the period of 1974-78 - and in relation to some non-EMS countries. Constructing the

European non-EMS countries as "control group" is misleading because a number of European countries such as Austria and Switzerland are quasi-members of the EMS, and others such as the United Kingdom have tacitly accepted exchange rate targeting in recent years. These two comparisons are a crude substitute for a reference system. The real question is: "what would have happened if the EMS had not been created?". The construction of the counterfactual is impossible for many reasons: the lack of a theory explaining the exchange rate movements, the size and magnitude of disturbances due to the numerous external shocks and policy regime changes, and the unpredictability of policy reactions and their repercussions for other countries in a world without the EMS. The available analytical techniques and the relative short time series do not allow detailed model building and simulations of counter-factual developments.

The following remarks offer a review of some of the main contributions of the EMS to the objectives defined by the Resolution of the European Council in December 1978, namely to create a zone of monetary stability in Europe and to induce a greater degree of economic policy convergence.

Exchange Rate Performance and Variability

There is now widespread agreement that the EMS has achieved its immediate objective, namely to reduce the short-term variability of nominal and real exchange rates. Empirical studies on the *relative stability* of bilateral exchange rates within and outside the EMS have been carried out by the EC Commission (1982, 1984), the IMF (1983, 1986) and others (Padoa-Schioppa 1985, Rogoff 1985, and see Figure 1). They use several measures of variability such as averages of absolute changes, standard deviations and deviations from medium-term trends. Most measures show the same basic pattern over time and across countries.

The findings - based on unconditional or conditional variances (Rogoff 1985) - are robust and they all come more or less to the same conclusion:

- the short-run volatility of the dollar, the pound sterling and much less the yen has increased since 1979 in nominal bilateral and effective but also in real effective terms;

Fig. 1: Variances of Exchange Rates Against EMS Currencies

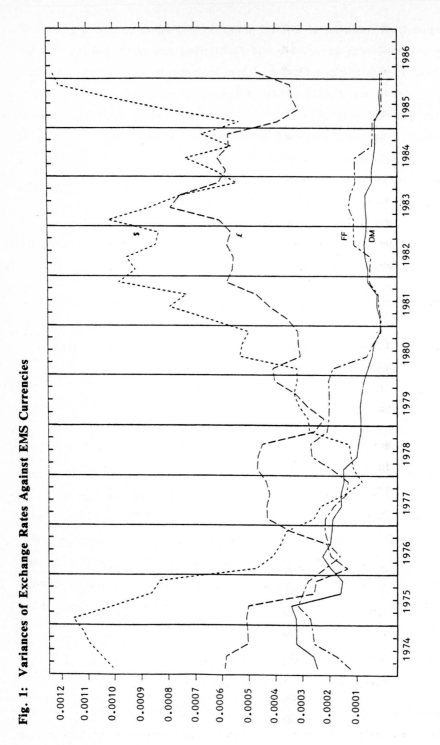

Source: E.E.C.

- the variability of bilateral nominal and nominal effective rates amongst EMS currencies has been significantly reduced since 1979 and was approximately half that recorded for non-EMS currencies;

- The EMS succeeded not only in generating greater stability in nominal exchange rates but has led to an increasing convergence of cost and price developments and to less variability of real intra-EMS exchange rates, but these gains have been less dramatic;

- the trend towards greater exchange rate stability has been substantially re-inforced in the last years.

Greater stability of intra-EMS exchange rates does not necessarily carry over to effective exchange rate movements against third countries. There are some indications (Rogoff, 1985) that the stability of intra-EMS bilateral rates was purchased at the price of greater variability in exchange rates between EMS currencies and those of third countries. However, the evidence is weak. Indeed, close study of the tables 16 to 30 in Ungerer et al. (1986) shows that the variances of the yen, U.S. dollar and pound sterling, that is, of the three main currencies independent of the EMS, against other non-EMS currencies has risen at least as much as that of EMS currencies since 1979. This fact suggests that most of the "news" (shock) originate outside the EMS, and that countries outside the EMS are largely responsible for the increased volatility since 1979.

The powerful evidence in favour of a greater short-run stability of both nominal and real exchange rates among the EMS currencies is not much of an achievement in itself. Exchange rate fluctuations could average out over several months or quarters or the short-term risks can be hedged by appropriate techniques. The proponents of the EMS claim that the "spectacular success" of the system is based on the offsetting of national inflation rates by smooth realignments, "thus pre-serving or restoring reasonably rapidly the stability of real exchange rates at competitive levels" (Triffin, 1985). The persistent deviations from the long-term equilibrium path and the protracted swings of exchange rates (misalignments) prob-ably create costly shifts in capital and labour resources and protectionist pressures which would damage the cohesion of a highly integrated economic region such as the European Community.

Real effective exchange rates are used as a rough indicator of *price competitiveness* and as a composite indicator of the behaviour both of nominal exchange rates and relative inflation vis-à-vis EMS and non-EMS countries.

The calculation of real effective exchange rates is fraught with many statistical and methodological difficulties. More stable real exchange rates can be the result of the disciplinary forces of the EMS leading to converging and lower inflation rates - but they can also be an indication of offsetting price increases due to nominal devaluations.

Table 2 provides some empirical evidence that the real effective exchange rate movements of EMS currencies have avoided excessive changes in relative competitiveness and responded well to the different economic fundamentals and internal and external adjustment needs of the member countries. The patterns in the changes of real effective exchange rates measured by relative unit labour costs and consumer prices in relation to the other EMS countries and to the broader base of 16 industrial countries are the following:

- for the Federal Republic of Germany and for France the realignments in the seven years from 1979 to 1986 have offset more or less the unit labour cost differentials relative to EMS partners and also the consumer price differentials in France; both countries appear to have followed in their exchange rate adjustments in the EMS a medium-term purchasing power parity rule;

- in Italy and Ireland the realignments have not compensated the price and cost differentials, both countries accepting large competitiveness losses for the price of lower import prices;

- all other EMS partners, especially Belgium and partly Denmark (in the years 1979 - 1984) and the Netherlands, have profited from competitive improvements within and outside the EMS; Belgium and Denmark are both countries with large current account deficits; it is worth noting that Denmark has reversed its devaluation stance since 1984.

Table 2:

Indicators of Competitiveness

(in Relation to EMS Partners and to 16 Industrial Countries)[1]

1979/I = 100

		as measured by Unit Labour Costs in Manufacturing		as measured by Consumer Prices	
		EMS	16 IC	EMS	16 IC
F.R. Germany	1982/I	97.0	87.5	92.5	84.4
	1984/I	103.6	90.6	94.8	83.3
	1986/I	103.9	92.9	90.8	83.4
France	1982/I	107.9	97.1	106.4	96.0
	1984/I	101.6	90.9	97.6	86.7
	1986/I	105.4	96.3	102.7	93.8
Italy	1982/I	112.8	102.5	115.0	104.1
	1984/I	123.3	109.9	126.6	110.4
	1986/I	115.4	105.8	126.7	114.3
Netherlands	1982/I	89.5	81.2	97.3	88.1
	1984/I	83.0	74.3	96.5	85.3
	1986/I	78.4	72.0	94.2	86.0
Belgium	1982/I	83.9	77.3	88.0	81.1
	1984/I	72.3	66.0	84.2	76.0
	1986/I	77.6	72.1	86.1	80.0
Denmark	1982/I	87.7	78.7	96.0	85.3
	1984/I	83.2	75.3	95.0	83.8
	1986/I	91.3	83.8	96.6	87.5
Ireland	1982/I	132.1	107.4	126.9	103.8
	1984/I	119.6	97.8	130.7	105.0
	1986/I	115.3	97.3	135.0	116.7

[1] Unit labour costs or consumer prices against the weighted average of unit labour costs or consumer prices of the other countries participating in the EMS exchange rate mechanism (in common currency) or of 16 industrial partner countries.

Source: Ungerer et al., 1986 (tables 11 to 14), quarterly data.

The experience of the EMS has shown that countries with higher inflation rates than their partners have lost competitiveness relative to their partner in two ways:

- between successive realignments higher inflation rates resulted in a temporary appreciation of the real exchange rate which fluctuated over time around PPP (French case) and/or

- the various realignments produced a more permanent real exchange rate appreciation by not fully accommodating the loss of competitiveness (Italian case).

On balance, the medium-term performance of nominal and real exchange rates reveals that the EMS works as an effective disciplinary device, and that their smooth adjustment is consistent with underlying economic fundamentals. This relative achievement contrasts sharply with the wide swings and persistent overshooting of some individually floating currencies, such as the U.S. dollar and the pound sterling.

Economic Policy Convergence and Policy Coordination

Progress towards convergence of economic policies and intermediate monetary objectives (such as at the growth of monetary aggregates and interest rates) and towards the coordination of economic policy-making within the EMS can best be assessed in comparison with the final objective: the reduction of price differentials between participating countries and a higher degree of price stability for the system as a whole. Both developments are an objective of the EMS and at the same time the prerequisite for the efficient functioning of the system.

Over the eight-year period the EMS made only slow progress on the inflation front (see Table 3). The *convergence of national inflation rates* among the participating countries was modest in the early years of the EMS. Due to the impact of the second oil price shock and the rapid appreciation of the dollar the average inflation for the EMS countries and the standard deviation widened in the first two years 1979 and 1980 relative to the pre-EMS period. Only in the following years have the average consumers price changes started to slow down. The price trend differentials between EMS countries narrowed only slightly in the years 1982 and 1983.

Table 3:

Consumer Price Changes in the EMS

(quarterly data, annual changes in %)

	1960–1973	Before EMS 1973/I–1979/I	After EMS			
			1979/I–1982/I	1981/IV–1983/IV	1983/IV–1986/IV	1985/IV–1986/IV
F.R. Germany	3.4	4.6	5.6	3.6	1.1	-1.1
France	4.6	10.6	13.3	8.7	4.6	2.1
Italy	4.7	16.2	19.1	14.9	7.2	4.7
Netherlands	4.9	7.2	6.5	3.7	1.5	-0.2
Belgium	3.6	8.6	7.0	7.9	3.4	0.6
Denmark	6.2	9.6	9.7	7.8	4.5	3.4
Ireland	5.9	14.8	18.4	11.3	4.9	3.2
Average EMS (weighted)[1]	4.3	9.2	10.9	7.8	3.6	1.4
Standard Deviation	1.3	4.2	5.1	4.2	2.3	2.2
United Kingdom	5.0	15.2	14.3	5.5	4.7	3.3
Average EC-10	4.6	10.4	11.8	7.5	4.2	2.1
U.S.A.	3.2	8.2	10.9	3.7	3.2	0.9
Japan	6.2	10.5	5.6	2.1	1.1	-0.2

[1] Without U.K.

Source: OECD (weights for EMS averages before EMS: 1980; after EMS: changing).

Substantial progress in reducing the average rate of inflation and differentials has become evident since 1984. During 1986, the average inflation rate in the EMS reached a record low of 1.4%, greatly helped by the decline of oil prices and the dollar. The standard deviations had been reduced by almost half compared with the variance of the pre-EMS period 1973-1978. The national inflation rates converged as is indicated by the bilateral correlation coefficients (Table 4) for the major countries.

It would be wrong to attribute this relative success uniquely to the establishment and discipline of the EMS. After the second oil price shock most industrial countries attached higher priority to price stability and implemented strongly restrictive monetary and - in many European countries - also stricter budgetary policies. Yet more formal empirical tests seem to support the hypothesis that the EMS "provided a framework in which anti-inflationary policies could be pursued more effectively" (Ungerer et al., 1986) and that the monetary discipline of the EMS has "induced several countries to disinflate more than they otherwise would have done" (Melitz, 1987).

The growing economic convergence is mirrored in the growth rates for narrow and broad money which decelerated drastically on average in the 1980s as compared with 1974-1978. In the late 1970s, the annual rise of the broad money aggregate amounted to 13-14% for the EMS on average and has been reduced in 1986 to less than 7%. The standard deviation was more than halved during this period comparable with the variance of the 1960s.

A similar convergent development can be observed for the nominal short and long-term interest rate levels in the EMS countries (as one expects from uncovered interest parity) (see Table 4); short-term and long-term interest rates moved more closely with those of partner countries in the post-EMS period than before. The dependence on the German interest rates has grown , especially for the smaller countries, Belgium, the Netherlands and Denmark, with very open economies.

Several empirical studies have provided evidence that the close interest rate linkage can be broken by *capital controls*. It has been argued that extensive capital controls have been a major factor contributing to the relative stability of EMS exchange rates. They are claimed to be essential in defending weak EMS currencies from speculative attacks and in avoiding excessive domestic interest rate fluctuations.

Capital controls in effect increase transaction costs, thus imposing obstacles for international portfolio diversification and reducing the degree of asset substitutability. Behind these institutional barriers countries can then pursue more independent monetary policies even with pegged exchange rates; capital controls are a reflection of the unwillingness - up till now at least - of some EMS members to conform thoroughly.

Capital controls were operative both before and after the inception of the EMS in many European countries, especially in Italy, France and Ireland, but also in Belgium with its two tier exchange rate markets and Denmark, and they were even strengthened in France after May 1981. The argument that capital controls could suspend the link between interest rates is based on the observation that intra-European real interest rate differentials have become more volatile since the formation of the EMS (Rogoff 1985) and that outside disturbances have led to asymmetric exchange rate responses within the EMS (Giovazzi and Giovannini, 1986a). A further argument revealing the important role of capital controls in the EMS can be seen in the growing exchange rate tensions during the second half of 1986 when some measures to liberalize capital movements were taken in France and Italy. The counter-argument is to be found in Denmark which abolished exchange controls and liberalized portfolio investments some time ago without inducing speculative capital outflows. The planned full liberalization of capital markets in the European Community will have important consequences for the functioning of the EMS and will be a serious test for the system in its current form.

The convergence of economic performance is a necessary but not sufficient condition for achieving greater exchange rate stability. Prolonged inconsistencies in the policy mix of fiscal and monetary policies have been the root cause for the persistent misalignments of key currencies in the 1980s (Wegner 1987). Balancing the often conflicting requirements of internal and external balance and minimizing the negative spill-over effects of national policies requires effective rules in the co-ordination of macro-economic policies.

Table 4:

Correlation Between Inflation Rates, Real GDP Growth and

Interest Rates in the EMS Countries Before and After the EMS

(based on quarterly data)

	France 1973–78	France 1978–86	Italy 1973–78	Italy 1978–86	United Kingdom 1973–78	United Kingdom 1978–86
Consumer price inflation rates						
Germany	0.78	0.97	0.34	0.93	0.60	0.74
France	-	-	0.64	0.94	0.37	0.75
Italy	-	-	-	-	0.29	0.80
Real GDP growth rates						
Germany	0.87	0.61	0.69	0.77	0.69	0.37
France	-	-	0.90	0.66	0.52	0.31
Italy	-	-	-	-	0.21	-0.06
Nominal short-term interest rates						
Germany	0.54	0.74	0.61	0.59	-0.01	0.30
France	-	-	0.09	0.81	-0.15	-0.03
Italy	-	-	-	-	0.07	-0.17
Nominal long-term interest rates						
Germany	-0.23	0.82	-0.78	0.69	0.48	0.81
France	-	-	0.64	0.94	0.47	0.60
Italy	-	-	-	-	-0.02	0.49
"Real" short-term interest rates						
Germany	0.06	0.34	-0.25	0.39	0.49	0.46
France	-	-	0.11	0.46	0.16	0.29
Italy	-	-	-	-	0.20	0.40
"Real" long-term interest rates						
Germany	-0.25	0.59	-0.10	0.57	0.61	0.69
France	-	-	0.87	0.77	0.22	0.82
Italy	-	-	-	-	0.31	0.91

Sources: EC Commission and OECD.

Short-term interest rates: Call money rates or, for Italy, the official discount rate.
Long-term interest rates: Yield on long-term government bonds.
"Real" interest rates: Nominal rate minus current inflation.

The EMS has agreed upon clearly defined rules for the working of the exchange rate intervention system. But no well established lines of action for the *coordination of macro-economic policies* to ensure cooperative outcomes instead of beggar-thy-neighbour policies or free-rider attitudes have been settled.

In the previous "snake" arrangement the deutsche mark was already regarded as an "attractive pole", guiding the monetary and interest rate policies of the smaller countries. With the gradual establishment of a zone of monetary stability the EMS, too, became the anchor for the formerly weak currencies and made Germany the monetary centre of gravity (Micossi and Padoa-Schioppa, 1984) in which the Bundesbank exercises a dominant influence. German economic policy leads the disinflationary process within the EMS and makes the German exchange rate the reference point which implicitly determines who should adjust, when and by how much. That Germany can play such a role is based on a record of superior price performance established long before the inception of the EMS.

But what can explain the attractiveness of the German stability course and the voluntary commitment to it of other countries within the EMS? Why have the inflation-prone countries accepted a more restrictive monetary policy? Convergence towards the German policy stance and a low inflation objective was not the initial intention of most partners, who would have preferred the adoption of a more moderate guide-line for their policies. Some authors (Giavazzi and Giovannini, 1986b; Padoa-Schioppa, 1985) have argued that the main reason for the EMS commitments is the large gain in credibility for policy makers and monetary authorities in high inflation countries.

"Tying one's hands" in the EMS has the welfare-improved advantage of alleviating the "time-inconsistency" problem of policy makers. The "time-inconsistency" problem arises because policy makers are unable to make a binding commitment to anti-inflationary policies due to incentives to renege. Suppose that policy makers and especially the monetary authorities could achieve an increase in output and employment were they able to engineer a positive price "surprise" and thus exploit short-term nominal rigidities. Then there is an inflationary bias to policy which, however, never achieves any real good because the public anticipates the government's behaviour; surprises are necessarily unsystematic but the inflation persists.

Joining the EMS means restricting short-term manipulations of national policy makers and accepting competitiveness losses if inflation is relatively high, so policy can credibly be made less inflationary as the public recognizes that the potential benefit of an expansionary policy is reduced. If convergence is not complete (perhaps due to capital controls) then a country must bear the cost of reduced international competitiveness between realignments, but the benefits of greater price stability may be more than offsetting.

What are the gains for a stability oriented country such as Germany to be part of a pegged exchange rate system? Has the deutsche mark been shielded from rapid portfolio shifts in phases of a declining dollar which may put excessive upward pressure on the DM and disturb the EMS? It is often argued that the relative smooth performance of the EMS was only possible because the DM, the only reserve currency, has been weak against the dollar most of the time. The weakness of the deutsche mark may have considerably reduced the exchange rate tensions within the EMS and made it easier for the other EMS partners to accept the disciplinary constraints of the system. Yet, the empirical regularity between the U.S. dollar movements and tensions in the EMS found by some observers (Micossi and Padoa-Schioppa, 1984) cannot be based on a mechanical link between the (weakening) dollar and the (strengthening) DM. This link exists only in the short run and holds during infrequent and short-lived periods of exchange rate strains. In periods of calm exchange rate expectations other EMS currencies have in general kept pace with the DM. Sterilized interventions, moderate movements in interest rate differentials or small exchange rate changes have been sufficient to shield the EMS as a whole.

For example, the growing and persistent speculative tensions in the second half of 1986 (leading finally to the realignment in January 1987) originated mainly from capital flows and not from inflation differentials. The main weapon used to defend the EMS parities were massive intra-marginal intervention (amounting net to $35 billion), especially by the Bundesbank, but without affecting bank liquidity (Pöhl, 1987). In general, the emergence of a "deutsche mark zone" has not undermined the Bundesbank's ability to determine monetary growth and to pursue strict anti-inflationary policies. German economic policy has profited from the more stable monetary environment in the EMS which has made the restructuring process in industry easier to realize during a most turbulent period. This experience has contradicted the scepticism at the start of the EMS shared by most observers in Germany, including the Bundesbank.

Some observers have argued that the EMS regime has not contributed to the growth and intra-European trade performance of the participating countries as hoped by the proponents (de Grauwe, 1985). But there are few doubts that the disinflationary stance and the high real interest rates of the 1980s were not conducive to investment and growth in the Community. The EMS arrangement is still too fragile and incomplete to offer more than a framework in which a co-ordinated mix of macro-economic policies (Oudiz, 1985 and an employment-oriented growth strategy (EC Commission, 1986) combined, it is hoped, with the positive supply shock of creating the large internal market by 1992 may generate a forceful dynamic impetus. The EMS alone is a necessary but not sufficient part of a more general move to revive the economies of the Community.

IV.   Conclusions and Perspectives

Over the eight years since 1979 the EMS has shown an unexpected resilience in coping with many unforeseen circumstances: diverging policy preferences and new governments in the major countries, the fall of the U.S. dollar followed by a steep rise and a new decline and a serious recessionary period relieved by a sustained albeit moderate recovery in Europe. The hopes for a quick move towards monetary unification in the Community have not been fulfilled. The commitments of the founding fathers of the EMS to proceed to a more definite institutional framework were set aside. But also the widespread expectations that the EMS would not hold together for long or degenerate into a soft and unbinding arrangement have proved wrong.

Although valuable insight about the working of a managed exchange rate system has been gained, our knowledge about the real causes of exchange rate movements and the links with macro-economic policies is still limited. Nevertheless, a number of tentative conclusions about the experience in managing the EMS can be drawn:

- the variability of bilateral exchange rates among EMS currencies has fallen considerably; exchange rate adjustments and the intervention arrangements allowed a flexible response to internal and external pressures; the EMS has proved to be much less rigid than the Bretton Woods system;

- the collective setting of new central rates has developed into "the most important aspect of constitutional practice" (Padoa-Schioppa 1985) promoting a common learning process in policy cooperation and ruling out competitive devaluations and related protectionist measures;

- in general, realignments have tended to offset the inflation differentials between EMS countries, thereby avoiding overshooting of real exchange rate and improving the accuracy and stability of exchange rate expectations;

- the commitment to more stable exchange rates has helped the partner countries to gain control over inflationary tendencies at home and to avoid the vicious circle of depreciation and inflation; the disciplinary forces imposed by the EMS and the growing weight given to price stability have contributed to the reduction of inflation and inflation differentials, particularly in the most recent period;

- the established rules of the EMS and the evolving balance with discretionary measures in supporting the macro-economic adjustment have raised the intensity and the quality of policy coordination in the European Community; the stronger convergence of monetary policies was accompanied by a corresponding moderation of wage incomes and the abolishing of widespread wage indexation systems; only the fiscal policies are lagging behind the progress in the monetary field.

The EMS experience has shown that there is room for a system between unmanaged flexible rates and fixed rates which leads to more predictable exchange rates and to credible adjustment policies. The EMS is a showpiece for a mixed system sui generis functioning on a regional base. But could it become a model for a more stable international monetary order? One can have doubts whether a formal commitment to a new international monetary regime could be expected at present as long as the major industrial countries are not willing permanently and more

credibly to subordinate their monetary and fiscal policies to international requirements.

The EMS is one aspect of a wider and deeper economic and political confederacy,
the European Community, which consists of countries with close economic and
cultural links, sharing common principles and basic convictions. The interdependence here between monetary, trade, financial and macro-economic policies is much
stronger than elsewhere. Every institution, and not least an extended European
institution, is the product of the political economy, and it is to the political economy that the EMS still has much to contribute.

The EMS is still an incomplete and voluntary arrangement based on the mutual
benefits recognized by its members. Only seven out of twelve EC countries are
fully committed to the narrow fluctuation bands; one member enjoys some special
treatment. The consolidation and strengthening of the EMS has to go hand in hand
with the programme to complete the internal market, the "Europe without fron-
tiers", by 1992. This Community-wide liberalization and deregulation concept
includes the removal of all capital and exchange controls. Moving towards an integrated European money and capital market will have profound implications for the
EMS and require strengthening both the monetary coordination and the institutional framework. A Study Group appointed by the Commission has recently
presented recommendations for "Stage Two" (see EC Commission, 1987). They
include the joint setting of monetary policy targets, an enhanced role for the EMS
in international monetary relations and the further development of the ECU. It
could be that realizing the internal European market in the next decade will restore
momentum towards greater economic and monetary unification. Certainly full
British participation would add more weight and a new quality to the EMS, not
only due to the vitality of the London capital market but also as an act of political
will.

The gradual evolution of the EMS is a very long-term perspective. Nevertheless the
final objective of the Community should not be lost: a single European currency
issued and controlled by an independent European central bank.

References

Commission of the European Communities (1982), Documents Relating to the European Monetary System, in: *European Economy*, No. 12, Brussels, July.

Commission of the European Communities (1982), Exchange Rate Variability and Interventions within the European Monetary System, Brussels, mimeo.

Commission of the European Communities (1984), *Five Years of Monetary Cooperation in Europe*, Communication from the Commission to the Council, Brussels, March.

Commission of the European Communities (1986), Annual Report 1986/87, in: *European Economy*, No. 30, Brussels, November.

Commission of the European Communities (1987), Efficiency, Stability and Equity, Report of a Study Group Presided by T. Padoa-Schioppa, Brussels, April, mimeo.

Crocket, A. and M. Goldstein (1987), Strengthening the International Monetary System: Exchange Rates, Surveillance, and Objective Indicators, International Monetary Fund, Occasional Paper No. 50, Washington D.C., February.

Dam, K.W. (1982), The Rules of the Game, Reform and Evolution in the International Monetary System, Chicago.

Giavazzi, F. and A. Giovannini (1986a), The EMS and the Dollar, in: *Economic Policy* No. 2, London, April.

Giavazzi, F. and A. Giovannini (1986b), Monetary Policy Interactions under Managed Exchange Rates, Discussion Paper Series No. 123, Centre for Economic Policy Research, London.

De Grauwe, P. (1985), The European Monetary System During 1979-84. An Evaluation. International Economics Research Paper No. 47, Leuven.

Ifo-Institut für Wirtschaftsforschung (1985), Das Europäische Wirtschaftssystem - Erfahrungen und Perspektiven (with contributions by Triffin, Wegner, Mohr and Herrmann), Ifo-Schnelldienst 17/18, June.

Kenen, P.P. and D. Rodrick (1984), Measuring and Analyzing the Effects of Short-term Volatility in Real Exchange Rates, Princeton University, Working Papers in International Economics, March.

Kindleberger, C.P.K. (1986), International Public Goods without International Government, in: *The American Economic Review*, Vol. 76, No. 1, March.

Melitz, J. (1987), Monetary Discipline, Germany, and the European Monetary System, CEPR Discussion Paper No. 178, London, April.

Micossi, S. and T. Padoa-Schioppa (1984), Can Europeans Control Their Interest Rates? Centre for European Policy Studies, CEPS Papers No. 17, Brussels.

Obstfeld, M. (1985), Floating Exchange Rates: Experience and Prospects, in: *Brookings Papers on Economic Activity* 2, Washington, D.C.

Oudiz, G. (1985), European Policy Coordination: An Evaluation, Centre for Economic Policy Research, Discussion Paper Series No. 81, London, October.

Padoa-Schioppa, T. (1985), Policy Cooperation and the EMS Experience, in: W.H. Buiter and R.C. Marston (eds.), *International Economic Policy Coordination*, Cambridge.

Peeters, T., P. Praet, and P. Reding (1985), (eds.), *International Trade and Exchange Rates in the Late Eighties*, Amsterdam.

Pöhl, K.O. (1987), The European Monetary System - a Model for a More Stable International Monetary Order? (Paul-Henri Spaak Lecture at the Center for International Affairs, Harvard University, May 4), in: Deutsche Bundesbank, Auszüge aus Presseartikeln, No. 33, Frankfurt /M.

Rogoff, K. (1985), Can Exchange Rate Predictability be Achieved without Monetary Convergence? Evidence from the EMS, in: *European Economic Review*, 28.

Steinherr, A. (1985), Competitiveness and Exchange Rates: Policy Issues for Europe, in: Peeters/Praet/Reding (eds.)

Thygesen, N. (1981), Are Monetary Policies and Performances Converging? Some Elements of an Evaluation of Constraints and Performances in the First Two Years of the EMS, in: *Banca Nazionale del Lavoro, Quarterly Review*.

Thygesen, N. (1984), Exchange-Rate Policies and Monetary Targets in the EMS Countries, in: R.S.Masera and R. Triffin (eds.), *Europe's Money: Problems of Coordination and Integration*, Oxford.

Triffin, R. (1985), Before and After the Bonn Summit Meeting, in: Peeters/Praet/Reding (eds.).

Ungerer, H., O. Evans, and P. Nyberg (1983), The European Monetary System: The Experience, 1979-82, IMF, Occasional Paper No. 19, Washington, D.C., May.

Ungerer, H., O. Evans, T. Mayor, and P. Young (1986), The European Monetary System: Recent Developments, IMF, Occasional Paper No. 48, Washington, D.C., December.

Wegner, M. (1985), External Adjustment in a World of Floating: Different National Experiences, in: L. Tsoukalis (ed.), *The Political Economy of International Money*, London.

Wegner, M. (1987), Problems and Instruments of International Coordination, in: *The World Economy*, Vol. 10, No.3 (forthcoming), London.

Ypersele, J. van, and J.-C. Koeune (1984), The European Monetary System, Commission of the European Communities, European Perspectives Series, Luxembourg.

COMMENTS

Roland Vaubel

Manfred Wegner's description and appraisal of the European Monetary System (EMS) shows only one side of the coin: its success in reducing exchange rate fluctuations among the member currencies participating in the exchange rate mechanism (ERM). What is the other side of the coin? Let us compare the years before and after the establishment of the EMS.

1. *Nominal and real exchange rate variations vis-à-vis (eight) other major OECD currencies have on average increased more for the ERM currencies than for the other OECD currencies or the other European OECD currencies* (Ungerer et al., 1986, Tables 22 and 25).

2. *Nominal effective exchange rate variations have on average decreased less for the ERM currencies than for the other European OECD currencies* (Ungerer et al., 1986, Table 28).[1]

3. *The average annual rate of depreciation vis-à-vis the Deutschmark has on average decreased less for the ERM currencies than for other major European OECD currencies* (calculated from Lehment, 1987, Table 2a).

4. *Expected exchange rate changes as proxied by the standard deviation of long or short-term interest rates have increased among the ERM currencies; they have grown a little less, but since 1979 have been larger than among the other major OECD countries* (Ungerer et al., 1986, Tables 43 and 44; Harbrecht, Schmid, 1987, Figures 12 and 15).

---

[1] This cannot be explained by the fact noted by Wegner that "a number of European countries such as Austria and Switzerland are quasi-members of the EMS, and others such as the United Kingdom have tacitly accepted exchange rate targeting in recent years." (III, 2nd paragraph).

Studies in International Economics and Institutions
Vosgerau (Ed.) New Institutional Arrangements for the World Economy
© Springer-Verlag Berlin Heidelberg 1989

5. *The weighted average of the inflation rates decreased much more slowly, and in 1986 was still a little higher, in the ERM countries than in the rest of the OECD* (Scheide, Sinn, 1987, Table 1; de Grauwe, 1987, Table 1; 1985, Figure 4; Collins, 1987, Table 2; Harbrecht, Schmid, 1987, Figure 3). It also decreased more slowly in the EMS than in the other *European* OECD countries although it is still lower in the former than in the latter group (Scheide, Sinn, 1987, Table 1; de Grauwe, 1987, Table 1).

6. *If the seven years before and after the establishment of the EMS are compared, the standard deviation of inflation rates shows an increase among the ERM currencies but a decrease among the other major OECD currencies* (Collins, 1987, Table 2). *Over the whole life of the EMS*, the dispersion of inflation rates has also been much larger among the ERM currencies than among the major OECD currencies (Collins, 1987, Table 2; Harbrecht, Schmid, 1987, Figure 5; de Grauwe, 1985, Figure 3). For the more recent past, this is not true any longer (Collins; Harbrecht, Schmid, ibid.) but there remains the fact that *inflation convergence took longer in the EMS than in the rest of the OECD.*

7. *From December 1978, bid-ask spreads vis-à-vis the Deutschmark increased for the average of ERM currencies, and they increased more for the ERM currencies than for an average of other major European OECD currencies* (Lehment, 1987, Tables 4a and 4b).

8. *Since the establishment of the EMS, all old members of the EEC[2] have experienced larger growth rates in their trade with non-ERM countries than with other ERM countries* (de Grauwe, 1985, Table 2).

9. *Real growth of investment and GDP was much slower in the ERM countries than in the other OECD countries; compared with 1973-78, it declined more in the ERM countries than in the other major OECD countries;* in the other

---

[2] As de Grauwe points out, this is not true for Denmark and Ireland which joined the EC customs union at a later stage and may still have been benefiting form entry-induced trade creation.

European OECD countries, investment has even increased (de Grauwe, 1987, Table 1).[3]

To sum up: the exchange rate mechanism of the EMS does not seem to have contributed to reducing nominal effective exchange rate variations, inflation and inflation differences of the member currencies, or to increasing intra-ERM trade, investment and growth in the member countries.

The EMS exchange rate arrangement is a cartel of national money producers with a price leader. Cartels are inherently unstable; ceteris paribus, they raise prices (here: the price of holding money) and reduce the output (here: real money balances). The EMS money supply cartel is neither a necessary nor an efficient step on the way to a common European currency.

Whether such a single European currency should be "the final objective of the Community", as Wegner suggests, is an open question to which politicians and economists cannot know the answer. It depends on the trade-off between price level stability and transaction costs. As I have argued elsewhere (Vaubel 1987), only individual money users possess the knowledge and incentive required to make that choice. The optimal way of finding out whether currency union is efficient and, if so, of bringing it about is unrestricted currency competition or "choice in currency" (Hayek 1976). The European Currency Unit (ECU) can be instrumental in this process, especially if its weights are permitted to respond to revealed currency preferences (Vaubel 1987).

---

[3]   "The disinflationary stance and the high real interest rates of the 1980s" emphasized by Wegner do not explain this difference, since disinflation was faster in the other OECD countries.

References

Collins, Susan M. (1987), PPP and the Peso Problem: Exchange Rates in the EMS. *Workshop on the International Monetary System, the European Monetary System, the ECU and Plans for World Monetary Reform*, European University Institute, Florence, April (forthcoming: E.M. Claassen, ed.).

Grauwe, Paul de (1985), Memorandum, in: *Memoranda on the European Monetary System*, House of Commons, Treasury and Civil Service Committee, The Financial and Economic Consequences of UK Membership of the European Communities, London, pp. 5-11.

Grauwe, Paul de (1987), Fiscal Policies in the EMS: A Strategic Analysis, *Workshop on the International Monetary System, the European Monetary System, the ECU and Plans for World Monetary Reform*, European University Institute, Florence, April 1987 (Forthcoming: E.M. Claassen, ed.).

Harbrecht, Wolfgang, Jürgen Schmid (1987), Die Monetären Konvergenzwirkungen des EWS, in: H.-E. Scharrer, W. Wessels (eds.), *Stabilität durch das EWS?*, Bonn 1987, pp. 213-253.

Hayek, Friedrich A. von (1976), Choice in Currency. A Way to Stop Inflation, Institute of Economic Affairs, London, *Occasional Papers*, 48.

Lehment, Harmen (1987), Neue Gemeinschaftspolitiken: Währungspolitische Zusammenarbeit, in: H. Dicke et al., *EG-Politik auf dem Prüfstand. Wirkungen auf Wachstum und Strukturwandel in der Bundesrepublik*, Tübingen, pp. 152-167.

Scheide, Joachim, Stefan Sinn (1987), Internationale Koordination der Wirtschaftspolitik: Pro und Contra, *Kieler Diskussionsbeiträge*, 135.

Ungerer, Horst, Owen Evans, Thomas Mayer, Philip Young (1986), The European Monetary System: Recent Developments, International Monetary Fund, *Occasional Papers*, 48.

Vaubel, Roland (1987), Currency Unification, Currency Competition, and the Private ECU: Second Thoughts, Workshop on the International Monetary System, the European Monetary System, the ECU and Plans for World Monetary Reform, European University Institute, Florence, April 1987 (forthcoming: E.M.-Claassen, ed.)

Wegner, Manfred (1987), The European Monetary System: A Regional Bretton Woods or an Institutional Innovation?, in this volume.

II. International Financial Markets

Domestic Bank Regulation
in a World of International Banking

Kenneth E. Scott

It is a commonplace that the economic environment in which financial institutions operate has changed radically in the last two decades. Technological advances in the computer and communication industries have drastically lowered the costs of transmitting and processing information and thus of executing financial transactions. Financial services products have been re-defined; the efficient scale of operation has been increased, enlarging geographical market areas. The result has been a trend toward a world-wide integration of credit and capital markets.[1]

These economic forces have exerted pressure on a system of legal regulation of banking in the United States that was designed in large part over 50 years ago, in the aftermath of the Great Depression. In this paper I wish to consider some of the problems being encountered by that regulatory system, some of the proposed solutions being discussed, and the impact of the currently enlarged role of international markets in commercial banking. In the latter regard, my focus will be on the issues created for the regulation of U.S. banks by their foreign operations, and not on questions relating to regulation of operations in the United States of foreign banks. The regulation to be examined will be that dealing with the safety and soundness of the banking system, rather than with the implementation of monetary policy,[2] to the extent that distinction can be made.

---

[1] See introductory remarks of Governor Seger, 23rd Annual Conference on Bank Structure and Competition, Federal Reserve Bank of Chicago, May 7, 1987.

[2] See e.g. the complex efforts to prevent foreign dollar-denominated deposits from being used to circumvent domestic monetary actions: C. Lichtenstein, U.S. Banks and the Eurocurrency Markets: The Regulatory Structure, 99 Banking L. J. 484 (1982).

I

At the present time it is reasonably apparent that banking regulation in the United States is experiencing some major difficulties. For example, in the 35 years from the end of World War II through 1980 the Federal Deposit Insurance Corporation (FDIC) reported the closure on the average of six banks a year (the peak in 1976 was 17).[3] Since then the number has been increasing sharply, from 10 in 1981 to 42 in 1982, 48 in 1983, 79 in 1984, 120 in 1985, 138 in 1986, and 69 in just the first four months of 1987. The number of "problem banks" has also continued to mount, being currently at 1,555 or 10.7% of total banks.[4] As a result of its disbursements and losses, the $18 billion federal deposit insurance fund has stopped growing, and the ratio of the fund to insured deposits has declined to 1.1%, the lowest level since its inception.[5]

Most of the failures and problems have thus far been relatively small agricultural or energy banks, but the assistance list included the nearly $40 billion Continental Illinois National Bank in 1984. As to the future, there is the distinct possibility of trouble at some more large banks, due in substantial measure to the international debt situation.

During the 1970s, the foreign lending activities of U.S. banks expanded at a rapid pace, and by September 30, 1986 foreign loans constituted $301 billion or 11% of the total assets of the U.S. banking system.[6] The debt service problems of Brazil, Mexico and Argentina have attracted wide attention, but Peru, Chile, Bolivia, Venezuela, the Philippines, Liberia, Nigeria and others are in difficulty also. The consequences for the U.S. banking system are concentrated on a relatively small number of big institutions: as of September 30, 1986, for example, the nine largest

---

[3] FDIC, 1985 Annual Report, Table 122.

[4] Board of Governors of the Federal Reserve System, 73rd Ann. Rep. 1986 at 252.

[5] FDIC Chairman Seidman, Address to National Council of Savings Institutions, May 13, 1987.

[6] Statement of Deputy Comptroller of the Currency Bench before the Subcommittee on International Finance of the Senate Committee on Banking, Housing and Urban Affairs, April 2, 1987.

money center banks held $51 billion in Latin American loans, which represented 1.14 times their total capital.[7] Generally accepted accounting principles (GAAP) require mark-to-market accounting for assets held in trading portfolios but not for assets being held to maturity in a loan or investment portfolio. The balance sheets of most money center banks, therefore, do not reflect large losses in the market value of their international loans or their true solvency. Some indication of the extent of the hidden losses may be found in the decision announced by Citicorp on May 19, 1987, to sharply increase its loan-loss reserves (by $3 billion) to a total of $5 billion; that would correspond to a 40% writedown of its $12.8 billion in loans to its six biggest Third World borrowers.[8] The FDIC may yet have to confront the possible insolvency of another large money center bank.

The potential problems of the FDIC are dominated in the public view at this time, however, by the visibly urgent problems of the Federal Savings and Loan Insurance Corporation (FSLIC), which insures accounts at thrift institutions. Beginning in 1981, the thrift industry encountered adverse developments, first in money market interest rates and then in real estate markets, that rendered a majority of the industry insolvent. By 1983 it became apparent that the $6 billion FSLIC fund would not have the resources to close all the bankrupt institutions and pay off insured accounts, so it embarked on a program of keeping them in operation and postponing the day of reckoning.[9] Gradually the liquid resources of the FSLIC dwindled to a current level of about $500 million; in terms of existing claims, that left the insurance fund insolvent to the extent of about $6 billion, while the FSLIC's estimate of the amount required to resolve the industry's insolvency rose to $23 billion.[10] Other estimates of the amount ultimately required are on the order

---

[7]   Ibid.

[8]   Wall St. J., May 20, 1987, p. 1.

[9]   J. Barth, D. Brumbaugh, D. Sauerhaft and G. Wang, Insolvency and Risk-Taking in the Thrift Industry: Implications for the Future, 3 Contemp. Policy Issues 1 (Fall (1985).

[10] Wall St. J., May 6, 1987, p. 5.

of twice that sum, but Congress was finally brought to allow the FSLIC to borrow enough to increase its resources by only $10.8 billion.[11]

Enough has been said to suggest that the U.S. deposit insurance system is under considerable stress, and that leads to an inquiry as to the cause. One possible explanation is that the national and world economies have simply been undergoing some random shocks, more severe than most in some areas but the sort of thing that has to be expected over the long run. If the deposit insurance funds are showing signs of strain, it may indicate no more than that the annual insurance premium level (1/12th of 1% of the deposit base) was set at too low a figure 50 years ago when the statutes were enacted. For a long time the funds seemed adequate, but now the random fluctuations of events are catching up with them. There is no fundamental problem, except perhaps to correct an underestimation of the appropriate premium level.

A second explanation is that recent events have revealed a need for better supervision of banking. Indeed, banking supervisors are always saying that they need more regulatory authority - over capital ratios or conflicts of interest or international lending or enforcement techniques - and their critics are always saying that they don't exert their existing authority forcefully enough. But the premise common to both supervisors and their critics seems to be that, unlike other business enterprises, banking firms have an inherent tendency to self-destruct and require stringent supervision if they are not to be led by management into excessive risk and frequent insolvency.

What intellectual support can be offered for the proposition that banking firms are in especial need of external regulation? The standard argument asserts that banks are uniquely prone to runs, which spread and bring down even solvent institutions. So the random failure of a few can lead to general failure, and thus supervision is required to protect this industry from a tendency to collapse, by preventing the failure of individual institutions which trigger the process.

That argument is both familiar and important, and warrants more extended consideration than can be given it in the context of this paper. But a few observations

---

[11]   Competitive Equality Banking Act of 1987, 100th Cong. 1st Sess. (1987).

seem worth making nonetheless. The historical prevalence and extent of bank runs has recently been undergoing re-examination that suggests the problem has been over-emphasized.[12] In any event, deposit insurance has clearly been effective in dealing with this problem in the modern period; supervision has not prevented numerous individual bank failures, but no general runs have occurred. Of course, the argument can be reformulated, in terms of the need for better supervision and a reduced incidence of individual failures in order to protect the insurance system as presently funded - which returns the discussion to the appropriate level of funding also.

A third explanation finds the source of current difficulties in the deposit insurance system itself. The insurance premium is assessed at a uniform rate to all institutions; no recognition is taken of the variations in risk presented by variations in the composition of asset portfolios, in the matching of asset and liability durations, in leverage or "capital adequacy," in managerial competence or in other factors relevant to failure. The bank can raise insured deposits (which for the banking system represent close to 80% of total deposits) at something approaching the risk-free rate of interest, due to the implicit government guarantee, and invest them in risky loans and investments, keeping the higher expected rate of return. In short, the uniform premium structure creates an incentive for the bank to take higher risks than it would otherwise choose, and that incentive increases as the capital ratio of the bank diminishes.[13] In terms of the option-pricing model, deposit insurance can be seen as an option to "put" the bank to the insuring agency, and the stockholders can increase the value of that option (at no added cost) by increasing the volatility of the bank's assets and decreasing the bank's capital.

These explanations of current strains in the U.S. banking system are not mutually exclusive in theory and may all have a degree of validity. The one that I shall explore further in this paper concerns the incentives created by a mispriced premium

---

[12]   See, e.g., G. Kaufman, The Truth About Bank Runs (SM-87-3, Fed. Res. Bank of Chicago); B. Ely, The Big Bust: The 1930-33 Banking Collapse - Its Causes, Its Lessons (unpublished paper 2/26/87).

[13]   See E. Kane, The Gathering Crisis in Federal Deposit Insurance (1985); K. Scott, The Defective Design of Federal Deposit Insurance, 5 Contemp. Policy Issues 92 (Jan. 1987).

structure and the proposals that have been made to correct it, on the assumption that mandatory deposit insurance will continue to be a politically imperative feature of American banking. Four lines of approach will be discussed and evaluated, in relation to the trend noted at the beginning toward internationalized banking markets and greater foreign operations by U.S. banks.

II

One approach to the risk incentive problem is to endeavor to control the institution's risk so that it fits the statutorily-fixed, uniform insurance premium. That involves two main elements - control of asset risk and control of financial (leverage) risk - which are part of traditional bank regulation.

The control of asset risk is the objective of portfolio regulation. Banking law contains a number of ex ante restrictions on investments in securities: U.S. banks[14] generally cannot make equity investments (save in subsidiaries engaged in permissible "banking" activities) and can buy for their own account only "investment grade" debt securities.[15] There are some ex ante restrictions on loans (such as those dealing with real estate loans or limits on loans to a single borrower), but loan quality is regulated mostly through management's anticipation of ex post loan review and classification by examiners.

Several criticisms can be made of this body of asset regulation. The most fundamental one is that it focuses on the riskiness of individual investments and loans, or categories of investment and loan, in isolation. That is contrary to the basic tenet of modern portfolio theory that the riskiness of a portfolio is determined by the covariance of returns of the portfolio securities and not by a weighting of their

---

[14] Bank holding companies are also restricted in their activities and equity investments to those "closely related" to banking: 12 U.S.C. § 1843(c)(8). The precise location of that line is a matter of constant dispute. See G. Corrigan, Financial Market Structure: A Longer View, in Fed. Res. Bank of New York, Annual Report (1987).

[15] 12 U.S.C. § 24 (Seventh).

individual variance. The result of present law is to mandate inefficient portfolios with unnecessary risk.

And even in individual terms, the legal rules are not well adapted to foreign loans and investments, for which they were not designed. The constraints on equity investment and lines of business are less narrow when a bank operates abroad, for example through Edge Act subsidiaries or securities affiliates, or even through direct branches.[16] Foreign activities are merely confined to those of a "banking or financial nature," which includes general securities underwriting.[17] The 15% of capital limitation on loans to a single borrower[18] was interpreted to apply separately to a sovereign government and its various agencies and instrumentalities, provided the "purpose" of the loan is represented by the borrower to be "consistent with the purposes of the borrower's general business."[19] In the case of foreign government lending, therefore, the legal lending limit would not prevent banks from making loans to a single country in amounts exceeding their total capital.

Furthermore, the process of examination and supervision operates at a major disadvantage with respect to foreign credits, since the information required for a review of a project's value or a borrower's current creditworthiness is often more difficult to obtain and evaluate. In principle, the information problem can be reduced by cooperation between supervisory authorities in different countries, and that is the objective of the Revised Basle Concordate of 1983, issued by the Committee on Banking Regulations and Supervisory Practices under the auspices of the Bank for International Settlements.[20] But in practice, the barriers are substantial and supervision of foreign credits is less effective.

The result is that, despite the existence of a number of restrictions and controls, a bank can establish approximately the asset risk level that it desires. The one-ninth

---

[16] See 12 C.F.R. § 211.1-7 (1987).

[17] 12 C.F.R. § 211.5 (1987).

[18] 12 U.S.C. § 84(a)(1).

[19] 12 C.F.R. § 32.5(d)(1) (1987).

[20] For the text, see 22 Int'l Legal Materials 901 (1983).

of banking system assets represented by foreign claims[21] is substantially outside domestic regulation, and that has an especially large impact on the big money center banks. But even the smaller, country banks can - both by choice and by virtue of geographical constraints on operations - create portfolios with a great deal of non-systematic or diversifiable risk, through concentration on some local industry such as oil or agriculture.[22]

The second line of institutional-risk control is to focus on the bank's capital position or leverage. In the strongest form of this technique, one could let the institution choose the asset composition and risk level it preferred (since that is difficult to prevent in any event), but then adjust the required capital accordingly.

How would the adjustment determination be made? In theory, one could set the capital ratio which makes the statutorily-fixed insurance premium actuarially correct for a particular level of asset risk. Using option pricing theory, Merton has calculated the cost of deposit insurance under different assumptions as to capital ratio and asset volatility;[23] working the other direction, from a given asset volatility and a fixed premium, one could ascertain the implied capital ratio.[24] In practice, such a procedure would again impose a severe information problem on the regulators, since they would have to be able to calculate accurately the asset volatility in order to require the right minimum capital for the bank.

---

21   See n. 6 supra. There are several sources and definitions of foreign claims; the Fed's own series reports a figure of $400 billion rather than $300 billion. See Foreign Lending by Banks: A Guide to International and U.S. Statistics, October 1986 Federal Reserve Bulletin 683 and Table 3.21 at A62.

22   The classic example would be the Penn Square Bank, which failed in 1982.

23   R. Merton, An Analytic Derivation of the Cost of Deposit Insurance and Loan Guarantees, 1 J. Banking and Finance 3 (1977).

24   Otherwise, of course, there is no basis for requiring any particular capital level - that is the lesson of Modigliani and Miller, The Cost of Capital, Corporation Finance and the Theory of Investment, 48 Am. Econ. Rev. 261 (1958). The firm's leverage just distributes the asset risk between equity and debt claims, and in the absence of deposit insurance the market rates of return and security prices would adjust to whatever capital ratio was chosen.

Instead, the U.S. banking agencies have established a general minimum total capital requirement of 6% of assets,[25] while retaining the right to set higher ratios in individual cases and enforce them through a procedure for issuing capital directives.[26] The individual determinations are not based on the option pricing approach outlined above or any other "rigid mathematical formula," but are "necessarily based in part on subjective judgment grounded in agency expertise."[27]

The banking authorities have indicated from time to time their belief that the basic 6% minimum was too low and ought to be raised; banks have objected that the cost of additional capital would put them at a competitive disadvantage vis-a-vis less-capitalized domestic non-bank alternatives and foreign banks in international markets. Critics of the regulatory capital standard also pointed out that it treated all bank assets alike, thereby contributing to the incentive for the bank to shift toward higher-risk, higher return portfolios.

To address those issues, the Fed in January 1986 issued a proposal for a supplemental risk-based minimum capital requirement.[28] Discussions with the Bank of England led to an agreement in January 1987 for the banking agencies in both countries to propose jointly a revised version of the risk-based capital regulation, as "an important concrete step in the direction of greater harmonization and convergence of supervisory policies among countries with major banking institutions."[29] To put it in less diplomatic terms, there is competition for market share not only among financial institutions but also among bank regulators, within a

---

[25] 12 C.F.R. 3.6 (1987). Total capital consists of common and preferred stock and, to a limited extent, subordinated debt and mandatory convertible debt. More dubiously, it includes reserves for loan losses. 12 C.F.R. 3.2 (1987).

[26] 12 U.S.C. § 3907; 12 C.F.R. §§ 3.9-21 (1987).

[27] 12 C.F.R. § 3.11 (1987).

[28] 51 Fed. Reg. 3976 (1986).

[29] Statement by Chairman Volcker before the Subcommittee on General Oversight and Investigations of the House Committee on Banking, Finance and Urban Affairs, April 30, 1987.

single country[30] and internationally.[31] The U.S./U.K. Agreement is an effort to form a regulators' cartel, and will face the usual cartel problems.[32]

As for the substance of the new risk-based capital proposal, it suffers from familiar deficiencies. Assets are sorted by type into five risk categories and assigned a corresponding weight (0%, 10%, 25%, 50%, 100%) to calculate an adjusted asset number, against which an as yet unspecified percentage of capital is to be maintained. The structure is analytically quite crude. Book values, not market values, are used to calculate the asset figures and capital position of the bank. All commercial loans and foreign government debt are assigned to the same (100% weight) risk category, without differentiation as to borrower creditworthiness or collateral. Portfolio diversification is ignored. Interest rate risk is to be treated later, but apparently on the basis of the maturity of the particular instrument rather than on the extent of mismatch between assets and liabilities considered together. And the manner in which the actual figure for the required capital ratio is to be derived remains a mystery; presumably it will be founded, not on any intelligible economic theory, but on the regulators' perennial desire to judge capital levels up another notch.[33]

The need for concern over joint action seems questionable,or at least overstated. The problem is supposed to be one of competitive equality - the well-known "level playing field." But in the world of Modigliani and Miller, if a firm chooses to operate with less real equity, its (noninsured) obligations and commitments become more risky or less valuable, and its debt costs rise. That is what levels the playing field - not mandated uniformity. Even in the world of FDIC, for large banks most

[30] Scott, The Dual Banking System: A Model of Competition in Regulation, 30 Stan. L. Rev. 1 (1977).

[31] E. Kane, Competitive Financial Reregulation: An International Perspective, in Threats to International Financial Stability (R. Portes and A. Swoboda, eds., 1987).

[32] Discussions began in June 1987 with Japan's Ministry of Finance, to attempt to bring it into the cartel.

[33] Cf. FDIC's 9% proposal, 50 Fed. Reg. 19088 (1985); President Parry, The Bank Capital Dilemma, Federal Reserve Bank of San Francisco (1/16/87).

of their liabilities and commitments are not legally insured, including both all off-balance-sheet commitments (such as letters of credit, guarantees, repurchase obligations, lines of credit) and on-balance-sheet liabilities such as borrowings and deposits over the $100,000 insurance ceiling.[34] It is quite possible to operate competitively at higher capital ratios than characterize U.S. banks, as both Swiss and German banks can attest.

Whether a banking authority relies on controlling asset risk or controlling financial risk, or on some mix of both, it needs to be able to measure an institution's risk in a fairly accurate and defensible manner. Modern portfolio theory affords the analytical tools for doing so, but the necessary empirical data are only partially available. That makes fine distinctions hard to justify, and leads regulators to use broad categories or uniform requirements. So a distortion of managerial incentives seems certain to persist under this approach, though it should be possible to make it less severe than under the existing uniform insurance premium system.

III

A second avenue of approach to the risk incentive problem is to vary the insurance premium to fit an institution's risk. Rather than making the institution fit the premium, the objective would be to make the premium fit the institution.

Under this approach, it is even more essential to be able to measure the risk of each institution. As already noted, that is a difficult assignment for a bank regulator, in both an empirical and a political sense. Empirically, the data on asset return variance and covariance are often lacking, though a concerted program by the agencies could over time help fill the gap. Politically, a variable premium does not possess the apparent "fairness" of uniformity (even in a non-uniform world). Con-

---

[34] For banks with over $10 billion in deposits, accounts with balances above $100,000 account for about 70% of total deposits. FDIC, Deposit Insurance in a Changing Environment App. F-3 (4/15/83).

sequently, the banking insurance agencies have fluctuated between tepid support and outright hostility to the concept of risk-based insurance premiums.[35]

The alternative to public agency discretion in assessing risk and premiums would be to rely on a private market consensus. One suggestion for creating a private market pricing mechanism is to require partial private insurance - for example, of 5% of the deposit liability, leaving 95% for the government insurance system.[36] Complete private insurance of the entire banking system would require a huge capital base to be fully credible against a correlated wave of failures, and has usually been ruled out on that basis.[37] A simpler device in my view would be to require at least the larger insured banks to issue short term unsecured debt, on a parity with the status of FDIC as subrogee of insured deposit claims. Since the insolvency risk position of the debtholders would be the same as that of FDIC - both would be unsecured general creditors - the risk premium demanded by the debtholders would be equivalent to the appropriate insurance premium for FDIC to charge, with two caveats noted below.

The first caveat relates to information costs and disclosure policies. Bank examination and supervision has functioned historically in an atmosphere of secrecy and confidentiality, lest the public be unduly alarmed and cause unnecessary runs and damage. The thrust of regulation in the securities markets, on the other hand, has been toward full disclosure and reliance on the judgments of investors and markets. These two opposing modes of regulation collided in the late 1960s in the wave of bank holding company formations; bank holding companies were under the jurisdiction of the Securities and Exchange Commission in the public offering of their securities, but prospectus disclosure was centered on their only significant business, the bank. The outcome is still being determined, but gradually the banking auth-

---

[35] See, e.g., FDIC, Deposit Insurance in a Changing Environment (1983); Federal Home Loan Bank Board, Agenda for Reform (1983).

[36] H. Baer, Private prices public insurance: The pricing of federal deposit insurance, 9 Economic Perspectives 45 (Federal Reserve Bank of Chicago, September/October 1985).

[37] But see B. Ely, Private Sector Depositor Protection Is Still a Viable Alternative to Federal Deposit Insurance, 10 Issues in Bank Regulation 40 (Winter 1986).

orities have been accepting greater disclosure of the real condition of the banks they supervise, though by no means of the full picture available to them through examination reports.[38]

Even with restricted information, the market is currently able to make significant differentiations among banks and assess varying risk premiums. Data on the interest rates on $1 million certificates of deposit offered by 54 money market banks were collected over two different periods in 1986; the average deviation of a bank from each week's mean rate is given in Appendix I. The spread among these banks is 230 basis points, without adjustment for the fact that one-tenth of each CD is FDIC-insured or for other circumstances that might affect a particular offering. (By way of comparison, the present[39] FDIC premium is a bit over 8 basis points.)

If the FDIC insurance premium were to be drawn from a debt market risk premium, it would make sense to improve disclosure to the market. Particularly would that be true with respect to international operations, where the information barriers are greatest. An important first step in that direction was taken by Section 907 of the International Lending Supervision Act of 1983, which required banks to disclose to the public material information regarding the composition of their foreign country exposure.[40] The banking agencies began developing a regulatory system for country risk evaluation in 1977 when the Country Lending Exposure Survey was added to the reporting schedule,followed by the establishment of the Interagency Country Exposure Review Committee to analyze and comment on the data.[41] The United States General Accounting Office criticized this commenting

---

[38] See, e.g., G. Coombe and J. Lapic, Problem Loans, Foreign Outstandings, and Other Developments in Bank Disclosure, 40 Bus. Law. 485 (1985); FDIC proposal on June 17, 1987 of a rule on disclosure of financial and other information: 12 C.F.R. Part 350.

[39] In 1985 and 1986, unlike prior years, the FDIC gave member banks no rebate credit on insurance assessments, and none is expected in 1987.

[40] 12 U.S.C. § 3906.

[41] See J. Ongman, Federal Regulation of Lending Abroad: Past History, Current Practice and Future Prospects, 17 Law & Pol'y Int'l Bus. 679, 690-94 (1985).

procedure as ineffectual,[42] and after the Mexican debt crisis of 1982 the Congress responded by enacting the International Lending Supervision Act of 1983.[43] The Act requires the banking agencies, on the basis of their evaluation of foreign country exposure and transfer risk, to require banks to establish special reserves against impaired foreign credits and to factor those risks into their determination of a bank's capital adequacy. To implement those provisions, the agencies promulgated regulations for "allocated transfer risk reserves" to be held against loans due from designated countries, in amounts dependent on their classification (loss, value impaired or debt service impaired), but neither the countries nor the reserve percentages are public information.[44] Likewise, there could be greatly improved disclosure of banks' off-balance-sheet contingent liabilities, which in large banks may exceed book liabilities.[45]

The second caveat to reliance on private debt market pricing of the risk premium lies in precise definition of the risk. In the usual business enterprise, the creditor's risk is that of receiving partial or no payment in the event of insolvency. But in the case of a bank, different insolvency rules and procedures are followed. Closure is a supervisory decision involving substantial discretion, and the perception has grown that the banking authorities will not allow the outright failure of a large bank. It is to those issues that we now turn.

IV

A third line of approach to the risk incentive problem of the present deposit insurance system would be to close the bank at or just before the point at which its liabilities exceeded its assets. If that were done consistently and accurately, there

---

[42] U.S. General Accounting Office, Report on Bank Examination for Country Risk and International Lending 20 (September 2, 1982).

[43] Pub. L. No. 98-181, 97 Stat. 1153, 1278 (1983) (codified at 12 U.S.C. §§ 3901-3913.

[44] See, e.g., 12 C.F.R. §§ 20.6-10 (1987); J. Guttentag and R. Herring, The Current Crisis in International Lending (1985).

[45] Rowe, FDIC Urges Coverage of Foreign Funds, Wash. Post, June 7, 1985, at B1.

would be no depositor (or creditor) loss for the insurer to bear, so premiums could be uniformly nominal without a distortion of managerial and owner incentives.

The grounds for closure of a bank are specified by the law of the jurisdiction in which it is organized, so there are differing provisions across the federal government and fifty states. In general, a bank may be closed if it is insolvent, or in an unsafe or unsound condition, or unable to pay a judgment or meet the withdrawal of a deposit when due.[46] The authority to make that determination is vested in the bank's primary supervisor (chartering agency), but the primary supervisor's action is greatly influenced by the willingness of the Federal Reserve Board to provide liquidity to stay open and the willingness of the FDIC to provide assistance to a supervisory merger or deposit assumption. The insolvency determination is usually made on the basis of the book value of assets and liabilities, as defined by regulatory accounting principles (which are similar in many respects, but not identical, to generally accepted accounting principles).

The result is that closure is viewed by the supervisors as a discretionary action, generally taken around the time of book value insolvency but sometimes much later.[47] Book value insolvency usually indicates a substantial loss to the insurer upon liquidation; the market value of the equity of large banks has been below book value for more than the last 10 years, as shown in Appendix II.[48] In essence, the market value of bank assets has consistently been less than their book value, which is the result to be expected from the degree of flexibility afforded by accounting principles to recognize gains and income and defer losses and expenses, when it is in management's interest to do so.

---

[46] See, e.g., 12 U.S.C. § 191; Cal. Fin. Code § 3100(g).

[47] The Federal Home Loan Bank Board has for several years been keeping hundreds of insolvent thrift institutions in operation, because of insufficient funds in the FSLIC to handle their closure. See J. Barth, D. Brumbaugh, & D. Sauerhaft, Failure Costs of Government-Regulated Financial Firms: The Case of Thrift Institutions (unpublished paper July 1986); J. Barth, D. Brumbaugh, D. Sauerhaft, & G. Wang, Insolvency and Risk-Taking in the Thrift Industry: Implications for the Future, 3 Contemp. Policy Issues 1 (Fall 1985).

[48] See also U.S. General Accounting Office, 1 Deposit Insurance: Analysis of Reform Proposals 111 n. 12 (September 30, 1986).

When it comes to large banks, FDIC has adopted an implicit policy that it will avoid liquidation or deposit insurance payout, using instead an assistance or purchase-and-assumption procedure that gives full protection to uninsured depositors and creditors. In 201 failing bank situations between 1979 and 1984, the FDIC afforded de facto 100% coverage of all liabilities in all but one case when the size of the bank was greater than 1% of FDIC's reserves.[49] Justifications for this policy have been offered in terms of the limitations of FDIC's financial and personnel resources and avoiding losses to correspondent banks.[50]

Thus the insurance premium is a function, not just of an institution's asset risk and leverage, but even more of the timing of supervisory action - or in option-pricing terms, of the duration of the option. The purchaser of a bank's debt securities, in setting the risk premium, must be concerned with estimating not only the likelihood and extent of market value insolvency during some time period, but also the probability that the bank will actually be closed when insolvent and that the FDIC will actually impose part of the loss on uninsured creditors. Under such circumstances, the private risk premium is an underestimation of the actual expected loss and would not be the correct rate for the government insurer to use.

To address these shortcomings, the banking agencies have been urged to adopt market-value accounting requirements and an automatic closure rule at the point of market-value insolvency.[51] If there were no measurement error and no time lag in supervisory response, the only loss to creditors and the insurance fund would come from the administrative and transactions costs of handling the failure. Critics focus on the conditions contained in the "if" clause and the difficulty of their fulfillment.

The obstacle to market value accounting, it is asserted, lies in the absence of the needed markets to give valuations for many categories of bank assets. The objection is both valid and susceptible to exaggeration. Secondary trading markets are

---

[49] The exception was the $500 million Penn Square Bank in 1982. Id. at 31, Table 2.1.

[50] Id. at 33-42.

[51] See E. Kane, The Gathering Crisis in Federal Deposit Insurance 124-28, 148-51 (1985).

being developed in previously rarely traded assets, such as foreign government loans or (through securitized pools) consumer mortgages and other receivables. The process could be deliberately encouraged or even mandated - for example, a portion of all foreign sovereign borrowings above a given size could be required to be sold through a public underwriting. Nonetheless, actual market values will never be available for all bank assets, so an element of supervisory judgment and possible measurement error would remain. It would surely be reduced below present levels, however, if market values were made the goal. For instance, although there might be no objective estimate of a loan's changing credit risk, its interest rate risk and corresponding premium or discount could be calculated from secondary market data on government securities of comparable maturity.

An automatic closure rule based on market value insolvency is also met with several objections. One is that such a rule is simply impossible in the political environment in which even the relatively independent banking agencies must operate. There seems to be an inherent political pressure to delay taking action detrimental to the recipients of government credits and guarantees, both in the aggregate and in individual cases. The tendency to defer resolution of massive insolvencies of government guarantee programs can be illustrated by not only the FSLIC but also the Pension Benefit Guarantee Corporation and the Farm Credit System.[52] On the level of individual institutions, the Majority Leader of the House of Representatives has recently set an unedifying example by trying to block FSLIC recapitalization unless given some assurance that the additional funds would not be used to close some of the insolvent savings and loan associations run by his Texas constituents and supporters.[53]

Another objection to an automatic closure rule of any sort is the fear of having to deal with the failure of a very large bank. The most dramatic example was provided by the $40 billion Continental Illinois National Bank in 1984, when the FDIC kept the bank open by furnishing several billion dollars in immediate assistance

---

[52] Perhaps a rational explanation lies in politicians with relatively short expected terms of office setting a high discount rate on future as compared to present costs.

[53] N.Y. Times, February 9, 1987, p. 22; Wall St. J., February 11, 1987, p. 6.

and guaranteeing full protection to all the bank's depositors and other general creditors.[54] The justification given by FDIC is as follows:

> "Permitting Continental to fail and paying off insured depositors was never a feasible option for the regulators. Insured accounts totalled only slightly more than $3 billion. This meant that uninsured depositors and other private creditors with over $30 billion in claims would have had their funds tied up for years in a bankruptcy proceeding awaiting the liquidation of assets and the settlement of litigation. Hundreds of small banks would have been particularly hard hit. Almost 2,300 small banks had nearly $6 billion at risk in Continental; 66 of them had more than their capital on the line and another 113 had between 50 and 100 percent."[55]

Other considerations may have been the fact that the alternative of a modified payout plan, in which uninsured claimants would be advanced a portion of their claims based upon estimated liquidation proceeds,[56] would have necessitated an outlay by FDIC larger than its entire insurance fund,[57] and the concern that not only domestic but international banking relationships would have been disrupted.

Continental gave rise to the understanding that very large banks would have to be bailed out with full protection to all creditors, but the reasons for such a position do not seem adequate. The costs and incentive problems created by a policy of non-closure and full protection can be still greater, as the FSLIC situation suggests. And the FDIC is not limited to a choice between a species of receivership liquidation (with its large initial expenditure and lengthy delays) on the one hand and assisted merger or purchase-and-assumption (which requires an acquiring partner large enough to handle the transaction and small enough to not raise antitrust problems) on the other. Another option would be for the insurer to take over the bank, make whatever capital infusion and management replacement it deemed

---

[54] A description of the bailout plan may be found in FDIC, 1984 Annual Report 28-29.

[55] Id at 4.

[56] See FDIC, Deposit Insurance in a Changing Environment III-5 (April 15, 1983). In 1984 FDIC employed this procedure eight times prior to the Continental crisis.

[57] See U.S. General Accounting Office, 1 Deposit Insurance: Analysis of Reform Proposals 40, Table 2.4 (September 30, 1986).

necessary, and then sell the bank in a public offering.[58] If the sale proceeds were less than the insurer's outlays, the loss would have been promptly realized and could be shared pro rata with the uninsured creditors; if sale proceeds exceeded the insurer's costs, the surplus would go to subordinated debtholders and then the former stockholders. Going concern values and ongoing relationships would have been preserved; uninsured creditors would share the loss (and hence have reason to exert greater market discipline on the bank's management prior to closing) but suffer from the illiquidity of only a portion of their claim (based on the receiver's estimate of potential loss) for only a limited period of time (to arrange the restructuring and sale). In short, perfect implementation of a regime of market value accounting and closure rules is not achievable, but it seems a proposal worth serious investigation.

V

A fourth approach to the deposit insurance problem is more radical - to create "riskless" banks through a separation of their payments and investment functions.[59] Deposit banking would be carried on in a "narrow" bank, which could invest only in virtually riskfree assets, such as short term Treasury securities or perhaps commercial paper; checking and savings accounts offered by such a bank would be covered by federal deposit insurance. Commercial and consumer lending and other riskier assets would be transferred to an affiliated non-bank institution and funded by uninsured investments and instruments; since federal deposit insurance would not apply to the affiliate, it would raise its funds at market rates commensurate with its portfolio risk and not be restricted as to its permissible investments or activities.

---

[58] See K. Scott, The Future of Bank Regulation, in To Promote Prosperity: U.S. Domestic Policy in the Mid-1980s (J. Moore, ed. 1984).

[59] See, e.g., J. Kareken, Federal Bank Regulatory Policy: A Description and Some Observations, 59 J. Bus. 3 (1986); R. Litan, What Should Banks Do? (forthcoming 1987).

This proposal can be seen as an intellectual descendant of earlier suggestions of 100% reserve banking[60] or as an extension of recently developed money market mutual funds. It undertakes to break the link between risky assets and riskless claims that is the vulnerable spot in the present structure of banking and deposit insurance. The role of deposit insurance would be diminished, but not necessarily eliminated. If a bank failed, due to short term rate movements or fraud losses, the insurance corporation would provide continued access to checking account balances and uninterrupted clearance of transactions, while the securities pool was being marshalled and liquidated. For these functions, the cost would presumably be low and hence a small premium sufficient. There would probably be no necessity for the insuring agencies to make risk determinations for individual institutions; if the portfolio restriction for investment of deposit balances permitted little variation in risk, a uniform premium would be quite feasible.

Criticism of the riskless bank concept centers on two aspects. The first is the question of economic inefficiency, engendered by segregating deposit services from nondeposit services with a resulting loss of economies of scale or scope. The extent of such economies is of course an empirical matter, about which it is hard at present to form a reliable estimate, but developments generally in the field of financial services suggest they are significant. The efforts on the part of both securities firms and banks to penetrate the Glass-Steagall Act and Bank Holding Company Act barriers to joint production and marketing indicate as much.[61] The point has less force in the context of the riskless bank proposal, however. In this instance, the separation is not necessarily of production or delivery, but only of investment risk. Although proponents formulate their proposal in terms of separate incorporation, that does not seem essential; the needed separation could be accomplished in the setting of a single institution, simply by requiring that "deposit" or "transaction" account balances be invested in and secured by a lien on a pool of

---

[60]   H. Simons, Economic Policy for a Free Society 62-65 (1948); M. Friedman, A Program for Monetary Stability 65-75 (1960).

[61]   See the extensive discussion of such efforts in M. Eisenberg, Financial Services: Litigation and Regulatory Developments (unpublished paper March 1987).

relatively riskless assets. That should not give rise to substantial production inefficiencies.

The second line of objection calls into question the operational practicality of the intended separation. Since deposit account balances would earn only at the riskfree rate of return and would generate large costs from the payment clearance process, the return to the customer would be lower than it is at present and might at times be negative. That, it is said, would create incentives to avoid the separation by devising new payments instruments, uninsured but offering higher returns, so the outcome would be a payments system comprising both riskless (insured) and risky (uninsured) instruments. Such a system would again be vulnerable to panics and general runs on solvent but illiquid institutions - the very result deposit insurance was instituted to forestall.

This objection is not without merit, and a full discussion of the bank run issue would greatly extend this paper, but a few observations may be in order. The general run or panic phenomenon is basically an information externality problem, and would best be dealt with as such. It grows out of an inability on the part of creditors to distinguish confidently between solvent and insolvent institutions, and the traditional "bank secrecy" treatment of examination reports certainly does nothing to overcome that inability. As for a run on an individual bank of dubious solvency, it is wholly appropriate; indeed, it is an integral part of that "market discipline" which the banking agencies are now starting to promote.

Under the narrow bank concept, the extent of international lending or activities is irrelevant, since it falls in the domain of the affiliated nonbank (or does not affect the deposit security pool). Would the nonbank affiliate be at a competitive disadvantage in carrying on such activities, because it would be deprived of the core deposit base? Perhaps, but only in the sense that it was deprived of an existing subsidy obtained from the government in the form of an insufficient deposit insurance premium. Only a banker could regard that change as unjust.

VI

This paper has considered some of the currently pressing issues in U.S. bank regulation and attempted to evaluate them, keeping in mind the growing internationalization of banking markets. Ultimately, they seem to me to present us with two distinct choices: to make the deposit insurance system viable, or to make it largely superfluous.

The first alternative probably involves a synthesis of the initial three approaches discussed above. Portfolio regulation, or control over asset risk, has always been the least satisfactory form of bank regulation - conceptually defective, limited in coverage and historically ineffectual. It is not likely to be more effective in the evolving international markets. But capital requirements, market value accounting and closure rules, and variable insurance premiums can be combined in a number of ways to yield an insurance system that is sounder and less incentive-distorting.[62] That is the direction the banking authorities are likely to take, though no doubt in a slow-moving and erratic way.

The second alternative is to separate deposit banking from risky lending and investment activities. If successful, bank regulation, including concern over international operations, would be greatly simplified or eliminated. Neither banks (with a subsidy to protect) nor bank regulators (with careers to protect) could be expected to be enthusiastic about the concept - which makes it a fitting subject for academic attention and further exploration.

---

[62] See, e.g., D. Pyle, Capital Regulation and Deposit Insurance, 10 J. Banking & Finance 189 (1986).

Appendix I
ANALYSIS OF CD RATES

BANK	NO. OF WEEKS	MEAN OF DEVIATIONS	STANDARD DEVIATION
First Deposit National Bank	11	+1.187	.397
United Bank of Texas, Austin	11	+1.083	.358
Alaska Mutual Bank Anchorage	10	+1.015	.256
Colonial National Delaware	11	+ .958	.168
Banc Texas Dallas	11	+ .742	.207
People's Bank of Cleveland, GA	11	+ .405	.124
First National Bank of Gainesville, GA	11	+ .404	.124
Merchants Bank Kansas City	10	+ .366	.328
Colonial Naitonal Ft. Worth	11	+ .355	.148
Florida National Bank of Jacksonville	11	+ .278	.223
MBank Texas	10	+ .266	.115
Capital Bank of Miami	11	+ .207	.196
Republic Bank Dallas	9	+ .177	.089
First National Bank of Tulsa	11	+ .169	.111
Bank of Cirpple Creek, Co.	10	+ .167	.401
Pacific Bank San Francisco	11	+ .154	.086
First National Bank of Oklahoma City	9	+ .092	.328
Gulf National Bank Miami	11	+ .071	.105
Peoples Bank of Tupelo, Miss.	11	+ .037	.180
Continental Illinois	10	+ .017	.272
Citizens Bank & Trust	11	+ .001	.173
Old Kent Bank, Grand Rapids, MI	10	+ .001	.113
National Bank of Commerce	11	- .008	.200
Centerre Bank, St. Louis	10	- .008	.162
IBJ Trust	9	- .030	.179
Commercial Center Bank, CA	11	- .040	.213
Deposit Guaranty	11	- .045	.212
First Interstate Arizona	10	- .050	.123

BANK	NO. OF WEEKS	MEAN OF DEVIATIONS	STANDARD DEVIATION
Imperial Bank LA	11	- .085	.127
Wachovia Bank & Trust	10	- .138	.119
First National Bank of Chicago	9	- .139	.082
European American Bank	11	- .140	.098
First National Bank of Minneapolis	11	- .158	.096
Bank of Tokyo Trust Co.	11	- .167	.151
Rainier National Bank	10	- .180	.068
Lake Shore National Bank Chicago	10	- .194	.102
National Bank of Washington	11	- .203	.078
Fleet National, R.I.	11	- .213	.134
First American, Washington, D.C.	10	- .228	.078
City National, Beverly Hills	11	- .238	.158
Chemical Bank	9	- .244	.205
Irving Trust	11	-.285	.115
Dominion Bank, Virginia	11	- .308	.104
Ameritrust Cleveland Corp.	9	- .319	.134
Bank of Virginia	11	- .354	.077
Balboa National Bank	10	- .369	.241
Schroder Bank & Trust	11	- .404	.165
U.S. Trust Co.	11	- .408	.127
Bankers Trust New York	11	- .429	.464
Bank of New York	11	- .440	.095
Chase Manhattan Bank New York	11	- .454	.173
Citibank	11	- .463	.124
Marine Midland	11	- .472	.069
Firstier Bank, Omaha	10	-1.115	.521

Appendix II

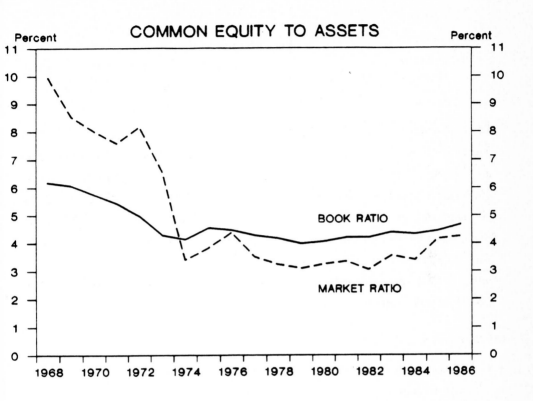

Data are unweighted averages for the ratios of common equity to assets for the twenty largest U.S. banking organizations based on assets as of September 1986. Data are year end figures except for 1986 which is a third quarter figure.

Source: Federal Reserve Bank of San Francisco.

COMMENTS

Karl Kreuzer

To complement Professor *Scott*'s contribution to our symposium focused on crucial questions of the present U.S. deposit insurance system, I would like to concentrate my remarks on the legal problems national authorities face in consequence of the internationalization of banking operations and will demonstrate this by using the pertinent reform of German legislation, effective since January 1, 1985, as an example. I shall shortly present its main features as a concrete example of Domestic Bank Regulation in a World of International Banking. This will give us the possibility to raise some difficult legal questions originating in the worldwide integration of banking markets.

1. Supervision Problems in Transnational Banking Operations: An Overview

1.1 General Background

1.1.1 Internationalization of banking does not only require domestic financing of international operations, international trade transactions in particular, but also establishment abroad.

It is well known that after World War II, U.S. banks were the first to cross the national borders by founding foreign establishments, i.e. branches, (wholly or majority-owned) subsidiaries and (minority participation-) joint ventures abroad. Banks in other countries followed the U.S. example. Thus national banking systems were mutually penetrating each other. During the 1960s "going international" became a common feature of major and middle sized banks. The establishment of an international, indeed of a worldwide banking system was emerging.

Studies in International Economics and Institutions
Vosgerau (Ed.) New Institutional Arrangements for the World Economy
© Springer-Verlag Berlin Heidelberg 1989

As far as domestic regulation of banking activities is concerned, transnational banking operations occur in the form of foreign activities of domestic banks and - vice versa - domestic activities of foreign banks. In both cases the cross-border establishment of the investing (parent) bank may be realized by foreign branches, by separate foreign subsidiaries or by joint ventures, established as separate legal entities under the legal system of the host country.

Internationalization of banking, understood here in the sense of setting up establishments of banks abroad, has created new problems for supervisory authorities. De iure[1] or de facto[2], transnational banking groups form - roughly speaking - *risk units* as far as liability is concerned.[3] To be more specific, parent banks are considered to be answerable for debts of branches, subsidiaries and - to a certain extent - even minority joint venture participations, irrespective of the country in which the need for help occurs.[4] Operations of foreign establishments cause risks for the parent bank at least as high as the purely domestic banking activities. Therefore, national supervisory authorities of the parent bank's registered office country (parent authorities) cannot merely rely on the supervisory authorities of the foreign State to oversee the operations made by the parents' foreign establishments in the host country (host authorities), but must take a strong concern in informing itself of the economic situation of both the parent and its foreign establishments. As a consequence of this situation, supervision of the parent bank must be enforced not only on the parent but on its foreign establishments as well, at least on a consolidated basis. Otherwise it would be possible for the banks to circumvent

---

[1] Cf. letters of comfort or of awareness; see e.g. *K. Wagner*, Die internationale Tätigkeit der Banken als aufsichtsrechtliches Problem, Baden-Baden (1982) p. 23 et seq.

[2] Cf. e.g. *M. Schneider*, Internationale Aspekte der Bankenaufsicht, in: Wirtschaftsprüfung und Wirtschaftrecht. Beiträge zum 75jährigen Bestehen der Treuhand-Vereinigung AG (1980) p. 94.

[3] Supervisory authorities of certain international finance centres increasingly require comfort letters from the parent as a prerequisite for licensing a domestic subsidiary; see *I. L. Bähre*, Eurobanken und Bankenaufsicht, in: Off-shore-Kreditmärkte, Frankfurt/m. (1984) p. 194.

[4] See *D. Bester*, Aufsichtsrechtliche Kontrolle internationaler Bankkonzerne (1986) p. 92; *M. Schneider*, Praxis der Bankenaufsicht (1978) p. 104.

national (credit) restrictions by shifting operations abroad.[5] Therefore, in principle, parent authorities try to extend their supervision to foreign establishments of domestic banks.

Vice versa, supervision of domestic branches belonging to foreign parent banks causes difficulties. From the point of view of the host authorities, such branches are considered *domestic* enterprises and therefore are subject to the host authorities' supervision. The fact that the domestic supervisory authorities are fictitiously treating the domestic branches of foreign parents as separate (domestic) banks[6] will not exclude the branch from being affected by the foreign parents' fate. On principle, the same proves true for domestic subsidiaries of foreign parents. Host authorities may require information from domestic branches or subsidiaries of foreign banks regarding the financial situation of the foreign *parent* bank in order to prevent detrimental effects of the foreign parent's financial difficulties on their domestic establishments. This has been done, for instance, by the U.S. Board of Governors in respect of U.S. subsidiaries of foreign banks.[7] On the other hand, host authorities do not hesitate to ask the parents to help their branches if needed.[8]

The result of this internationalization of banking through foreign establishments (branches, subsidiaries, joint ventures) is that the venture as a *whole* concerns *both* parent authorities and host authorities. Therefore, both states principally have a legitimate interest not only in the supervision of the domestic activities, but also in the supervision of the *whole* transnational group as a risk bearing unit. The safety and soundness of the transnational group concerns both the parent and the host supervisory authorities, because failure of one part may well affect the other members of the group. Thus, there is a need for transnational cross supervision - notwithstanding the fact that the majority of the opinions expressed seem to favour

---

[5]   Cf. *Bester* ibid. (last fn.) p. 97.

[6]   See, e.g., section 53 of the German Banking Act.

[7]   See *Kl.-A. Bauer*, Das Recht der internationalen Bankenaufsicht (1985) p. 55 fn. 64 with ref.

[8]   See *Bauer* ibid. (fn. 7) p. 55 fn. 64 with ref.

the primary responsibility of the parent bank's registered office country at least for *branches* in foreign countries.[9]

1.1.2 In spite of the transnationalization of banking operations, supervision has remained *national*. The internationalization of banking has no counterpart in a formal (institutionalized) internationalization of banking supervision. As Professor *Scott* put it in the title of his contribution, we face *domestic* bank regulation in a world of *international* banking. International (transnational) supervision does not exist. International (or European) supervisory authorities have not been established. Neither written nor unwritten rules (state practice) of international law exist in our special field. Transnational (extraterritorial) *extension* of ordinary *national* supervisory regulations or enactment of special national rules for transnational banking groups[10] can be in accordance with the international law "Effects Principle" and "Balancing Rule of Non-Interference", provided that the operations concerned have substantial, direct and foreseeable domestic effects and do not interfere with greater foreign interests.[11] However it may be, *general* rules delimiting the scope of *domestic* banking regulations do not seem to exist as in the German antitrust law[12], for example. In so far as they may exist, such as in the conflict of law rules concerning the applicability of *domestic*[13] banking supervisory regulations on transnational banking cases, they are restricted to specific situations. At least in

---

[9] See *Bauer* ibid. (fn. 7) p. 55 et seq.

[10] Relevant provisions have been enacted, e. g., in the U.S.A., in the Fed. Rep. of Germany and in Switzerland; for example: prescription of reporting duties for domestic parents and their foreign establishments in relation to the group's total lending volume or large-scale credits to single borrowers.

[11] For these principles see *Meessen*, Kollisionsrecht der Zusammenschluß-kontrolle (1984) p. 21 et seq., 86.

[12] Under the general (unilateral) rule of conflict of laws of section 98 (2) sentence 1 of the German Act Against Restraints of Competition German antitrust law is applicable, if the business practice has (sc. substantial, direct and foreseeable) domestic effects.

[13] Until today, (multilateral) rules of conflict of laws prescribing the applicability of *foreign* banking supervisory regulations seem to have been enacted or suggested. Normally, national authorities do not apply foreign economic law which is generally too closely bound to the specific national economic system, as in our particular case, to the existing national banking structure.

German law, it is mainly a question of special banking supervisory rules reserved either for domestic branches of foreign parent banking institutions or for domestic parent banks in respect of their transnational banking operations through foreign branches, subsidiaries or joint ventures. In any case, *jurisdiction* (and de facto possibility) of *enforcing extraterritorially* binding *national* rules (e.g. to report) will be lacking. As a general rule, extraterritorial enforcement of supervisory regulations upon domestic banking operations, either of the parent or host country, has no basis in international law. This is particularly true for audits which are conducted abroad to verify the correctness of reported data. But if the host country refuses such measures, no national supervisory authority is entitled or able to carry out supervisory activities abroad, as far as the legal and de facto aspects are concerned. Thus, none of the national authorities is able to effectively supervise the operations of transnational groups with the purely national supervisory means available. This heavily restricts the supervisory activities of national authorities in respect of transnational banking. Mere national supervision, restricted to operations carried out on and from the national territory, turns out to be insufficient to guarantee the safety of national credit institution systems.[14] Thus, on the one hand we have a substantial *common interest* of both the parent and the host authorities in the safety and soundness of the *whole* transnational banking group, the safety of any single establishment depending heavily on the group's good economic condition. On the other hand, we have to state the *impotence* of each single national authority to carry out alone the necessary measures to reach the common objective. The interest of the national states in the safety of their banking systems calls for transnational supervision of transnational banking groups. As national authorities are not in a position to afford transnational supervision, they are left to coordinate their supervisory measures with other national authorities. *Rebus sic stantibus*, co-operation and co-ordination between the national supervisory authorities concerned is a *conditio sine qua non*, and it turns out to be a "must" for supervisory success.

---

[14] See also *C. Köhler*, Internationale Aspekte der Bankenaufsicht, Betriebswirtschaftliche Blätter 1983, 370. Professor Köhler is a member of the Board of Directors of the German Bundesbank.

Adequate supervision of transnational banking establishments requires the co-operative participation of both parent and host authorities[15] - and a harmonization of supervisory regulations in order to avoid the evasion of supervision[16]. As *Peter Cooke*, the chairman of the Committee on Banking Regulations and Supervisory Practices' stated, "within a global banking system, safety is indivisible"[17]. The internationalization of banking activities renders the internationalization of banking supervision necessary. The lack of efficient transnational supervision would compel national authorities to take efficient national measures. This inevitably means the restriction of transnational banking activities. Thus, transnationalization of banking supervision appears to be an indispensable prerequisite for the transnationalization of banking activities.[18]

As a matter of fact, our area is a good example of co-operation between authorities of different states in economic law with transnational effects. Common interest has led to several more or less formal new institutional arrangements, fostering co-operation and co-ordination between national supervisory authorities on three levels:

- on the level of the Bank for International Settlements

- on the EEC level

- on a bilateral level.

---

[15] Basle Concordat on Principles for the Supervision of Banks' Foreign Establishments, sub III. Text: International Legal Materials 1983, 900.

[16] Cf. *R. Dale*, Bank Supervision around the World, New York (1982) p. 1.

[17] Quoted by *U. Damm*, Die Internationalisierung der Bankenaufsicht, Die Bank 1985, 212. For the Committee see infra 1.2.1.

[18] See also *C. Köhler* ibid. (fn. 14).

1.2 New Institutional Arrangements Fostering Cooperation Between National Supervisory Authorities

1.2.1 The Bank for International Settlements

The 1983 Basle Concordat on Principles for the Supervision of Banks' Foreign Establishments[19], issued by the Committee on Banking Regulations and Supervisory Practices[20], are neither themselves legally binding rules nor necessarily embodied in national legal orders. They only constitute strongly "recommended guidelines of best practices in this area"[21]. The Concordat incorporates the principle of supervising banks on a consolidated world-wide basis and emphasizes the mutual responsibilities of both home and host state as well as the need for co-operation and co-ordination between the respective supervisory authorities.[22] The Concordat suggests an appropriate allocation of responsibilities between parent and host supervisory authorities.

---

[19] See fn. 15. A first (in substance very similar) version of the Concordat had been issued in 1975, see *I. L. Bähre* ibid. (fn. 3) p. 195 et seq.

[20] Called the "Cooke Committee", after its British chairman, inaugurated in 1974, after the *Herstatt* breakdown, under the auspices of the Bank for International Settlements (BIS). Members are the chairmen of the banking supervisory authorities mainly of the "Group of 10", i.e. Belgium, Canada, France, FR Germany, Italy, Japan, Luxembourg, Netherlands, Sweden, Switzerland, United Kingdom, U.S.A. The Committee meets three times a year in Basle, at the headquarters of the BIS. At the initiative of the Cooke-Committee, conferences of national banking supervisory authorities were organized in London (1979), Washington (1981) and Rome (1984). Under the influence of the said Committee, the group of "Offshore Banking Supervisors" was founded in 1980 and a commission of banking supervision authorities of Latin America and the Caribbean met for the first time in 1981.

[21] See ibid. (fn. 15) p. 901.

[22] Cf. *I. L. Bähre*, Probleme der Bankenaufsicht internationaler Finanzmärkte, in: *v. Krümmel* (ed.), Internationales Bankgeschäft, supplement 8 to *Kredit und Kapital*, Berlin (1985) p. 63, 68; *Bester* ibid. (fn. 4) p. 174 et seq.

1.2.2 The Law of the European Communities

Taking into account the difficulties that the enforcement of unified European banking supervisory regulations by a centralized European authority would encounter, up to now the EEC has acquiesced in harmonizing the relevant legislation.[23] The Council of Ministers has enacted two Directives[24] pertinent to the supervision of banking operations:

- First Council Directive of 12 December 1977 on the Coordination of the Laws, Regulations and Administrative Provisions Relating to the Taking up and Pursuit of the Business of Credit Institutions[25] and

- Council Directive of 13 June 1983 on the Supervision of Credit Institutions on a Consolidated Basis.[26]

These Directives are, world-wide, the first realization of transnational (regional) harmonization with respect to banking supervisory rules.

For our purposes, the Directive of 13 June 1983 on the Supervision of Credit Institutions on a Consolidated Basis[27] is particularly interesting. The Directive is understood as a step towards an EEC-wide, co-ordinated supervisory system in which the supervision of a parent bank operating in other EEC member countries will be entirely conducted by the authorities of the parent banks' registered office. This requires a harmonization of the controls and supervisory measures within the

---

23   In the beginning, the EEC had planned to introduce a complete European Banking Law, a preliminary draft had been completed in 1972, see *P. Troberg*, Angleichung des Bankenaufsichtsrechts in der Europäischen Gemeinschaft, Nachrichten aus dem Institut für Kreditwesen der Westfälischen Wilhelms-Universität Münster, 28 (Winter 1984/1985) p. 5.

24   Proposal for a Council Directive Concerning the Annual Accounts of Banks and Other Financial Institutions, Official Journal no. C 130 of June 1, 1981, p. 1.

25   Official Journal no. L 322/30, 17 December 1977.

26   Official Journal no. L 193/18, 18 July 1983.

27   See fn. 26.

EEC. Therefore, the said Directive binds[28] the EEC member states to introduce a consolidation procedure in case of foreign subsidiaries established in EEC countries and to make sure[29] that a subsidiary is not hampered in freely transmitting across state borders the data necessary for the implementation of the consolidation. Furthermore, the member countries must allow the exchange of data necessary for supervision on a consolidated basis between their authorities.[30] Finally, if supervisory authorities of one member country want to audit information concerning a banking institution registered in another member state, they are bound to ask the competent authorities of the host state to conduct the audit. The host authorities have to conduct the audit themselves or empower the (foreign) parent's authorities to audit or allow it to be done by an auditor or other expert.[31]

The First Council Directive of 12 December 1977 on the Coordination of the Laws, Regulations and Administrative Provisions Relating to the Taking up and Pursuit of the Business of Credit Institutions[32] instituted an Advisory Committee of the competent authorities of the member states whose main objective is the coordination of national supervisory exigencies as a prerequisite for enforceable European legislation.[33] The so-called Contact Group,[34] composed of representatives of all EEC banking supervisory authorities, serves, inter alia, as an expert team for the said Committee.

---

[28] Art. 3 and 4 Directive no. L 193/18 (fn. 26). The Directive contains the obligation to introduce a consolidation procedure only if one bank effectively controls another bank. This control is presumed in cases of majority positions (exceeding 50%); in the case of participations between 25 and 50% a dominant influence has to be established.

[29] Art. 5 (1) Directive no. L 193/18 (fn. 26).

[30] Art. 5 (2) Directive no. L 193/18 (fn. 26).

[31] Art. 5 (4) Directive no. L 193/18 (fn. 26).

[32] Art. 11, See fn. 25.

[33] The Committee has been operative since 1979.

[34] Or Contact Committee, founded in 1972 and recognized by the Preamble of the First Council Directive of 12 December 1977 on the Coordination of the Laws, Regulations and Administrative Provisions Relating to the Taking up and Pursuit of the Business of Credit Institutions (fn. 25).

1.2.3 Co-ordination on a Bilateral Level

Actual German banking regulations permit the *transmission of data* between German establishments (branches, subsidiaries, joint ventures) and foreign parent banks holding at least 25% of the capital, if the information transfer is necessary in order to satisfy the requirements of parent authority banking supervision on a consolidated basis.[35] An exception is made when reciprocity is not guaranteed, in which case the FBSA (Federal Banking Supervisory Authority) may prohibit a domestic credit institution from transmitting data.[36] Besides the EEC member countries[37], reciprocity is guaranteed between Germany and some non-EEC States, presumably[38] including the U.S.A., on the basis of bilateral agreements.

In contrast to EEC member countries[39], the auditing of foreign non-EEC banking supervisory authorities within German territory is not granted by the German Banking Act, but requires a special international agreement.[40] As a matter of fact, Germany has concluded such (unpublished) agreements in the form of an exchange of "Notes Verbales" guaranteeing reciprocity[41] with numerous states. Such agreements regulate reciprocal extraterritorial auditing rights particularly with the

---

[35] Section 44a (1) sentence 1 Banking Act.

[36] Section 44a (1) sentence 2 Banking Act.

[37] Cf. art. 5 (1) Directive no. L 193/18 (fn. 23).

[38] The agreements are not published.

[39] Section 44a (2) sentence 1 Banking Act. The domestic credit institutions concerned must allow such examinations (section 44a (2) sentence 3 Banking Act).

[40] Section 44a (2) sentence 4 Banking Act.

[41] *Bauer* ibid. (fn. 7) p. 159.

U.S.A.[42]. Thus, U.S. authorities are allowed to audit German branches since 1971/72[43] and (wholly) owned subsidiaries since 1979[44] of U.S. parent banks.[45]

One might ask if we are entering a period of transnational regulation by means of co-ordination and co-operation in international banking and if we could call this model a "New International Arrangement for the World Economy". The reported regional and bilateral models may form a transitory stage preceding the appearance of a global approach to the problems of bank safety and soundness created by the increasing internationalization and the transnational interdependence of banks and banking systems.[46]

2.   Regulation of Transnational Banking: The German Example

2.1   Outline of General German Banking Legislation

A general administrative supervision of the banking sector was introduced in Germany after the banking crisis of 1931. The law actually effective, the *Kreditwesengesetz* (KWG; hereinafter: Banking Act), was enacted in 1961. The Act was substantially reformed by two major amendments in 1976 and 1985 respectively, both being "emergency amendments" following spectacular collapses of major banks.[47] The dual banking system does not exist in Germany. Banking law is a matter which lies in the domain of the Federal State. Therefore, all banks are federally char-

---

[42]   See *Bähre* ibid. (fn. 22) p. 67 et seq.; *Bauer* ibid. (fn. 7) p. 127, 159 with ref.

[43]   Cf. Notes Verbales of October 20, 1971 and March 16, 1972 between the Embassy of the U.S.A. (Bonn) and the Foreign Office of the Federal Republic of Germany.

[44]   Cf. Notes Verbales of June 22, 1979 and September 28, 1979 between the Embassy of the U.S.A. (Bonn) and the Foreign Office of the Federal Republic of Germany.

[45]   *Bähre* ibid. (fn. 22) p. 67 et seq.

[46]   See also *R. Dale* ibid. (fn. 16) p. 1.

[47]   See the text in the next section.

tered. Within the Ministry of Finance, the Banking Act has established a separate but not independent supervisory agency, the *Bundesaufsichtsamt für das Kreditwesen* (BAK; Federal Banking Supervisory Authority: FBSA). The overall objective of the supervision by this authority is the preservation of an operating credit system as an indispensable element of the economy. Therefore, supervision is restricted to secure the safety and soundness of the banking system (*Liquidität und Bonität*), to keep away dubious enterprises, to guarantee an appropriate ratio between capital and assets and to ensure, in case of insolvency of an institute, that the whole credit system will not be detrimentally affected (section 6 (2) Banking Act).

Every bank is required to have an adequate amount of capital (section 10 Banking Act). What "adequate" means, is determined in the principles enacted by the FBSA with the consensus of the *Bundesbank* (German Central Bank: CB). Accordingly, loans and shareholding in subsidiaries should not exceed 18 times the capital. *One loan may not be greater than 50% of the capital and the sum of all large loans must not exceed 8 times the capital* (section 13 (3) and 4 Banking Act). Credits exceeding one million DM have to be reported to the Bundesbank (section 14 Banking Act). If a bank does not comply with the requirements of the Banking Act the FBSA is authorized to take measures in order to secure the safety of the banking system (section 45 et seq. Banking Act).

The Emergency Amendments of 1976 and 1984

The collapse of the *Herstatt*-Bank[48] in 1974, induced by losses on business in foreign currency, was the cause for the 1976 *emergency* amendment of the Banking

---

[48] For a list of the 33 banks compulsorily closed (1962-1985) by the FBSA see *Reischauer/Kleinhans*, Kreditwesengesetz (loose-leaf) Einl. 112 p. 12.

Act[49], mainly concentrating on provisions limiting the risks of day to day banking operations, especially focusing on restrictions for large loans.[50]

Motivated by this major collapse the German legislators had also planned the introduction of a compulsory deposit insurance system. However, this institution was made superfluous by the establishment of a so-called *Einlagensicherungsfonds*[51] by the Association of German Private Commercial Banks, i.e. a separate emergency pool of assets to prevent disturbances in the case of bank breakdowns. The other groups of German banking institutions have similar emergency funds.[52] In consequence of the *Herstatt* case no non-bank depositor has suffered damage due to the relevant *Einlagensicherungsfonds*.

The *Herstatt* case of 1974 also brought about the so-called Bank Structure Commission ("Grundsatzfragen der Kreditwirtschaft"). The Commission submitted its Report in 1979 and, with regard to the fundamental choice of the German banking system in favour of "universal banking", came to the conclusion that no change was called for.[53] However, the Report contained decisive proposals on the amendment

---

[49] 2nd Gesetz zur Änderung des Gesetzes über das Kreditwesen of March 24, 1976 Bundesgesetzblatt I p. 725, in force May 1, 1976; Bill (= Regierungsentwurf) Bundestags-Drucksache 7/3657. The FBSA's introduction of the Ia Principle (Bundesanzeiger no. 166 of September 6, 1974) which heavily restricts business in foreign currency as well as the institution of the *Liquiditäts-Konsortialbank GmbH* by the German Central Bank and several German bank groupings in September 1974 whose objective is to provide emergency loans to banks which are in difficulties yet otherwise healthy, have to be seen in the same context.

[50] 17 of the 21 breakdowns of banks in Germany between 1962 and 1976 were caused by failure of large loans: cf. Bundestags-Drucksache 7/3657 (Gegenäußerung der Bundesregierung ad 3. a).

[51] Established in 1966 and enlarged later on. See art. "Einlagensicherung", in: *Gablers* Banklexikon, 9th ed. (1983) p. 598 et seq.

[52] An emergency fund of the *Kreditgenossenschaften* (co-operative banks) has functioned since the 1930s. A similar fund has been created by the group of (municipal) Saving Banks. For details see the ref. in last fn.

[53] Report, no. 89.

of supervision regulations[54] which substantially influenced the 1984/1985 amendment of the Banking Act.[55] This amendment in particular is closely concerned with the problems we are discussing at this symposium. The amendment was under consideration for about 10 years but became urgent in consequence of the difficulties of a large private bank (*Schroeder, Muenchmeyer, Hengst & Co*) caused by non-performing credits granted to one single borrower which were far beyond the limits, and which had not been detected because a portion of the loans had been granted via the bank's Luxembourg subsidiary.

2.2 Consolidated Supervision

With regard to our topic, the outstanding novelty of the 1984/1985 amendment of the Banking Act[56] consists in a supervisory *consolidation procedure* both *for capital adequacy requirements* and *large credits*.

The consolidation procedure extends the supervision of the FBSA, which until 1985 was restricted to individual banks, to national and particularly transnational *groups* of banks. It tries to make sure that not only the single member bank of a banking group but also the group as a whole has adequate liable equity capital (capital ad-

---

[54] Report, no. 121.

[55] 3rd Gesetz zur Änderung des Gesetzes über das Kreditwesen of December 20, 1984 Bundesgesetzblatt I p. 1693; Regierungsentwurf (bill), Bundestags-Drucksache 10/1441; Beschlußempfehlung des Finanzausschusses, Bundestags-Drucksache 10/2459; Bericht des Finanzausschusses, Bundestags-Drucksache 10/2510.

[56] The Act carries out the principles of the above-mentioned (fn. 26) European Directive of 13 June 1983 on the Supervision of Credit Institutions on a Consolidated Basis.

equacy requirements for banking groups)[57] and that the entire group is subject to the limitation of large-scale loans (large credit requirements for banking groups)[58].

Under the consolidation procedure, lending ratios are measured not only in relation to the capital of the individual bank concerned but also in relation to the aggregate capital and the combined credit volume of the whole banking group. The reason for this procedure is that the parent bank is liable for the liabilities of its subsidiaries which may substantially exceed the loss of the participation capital. It does not matter if this parent risk of liability is based on law (e.g. Patronatserklärungen, i.e. letters of comfort or of awareness)[59] or on factual grounds. This requirement originated in the so-called credit pyramids built up by German banks through the establishment of subsidiaries, especially abroad. Credit pyramid means the multiple utilization of the same capital fund as a basis for loans - on the one hand in the form of equity shares (parent bank, first level subsidiary etc.) and, on the other hand, in the form of "real" capital (lowest level subsidiary).[60] The more foreign subsidiaries are involved, the higher the multiplication of the parent banks' capital amount.[61] As a result, the total credit of a banking group could substantially exceed the amount that would have been allowed if the legally prescribed maximum capital/credit ratio had been applied to the whole group.

Scope of the Consolidation Procedure

For the purposes of *capital adequacy requirements* credit institutions belong to a banking group if one credit institution (parent bank) directly or indirectly holds at

---

[57] Section 10a Banking Act. Whether banking groups in the aggregate have adequate liable equity capital has to be evaluated based on a quota consolidation of the liable equity capital (section 10a (3) Banking Act).

[58] Section 13a Banking Act.

[59] See, e. g., *Wagner* ibid. (fn. 1).

[60] See *Bester* ibid. (fn. 4) p. 67 et seq.; *H. Mayer'* Das Bundesaufsichtsamt für das Kreditwesen, Düsseldorf (1981) p. 199 et seq.; *Wagner* ibid. (fn. 1) p. 65 et seq.

[61] For an example see *Bester* ibid. (fn. 4) p. 69 et seq.

least 40% of the shares or voting rights (*erhebliche Beteiligung* = significant holding) of another credit institution (subsidiary bank), or if the parent bank is in a position where it can exercise a dominant influence either directly or indirectly.[62] Enterprises registered abroad (foreign enterprises) conducting a banking business pursuant to section 1 of the Banking Act or a factoring or leasing business are expressly deemed to be subsidiary banks, i.e. they belong to a *banking* group.[63] Thus, banks based in another State are expressly included in the consolidation procedure if a significant (= 40%) participation is held by a German parent bank or if the German parent is able to exercise a dominant influence. This inclusion has been considered to be indispensable in view of the fact that the establishment of foreign subsidiaries and the acquisition of participation by foreign based banks play an increasing role within the German banking system; this is especially true for places such as Luxemburg where administrative restrictions are not as severe as in Germany.[64] Recent field studies show that German banks take full advantage of this legal East/West supervision decline.[65]

For the purposes of *large credits consolidation procedures,* the definition of the banking group is the same as for the capital adequacy requirements, except that the limit of the participation (shares/voting rights) percentage has been fixed at a minimum of 50% (instead of 40%).[66] Thus, foreign subsidiary banks will belong to a large credit consolidation group if the German parent bank directly or indirectly holds 50% of the capital (or voting rights) or if the parent is able to exercise a dominant influence.

---

[62]   Section 10a (2) sentences 1, 3 Banking Act.

[63]   Section 10a (2) sentence 5 no. 3 Banking Act.

[64]   *I. L. Bähre* ibid. (fn. 3) p. 189, 190.

[65]   For statistical data see bill (Regierungsentwurf) Bundestags-Drucksache 10/1441, ad no. 7 (section 10a Banking Act).

[66]   Section 13a (2) sentence 1 Banking Act.

2.3 Procurement of Necessary Data for Supervision

Under German law, the (German) parent bank of a banking group has to provide the FBSA and the Central Bank with the necessary data in order to allow the review of the adequacy of the capitalization and of the respecting of large-scale credit limits.[67] Subsidiary banks based in Germany are required to provide the (German) parent bank with the necessary information for quota consolidation purposes (capital adequacy, large credit).[68]

As far as the *foreign* subsidiaries of German parent banks are concerned, the duty to report can not be imposed by the German legislator.[69] Yet, in order to guarantee the necessary data supply from foreign subsidiaries, section 12a (1) of the Banking Act obliges every future German parent that acquires a significant (= at least 40%) or material (= at least 50%) holding, or another position giving control over a foreign subsidiary bank (incl. leasing or factoring business) to secure all the information necessary to meet the consolidating and reporting requirements[70] prescribed by the German Banking Act. For bank-to-bank participation within the EEC the above-mentioned Directive[71] provides the legal basis for the necessary flow of data. Even for other countries in which German parent banks hold interests, difficulties regarding reporting requirements are not known.[72]

---

[67]   Section 10a (4) sentence 3, section 13a (4) Banking Act.

[68]   Section 10a (5) sentence 1, section 13a (5) Banking Act).

[69]   *Troberg* ibid. (fn. 23); *Wagner* ibid. (fn. 1) p. 190; but for a dissenting opinion see *Mülbert*, Bankenaufsicht über internationale Bankkonzerne - Informationsrechte und -pflichten nach der KWG-Novelle 1984, Die Aktiengesellschaft 1986, 1, 10.

[70]   See sections 10a, 13a and 25 (2) Banking Act.

[71]   Directive no. L 193/18 (fn. 2).

[72]   Motivation for section 12a in the *Regierungsentwurf* (bill) of the 3rd Gesetz zur Änderung des Gesetzes über das Kreditwesen of December 20, 1984, Bundestags-Drucksache 10/1441 p. 36 et seq.

If a parent bank is unable to obtain the necessary data, another (=an emergency) calculating method is provided.[73] If this method proves to be inadequate or if it is not possible for the FBSA to review the adequacy of this procedure, the FBSA can prohibit the continuation of a holding in or a relationship with the subsidiary bank.[74]

3. Scope and Enforcement of German Domestic Banking Supervision Regulations on Transnational Banking Activities

Significantly, the 1961 German Banking Act did not contain, until its 1984/1985 amendment, any provision regarding foreign activities of German banks. Before the enactment of the said amendment only the activities of foreign banks in the Federal Republic of Germany were regulated and this just to a limited extent.[75]

3.1 German Parent Authority Supervision of German Establishments Abroad

3.1.1 Foreign Branches of German Banks

With regard to supervisory regulations, foreign branches of German banks have always been considered components of the German parent.[76]

---

[73] Section 10a (5) sentence 2 Banking Act: deduction from the liable equity capital of book values of the non reporting subsidiary bank.

[74] Section 12a (2) Banking Act.

[75] Section 53 Banking Act (fictitious treatment of foreign parents' German branches as separate German banks) and, since 1976, Section 53a Banking Act (notification duty for German representatives of foreign banks).

[76] Cf. *Bähre* ibid. (fn. 3) p. 206; *Schneider* ibid. (fn. 2) p. 86.

The European Directive no. L 193/18 of 13 June 1983 on the Supervision of Credit Institutions on a Consolidated Basis[77] guarantees the free *flow of data* from German branches operating in EEC member states to the German parent bank in so far as the information is necessary to comply with the German rules of banking supervision on a consolidated basis. For non-EEC countries the relevant data transmission may be secured by bilateral administrative agreements.

Under section 44 of the Banking Act the FBSA may *audit* branches of German parents based abroad provided that international agreements or the domestic law of the host state allow such measures. The European Directive already mentioned generally guarantees the audit procedure of the German parent authority regarding branches of German parent banks in all EEC member countries in respect of the supervision on a consolidated basis.[78] As for non-EEC countries, there are bilateral agreements which permit the German parent authorities to audit branches of German banks in the countries concerned. In the past, audit procedures concerning German foreign branches of domestic banks were directly carried out by German parent authorities abroad, for example in New York and London.[79]

However, it is generally admitted that the host state of a foreign banks' branch has the authority to regulate the domestic banking operations of the branch. Thus, we have to recognize that an overlapping of different and even incompatible legal systems is possible.

3.1.2 Foreign Subsidiaries of German Banks

Traditionally, the scope of German supervisory regulations was territorially restricted to domestic banking institutions including foreign branches of German banks, but it did not include provisions regarding foreign subsidiaries or joint

---

[77] Art. 5 (1) Directive no. L 193/18 (fn. 26).

[78] Art. 5 (4) Directive no. L 193/18 (fn. 26).

[79] *Bauer* ibid. (fn. 7) p. 159; see also *Schneider* ibid. (fn. 2) p. 106.

venture participations of German banks. The situation only changed in 1984/85 with the last Banking Act amendment.[80]

Foreign (wholly or majority-owned) subsidiaries of German parent banks or foreign banks in which a German bank holds a minority position (joint ventures) are beyond the direct grasp of German supervisory authorities.

With regard to the *data flow* from foreign subsidiaries or joint ventures to German parent banks the pertinent supervisory rules correspond to those governing foreign *branches* of German banks: referring to EEC-subsidiaries, the transfer is guaranteed by the above-mentioned European Directive on the Supervision of Credit Institutions on a Consolidated Basis[81] for supervision on a consolidated basis, otherwise by bilateral agreements.

Until 1985 the FBSA was entitled by section 44 of the Banking Act to conduct audits only concerning foreign *branches* of German parent banks; the 1985 amendment section 44a (3) of the Banking Act extended the auditing powers to foreign *subsidiaries* of German parent banks if the latter hold at least 40% of the shares or are otherwise in a position to exercise a dominant influence. Auditing measures are allowed particularly to review the correctness of the data transmitted in order to permit quota consolidation in accordance with the section 10a (3), section 13a (3) and section 25 (2) of the Banking Act, provided the audit is permitted under the law of the host state. Evidently under international law, section 44a of the Banking Act may not empower the German authorities to conduct audits abroad.[82] This auditing permission is generally guaranteed in respect of foreign *subsidiaries* (and joint ventures) of German parent banks in all EEC member countries, by the European Directive already mentioned, as far as supervision on a consolidated basis is concerned.[83] In regard to non-EEC countries, bilateral agreements may permit

---

[80]   See fn. 53.

[81]   Art. 5 (1) Directive no. L 193/18 (fn. 26).

[82]   *Bähre* ibid. (fn. 22) p.73/74.

[83]   Art. 5 (4) Directive no. L 193/18 on the Supervision of Credit Institutions on a Consolidated Basis (fn. 26).

German parent authorities to audit foreign German establishments other than branches of German parent banks in the respective countries. In consequence of the non-disclosure of the pertinent agreements it is not clear whether, where and in which cases German parent authorities are entitled to such audits in foreign states. As U.S. parent authorities are allowed to conduct audits in respect of wholly owned German subsidiaries of U.S. parent banks, I presume that, on the basis of reciprocity, an analogous right of German parent authorities in respect of U.S. establishments wholly owned by German parent banks is granted.

We will now turn to the vice versa situation, i.e. to German establishments (branches, subsidiaries and joint ventures) of foreign registered banks.

3.2 German Host Authority Supervision of Foreign Establishments in Germany

3.2.1 German Branches of Foreign Banks

Foreign banks (i.e. having the head office in a foreign state) operating in Germany from abroad are subject to German banking regulations only when they are operating from a branch situated in Germany.[84] In spite of their lack of juristic corporate character, domestic branches of foreign banks are basically treated under German banking supervisory law as a separate (German) bank which needs a written licence by the FBSA for conducting banking transactions .[85]

Nevertheless, it is recognized under German law that German branches of foreign banks legally form part of the foreign company and therefore are *also* subject to the foreign banking supervision regulations applicable to the *parent* bank. Correspondingly, section 44a (1) sentence 1 of the Banking Act provides that legal provi-

---

[84]   Section 53 Banking Act; *Bähre/Schneider*, Kreditwesengesetz, 3rd ed. (1986) § 53 no. 1, § 32 no. 1. Representative offices established in Germany by a banking institution with its head office in a foreign state, have to be notified to the supervisory authorities without delay (section 53a Banking Act).

[85]   Section 32 Banking Act.

sions limiting the *transmission of data*[86] shall not apply if the transmission is necessary in order to satisfy the requirements of banking supervision on a consolidated basis relating to a foreign bank which holds at least 25% of the capital share of the domestic establishment. While the relevant European Directive on the Supervision of Credit Institutions on a Consolidated Basis of June 13, 1983[87] prescribes this lifting of communication barriers only with EEC member countries, German law *generally* removes the legal obstacles under the condition of reciprocity.[88] Reciprocity is guaranteed, on the one hand, under the said European Directive of June 13th 1983[89] between the EEC member countries and, on the other hand, on the basis of bilateral agreements, between Germany and non-EEC States, e.g. presumably the U.S.A.

As far as official assistance is concerned, at the request of another EEC (parent) country's supervisory authority, the FBSA is bound to review the correctness of the data transmitted (for the purposes of banking supervision on a consolidated basis) or to permit the requesting foreign authority a qualified auditor or an expert to review the data concerned.[90] Authorization of foreign non-EEC banking supervisory authorities to conduct *audits* within German territory are not granted by the German Banking Act but need a special international agreement.[91] As a matter of fact, Germany has concluded such (unpublished, purely administrative) agreements guaranteeing reciprocity[92] with several states. This is particularly true, for the U.S.A. Thus U.S. authorities are allowed to audit German branches (and wholly

---

[86] E.g. section 3 Federal Data Protection Act.

[87] Directive no. L 193/18 (fn. 26).

[88] Section 44a (1) sentence 2 Banking Act.

[89] Art. 5 (1) Directive no. L 193/18 (fn. 26).

[90] Section 44a (2) sentence 1 Banking Act. The domestic credit institutions concerned must allow such examinations (section 44a (2) sentence 3 Banking Act).

[91] Cf. section 44a (2) sentence 4 Banking Act.

[92] See *Bauer* ibid. (fn. 7) p. 159.

owned subsidiaries) of U.S. parent banks.[93] This implementation of U.S. supervisory regulations by the U.S. authorities in Germany pertaining to operations conducted by the German branches of U.S. banking institutions clearly constitutes an
example of extraterritoriality. It is probably this practice which explains the fact
that until now, cases on extraterritorial application of foreign banking supervisory
law or requirements of data transmission from abroad are unknown. And this is
true in spite of the fact that in the case of (German) domestic branches of foreign
banks both (German) host and foreign parent supervisory authorities are responsible and two different sets of regulations apply to the (German) branch. Hitherto,
co-ordination seems to work in this area.

3.2.2 German Subsidiaries of Foreign Banks

If a foreign bank establishes a (wholly or majority owned) subsidiary or participates in a joint venture registered in Germany, German supervisory regulations on
the foreign banks' German establishment primarily apply. However, the provisions
on permitting *data transmission and audits* across the borders[94] are just as applicable to (German) subsidiaries and joint ventures of foreign banking institutions as
to German *branches* of foreign banks. An administrative agreement regulates reciprocal extraterritorial auditing rights[95] with the U.S.A. in particular, and reciprocity
is presumably guaranteed as far as information flow is concerned. U.S. audit in
Germany is allowed, however, only for *wholly* owned German subsidiaries of U.S.
parent banks.

---

[93] *Bauer* ibid. (fn. 7) p. 127, 159 with ref.

[94] Section 44a (1) and (2) Banking Act.

[95] *Bauer* ibid. (fn. 7) p. 127, 159 with ref.

4.   Some Questions

Finally, I would like to ask a few questions, partly regarding Prof. *Scott*'s report, which may be answered during the discussion:

1.   Are the problems of the present U.S. deposit insurance system of domestic origin or imported, i.e. caused by the internationalization of the banking (credit) market?

Prima facie, it seems that the problems are self-inflicted and have not been caused by the internationalization of banking operations. The potential causes discussed in the paper concerned, i.e. the unfavourable economic conditions, the insufficient supervision of banking and the difficulties in the deposit insurance system itself, are substantially domestic. I would like to ask whether *one* cause of the difficulties, actually faced by the U.S. banking system, may be found in the very structure of the U.S. banking system characterized by unit banking, limited area branching and prohibition of interstate branching, by the separation of investment and commercial banking. The consequences seem to be a fragmented banking system with a relatively large number of small separate banks operating in restricted areas and, therefore, in restricted sectors of the economy. Does this structure prevent intra- and inter-bank risk spreading? Is the creation of a large state institution such as the FDIC a consequence of this structure? Are such huge centralized agencies able to cope with problem-banks spread union-wide? Would it be imaginable that the best possible deposit insurance system is not enough to match the problems caused by the intrinsic structure of the banking system? Does not a functioning deposit insurance system presuppose a bank structure with stronger banking units, with branches spread nation-wide and operating both as commercial and investment banks? In that case, a private insurance system established by the banks themselves could possibly master the problems.

As you are all aware, the model outlined here is the German solution. The results are satisfactory without almost any public intervention.

2. Were the non-performing U.S. loans given to foreign countries directly by U.S. banks or via foreign subsidiaries? Were they in accordance with the relevant banking supervisory regulations? If so, does one consider the regulations inadequate? Are amendments under consideration ? And if so, in which direction?

3. Does a foreign loan insurance system exist? To be more explicit, is the Overseas Private Investment Corporation (OPIC) involved, or is OPIC's operation area restricted to capital investment, as will be the case with the Multinational Investment Guarantee Agency (MIGA)?

4. A last set of questions, addressed particularly to our economists: What about the role of the World Bank/IMF as a world supervisory authority? To what extent may they serve as a (hidden) supervisory authority and to what extent do they actually do so? Would it be worthwhile testing or scrutinizing the idea of a new institutional arrangement for the world economy in the form of a "loan MIGA", that is to say a Multinational Foreign Loan Guarantee Agency (MuLGA)? Could such an institution - *de facto* - serve as an international supervisory authority and as a tool for spreading risk amongst countries?

The Internationalization of Financial Markets and the Regulatory Response

David Folkerts-Landau[1]

I.   Introduction

Domestic and international finance - markets, institutions, and practices - is undergoing a major transformation in response to changes in economic and technological conditions. Markets have expanded through the increased securitization of the liabilities of non-financial entities, through the increased internationalization of participants, and through the globalization of trading in certain securities. Changes in the relative importance of various activities (both on- and off-balance sheet), and the emergence of new activities, is transforming the industrial organization of financial firms. Finally, and perhaps most important has been the institutionalization of innovation in financial products and practices. Financial engineering, in the form of new products and practices, and financial entrepreneurship, in the form of restructuring of the balance sheets of non-financial firms through mergers, acquisition, leveraged buy-outs, and divestitures, has become institutionalized with the growth of new-products departments and merchant-banking departments alongside the traditional departments in financial institutions. These on-going developments, more advanced in some countries than in others, have made fundamental modification necessary, and in some instances a complete redesign, of national and international financial supervisory and regulatory policy. Some countries, most notable the United Kingdom, have successfully implemented such a complete restructuring of their supervisory and regulatory policy, while others have taken a more gradualist approach.

---

[1]   The author has benefited from comments of other authors at the symposium and from comments by the discussant, Professor N.K.A. Läufer. The views expressed here are those of the author and should not be taken as reflecting the views of the International Monetary Fund.

Studies in International Economics and Institutions
Vosgerau (Ed.) New Institutional Arrangements for the World Economy
© Springer-Verlag Berlin Heidelberg 1989

The developments in financial markets since the early 1970s do not fit easily into the traditional analytical mold of financial and regulatory economics which is largely concerned with questions of pricing and allocation of risk under various information and market structures rather than with institutional innovation.

This paper discusses recent developments in finance and the implications of these developments for financial policy. In keeping with the subject matter of this conference we place particular emphasis on the internationalization of finance and its implications for national supervisory and regulatory policy and for the coordination of such policies.

II. Forces Creating Change in Financial Markets

The extensive changes in financial instruments, financial institutions, and regulatory structures of the previous decade represent the competitive response of market participants (in both the private and public sectors) to a growing stock of financial claims and to a series of macroeconomic disturbances and technological advances. In a number of respects, borrowers and lenders operating in international financial markets in the 1970s and 1980s were confronted with macroeconomic conditions that were less stable and more uncertain than those in the 1960s - in particular, higher and more variable rates of inflation and interest rates, greater exchange rate variability, the presence of large fiscal and external imbalances in both developing and industrial countries, and the emergence of external payments difficulties for many developing countries.

More uncertain macroeconomic conditions led to the development of new financial instruments, which were designed to allow market participants to hedge the new risks better, as well as to arbitrage cross-country differences in financial market conditions. Floating rate notes and exchange rate and interest rate swaps, as well as futures and options markets, emerged to provide new means for hedging greater interest rate and exchange rate variability.[2] Moreover, there were, at times, strong

---

[2] These instruments could also be used to take on additional risk in order to earn a higher return.

incentives for borrowers and lenders to arbitrage cross-country differences in the returns and risks of financial investments as well as in tax structures and regulatory restrictions. In particular, residents in some countries at times found it profitable to undertake transactions with other residents of the same country through the off-shore markets. This arbitrage process was facilitated by technological change, which lowered the cost of telecommunications and of data processing. In addition, activities in international markets were also stimulated by the recycling of the current account surpluses of the oil exporters in the 1970s, and the emergence of large fiscal deficits and current account imbalances in the industrial countries in the late 1970s and the early 1980s. During the late 1970s and 1980s, the pace of these structural changes in financial markets accelerated as all major countries undertook financial liberalizations designed to increase market efficiency and to adapt domestic financial structures to the new financial instruments and techniques that had emerged in other domestic and offshore markets.

1. Macroeconomic Disturbances

In the early 1970s, the structure of the major financial markets across the larger industrial countries was quite diverse. Although these countries had shared an extended experience with sustained growth and low inflation during much of the late 1950s and 1960s, each nation's financial markets developed largely independently of others, reflecting both economic factors and government policies. Communication and transportation costs, differences in financial and legal arrangements, and even cultural and social traditions made it costly to undertake new financial operations in different national markets. In addition, capital and exchange controls on external financial transactions in France, Japan, and the United Kingdom discouraged financial integration. In this environment of relative macroeconomic stability and of incomplete cross-country linkages between financial markets, the structure of domestic financial institutions, and the attendant regulatory arrangements, primarily reflected domestic concerns.

Nonetheless, international financial intermediation grew rapidly during the late 1950s and 1960s, as financial institutions attempted to service the needs of domestic nonfinancial firms engaged in international trade in goods and services, and as market participants attempted to arbitrage the differences between yields on financial transactions in various markets. The offshore (Eurocurrency) markets expanded rapidly, in response both to attempts to evade certain financial restrictions imposed by the authorities and to the need for international financial intermediary services. The decisions by the United Kingdom to place restrictions on the use of sterling for financing third country trade (in 1957), and by the United States to impose a penalty (interest equalization tax) on purchases by U.S. residents of securities issued by foreigners (in 1963), encouraged borrowers to seek financing in the Eurocurrency markets.

Financial systems have been forced since the early 1970s to adapt to increased uncertainty about macroeconomic conditions, and to the need to finance large fiscal and current account imbalances in many countries. The greater uncertainty about macroeconomic conditions reflected the emergence of a series of historically large and unanticipated shocks to the international economy. The abandonment of the Bretton Woods system of fixed exchange rates was accompanied by a sharp expansion of cross-border financial flows and by the increased variability of nominal and real exchange rates - a factor that was to continue, albeit to varying degrees - throughout the floating rate period. Moreover, the uneven pattern of growth and recession in economic activity that was evident in the 1970s and 1980s may have further contributed to uncertainty about future developments.[3]

Inflation in the 1970s was higher and more variable than in the 1960s.[4] After a period of historically low real interest rates in the mid-1970s, nominal and real interest rates reached levels in the early 1980s not experienced in most industrial

---

[3] The average rate of growth in the industrial countries fell from 4.8 percent per annum in the 1960s, to 3.3 percent and 2.3 percent in the 1970s and the period 1980-86, respectively. In contrast, the variability of GNP growth rates (as measured by the variance) was ten times as high in the 1970s and 1980s (4.1 percent) as in the 1960s (0.4 percent).

[4] The average rate of inflation in the industrial countries in the 1960s was 3.1 percent per annum but rose to 7.9 in the 1970s before declining to 5.0 percent in the period 1980-86. The variance of inflation rates also increased from 0.6 percent in the 1960s to 6.7 percent in the 1970s, before declining to 5.5 percent in the 1980s.

countries since the post-World War II period. The scale of the debt-servicing difficulties encountered both by many developing countries and by interest-sensitive sectors of major industrial countries, was also outside the range of experience since the 1930s.

Taken together, these developments implied a fundamental adverse shift in the degree of macroeconomic instability in comparison with the late 1950s and 1960s. Since the instruments and financial arrangements in the major industrial countries were developed during periods of lower inflation and more stable conditions, immediate pressures were created for adapting instruments, institutions, and regulations.

The level of activity in international financial markets was sharply stimulated by sectoral imbalances that emerged as a result of the macroeconomic shocks. The recycling of the current account surpluses of the oil-exporting countries associated with the oil price increase of 1973 and 1979 was accomplished primarily by private rather than public sector intermediaries. Most of the reserves accumulated by oil-exporting countries as a result of current account surpluses were initially held as deposits in banks in offshore financial markets and in the major industrial countries. During the same period, the current account deficit of the industrial countries and that of the non-oil developing countries rose sharply. Lending from banks and other private creditors financed nearly half of the current account deficits of the non-oil developing countries.

In the early 1980s, sharp changes in access to these markets for many developing countries also had a major impact on the scale and distribution of credits through these markets. For countries with external payments difficulties, most additional credits from private financial markets were obtained through new money packages accompanied by Fund-supported adjustment programs. In contrast, flows between borrowers and lenders in the industrial countries accelerated sharply, with much of the growth being in the securities markets as opposed to bank lending. In addition, the emergence of large fiscal deficits in some major industrial countries in both the mid-1970s and early 1980s led over time to sharp increases in the stocks of government securities outstanding. In order to market those securities, governments removed restrictions on purchases by both the domestic nonfinancial sector (especially of short-term securities) and foreigners. In some countries, foreign purchases also began to account for an increasingly larger share of the sales of new issues.

2. Technological Advances

The ability of financial institutions to adjust to these changes in macroeconomic conditions was influenced profoundly by innovations in telecommunications and data processing. New developments in such areas as computer technology, computer software, and telecommunications permitted more rapid processing and transmissions of information, completion of transactions, and less costly confirmation of payments. These advances made possible 24-hour a day trading by linking exchanges in different time zones. Moreover, information about financial conditions in all major markets became much more readily available. Such changes basically enlarged the set of markets in which financial institutions could provide intermediary services. Since more institutions could efficiently service the various markets, competitive pressures naturally increased. In addition, improved computer technology made possible new hedging instruments, including options and financial futures, whose initial pricing required the solution of complex mathematical and statistical problems.

3. Differences in Regulatory, Supervisory, and Tax Structures in the Mid-1970s

While macroeconomic shocks, payments imbalances, and technological changes provided the principal stimulus for the rapid expansion of activity in international financial markets during the 1970s and 1980s, attempts to arbitrage financial conditions (including regulatory and institutional differences) between the offshore and domestic markets of the major industrial countries often played a role in determining the scale and composition of the flows between particular markets. In general, financial structures in the major industrial countries differed most in terms of: (1) regulations concerning yields on financial instruments, the activities and location of financial institutions, and access to markets; (2) prudential supervision of the financial sector; and (3) tax, legal, and disclosure systems. The liberalizations of domestic financial markets were to play an important role in removing many of these differences.

a.   Regulations on Yields, Activities, and Market Access

In the mid-1970s, interest rate ceilings were important constraints in France, Japan, and the United States, but were not present in the Federal Republic of Germany or in the United Kingdom. In Japan, interest rates on most financial assets were closely linked to the official discount rate charged by the Bank of Japan on discounts of commercial bills and on loans secured by eligible paper. The ability of Japanese borrowers and lenders to evade those interest rate ceilings was constrained by the limited availability of short-term money market instruments and by a comprehensive system of exchange controls. However, the need to sell larger volumes of government securities when bond-financed central government fiscal deficits emerged in the mid-1970s, put considerable pressure on the system. As fiscal deficits created alternative portfolio instruments and exerted upward pressure on free market interest rates, strong incentives were created to shift away from assets with low fixed yields.

In the United States, statutory restrictions (Regulation Q) prohibited the payment of interest on demand deposits and set interest rate ceilings on savings and time deposits at depository institutions. As inflation and market interest rates rose in the late 1960s and early 1970s, relative to the Regulation Q ceiling rates, there were repeated episodes of withdrawal of deposits (disintermediation) from financial institutions, with the result that the availability of credit (especially for housing) was often sharply reduced. Depositors sought higher yields through direct purchases of U.S. government securities and money market funds. In addition, large borrowers and lenders turned to the Eurocurrency market to obtain additional funds and to earn a market return on their financial assets.

Restrictions on the products, activities, and location of financial institutions differed significantly between financial systems with universal banks and those with more segmented markets and activities. In the Federal Republic of Germany and in Switzerland, banks were allowed to undertake both commercial and investment banking activities, and they have extensive branch networks in their domestic economies. In contrast, commercial banks in the United States and Japan were more restricted, especially with respect to investment banking activities. In the United States, the Banking Act of 1933 (frequently referred to as the Glass-Steagall Act) prohibited commercial banks from underwriting either nonpublic bond issues or revenue bonds of state and local governments. In addition, under the McFadden Act of 1922, national banks in the United States could branch no farther in a particular state than was allowed for the state chartered banks. In a number of states, no branching was allowed. In Japan, commercial banking was formally separated after World War II from underwriting and trust business by Article 65 of the Japanese Securities Law. However, Japanese banks were legally permitted to branch nationwide.

During the early and mid-1970s, the maintenance of extensive capital controls and limitations on entry of foreign financial institutions into the domestic market were part of the effort to isolate domestic financial systems from external developments. As noted earlier, France, Japan, and the United Kingdom placed a variety of controls on capital flows, especially those involving short-term instruments.

There was nonetheless a movement toward a national treatment of foreign financial institutions (especially banks). Foreign financial institutions became subject to the same regulations as comparable domestic institutions. For example, in the United States, the International Banking Act of 1978 provided for a uniform national treatment of foreign banks.[5] In this situation, the number of foreign banks in the United States expanded rapidly, rising from about 150 banks in the mid-1970s (with $40 billion in assets) to 369 banks (with $223 billion of assets) by 1981. They brought new competitive pressures to the major financial centers in the United

---

[5] Foreign banks were made subject to federal supervision in a manner similar to U.S. domestic banks, required to hold minimum reserves, faced with Regulation Q ceilings, required to have deposit insurance if they accepted retail deposits, and confronted with new limitations on branching.

States. A number of other countries have also expanded the scope of activities, especially in the stock exchanges, for foreign financial institutions.

In the United Kingdom, foreign banks played active roles in both the London Eurocurrency market and in the domestic markets. As the Eurocurrency market expanded, the number of foreign banks either directly or indirectly represented in London grew from 138 in 1969 to 335 in 1975. In the Federal Republic of Germany, foreign banks could compete with domestic banks in most areas, but they were restricted in their ability to lead manage securities issues. Foreign banks in Japan represented only about 3 percent of total commercial bank assets in the mid-1970s, and their primary focus was on international rather than domestic banking. These banks were not allowed to branch; they were restricted in their solicitation of yen deposits, and their access to the discount facilities of the Bank of Japan was sharply limited.

b.   Prudential Regulation and Supervision and Taxation

In some cases, prudential regulations created incentives for institutions to adjust the location or types of their activities. Some financial institutions used off-balance-sheet activities (e.g., guarantees or currency swaps) or operations in the external markets to minimize the costs of satisfying capital requirements. In particular, to the extent that the operations of branches or subsidiaries in the Euro-currency markets were not consolidated, booking business offshore often reduced the effective level of capital needed for the firm as a whole.

Accounting standards also differed significantly across the major countries. One key difference, for example, was associated with the extent of "hidden" reserves (typically associated with below market valuation of assets) in the accounts of financial and nonfinancial institution. In countries such as the Federal Republic of Germany, Switzerland, and Japan, these reserves were more important than in other countries. Unreported charges against, and additions to, such reserves made it difficult to compare profit and loss statements across countries.

Disclosure requirements were also diverse. In part, this difference reflected alternative philosophies about the types of borrowers that should be allowed to access financial markets. One view was that market participants should be allowed to take on whatever risks (at a market related price) that they desired so long as there was full disclosure of the relevant financial information about the borrower's condition. The alternative view was that market access should be limited to more creditworthy borrowers (i.e., through merit-regulation often imposed by the market); with the quality of the borrower being more assured, less detailed disclosure could be required. In the mid-1970s, the disclosure requirements established by the U.S. Securities and Exchange Commission (SEC) came closest to the first view. In contrast, borrowers in the Eurobond markets were traditionally limited to the more well known firms, banks, and governments whose credit standing was considered sufficient. In line with the second view, that market, therefore, required less detailed disclosure, although to some degree additional disclosure existed when bonds were also issued in domestic markets.

Differences between the taxation of financial transactions and income from financial assets often led to a situation where financial transactions would take place (be "booked") in a given market or country solely to reduce a tax liability. The withholding tax typically levied in domestic markets on payments of interest to foreign holders of domestic securities or deposits also stimulated the issuance of Eurobonds (not subject to any withholding tax) and acquisition of Eurocurrency deposits. In addition, transfer taxes on security transactions (such as existed in the Federal Republic of Germany and Switzerland) discouraged the use of domestic money market instruments and encouraged the use of external money markets.

III. Dynamics of Change

Given the structural differences that existed in major domestic and offshore markets in the 1970s, three elements appear to have been the main factors influencing how rapidly the effects of structural changes and financial innovations moved across national boundaries or between domestic and offshore markets: the degree of competition in various financial markets; the method of regulatory enforcement;

and the prevalence of restrictions on financial yields, the types of activities allowed for certain institutions, and international capital flows.

Perhaps the most important factor that affected the speed with which new innovations were transmitted was the degree of competition both within a given domestic financial system and across financial markets. At the firm level, for example, the introduction of an innovation by one firm in a highly competitive industry lead other firms to quickly change their products in order to retain customers and market shares. At the industry level, such competition has meant that innovations in one sector of the financial system lead to new products in other segments. At the regulator's level, the desire to avoid either sharp shifts in market shares of certain sectors of the domestic financial system or transfers of financial activity to external markets at times induced significant regulatory changes.

An important force generating regulatory change through indirect competition among regulators has been the development of offshore markets. While capital controls at times inhibited the use of offshore markets, they proved difficult to enforce and, where effective, produced significant distortions. When such controls were ineffective or absent, the cost imposed by existing domestic regulatory requirements or taxes could frequently be lowered by moving an activity to an offshore market. For example, the separation of commercial banking and investment banking was weakened by commercial bank ownership of investment banking subsidiaries in offshore locations. The loss of financial activity to offshore markets often resulted in modifications of domestic regulatory constraints.

The response of regulatory agencies to structural changes in financial markets was strongly influenced by the extent to which the regulatory structure and its legislative oversight has been concentrated or diffused. In the United States, the regulatory structure was specialized not only by industry such as securities (Securities and Exchange Commission), banking (Federal Reserve, Federal Deposit Insurance Corporation, and the Comptroller of the Currency), and future markets (Commodity Future Trading Commission) but also along geographic lines (e.g., federal and state). Moreover, the federal legislative oversight was lodged with several congressional committees. This dispersed system of regulatory agencies and legislative oversight at times created incentives for institutions to switch from one regulatory domain to another and for regulators to take actions to maintain the competitive positions of the institutions which they regulated. In contrast, the financial systems of continental Europe tended to have one or two main supervisory agencies and a single legislative group that provided regulatory structure. In such financial systems, financial firms had a more limited ability and incentive to shift their regulatory jurisdiction within the country by changing their product line, legal form, or domicile.

Finally, an important distinction among financial systems is that in some systems the enforcement of regulatory restriction tends to be primarily through the court system and legislative action whereas in other cases, enforcement is done through "moral suasion". The U.S. financial system is the best example of the first case, while the financial systems of Japan and continental Europe fall into the second category. The legislative, or statute based system, appears to have sanctioned the active exploitation of so-called loopholes in the regulatory structure, whereas in the moral suasion system, such behavior has not been condoned. Hence the legislative system has generally encouraged financial firms to be more innovative in bringing products to the market and to challenge the rules of the game more so than the "moral suasion" system.

IV.   The Internationalization of Financial Markets

The internationalization of financial markets during the past decade reflected two broad trends: the securitization of international finance and the liberalization of national financial markets.

During the 1960s and 1970s, the trend toward the internationalization of financial activity was most evident in the growth of the Eurocurrency markets. Internationalization continued with the progressive integration of these offshore markets with domestic markets as restrictions on capital flows were liberalized by the United States in 1974, the United Kingdom in 1979, and other countries, most notably Japan and France during the 1980s. Another aspect of this internationalization has been the entry of foreign financial firms (e.g., in banking, insurance, and securities) into domestic markets. Finally, the spread of new financial instruments and techniques from the Euromarkets to the domestic markets reduced further the segmentation between domestic and international markets.

The internationalization of financial activity is readily apparent in the financial statistics of the past decade. Total lending through international bank credit (net of redepositing) and bond markets grew from $96 billion in 1976 to $245 billion in 1986. International bank lending (net of redepositing) rose from $70 billion in 1976 to $160 billion in 1986.[6] The net issue of international bonds increased at a somewhat faster pace, i.e., from $26 billion in 1975 to $85 billion in 1986. Medium-term borrowing in the form of note issuance facilities expanded from nearly $3 billion in 1982 to $39 billion in 1985, but fell $21 billion in 1986 due to the emergence of the Eurocommercial paper programs; while the Eurocommercial paper programs grew to $57 billion in 1986 from their first issue in 1984. Finally, the issue of international equity (initial public offerings of shares and other equity-linked instruments) has grown from about $2 billion in 1984 to $8 billion during 1986. The expansion of the international equity market in 1986 and 1987 provides the most recent example of the continuing internationalization of financial activity.

The greater participation of foreign financial entities in domestic markets has also been evident in most major markets. The number of foreign banking firms in the major industrial countries increased sharply and accounted for a considerably greater share of total bank assets. The introduction of foreign securities firms into domestic markets also proceeded at a rapid pace. For example, several stock exchanges (e.g., in Japan and the United Kingdom) further expanded their membership in 1986 and 1987 to include foreign firms. Moreover, the standardization of market practices, such as bond ratings, settlement procedures, and codes of conduct, served to facilitate cross-border transactions.

---

[6] Total international bank lending (including interbank activity) grew even more rapidly from $100 billion in 1976 to $562 billion in 1986. Interbank flows have grown rapidly in response to increased activity in the major financial centers and to arbitrage of regulatory restrictions.

Securitization

Securitization has contributed to the internationalization of financial activity. Securitization has involved a greater use of direct debt markets - in which the lender holds a tradable direct claim on the borrower, and a shift away from indirect finance - in which an intermediary holds a nontradable loan asset and the saver holds a liability (which may be tradable) of the intermediary. In particular, syndicated loans have been increasingly displaced by issues of international bonds or, more recently, by the use of note issuance facilities or nonunderwritten Eurocommercial paper.[7] In all major countries, the funds raised in the bank loan market as percentage of GNP have declined from 1980 to 1986 (except in Japan), while funds raised through securities markets have increased.[8]

The role of banks in the securities markets has changed with the trend toward securitization. The total holding by banks of international bond and other long-term securities rose from $47 billion in 1981 to $158 billion by the end of 1985, while the volume of securities (excluding certificates of deposits) issued by banks rose from about $7 billion in 1981 to $43 billion by the end of 1985. In addition, banks provided almost all the lines of credit used to secure note-issuance facilities. It therefore appears that, while securitization has changed the form in which

---

[7]   Syndicated lending (excluding reschedulings) declined from its peak of $98 billion in 1982, to $58 billion in 1986, while the international bond market grew from $76 billion to $226 billion over the same period and the volume of Euro-note borrowing facilities (including non-underwritten Eurocommercial paper) grew from $5 billion in 1982 to $84 billion in 1986. Moreover, the structure of borrowing in the Euronote market has shifted significantly away from underwritten note issuance facilities towards the nonunderwritten Eurocommercial paper market. Part of the decline in the note facilities appears to be associated with the proposal to apply capital requirements against facilities arranged by banks in the U.S. and the U.K. In 1984, underwritten facilities amounted to $29 billion, while Eurocommercial paper was not yet significant; by 1986 the importance of the two sources of funds had been reversed and underwritten facilities amounted to $27 billion while Eurocommercial paper had grown to $57 billion.

[8]   In some countries, this decline may have reflected the general improvement in the liquidity positions of nonbank firms (which reduced the need for bank borrowing) due to a recovery from cyclical downturns and improvements in conditions in the securities markets (reflecting lower interest rates).

banking institutions provide credits, banks have remained an important source of credit.

In addition to the shift of credit flows from bank lending to securities markets, a second form of securitization has involved the packaging of assets that are normally not traded (e.g., bank loans, corporate receivables, and household liabilities) into tradable securities. This has been done either by using the original assets as collateral for a new tradable securities issue (collateralized obligation) or by issuing a new tradable security that is being serviced by the proceeds of the original assets (pass-through security). For example, the sale of loans, notably residential mortgages, has continued to grow in the domestic as well as the external markets. The share of new mortgages being securitized in the United States has grown from 15 percent in 1981 to over 50 percent in 1986. In addition, many lending instruments, which are technically not securitized, carry provisions allowing for their transfer to third parties (e.g., transferable loan certificates).

A third form of securitization has involved the creation of exchange traded futures and options contracts. In this case, a certain type of risk, usually one associated with price volatility, is securitized. During 1986 and early 1987, several new contracts for financial futures and options were introduced on major exchanges and the turnover volume of existing contracts showed unprecedented increases. A relatively new development was the progressive introduction of embedded options in international bonds, where the bond's principal redemption is typically linked by a specific formula to an index or the price (including exchange rates) of another instrument. Several countries introduced new financial futures and options contracts, and trading volume increased significantly in 1986; e.g, the total financial futures trading volume on all U.S. exchanges increased by 23 percent in 1986 and the total trading volume of financial options increased by 64 percent in 1986. The fastest growth, by way of turnover volume and outstanding contracts, has been in the currency option markets.

Yet a further aspect of the securitization of international financial markets has been the increased volume of secondary trading in various securities markets. For example, the volume of secondary market trading in Eurobonds (such trading takes place in the over-the-counter market) was $2.2 trillion in 1985 and $3.6 trillion in

1986. Since 1980, the primary issue of Eurobonds has grown at an annual rate of about 45 percent, while secondary market trading has expanded by nearly 60 percent.

Liberalization and Innovations

The liberalization of financial markets during the past decade has proceeded along four avenues: the liberalization of cross-border financial flows, the growing foreign participation in domestic markets, the introduction of new instruments, and the removal of domestic price and quantity restrictions.[9] This section provides an overview of the major trends in the liberalization of financial markets.

The liberalization of financial markets during the past decade has involved the gradual removal of capital controls in the major economies and the more recent removal of restrictions on the participation of foreign financial firms in domestic financial markets. Heretofore, a variety of legal and fiscal restrictions on international transactions had been used to control both capital inflows and capital outflows for the purpose of macroeconomic management.

An early but significant step towards the liberalization of capital flows came with the removal of controls on capital outflows from the United States. An Interest Equalization Tax had discouraged foreign borrowers from issuing securities in U.S. financial markets and a Voluntary Foreign Credit Restraint Program may have inhibited U.S. banks and financial institutions from increasing the level of loans to foreign entities. By 1974, these measures and various other administrative guidelines had been removed. Foreign banks and other financial entities have generally had access to U.S. domestic markets, and the access for banks has been on the basis of national treatment since the International Banking Act of 1978. The U.S. authorities

---

[9] A detailed discussion of recent liberalization measures in selected countries was provided in Maxwell Watson, Russell Kincaid, Caroline Atkinson, Eliot Kalter, and David Folkerts-Landau, "International Capital Markets, Development and Prospects," World Economic and Financial Surveys, December 1986.

also abolished the withholding tax levied on nonresident holders of bonds issued by U.S. residents in 1984.

The United Kingdom undertook a major step toward the liberalization of sterling cross-border transactions by removal of exchange controls in 1979. The controls were designed to prevent capital outflows and their removal, along with the lifting of lending restrictions on banks (the so-called corset), opened the sterling banking and securities markets to foreign borrowers.

The German authorities too have significantly reduced restrictions on capital inflows. In the 1970s, these restrictions were principally authorization requirements for nonresident purchases of domestic bonds and money-market instruments and, for a few years, restrictions on payments of interest on bank deposits held by foreigners. Such restrictions were gradually removed in the 1980s. Access to the German capital markets was further liberalized with the recent replacement of the calendar for issues in securities markets with a simple notification system, and with the removal of a 25 percent withholding tax on interest payments on domestic bonds to nonresidents. However, it has been proposed that effective January 1989, a 10 percent withholding tax be reimposed on interest payments on bonds issued in the Federal Republic of Germany.

In the case of Japan, the authorities have, since the early 1980s, undertaken an extensive liberalization of cross-border financial activities. The set of foreign institutions allowed to borrow from Japanese banks, or to issue in the Japanese securities markets, has been gradually extended. In addition, the Euroyen bond market was opened to foreign corporations in 1984, and access to this market was further extended to foreign banks in 1986. The depth and breadth of the Euroyen market was significantly increased by authorization of Euroyen floating rate notes, dual currency bonds, currency conversion notes, deep discount and zero coupon bonds.

Throughout the 1970s and early 1980s, French authorities employed controls on capital outflows for the purpose of monetary and exchange rate management. However, in the mid-1980s, the authorities undertook an extensive liberalization of cross-border financial flows. The Euro-French franc bond market was reopened and exempted from a 10 percent withholding tax applied in domestic markets, and foreign exchange repatriation and hedging restrictions were reduced. Furthermore, the activities that foreign financial firms could undertake were greatly expanded.

The past decade - and particularly the last six to seven years - have also witnessed a significant expansion of the instruments used in international and domestic financial transactions. Many of these innovations originated in either the domestic U.S. market or in the Euro-dollar markets, and then spread to domestic financial markets in other countries. The introduction of the floating rate note in the early 1970s represented one of the first major innovations. Over time, the volume of international lending through this instrument grew to exceed the volume of lending through the syndicated loan market. The introduction in 1981 of note-issuance facilities - medium-term arrangements which allow borrowers to issue short-term notes in the Euromarkets backed by underwriting commitments of commercial banks - represented another important broadening of the choice of instruments. Currency and interest rate swaps - first undertaken in 1981 and amounting to over $500 billion by 1986 - are particularly significant, because of both their scale and their apparent availability.

The range of financial instruments available in domestic securities markets has also expanded. Innovations have generally occurred in financial instruments that compete closely either with bank liabilities, such as mutual funds or short-term government bills, or with bank assets, such as commercial paper.

In France, the volume of mutual fund assets quadrupled between 1982 and 1986. French banks started issuing negotiable certificates of deposits in 1985. In addition, the government made short-term treasury securities available to nonbanks and banks. Also, to complement the domestic bond market, the financial authorities opened a financial futures market (MATIF).

In the Federal Republic of Germany, the range of new instruments was extended by granting permission for zero-coupon bonds with debt-warrants, floating rate notes, certificates of deposits, dual currency bonds, and currency and interest rate swaps. In Japan, the liberalization effort centered on the creation of money market instruments. The authorities authorized negotiable certificates of deposits, removed restrictions on the interbank call and bill discount markets, and permitted repurchasing of bonds and certificates of deposit to grow. The maturity spectrum of money market instruments was broadened further with the introduction of money market certificates and of auctioned, discount, short-term government refinancing bonds. In the United Kingdom, commercial paper and asset-backed instruments were introduced into domestic financial markets, while in the United States, the introduction of exchange-traded financial futures and options was noteworthy.

The structure of principal financial markets was also reformed, either directly or indirectly. In the United States, the New York Stock Exchange was induced in 1975 to replace fixed with negotiated brokerage commissions; and the so-called shelf registration, which allowed borrowers in U.S. securities to register a proposed issue up to one year in advance of the issue day, was introduced in 1983 by the U.S. Securities and Exchange Commission, thus allowing for a flexible response to market conditions. Furthermore, the U.S. Commodities Futures Trading Commission authorized many new types of exchange-traded futures and options contracts. Perhaps most important of all, interest rate ceilings on bank liabilities were removed. Banks were also authorized to issue money market deposit accounts and to underwrite mutual funds. In addition, geographic constraints on bank expansion were relaxed.

The U.K. authorities have undertaken a major regulatory reform and liberalization of their financial markets (the so-called "Big Bang"). The authorities induced the Stock Exchange to end a fixed schedule of brokerage commissions in favor of negotiated commissions. In addition, the Exchange's operations have been liberalized through the introduction of new trading practices and systems, and the participation of foreign institutions has been greatly expanded. Stock exchange members are now permitted to deal directly with investors (i.e., to act as agents and principals). The gilt-edged market has been reorganized along the lines of the market for U.S. government securities, i.e., a system of primary dealers served by a number of interdealer brokers.

V.   The Regulatory and Supervisory Response

These changes in international financial markets had a number of implications for existing regulatory and supervisory polices. As the share of financial activity taking place in the offshore markets increased, the authorities were unable to attain as comprehensive a view of the overall activities of major financial institutions as in the past. This situation was accentuated by the growing use by many financial institutions of off-balance sheet business (e.g., the provision of guarantee and swaps) that was often not fully incorporated into such supervisory measures as minimum capital-asset ratios. The response of the authorities to these developments has involved removing some of the incentives for using offshore markets through liberalization of the regulatory structures in domestic markets, a broadening of the supervisory net to include more of the external and off-balance sheet activities, and attempts to better coordinate changes in regulatory and supervisory policies with other countries.

Three major changes in the institutional and regulatory environment of international financial markets have been evident. First, the authorities have placed greater reliance on measures to promote competition both within and across major markets as a means of obtaining greater efficiency within financial systems. Competition has been enhanced by the weakening of capital controls and restrictions on the entry of foreign firms into domestic markets. In addition, most industrial countries have also undertaken extensive domestic financial liberalizations focused on either removing or weakening restrictions on interest rates that could be paid on financial institution deposit liabilities, the use of instruments, and access to markets.[10]

The reductions in these restrictions have enabled domestic financial institutions to compete more readily in nontraditional markets. This liberalization has created a tendency toward the emergence of more universal financial institutions. Such in-

---

[10]   During these reforms, tax policies have also been modified to some extent to avoid creating incentives for undertaking offshore activities. All major industrial countries have removed withholding taxes on foreign-held domestic securities in order to reduce the tax advantage associated with using Eurobonds as opposed to domestic bonds.

stitutions have had the ability to achieve a better diversification of activities and a broad range of financial services and funding options. While there are still important specialized or sector-specific financial institutions, the viability of these institutions increasingly depends on economic factors (e.g., market and economies of scale) rather than official restrictions on entry or competition.

A second major change in the regulatory environment has been to remove restrictions on the use of financial instruments. One aspect of competitive behavior in the Eurocurrency market has been a willingness to try a variety of novel techniques and instruments (e.g., syndicated loans, floating rate notes, Eurocommercial paper, and interest rate and exchange rate swaps) have had characteristics closely tailored to the portfolio preferences of borrowers and lenders and have been introduced in other domestic markets. Many of those new instruments can now be used in the major domestic markets.

A third major change in the evolution of supervisory policies has involved a response to the increased internationalization of financial transactions. Some of the most significant changes in this area, especially as they have related to the cross-country agreements, have occurred in periods following major crises. For example, the disturbances surrounding the failures of Bankhaus I.D. Herstatt and Franklin National Bank in 1974 led to the formation of the Committee on Banking Regulation and Supervisory Practices (Cooke Committee), under the auspices of the Bank for International Settlements. The Committee's stated objective has been to try to establish comprehensive prudential practices including, notably, practices designed to ensure that banks' foreign operations do not "escape supervision." In December 1975, the Cooke Committee endorsed a concordat on international bank supervisory cooperation, indicating the division of supervisory responsibilities between parent and host country supervisors.

In 1978, the BIS Governors endorsed the Cooke Committee's proposal that banks' capital adequacy should be monitored on a consolidated basis, inclusive of foreign branches and of majority-owned subsidiaries, and, where possible, minority holdings and joint ventures.[11] Nonetheless, events such as the problems of Banco Ambrosiano Holding in 1982 indicated that there were still gaps in the supervisory net.[12]

In 1983, a revised version of the concordat was published[13] which examined ways of avoiding gaps in supervision that may arise as a result of inadequately supervised centers or the existence of intermediate holding companies within banking groups. By the end of 1986, consolidated supervision for purposes of capital adequacy of foreign branches and majority owned subsidiaries for capital adequacy purposes had been established among the G-5 and Switzerland.[14]

Since the emergence of widespread debt-servicing difficulties among developing countries and weaknesses in certain sectors of industrial economies during recessions in the early 1980s, there has been a coordinated effort to strengthen banks'

---

[11]   For a more detailed discussion of international coordination of bank supervision see Johnson and Abrams (1983).

[12]   Since Banco Ambrosiano Holding was a bank holding company - a 65 percent controlled subsidiary - and not a bank, under Luxembourg law, the Luxembourg authorities did not have supervisory powers. The Italian authorities felt limited responsibility for foreign subsidiaries whose activities they were unable to supervise. Subsequently, consolidated supervision was required by the Italian authorities of foreign banking and financial companies controlled, either directly or indirectly through the possession of more than 50 percent of capital.

[13]   This document ("Principles for the Supervision of Banks' Foreign Establishments") was published in Appendix I of R. Williams, et. al. (1983).

[14]   The Cooke Committee has also considered ways in which central banks could cooperate to provide official emergency assistance for temporary liquidity shortages in the Euromarkets. The communique of the Governors of the BIS issued in 1974 stated that

> [t]he Governors ... had an exchange of views on the lender of last resort in the Euromarkets. They recognized that it would not be practical to lay down in advance detailed rules and procedures for the provision of temporary liquidity. But they were satisfied that means are available for that purpose and will be used if and when necessary.

This statement, which has been reaffirmed on a number of occasions, remains the major policy statement on the lender of last resort function for international markets. See Guttentag and Herring (1983) for a detailed discussion of the issues surrounding the provision of lender of last resort assistance in an international setting.

balance sheets, reversing the downward trend that prevailed during the 1970s and early 1980s. Banks in industrial countries, except Japan, have increased their capital relative to total assets. However, these measures are not strictly comparable across countries due to accounting differences. Nonetheless, while the composition of assets and definitions of capital differ, there was a growing consensus among supervisors in major industrial countries that capital adequacy requirements should be strengthened and converge internationally.

Two principal supervisory techniques are used for assessing capital adequacy - a gearing ratio, which is the unweighted total of all on-balance sheet items divided by capital, or a risk asset ratio, which is a risk-weighted total of on- and off-balance sheet items relative to capital. During this period, agreement was reached among supervisors on the advantages of the risk-asset approach, especially for coping with off-balance sheet risks. At end 1986, France, the Federal Republic of Germany, Switzerland, and the United Kingdom utilized a risk-asset approach, and this approach was also applied to overseas activities of Japanese banks with foreign branches. U.S. Federal regulators circulated in 1986 a proposal for a risk-asset ratio approach. Nonetheless, substantial differences remain among major industrial countries in the risk weights assigned and in the definition of capital.

In 1986 the Cooke Committee published a report[15] that outlined a framework for supervisory reporting systems that sought to integrate off- and on-balance sheet risks. It was argued that risks associated with most off-balance sheet activities - market risk, credit risk, and management risk - are not different in principle from those risks arising from on-balance sheet business. In order to develop an integrated approach to assessing a bank's risk exposure, the report suggested methods for translating the various types of off-balance sheet instruments into their rough "equivalent" on-balance sheet credit risks.

The issuance in March 1987 of a joint United Kingdom/United States convergence proposal for monitoring capital adequacy marked a significant step toward a common supervisory framework for credit risk. In June 1987, Japanese authorities

---

[15] "The Management of Banks' Off Balance Sheet Exposures: A Supervisory Perspective," Committee on Banking Regulations and Supervisory Practices (Basle, March 1986).

announced their support, in principle, for the U.K./U.S. proposals. A common supervisory framework for monitoring capital adequacy would significantly diminish the opportunities for regulatory arbitrage by banks among the three largest international financial centers.

Recently, it has been reported that 17 countries, which are members of either the European Economic Community or the Group of 10, have been developing a set of common standards for capital adequacy of banks. Capital would apparently be defined to include ordinary paid-up share capital and disclosed reserves as well as some proportion of hidden reserves, property, equity holdings and subordinated debt. In addition, there would be different fixed weights for different types of on- and off- to balance sheet item used in calculating overall risk exposure. An overall ratio of bank capital to risk weighted bank assets of 8 percent would be established.[16]

The Commission of the European Communities has also proposed a "White Paper on the Internal Market," which was approved by the European Council in 1985 and which is now in the process of being ratified by the member states. This White Paper establishes as priority objective for the Community the completion of a free internal market by 1992 in goods and services, including financial services and capital. It sets out legislative agenda for achieving this goal. The White Paper contains about 20 proposals for directions concerned with banking and securities trading to be approved by the Council of Ministers with the consultation of the European Parliament before it becomes EC law.

The EC Commission's Proposals for Directives:

Banking

- Bank Accounting: Harmonization of bank accounting systems to improve their comparability. Will take effect in fiscal year 1993.
- Foreign Branch Offices: Elimination of the need for foreign branch offices of banks with head offices in the EEC to publish separate accounts for those branches. Proposal for directive not yet adopted by the Council of Ministers.

---

[16] Bank loans to any of the governments of 17 countries would apparently carry a zero weight.

- Reorganization of Credit Institutions: Specification of procedures involving the reorganization and winding-up of credit institutions with financial problems. The proposal for a directive assigns principal responsibility to the home-country authorities and seeks depositor-protection schemes to countries not currently covered by such schemes to branches of foreign banks in such countries. Not yet adopted.

- Own Funds: Harmonizes the concept of own-funds. These are classified into "internal" (those belonging to the credit institution) and "external" (at the disposal of the institution but not belonging to it). External items are restricted to 50 percent of the internal elements. Proposal for directive not yet adopted.

- Deposit Guarantees: Recommends establishment of a guarantee system of deposits within the EC. Recommendation adopted by the Commission.

- Payment Cards: Definition of common technical features of the payment cards.

- Solvency Ratios: Defines minimum capital adequacy ratios acceptable to bank regulators in member states. Proposal to be presented to council early 1988.

Securities Markets

- Disclosure of Large Positions in Securities: Defines information-disclosure requirements when a major holding in the capital of a listed company is acquired or disposed of. Proposal submitted to the council but not yet adopted.

- Prospectuses for Securities Listings: Mutual recognition of Stock Exchange prospectuses was adopted by council in July 1987. Another proposal calls for mutual recognition of public offer prospectuses presented to council but not yet adopted.

- Listing of Foreign Companies on Exchanges: Elimination of prohibitions against listing foreign companies on the exchanges of member states. Adopted by the council. Compliance by member states necessary by 1987.

- Insider Trading: Harmonises bans on insider trading, then extends them to areas not now covered by such a ban. Proposal sent to the council but not yet adopted.

Taxation and Liberalization of Capital Flows

- Long-Term Capital Flows: Extends obligation of member states to liberalize long-term commercial credits and transactions in securities not traded on exchanges (shares, bonds, and unit trusts). Requires that stock exchanges allow listing of member state companies. Proposal adopted by the council. Compliance by member states required by 1987.

- Collective Investment Undertakings: Provides for free circulation of units in collective investment undertakings (mainly unit trusts). Directive adopted by the council. Compliance required by 1989.

- Tax-Loss Carry-over: Harmonises member states' laws for carry-over of losses of undertakings. Submitted in 1985 but not yet adopted.

- Taxation of Mergers: Harmonization of taxation of mergers, division and contributions of assets. Submitted but not yet adopted.

The Commission's approach, as contained in the White Paper, is to achieve further liberalization of cross-border financial activity in two phases. The first phase is to achieve a complete liberalization of capital movements, initially in the medium and long-term credit markets and in the acquisition of residents of foreign securities and by nonresidents of domestic securities (seven member states of the EC - Belgium, Denmark, France, Luxembourg, the Netherlands, the Federal Republic of Germany, and the United Kingdom - have already undertaken these liberalizations) and then in the short-term market.

In the second phase, the Commission will propose a package of measures with broader implications. Financial transactions not directly related to trade or to the purchase of securities will be liberalized, including loans and deposits in both domestic and foreign currencies at home or abroad and to create a European securities market system based on the Community stock exchanges. The objective is to establish a common market in financial services in a deliberate, phased manner.

The Commission's strategy, both in the banking and in securities markets, is to combine a minimal basis of common rules for the protection of the users of financial services with the principle of "home country control," i.e., the supervision of the suppliers of services is left to the country of origin. This implies that each financial institution will be able to export freely its financial products to member states as long as it respects the regulations of its home country, which may well differ from those of the importing country. Thus, for example, Spanish banks would be able to offer their financial services to British residents and U.K. building societies can offer mortgages to residents in all member countries.

The main difficulty with the EC approach appears to be that the same type of institutions in one market place could operate under a different set of regulations. The widely diverging regulatory and supervisory structures in member countries' financial markets, which reflects the country's attitude toward the risk-efficiency trade-off, makes such an outcome likely. The main difference in financial regulation is the extent of the separation of banking and securities activities. While banks in all EC countries can be active in the primary markets, there are differences in the event of this involvement in secondary markets. There appears to be some convergence in recent years towards the universal banking system. Under the EC rules, a bank from a country without separation of securities and banking activities would be able to do banking and securities business in a country with such separation of the two types of activities. With regard to the United Kingdom, the question arises to what extent foreign institutions would be free to follow their home country regulations, which may be in conflict with current U.K. regulations. This problem has become more relevant with the inclusion of all euro-institutions into the new regulatory and supervisory structure created by the U.K. Financial Services Act. Thus, there may be large areas in which local banking and securities laws have to be further harmonized with less being left to mutual recognition.

An alternative method of achieving further liberalization in financial services transactions through a multilateral approach is through the principle of national treatment combined with some harmonization of prudential regulations. Under the principal of national treatment, foreign institutions abide by the regulations of the host country, thus all institutions in the same market face the same rules. National treatment has proved to be a significant obstacle, however, for banks from countries with a universal banking system desiring to operate in countries separating banking and securities markets. OECD member countries have accepted the obligations under national treatment.

VI.   Issues Raised by Recent Developments

Recent developments in international financial markets have affected the objectives of the financial authorities (especially as they relate to the regulation of domestic financial activity) and have introduced new complexities into the formulation and implementation of domestic macroprudential policies. While no central bank provides a detailed description of the circumstances under which it will provide emergency liquidity assistance, the growing integration of financial markets, and the blurring of the distinctions between banks and other financial institutions have raised questions about which institutions or markets may have to be supported during a crisis period and by whom. In particular, it has been argued that the close linkages between major short-term money markets (especially the interbank markets) may make it more difficult to confine the effects of a major domestic bank or non-bank financial institutional failure solely to the domestic market. Moreover, the extensive growth of international financial markets has lead some to conclude that the scale of emergency assistance needed (such as in the period surrounding the difficulties of the Continental Illinois Bank) could be significantly larger than in earlier periods.

One of the key issues in the formulation of these macro-prudential policies has been what should be the extent and nature of the "safety net" provided for the financial systems of the major countries in an increasingly liberalized and integrated world financial system. This issue has been discussed extensively in the other papers at this conference, and an "alternative" to the "traditional" view of the appropriate safety net in the case of the United States has been presented. However, recent proposals reflecting either the traditional and alternative views on the appropriate nature of the safety net have generally stressed the importance of strengthened supervision, especially with regard to enhanced capital adequacy. Our objective in this section is an examination of the implication of the growing integration of international financial markets for the implementation of macroprudential policies which focus on strengthening capital adequacy. This examination first briefly reviews the perceived rationale for strengthened capital adequacy under the various proposals, and then considers the problems associated with implementing such policies when financial institutions have the capability to undertake activity in a variety of corporate forms in a variety of international markets.

Concerns about the overall stability of the financial system, including maintenance of the payments system and protection of depositors and investors, have provided the traditional rationale for macroprudential policies that include not only the central bank's lender of last resort function and public sector deposit insurance guarantees, but also the supervision and regulation of financial institutions. It has been argued that the absence of lender of last resort assistance or deposit insurance could mean that even rational economic agents would rapidly withdraw their funds from financial intermediaries during a crisis period.[17]

The use of supervision to prevent or limit the extent of acts such as fraud, insider-trading, and self-dealing has been viewed traditionally as a complement to the provision of lender of last resort assistance. In part, this reflects the fact that knowledge of potential lender of last resort assistance (or in some countries of public sector deposit insurance guarantees) might encourage less prudent policies on the part of banks or other financial institutions, i.e., the problem of moral hazard.[18] In particular, troubled institutions could engage in high-return and high-risk activities in the hope of earning sufficient profits to avoid closure (a "double or nothing" strategy).

In addition to concerns about fraud and moral hazard problems, some have also argued that macroprudential policies should reflect the possibility that recent change in financial markets have not given financial institutions sufficient time to adjust their risk management techniques to the new environment and this might lead financial institutions to assume excessive risks due to inadequate experience with new financial instruments. However, there is a diversity of views regarding the issue of whether the liquidity and credit risks in newly liberalized financial markets have increased and what are the sources of any increased risks. While there has been increased volatility of some asset prices (including exchange rates and equity prices) in recent years, it has been difficult to identify the degree to which this greater volatility has been a response to unstable macroeconomic conditions or whether it reflects the activities of financial market participants. In particular,

---

[17] See Fama (1980 and 1985) and Diamond and Dybvig (1983) for a discussion of the conditions under which such runs are likely to occur, and Benston and Kaufman (1987) for a critique of the relevance of these models.

[18] The nature of this problem was stated clearly by Governor Henry Wallich of the Federal Reserve in testimony to the U.S. Congress:
There are dangers in trying to define and publicize specific rules for emergency assistance to troubled banks, notably the possibility of causing undue reliance on such facilities and possible relaxation of needed caution on the part of all market participants. Therefore, the Federal Reserve has always avoided comprehensive statements of conditions for its assistance to member banks. Emergency assistance is inherently a process of negotiation and judgment, with a range of possible actions varying with circumstances and need.

financial arrangements, institutions, and prices may show some evidence of instability as long as major macroeconomic imbalances remain.

It has been argued elsewhere that the traditional approach to macro-prudential policies has resulted in a safety net that leads to inefficiencies and may encourage risk taking on the part of some financial institutions. When public sector guarantees of financial sector liabilities and lender of last resort assistance are a part of the system and cannot be appropriately priced, then it has been noted that, in order to limit any exploitation of such guarantees and improve efficiency,[19] some minimum restriction would have to be imposed on the financial institutions' decisions regarding some aspects of their asset selection, the composition of their liabilities, the level of their required capital, and closure rules defining when the institution can remain in business. These restrictions would be accompanied by supervision of the asset side of the financial institutions, which in effect would mark assets to market and, in combination with capital requirements, determine whether the institution could remain open. A key issue is what constitutes the optimal level of such restrictions.[20]

Despite differences between the traditional and alternative approaches to designing the appropriate safety net for the financial system, most of the current proposals for improving financial system stability involve some steps for strengthening the supervision of enhanced capital adequacy. As already noted, the U.S./U.K. convergence proposals for capital adequacy have emphasized the use of a common risk-asset ratio in order to measure an institutions capital position and to inhibit regulatory arbitrage and provide a "level playing field."[21] Moreover, recent discussion among 17 industrial countries have reportedly focused on establishing a uniform risk-adjusted capital-asset ratio of 8 percent for banks across all countries. While the risk-weighting attached to bank loans to these governments apparently

---

[19] This discussion also applies to the mispricing of other services provided by the public sector such as access to the clearing system (Fedwire).

[20] For a discussion of the policy options in the United States, see Benston and Kaufman (1987).

[21] See Kane (1987) for a discussion of the view that such cooperation is designed principally to support regulatory cartels.

will be zero and certain types of hidden reserves will be included in measured capital, this could potentially require additional capital for banks in some countries, especially since risk-adjusted off-balance business would reportedly be included in the definition of assets. This proposal would also presumably involve the continued consolidation of foreign branches and majority-owned subsidiaries with the parent bank for purposes of assessing capital adequacy. Such harmonization and consolidation would be necessary if regulatory arbitrage is not to be encouraged. Similarly, although the proposals discussed at this conference generally regard the risk asset ratio approach as providing an inadequate measure of capital adequacy, they also envision some potential increases in required capital in a system where assets are marked to market and capital could include subordinated debt.

Recent developments in international financial markets raise the issue of whether these minimum capital-asset ratios (or other supervisory restrictions) can be effectively enforced in a world in which financial transactions can be undertaken in a variety of international markets through many alternative institutional arrangements with both on- and off-balance sheet transactions. Even if supervisory and regulatory policies are to be coordinated across countries, there could remain a number of obstacles to the successful implementation of such new prudential standards. First, depending on the extent to which higher capital-asset ratios raise the cost of funding for banks, there still may be an incentive to relocate activity under alternative corporate forms. While consolidation of branches and majority-owned subsidiaries currently helps limit this problem, a sharp rise in funding costs could induce the expanded use of minority-owned subsidiaries or affiliates in offshore markets. A key issue in this situation would be the nature of the guarantees that would be offered by the parent bank to depositors in the minority-owned subsidiary or affiliate. If a domestic institution extended guarantees to the activities of its foreign affiliates, for example, then this affiliate would have to be consolidated with its parent for supervisory and regulatory purposes. If a domestic institution has an interest in a foreign affiliate but was not obligated to stand by the affiliate, then its position in the affiliate could be treated for supervisory and regulatory purposes like any asset on its domestic balance sheet. However, monitoring the nature of the guarantees offered through affiliates may be no easy task. Moreover, if domestic institutions do provide guarantees to the activities of their minority-owned subsidiaries or affiliates, then consolidation may well have to be extended significantly beyond current practices.

A second potential issue in applying higher capital-asset ratios and enhanced supervision for banks is whether comparable treatment should be applied to other financial institutions such as securities houses. If the objective of these supervisory and regulatory policies is principally to limit any potential exploitation of lender of last resort assistance or public sector deposit insurance guarantees by those institutions benefiting from these services, then it has been argued that this requires consideration of the extent to which the benefits of the guarantees provided to one set of financial institutions (e.g. banks) also accrue to other sectors of the financial system. In particular, guarantees of public assistance to large banks in times of crisis could influence the activities of not only large banks (and their depositors) but also those of other institutions that are either dependent on banks as a source of funding or whose financial activities occur in markets where large banks are important participants (e.g., the money markets or clearing systems). If it was decided that enhanced supervision should be extended to other financial institutions, this could be difficult to achieve since there has been to date relatively little international coordination of supervisory policies relating to investment houses or other financial institutions (especially as it pertains to the monitoring of the consolidated positions of domestic securities houses and their foreign affiliates).

Finally, since the extent of lender of last resort assistance and public sector deposit insurance guarantees differs significantly across countries (e.g., the Federal Republic of Germany and Switzerland have private but not public sector deposit insurance), it is not clear that a common capital-asset ratio would provide the most appropriate constraint. Since significant differences between tax, legal, accounting, and disclosure requirements continue to affect the location of financial activity, the harmonization of capital-asset ratios would most likely be sustainable only if the other remaining structural differences between markets were also eliminated over time.

In considering future efforts at coordinating financial regulatory and supervisory policies, much of what is likely to occur depends on whether the current efforts at liberalizing domestic financial markets are sustained. For example, it could be difficult to reconcile further liberalization of international financial transactions if there should be a major expansion of protectionism in the major industrial countries. Moreover, a combination of protectionism and efforts to restrict external financial transactions would clearly be a "worst case" scenario, especially since it would be difficult to envision an effective set of capital controls that would not severely affect financial market efficiency. If recent financial liberalization measures are sustained or expanded, then the pressures for further coordination not only of prudential regulatory and supervisory policies but also of accounting, tax, and disclosure systems is likely to continue to grow. However, this will require solution of the analytical problem of deciding what common standards should prevail across still relatively diverse economic systems.

References

Aliber, R. (November 1984), International Banking: A Survey, *Journal of Money, Credit and Banking*, Vol. 16, Part 2.

Bank for International Settlements (1986), *Recent Innovations in International Banking*, Bank for International Settlements, Basle.

Benston, G., and G. Kaufman (August 1987), Risk and Solvency Regulation of Depository Institutions: Past Problems and Current Options, American Enterprise Institute, unpublished.

Black, F., M. Miller, and R. Posner (1978), An Approach to the Regulation of Bank Holding Companies, *Journal of Business*, Vol. 51, No. 3.

Bryant, R. (1987), *International Financial Intermediation*, The Brookings Institution, Washington.

Corrigan, E. (1986), Financial Market Structure: A Larger View, in: *Annual Report*, Federal Reserve Bank of New York.

Diamond, D., and P. Dybvig (1983), Bank Runs, Deposit Insurance, and Liquidity, *Journal of Political Economy*.

Fama, E. (1980), Banking in the Theory of Finance, *Journal of Monetary Economics*.

Fama, E. (1985), What's Different about Banks, *Journal of Monetary Economics*.

208

Flannery, M. (July 1987), Payments System Risk and Public Policy, American Enterprise Institute, unpublished.

George, A., and I. Giddy, eds. (1983), *International Finance Handbook*, Volumes 1 and 2, John Wiley and Sons, New York.

Germany, J., and J. Morton (October 1985), Financial Innovation and Deregulation in Foreign Industrial Countries, *Federal Reserve Bulletin*, No. 71.

Giddy, I. (1984), Domestic Regulation versus International Competition in Banking, *Kredit und Kapital*, Heft 8.

Golombe, C., and D. Holland (1986), *Federal Regulation of Banking, 1986-87*, Golombe Associates, Washington.

Guttentag, J., and R. Herring (1983), *Disaster Myopia in International Banking*, Essays in International Finance, No. 164, Princeton University Press, Princeton, New Jersey.

Guttentag, J., and R. Herring (September 1986), Emergency Liquidity Assistance for International Banks, unpublished working paper.

Guttentag, J., and R. Herring (1983), *The Lender of Last Resort Function in an International Context*, Essays in International Finance, No. 151, Princeton University Press, Princeton, New Jersey.

Haraf, W., and R. Kushmeider (September 1987), Redefining Financial Markets, American Enterprise Institute.

Johnson, G., and R. Adams (March 1983), *Aspects of the International Banking Safety Net*, Occasional Paper, No. 17, International Monetary Fund, Washington.

Kane, E. (May 1981), Accelerating Inflation, Technological Innovation, and the Decreasing Effectiveness of Banking Regulation, *Journal of Finance*, Vol. 36.

Kane, E. (May 1983), Policy Implications of Structural Changes in Financial Markets, *American Economic Review*, Vol. 73, No. 2.

Kane, E. (1987), How Market Forces Influence the Structure of Financial Regulations, American Enterprise Institute, unpublished.

Kareken, J. (1986), Federal Bank Regulatory Policy: A Description and Some Observations, *Journal of Business*, Vol. 59, No. 1.

Kareken, J., and N. Wallace (July 1978), Deposit Insurance and Bank Regulation, *Journal of Business*, vol. 51, No. 3.

Key, S., The Internationalization of U.S. Banking, in: R.C. Aspinwall and R.A. Eisenbeis (eds.), *Handbook for Banking Strategy*, John Wiley Interscience, New York.

Makin, J. (May 1987), The Third World Debt Crisis and the American Banking System, *The AEI Economist.*

Miller, M. (December 1986), Financial Innovation: The Last Twenty Years and the Next, *Journal of Financial and Quantitative Analysis*, Vol. 21, No. 4.

Pecchioli, R. (1983), *The Internationalization of Banking: The Policy Issues*, Organization for Economic Cooperation and Development, Paris.

Saunders, A. (June 1987), Bank Holding Companies: Structure, Performance, and Reform, American Enterprise Institute, unpublished.

Saunders, A., and L. White (eds.) (1986), *Technology and the Regulation of Financial Markets*, Lexington Books, Lexington, Massachusetts.

Silber, W. (May 1983), The Process of Financial Innovation, *American Economic Review*, Vol. 73, No. 2.

Spero, J. (1980), *The Failure of the Franklin National Bank: Challenge to the International Banking System*, Columbia University Press, New York.

Watson, M., R. Kincaid, C. Atkinson, E. Kalter, and D. Folkerts-Landau (December 1986), *International Capital Markets, Developments and Prospects*, International Monetary Fund, Washington.

Weston, R. (1980), *Domestic and Multinational Banking*, Croom Helm, London.

Williams, R., P. Heller, J. Lipinsky, and D. Mathieson (March 1983), *International Capital Markets, Developments and Prospects*, Occasional Paper, No. 23, International Monetary Fund, Washington.

Wilson, J., *Banking Policy and Structure* (1986), New York University Press, New York.

Wojnilower, A. (1980), The Central Role of Credit Crunches in Recent Financial History, *Brookings Papers on Economic Activity*, Vol. 2.

COMMENTS

Nikolaus K.A. Läufer

The paper discusses recent developments in financial markets and the implications of these developments for financial policy. Emphasis is placed on the internationalization of finance and its implication for national supervisory and regulatory policy as well as for the coordination of such policies.

The paper starts by describing the forces that created the changes in financial markets, and continues by describing the factors that determined the dynamics of these changes.

The paper then turns to its focal topic, the internationalization of financial markets and the regulatory and supervisory response. It concludes by describing some of the issues raised by the developments described.

The paper's approach is to treat the process of innovation and institutional change as a competitive response of market participants to a series of macroeconomic disturbances (inflationary policies, monetary shocks like the abandonment of the Bretton Woods system of fixed exchange rates, relative oil price shocks, external and fiscal deficits), to technological advances (changes in telecommunications and information processing) and to the arbitrage opportunities offered by differences in regulatory, supervisory and tax structural conditions across countries.

What I found missing in this list of causal factors are the developments in financial theory in, let's say the last 20 to 30 years which I would consider to be an important factor in the process of innovation. The tools of modern financial theory allow the systematic design of financial instruments to meet a demand arising for whatever reason. One may suppose that the reaction of market participants to macroeconomic disturbances is strongly shaped by the change in the opportunity set of financial arrangements that has come about by changes and innovations in

Studies in International Economics and Institutions
Vosgerau (Ed.) New Institutional Arrangements for the World Economy
© Springer-Verlag Berlin Heidelberg 1989

financial theory. The developments of financial theory have also changed the process of financial innovation. The invention and introduction of new financial instruments and institutions has changed from an uncontrollable creative process to a more systematic and target oriented design activity.

To my regret the present final version of the paper does not contain some interesting sections of the initial version. There, after a description of the various disturbances the pattern of reaction of various economic groups was analyzed. The most interesting part of that section dealt with the reaction of the regulatory agencies. To state it technically, regulatory constraints were endogenized. The response of regulatory authorities was described with a perhaps too implicit use of concepts of the theory of public choice, bureaucracy and the theory of joint maximization. Regulatory agencies were seen as watching the market shares of their regulatees and as adjusting their strategies, that is to say the regulatory structure of their industry, according to market share developments. In that perspective the self interest of bureaucrats in a competitive environment renders regulatory constraints as flexible and market dependent. The paper thus made the very important and general point that in order to understand market developments we should not only investigate the competitive structure on the demand and supply side of an industry but should also look at the competitive structure of the bureaucracies involved in regulating the industries. This point was well illustrated by the competition between bank regulation and securities regulation within the United States. Regulatory agencies were seen to operate within restrictions given by their enabling legislation. The bureaucrats of these agencies operate under the threat of being curtailed by the jurisdiction and by changes in the enabling legislation. However, the paper did not go as far as to endogenise the jurisdiction and the enabling legislation.

The point made in the initial version of the paper can also be formulated by means of concepts coming from the theory of production and the theory of international trade. Financial regulation can be seen as a product that serves as an input to the production of financial services. The quality of this input determines the comparative advantage of firms, industries and entire nations. This dependence is well known to the participants in the worldwide competitive game which are firms, bureaucrats and politicians. It is also taken into consideration on all levels of regulatory activity including the jurisdictional and legislative one.

Such a view may be fruitfully applied to recent events in the history of financial innovations, e.g. the attempts of the Federal Reserve to induce other governments to agree to controls of the Euromarkets. When these efforts failed the International Banking Facilities were created in the US. It is difficult to believe that the basic motives and interests of the American politicians and bureaucracies should have changed in this process over time.

The present version of the paper has been purged from contents of political economy. The author has decided to draw a picture of the phenomena and to eliminate his earlier attempts for a theory of their development. This bias for description as opposed to explanation becomes most conspicuous when the internationalization of financial markets during the past decade is described as a reflection of the broad trends of securitization of international finance and the liberalization of national financial markets.

The paper's merits are the description of broad trends with enough supporting factual details from the major industrial countries as to make the reading both informative and interesting without getting lost in the description of unimportant institutional details. It is a masterpiece of writing on recent financial history.

Economic Analysis of Debt-Equity Swaps

Günter Franke

The prospects to solve the financial problems of the heavily indebted less developed and developing countries are dim at present. With a few exceptions, these countries face substantial difficulties to pay the interest on their loans, not to speak about repayment of the principal. Apart from debt relief, economic growth of the indebted countries is viewed as the primary means of improving their financial status. Therefore debt-equity swaps (DES) have been greeted with enthusiasm in the financial press as a device to improve economic growth and, at the same time, to reduce the foreign currency-denominated debt of the troubled countries (see e.g. Economist, 1987, Schubert, 1987).

The typical mechanism of DES is as follows. Suppose that an investor wants to invest in an indebted country and that the proposed investment has been approved by the country's government. Then the investor can follow the conventional route and convert US-dollars into local currency (i.e. the currency of the indebted country) at the official exchange rate. The indebted country may add a subsidy to make the investment attractive for the investor. Alternatively, he can arrange a DES, i.e. he can buy outstanding dollar-denominated bonds (= $-loans) in New York, issued by the indebted country, at a price substantially below the face value. Then the central bank of the indebted country buys these loans from the investor for local currency such that the price equals the $-face value of the loan, multiplied by the official exchange rate. The central bank usually subtracts a discount from this amount, the size of which depends on the desirability of the investment from the viewpoint of the indebted country. The investor finally uses the local currency to finance the proposed investment. Usually the investor raises the equity capital of some local firm and the firm pays for the investment. Thus debt of the indebted country is converted into equity of a local firm. Alternatively, foreign currency-denominated debt of local firms may be converted into local currency-denominated equity. This explains the term "debt-equity swap".

Studies in International Economics and Institutions
Vosgerau (Ed.) New Institutional Arrangements for the World Economy
© Springer-Verlag Berlin Heidelberg 1989

A simple example illustrates a DES. Suppose Mexican $-loans sell in New York at 60 per cent of their face value. A multinational firm with a subsidiary in Mexico wants to expand its business there and thus the subsidiary needs more equity capital. Instead of simply buying Mexican pesos from the Mexican central bank at the official exchange rate, the multinational firm buys Mexican $-loans at a price of 60 per cent of their face value and sells these to the Mexican central bank. Thus it saves 40 per cent. If the Mexican central bank deducts 10 per cent, then the investor still saves 33 1/3 per cent, provided that the conventional purchase of pesos from the central bank is not subsidized.

This example illustrates what are considered to be the main advantages of the DES. First, it is argued that DES reduce the investment outlay and therefore increase direct investment in the indebted country. This stimulates economic growth and thereby improves the country's financial status. Second, it is argued that the foreign indebtedness of the country is diminished by DES so that the debt problems are reduced. Third, creditor banks can reduce their exposive to the risks of the indebted countries. Therefore DES are viewed as an ingenious tool to improve the financial situation of the indebted countries and of the creditor banks (Economist, 1987).

The purpose of this paper is to show that this favorable evaluation of DES is not well-founded. The main argument is as follows. DES can only be expected to improve the situation if they improve the situation as compared to conventional methods of financing investments. Such improvements can exist for three reasons:

(1) DES generate negative externalities. In other words, if DES allow investors and the indebted country, taken together, to gain something at the expense of others, of creditor banks e.g., then DES may prove valuable for the indebted country. In this paper it is argued, however, that DES do not allow the investor and the indebted country to reap appreciable gains from external effects imposed on others. The main reason is that in an efficient capital market the $-loans of the indebted country are priced such that their prices are not below the present value of the expected payments of interest and principal. Therefore DES do not allow investors and the indebted country, taken together, to gain something which they cannot gain by conventional financing of direct investments.

(2) The assumption underlying the preceding argument is that the capital market is efficient. This is questionable. It could be that the capital market and/or other institutional arrangements are inefficient and that DES remove part of these inefficiencies. Then DES would be beneficial even if they generate no externalities.

The problem with discussing inefficiencies is that we do not have a satisfactory theory of efficient arrangements. Hence the discussion of DES-effects on inefficiencies will be fragmentary. Given this caveat, we do not see any substantial improvements in efficiency, generated by DES, although minor improvements may exist.

(3) DES may, however, generate illusions about their nature. People may believe, for instance, that DES impose a burden on the country's creditors. In addition, accounting conventions, applied in setting up a country's budget, may favor DES as compared to conventional financing methods. Finally, DES may improve the indebted country's sovereignty. Thus politicians may prefer DES to conventional financing.

In summary, we do not see substantial improvements, generated by DES as compared to conventional methods of financing investments. Therefore the enthusiasm about DES does not appear to be well-founded. This scepticism is shared by Heller (1987).

The paper is organized as follows. Section 1 presents some facts about DES, section 2 describes the economic setting of the following analysis. Section 3 analyzes DES from the perspective of the investor, section 4 from the perspective of the indebted country. The results are summarized in section 5.

1.   Some Facts about Debt-Equity Swaps

First, some facts about DES will be summarized. In practice, many variants of DES exist. DES are quite complicated because the indebted country has to make sure that the DES are not abused to arrange profitable arbitrage. Suppose, for instance, one could buy Mexican $-loans at 60 per cent of their face value, convert them to pesos at the face value, multiplied by the official exchange rate, and then reconvert the pesos into dollars at the official exchange rate. This would yield a huge profit for the arbitrageur and reduce the dollar reserves of Mexico. Even if the investor purchases securities for the local currency, sells them after a few years and reconverts the money at the official rate, he might reap a substantial profit. Therefore the indebted country has to set up rules in order to prevent investors from these deals.

Mexico restricts DES to specified portfolio investments and direct investments such that disinvestment is not allowed before January 1998. In addition, DES have to be approved by the Mexican government. The government does not award the full face-value of the $-loan in Mexican pesos, but deducts up to 25 per cent, depending on the type of investment (UNCTAD, 1986, p. 144). Interestingly, the government converts the loans at the free rate, not the official rate. But it does it only if the free rate exceeds the official rate by less than 10 per cent (Euromoney, Sept. 1986).

Only rough estimates of the DES-volume are available. Through mid-1987, the Mexican volume is estimated at about .9 billion US-dollars, a small amount compared to the Mexican foreign debt of more than 100 billion dollars (see Morgan Guaranty 1987, Marton 1987, Fehr 1986). Perhaps the DES-volume would be greater if the Mexican bureaucracy acted faster and in a less restrictive manner. Moreover, Mexicans are not yet allowed to participate in DES. Thus, repatriation of flight capital is not yet supported by the official rules.

Brazil offered cash rewards to companies that convert debt into equity at face value, multiplied by the official rate. These rewards ranged from 5 to 10 per cent (UNCTAD 1986, p.144). To prevent speculation, dividends on the new equity were restricted to the level of the previously paid interest. The DES-volume for Brazil is estimated at 2.5 billion dollars. But Brazil has abandoned its DES-scheme in 1984. At present, DES are approved only exceptionally. The central bank claims that the foreign investments would have been the same without the scheme (Marton 1987).

In Chile DES-rules are less restrictive. Chile awards the full face value, multiplied by the official rate. The pesos can be used to pay domestic debts, purchase local assets or, in the case of foreigners or Chileans residing abroad, for direct investment (UNCTAD 1986, p.144). Foreign capital must remain in Chile for at least 10 years, profit remittances are not allowed in the first 4 years. Interestingly, Chile limits the monthly volume of DES and sells the rights for DES in an auction. The DES-volume through mid-1987 is estimated at about 1.9 billion US-dollars which is about 9 per cent of Chile's foreign debt (Morgan Guaranty 1987). A substantial part of this volume is attributed to the repatriation of flight capital. This may be explained by the generous treatment of flight capital, repatriated through DES. The Chilean government does not inquire after the sources of these funds and potential violations of the tax laws.

2.   The Economic Setting of the Analysis

The model economy for which DES will be analyzed will be specified now. In this economy there exists an official market for foreign currencies with fixed exchange rates. Foreign currency can be bought from or sold to the central bank at the official exchange rate. This rate is assumed to be the same for all transactions.

In order to simplify the exposition, besides the local currency of the indebted country only one foreign currency will be taken into consideration, say, for instance, the US-dollar. Moreover, without loss of generality, the fixed exchange rate is assumed to be 1. The exchange rate is defined as units of local currency per dollar.

Besides the official exchange market a black market exists. The black exchange rate is denoted b. For indebted countries which face a $-shortage, usually b F 1, i.e. the black rate is higher than or equal to the fixed rate. These countries usually buy unlimited amounts of dollars at the official rate, but sell only limited amounts. Suppose b > 1. Then everybody who wants to convert dollars into local currency, would prefer to do it in the black market. Everybody who wants to convert local currency into dollars would prefer to do it in the official market. In order to prevent arbitrage between both markets, the government has to restrict access to at least one market. It can, e.g., threaten the existence of the black market by high penalties for black trade, or it can force receivers of current account $-income to convert the dollars at the official rate, and it can restrict $-sales at the official rate to specific purposes. The separation of both markets is usually imperfect, however, there is always some leakage (Zedillo 1986).

DES represent a third market for buying local currency against dollars. This third market has various special features: (1) It is a one-way street since it is only possible to convert dollars into local currency, but not vice versa. (2) It can only be used with a special permission of the government which, apart from Chile, will be given only for specific purposes.

Let p denote the New York-dollar price for a $-loan of the indebted country, measured as a fraction of the face value of the loan. Hence a 1 000 $-face value-loan would sell at 1 000 p $ in New York. Let d denote the discount which the central bank subtracts when it buys the loan. This discount can be positive or negative. In the latter case, the central bank grants the investor a subsidy on DES. Hence, at an official rate of 1, the investor would get 1(1-d)·1 000 local currency units for a 1 000 dollar-face value-loan. Thus, the actual exchange rate in a DES, s, is

$$s = 1 \ (1-d)/p.$$

3. The Investor's Analysis

The investor looks for the cheapest way to finance his investment. The total investment expenses are determined by the net dollar amount required. This amount depends on the applicable exchange rate, on subsidies, on transaction costs and on potential arbitrage profits which can be derived from financing the investment. The following analysis will provide some insight into the investor's choice between the three exchange markets and into sustainable differences between the corresponding exchange rates.

Suppose that the transaction costs are the same in every exchange market. The transaction costs in the black market include potential penalties for black trade if this is prohibited. Can the official exchange rate be higher than the black rate and the DES-rate? If this were true, then every investor would buy local currency at the official rate unless the official exchange is associated with some disadvantages.

Such disadvantages exist, for instance, if all official exchanges are officially registered so that the investor cannot escape taxation of the future investment income or he cannot reconvert the money back into dollars. These disadvantages could motivate a premium of the official over the black rate. If exchange at the official rate was anonymous such that the government does not know the identity of the investor, then nobody would buy local currency at a rate below the official rate. Hence the black rate could not stay below the official rate.

As all DES are officially registered, the potential disadvantages of official conversion apply to DES, too. Hence the DES-rate s cannot be below the official rate if (1) the DES-market is active, (2) investors are allowed to change in the official market and (3) besides the difference in exchange rates no differences between both exchange markets exist.

The question then is whether the black rate exceeds the DES-rate. Governments usually prohibit black market conversions for financing direct investments. But this is not sufficient to render the DES-rate independent of the black rate.

Suppose $s > b > 1$. Then every local citizen who wants to invest in his country, would try to reap an arbitrage profit. Instead of investing local currency directly, he would buy $1/b$ dollars for one local currency unit at the black rate and then reconvert these dollars into local currency at the DES-rate s so that he can invest (s/b) local currency units. Thereby he reaps an arbitrage profit of $(s/b - 1) \cdot 100$ per cent. If local citizens have no access to DES, then they might have to arrange this transaction with the help of foreigners. This would create additional transaction costs, however. As long as the DES-volume is relatively small, the indebted country can tolerate this arbitrage between both markets and pay the arbitrage profit.

Now suppose $b > s > 1$, i.e. investors get most local currency for one dollar in the black market and the least in the official market. Then local citizens who want to invest their dollars in their country would change their dollars in the black market. Foreign investors usually get a permission for direct investments only if they prove that they change the invested money in a government-approved manner. Therefore $b > s$ would channel repatriated flight capital into the black market and foreign direct investment into the DES-market.

The question then is whether foreign investors, being barred from the black market, would be deterred from direct investments. If the black rate would emerge as the free rate in an unregulated exchange market, the foreign investors would regard the difference (b- s) as a government-imposed penalty on DES and adjust their investment decisions accordingly. It can be shown under fairly general conditions, however, that the free rate which would emerge after unifying the black and the official market, would lie between the black and the official rate (Lizondo 1987). Hence the black rate does not provide an unbiased estimate of the free rate. Thus foreign investors will not interpret (b - s) as a government-imposed penalty on DES. Therefore the government is free to choose a DES-rate below the black rate without necessarily deterring direct investments.

So far it has been assumed that conversion at the official exchange rate is not combined with any subsidies or penalties. As a result, no investor changes dollars at the official rate if s> 1. The preceding results remain the same if the government subsidizes conversion at the official rate, but only to an extent such that this deal is still more expensive for an investor than a DES.

4.   The Government's Analysis

The investor may regard the difference between the DES-rate s and the free rate f which would emerge in an unregulated exchange market, as a government subsidy (s > f) or penalty (s < f). If the government takes the same view on the difference (s - f), then the investor and the government together can benefit from DES as compared to a currency exchange at the rate f only if the DES provides advantages.

In a perfect international capital market such advantages do not exist. The Modigliani-Miller-Theorem holds. It makes no difference whether direct investments are financed by DES or by other financing methods. But the international capital market is far from perfect. Therefore we have to look for potential advantages of DES. These potential advantages can be split into three groups. The first group includes advantages which derive from external effects of DES forced upon third parties. The second group includes gains from reducing inefficiencies of the international capital market. The third group includes advantages which derive from the political process associated with DES.

Discussion of these potential advantages requires a standard of comparison. The standard of comparison for the evaluation of DES will be the conventional method of financing direct investments. This method entails conversion of dollars at the official rate plus, perhaps, a subsidy or penalty. The investor is indifferent between a DES and conventional financing if the latter implies conversion at the official rate 1 plus a subsidy of (s-1) local currency units per dollar.

4.1 External Effects of Debt-Equity Swaps

The investor and the indebted country together prefer DES if DES impose negative externalities on third parties. First, we will discuss external effects forced on the country's creditors, and second, external effects forced on others.

4.1.1 External Effects Forced On Creditors

Do the country's creditors suffer from DES as compared to conventional financing? As the creditors do not suffer from conventional financing, the question is whether the country and/or the investor gain from DES at the expense of the creditors. The DES implies conversion of long term-$-loans into long term-local currency-loans if the local money supply is to be held constant. Let us call this "loan currency substitution" (= LCS). If the central bank awards local currency in cash to the investor, then the money supply would increase thereby pushing inflation. In order to avoid this effect, the central bank either has to give the investor a long term-local currency-loan which is not regarded as a substitute for cash or it gives the investor cash and, at the same time, sells long term-local currency-loans in the open market, thereby withdrawing cash from other investors. Therefore the DES implies LCS if the money supply is held constant. Creditors of $-loans are replaced by creditors of local currency-loans.

As a DES affects the country's creditors only via LCS, DES can generate an externality, to be borne by the creditors, only if LCS does. Two types of externalities have to be distinguished. First, externalities which impair the creditors' wealth without benefiting the country and/or the investor. An example are costs of a creditor's financial distress, due to the country's debt servicing policy. These externalities, by definition, neither represent a gain to the country nor to the investor and, therefore, will be ignored. Second, externalities which benefit the country and/or the investor at the expense of the creditors. Such externalities, being created by LCS, can exist only if LCS reduces the market value of the country's total debt. *Hence the country or the investor cannot gain from a DES at the expense of the creditors if the market value of the country's total debt is not reduced by LCS.*

Does LCS reduce the market value of the country's total debt? For simplicity, let the DES-rate s be equal to the free rate f. From this and the definition of s follows $f = l(1-d)/p$ or $pf = l(1-d)$. Hence pf, the local currency-market value of the $-loan, converted at the free rate, equals $(1-d)$ local currency units. The government awards the investor $(1-d)$ local currency units in cash or in long term-local currency-loans with a market value of $(1-d)$ local currency units. Hence its local currency-denominated debt increases by $(1-d)$. At the same time, the local currency-market value of the country's foreign debt is reduced by pf. *Thus the market value of the country's total debt is not affected by LCS.*

The market value of the country's total debt is an ambiguous concept if the international capital market is imperfect. For many indebted countries a free exchange rate is unknown, local currency-loans are held only by local citizens. The LCS, associated with a DES, may reduce the welfare of the local creditors if, for instance, they are forced to buy the local currency-loans at unfavorable terms. But this does not generate an advantage for the indebted country as a whole, although it may redistribute wealth among local citizens. Hence the country and/or the investor, taken together, can gain from LCS only if the creditors of the $-loans lose. The essential question therefore is whether these creditors suffer a loss by selling their loans at the price p instead of the face value. Suppose, first, that the capital market in New York is informationally efficient and there exist no barriers to trading $-loans of indebted countries. Then the price p represents an unbiased present value of the expected payments on the loan. Expected payments include expected interest payments and repayments of principal, expected "fresh money" payments from the creditors to the country, being part of rescheduling agreements, have to be subtracted. If the indebted country and the creditors share homogeneous expectations, then the country expects to pay less than its contractual obligations. Hence the burden from these loans is smaller than the present value of the contractual obligations. The market price p is a measure of this burden. Thus a creditor does not suffer a loss if he sells his $-loan at the price p in an informationally efficient market.

A counterargument might be that the country faces costs of breaching the $-loan contract (default costs) and that, from the perspective of the country, these costs have to be added to p. Such costs are, for instance, additional transaction costs from international barter trade as compared to trade, financed by trade credit, if the banks react on a breach of contract by a reduction of trade credit. A DES could be valuable for the indebted country since the DES reduces the volume of $-loans and thus the expected default cost.

However, the DES involves LCS, therefore the costs of breaching the local currency-loan contract have to be considered as well. If the default costs are the same for both contracts, then the country does not gain from LCS. Default costs are irrelevant then. One might argue that the country can always repay its local currency-denominated debt by printing money. But then the default costs are replaced by the costs of additional inflation. It is not clear whether these costs are lower than those of breaching the $-loan contract.

So far it has been assumed that the price p is unbiased. This assumption may be incorrect. Primarily European and Japanese creditor banks sell these loans to other financial intermediaries or to investors who want to arrange a DES. US-banks which have a large portfolio of these loans but only low loan-loss reserves, are reluctant to sell loans at a price below the face value because they are afraid of being forced to write off their other loans. As a consequence, this accounting problem diminishes the loan supply so that the price p should be biased upwards. This hypothesis has been confirmed by the price drop which has been observed after some of the US-money center banks pushed up their loan-loss reserves. In addition, only specific loans are eligible for DES according to the rules of the indebted country so that the upward price bias may be reinforced.

Another bias may be generated by asymmetric information about the country's future debt servicing policy. The "market" might be overly pessimistic so that the price is downward biased.

In addition, moral hazard might bias the price downwards. The existence of DES might change the government's debt servicing policy in order to signal a lower loan quality which, in turn, reduces the loan price p. Similarly, the government may intervene in the $-loan market to reduce the price p. This may be easy since the loan market appears to be rather illiquid. The rationale behind such a policy is as follows: The lower the price p is, the higher is the DES-rate s, ceteris paribus. Alternatively, if a certain DES-rate s is needed to attract a certain volume of direct investments, then a lower price p permits the government to increase the discount d. Hence the government pays less local currency units per dollar. This explains why the very existence of DES creates an incentive for the government to reduce the loan price. Hence the existence of DES reduces optimal debt servicing. This produces an externality for the creditors.

The significance of this externality appears to be small, however. First, at present, the DES-volume as a fraction of a country's foreign debt may range between 1 to 10 per cent. Suppose the country changes its debt servicing policy such that the associated price drop enables it to reduce its local currency payments for DES by 20 per cent. Then multiplying 20 per cent by the fraction of 1 to 10 per cent yields savings of .2 to 2 per cent as a fraction of the country's foreign debt. This saving accrues once. Now consider the cost of a debt servicing policy change. Creditors may cut back trade credit lines, thereby imposing transaction costs of barter trade on the country. In extending loans, the creditors will require a larger spread over LIBOR which has to be paid annually. In addition, investors expect more restrictions on future profit remittances and require a higher DES-rate s. These costs may easily exceed the savings. Therefore it seems safe to conclude that the government's incentive for such a policy change is small.

The question then is why creditors push the indebted countries to set up DES-schemes. (1) A first answer would be that DES create additional demand for $-

loans so that the price p goes up. The price can rise above the expected present value of debt service payments if DES are so attractive for investors that they are ready to pay a premium for the $-loans. This premium enables the creditors to sell their loans for a higher price and reduces the pressure for write offs. But this answer is superficial. Demand for DES requires that DES-financing is cheaper for investors than conventional financing. If it is cheaper, then the country, its creditors or somebody else has to pay the difference. If the price p rises above the expected present value of debt service payments, then the creditors receive a *positive* externality. Hence they do not pay. If others do not pay, then the country itself has to pay.

This points to a strong reason for creditors to push for DES-schemes: They hope that the indebted countries grant more favorable terms (at their own expense) to investors on DES as compared to conventional financing and that they (the banks) can reap some of these benefits via a higher price p.

Some indebted countries appear to recognize this danger. They negotiate discounts on DES in order to extract investor rents. In a perhaps more effective manner, Chile sells the rights for DES in auctions so that investor rents from DES disappear to a large extent. The proceeds from the auction are earned by Chile, not by the investors nor by the creditors.

(2) DES increase liquidity in the secondary loan market by creating more demand. Thereby the efficiency of the market improves; the price volatility which still is substantial, is reduced presumably.

(3) DES tend to legitimate the secondary market discounts, since they are supported and utilized by some creditors. These discounts provide valuable information for future debt renegotiations.

Summarizing, in an efficient capital market DES do not generate externalities which benefit the indebted country at the expense of its creditors. Some reasons for inefficiencies have been mentioned so that a net pricing bias may exist. In addition, the market for $-loans is rather illiquid so that price volatility is substantial. But there is no evidence for a strong downward pricing bias which benefits the indebted country and/or the investor at the expense of the creditors.

4.1.2 External Effects Forced On Others

DES might create negative external effects at the expense of the creditors' domicile countries. This would be true, for instance, if DES provided opportunities for tax arbitrage which do not exist for conventional financing methods. In Germany, creditor banks can write off their loans so that their taxable income is reduced. Thus DES do not provide tax advantages. In the United States the creditors face a problem. If they raise their general loan-loss reserves, then this does not reduce their taxable income. If they write off a specific loan so that this becomes tax-relevant, then the debtors may interpret this as a partial debt relief. Hence tax-relevant write offs are undesirable. Selling a loan at a discount provides an immediate tax relief. Thus, a DES provides a tax advantage as compared to conventional financing.

But the Japanese banks have shown that such a tax advantage does not require a DES. They sold part of their loans to a newly founded firm, located at the Cayman Islands, at market prices and deducted the discount from their taxable income (Wirtschaftswoche 1987). Thus, it appears that taxation is not of major importance.

Another external effect could be that DES enable the highly indebted country to attract investments at the expense of slightly indebted countries and thereby derive benefits. A necessary condition for this effect to exist is that a DES as compared to conventional financing creates additional wealth for the highly indebted country and the investor, taken together. Then part of this wealth can be granted to the investor so that he shifts his investments from slightly indebted countries to the country with the DES-scheme. So far, no substantial arguments in favor of DES have been found. Thus investment shifts are unlikely.

Summarizing, this section shows that presumably DES do not generate substantial external effects for the indebted country and the investor at the expense of others. It may be, on the contrary, that creditors gain from DES at the expense of the indebted country.

4.2   Gains From Reducing Inefficiencies in the International Capital Market

Even if the indebted country and the investor do not benefit from externalities, they might benefit from DES if DES reduce inefficiencies in the international capital market as compared to conventional financing.

First, the creditors may prefer DES in order to reduce moral hazard of the indebted countries. With conventional financing, the country receives dollars but may use these for consumption rather than for debt servicing. With DES-financing, the dollars go directly to the creditors, thus eliminating consumption. The indebted countries may consider this, however, as a disadvantage.

Second, it is possible that the default cost is reduced by LCS so that DES are preferable. But, as has been argued before, available empirical evidence does not permit a definite conclusion.

Third, LCS might improve the international allocation of default risk. LCS means that the default risk is shifted from the $-loan creditors to the local currency-loan creditors. The latter are primarily local citizens. These citizens who own the local currency-loans, have to bear the default risk associated with these loans and the risk associated with their government's policy. These risks presumably reinforce each other. Hence an argument can be made that LCS impairs the allocation of risk.

Fourth, DES improve the liquidity of the secondary market (see section 4.1.1). Fifth, transaction costs of DES might be different from those of conventional financing. A DES involves the cost of purchasing the $-loan in New York and the costs of getting the approval of the government for the DES. Conventional conversion of dollars at the official rate and getting the approval of the government for the investment and the subsidy create transaction costs as well. If the government recognizes the equivalence of both arrangements, then the costs of getting the governmental approval should be about the same. If the political process is simplified by DES, then the transaction costs associated with DES may be smaller. On the other side, a DES requires the purchase of a $-loan in New York. This purchase is usually mediated by a marketmaker who commands a fee. It has narrowed down to about one per cent of the loan's face value (Marton 1987, Euromoney August 1986, p.73). Still this cost may be higher than that of conversion at the official rate. Thus a clear answer to the question which arrangement produces higher transaction costs, is not available.

Another transaction costs argument could be that the reduction of $-loans through DES simplifies the cumbersome and complicated rescheduling negotiations and thereby lowers the associated transaction costs. On the other side, issuing local currency-loans may not require negotiations so that a net transaction costs benefit exists.

A possible counterargument is that the indebted country could use the dollars, received from conventional financing, to repurchase $-loans at market prices and thereby simplify rescheduling negotiations, too. Although repurchase is discussed intensively, creditors banks are reluctant to do this at a large scale since (1) this endangers the principle of equal creditor treatment, (2) this might force the banks to grant a partial debt relief, and (3) this would motivate the debtor to use his available dollars for repurchases instead of serving the $-loans contracts. As a consequence, the value of the loans would be depressed even more. DES represent an indirect method of repurchase which avoids some of these problems.

Sixth, DES imply the existence of a third exchange market which augments the scope for profitable arbitrage between exchange markets as discussed before. This may be viewed as an inefficiency generated by DES.

Summarizing, DES may improve the efficiency of the international capital market as compared to conventional financing, but these improvements appear to be quite limited.

4.3   The Political Process and Debt-Equity Swaps

The government of the indebted country might prefer DES to substitute arrangements for political reasons. DES could improve the government's power vis-a-vis creditors and/or the country's citizens. These effects would not affect the country's wealth, but induce the government to prefer DES to substitute arrangements. The benefits accruing to the government could come from

a)   improvements in the government's ability to pay,
b)   improvements in the government's creditworthiness,
c)   improvements in the government's sovereignty,
d)   budget illusions.

Ad a): By LCS being part of the DES, $-claims are replaced by local currency-claims. As the country can always print local currency, it faces no liquidity problems servicing local currency loans. But it cannot print dollars, thus $-loans create a liquidity risk. Hence it appears that DES reduce the government's liquidity risk.

But this statement has to be taken with caution. Printing money represents an option of the government which may be exercised at the expense of the creditors. Exercising this option raises the inflation rate and thereby expropriates the holders of nominal claims. Creditors anticipate this, therefore they demand compensation for the expected inflation and the inflation risk. As a result, presumably the expected real interest rate is higher for local currency-loans than for $-loans. If the government refuses to pay a sufficiently high interest rate, then investors will move their funds out of the country and invest them abroad at more profitable terms.

The government can avoid the premium for inflation risk by issuing indexed local currency-loans such that interest and principal claims are always inflation-adjusted. Although indexed local currency-bonds are issued in various countries, foreign investors prefer $-bonds. The reason may be that (1) foreign investors face an exchange rate risk, (2) the government can cheat by manipulating the recorded inflation rate, and, (3) $-loans grant foreign investors some control by imposing a liquidity risk on the government. Thus the government's liquidity risk may be an important element of efficient contracting.

Ad b): The government's creditworthiness, i.e. its ability to obtain credit, cannot be assured by DES. A DES involves either LCS or printing money. It has been shown before that LCS does not alleviate the country's total debt burden. Printing money undermines creditworthiness. Thus there is no indication that DES improve the government's creditworthiness.

Ad c): The government's degree of sovereignty may increase through the use of LCS as printing local money for servicing local currency-loans is controlled by the government only whereas rescheduling $-loans requires the consent of the creditors. Another political argument in favor of DES could be that LCS as part of the DES amounts to an automatic partial debt relief since LCS is based on the $-loan's price instead of its face value. In other words, the argument is that LCS saves the government conflicts as compared to an agreement on debt relief, and thereby improves the government's sovereignty.

But this argument is misleading. First, there is an important difference between LCS and a debt relief. Banks today refuse a debt relief because the indebted countries try to get a relief for nothing. Thus the banks deny debt reliefs. A bank selling a $-bond at the price p does not grant a debt relief, it changes $-claims against $-cash. No gift is involved. Second, LCS implies for the indebted country the purchase of $-bonds against local currency-bonds. Again, no gift is involved. Therefore it is not surprising that the government need not spend much energy on LCS as compared to debt relief.

Ad d): Illusions associated with DES may explain part of their popularity. First consider the budget illusion. Suppose that, in the central bank's balance sheet, the country's $-loans are valued at face value, multiplied by the official rate. Hence a DES generates a profit to the central bank which equals the discount d, multiplied by the face value and the offical rate. Thus DES look favorable for the indebted country.

Alternatively, suppose the foreign investor converts dollars at the official rate 1 and gets a subsidy of (s-1) local currency units per dollar. This subsidy shows up in the current government's budget as an expense if the subsidy takes the form of a cash subsidy or it shows up in future budgets if the investor is granted future tax reliefs. In any case, the government has to declare a subsidy to the foreign investor which will be opposed by local competitors and by the International Monetary Fund which advocates a free market economy.

Although the foreign investor is indifferent between the DES and the substitute arrangement, the government's budget shows a profit for DES while it shows a loss for the substitute arrangement. Hence the DES appears to be much more favorable for the indebted country. If it is not recognized that this budget effect is generated only by specific accounting rules, then a budget illusion in favor of DES exists.

The budget illusion may be closely associated with the illusion that in a DES the creditors loose money, that the creditors' loss accrues as a gain to the investor and that this gain enables the government not to subsidize the investment. Hence the political opposition to DES can be expected to be weaker than that to substitute arrangements. Therefore governments which want to attract foreign investments may well prefer DES.

The politicians' preference for DES is evidenced by the following observation. Suppose the equity capital of a subsidiary, located in an indebted country, has been eroded . Then many indebted countries agree on a DES to raise the equity capital, but they refuse an equivalent conversion of dollars at the official rate, combined with subsidies.

Summarizing, the DES reduces the governments' liquidity risk, improves its sovereignty and facilitates political decisions in favor of foreign investments. Thus DES may well appear favorable to the governments of indebted countries as compared to substitute arrangements.

5.   Summary and Conclusion

The preceding analysis has shown that the effects of DES are similar to those of dollar conversion at the official rate, combined with a subsidy of (s-1) per dollar. DES do not permit investors and indebted countries to reap appreciable gains from forcing negative external effects on other parties. Hence they cannot expropriate creditors or others by DES. DES may improve the efficiency of the international capital market to some extent, but these improvements appear to be quite limited. The political aspects appear to be more important. The loan currency substitution which is part of the DES, reduces the indebted country's liquidity risk and increases its sovereignty. Illusions, associated with DES, may reduce political opposition to attracting foreign investments. Thus the governments of indebted countries may prefer DES. Apart from these political aspects, DES do not appear to increase the opportunity set of indebted countries and investors substantially. Thus the enthusiasm with which DES have been greeted is not well-founded. There is no evidence that direct investments in indebted countries will substantially grow and thereby improve the economic prospects of these countries.

Sometimes it is argued that DES will induce repatriation of flight capital. This argument is not well-founded, either. With respect to direct investments, it makes no difference whether the dollars are funded with flight capital or other foreign capital. The same is true of officially approved portfolio investments. The situation is different for portfolio investments, financed by secretly repatriated flight capital. Then DES are impossible, the owner of flight capital has to convert the money in the black market. Hence there is no reason to expect DES to foster repatriation of flight capital unless, as in the case of Chile, DES are associated with preferential treatment.

The conclusion to be drawn from the preceding analysis is that, depending on the circumstances, DES may provide some advantages as compared to conventional financing. But it is hard to identify substantial advantages which support expectations that DES will significantly alleviate the international debt problem.

References

The Economist (1987), A Lesson from Chile, March, pp. 87-90.

Euromoney (1986), The Debt Swappers, August, pp. 67-75.

Euromoney (1986), Mexico's Capital Idea, September, pp. 167-173.

Fehr, B. (1986), Debt-Equity-Swaps: Wie sich Schulden in Kapital verwandeln, *Frankfurter Allgemeine Zeitung*, December 17 1986, no. 292, p.13.

Heller, H.R. (1987), The Debt Crisis and the Future of International Bank Lending, *American Economic Review*, vol. 77, pp. 171-175.

Lizondo, J.S. (1987), Unification of Dual Exchange Markets. *Journal of International Economics*, vol. 22, February, pp. 57-77.

Marton, A. (1987), The Debate over Debt-for-Equity Swaps, *Institutional Investor*, February, pp. 115-117.

Morgan Guaranty Trust Company (1987), Debt-Equity Swaps, *World Financial Markets*, June-July, pp. 12-14.

Schubert, M. (1987), Trading Debt for Equity, *The Banker*, February, pp. 18-20, 31.

UNCTAD (1986), Trade Development Report 1986. United Nations, New York.

Wirtschaftswoche (1987), Lasten neu verteilt. No. 24, June 5 1987, pp. 148-154.

Zedillo, E.(1986), Capital Flight. Some Observations on the Mexican Case, Discussion Paper, Bank of Mexico.

COMMENTS

Silvio Borner

The paper before us is a showpiece of modern economic analysis: it starts with a real-world problem, applies simple but sound economic analysis to it and draws clear-cut conclusions. In other words, G. Franke's paper is highly relevant, analytically sharp and logically stringent. So why not stop here? G.F. places the debt-equity swaps into a framework of efficient financial markets. He shows that the debt-equity swap (DES) is a special case of a multiple exchange rate system and leads to a "loan currency" substitution (LCS). By assuming efficient international capital markets it is not surprising that a "twist" like a debt-equity swap does not really matter much - or at all. This result immediately calls to our minds the Modigliani/Miller Theorem.

But such a result as well as the route of reaching it should also arouse our critical instincts and maybe even some suspicions grounded in common sense rather than in traditional economic theory. In other words, does G.F. place the international debt problem into the appropriate framework? I have some doubts. Let me explain them shortly.

(1)   If international financial markets are efficient or at least near-efficient, why then could this excessive lending come into existence? Did not political incentives play a central role then (build-up of debts) and now (solving the debt crisis)? Certainly, the weight of the political aspects has greatly increased within the last years. In other words, the main problems may well be political. But if efficiency in the relevant international financial markets is not the basis of the analysis, then the model in G.F.'s paper is in great trouble. The argument hinges strongly on the parameter p, the market value of outstanding debt interpreted as the (correct) present value of all future interest/amortization payments. Once we drop the assumption of efficiency

Studies in International Economics and Institutions
Vosgerau (Ed.) New Institutional Arrangements for the World Economy
© Springer-Verlag Berlin Heidelberg 1989

in the capital markets, this centre-piece of G.F.'s analysis is in danger of collapsing. In other words, the average degree of inefficiency in financial markets at the present stage may well dwarf any marginal changes induced by DES.

(2) What Sachs calls the "debt overhang" produces real economic adjustment costs far in excess of those expected by economists measuring the debt burden simply as the discounted flow of resources that the debtor country must provide to its creditors. But over and above this transfer burden there is an enormous dead-weight-loss resulting from the way that the current debt overhang discourages investment in the debtor countries and exports in the industrial countries. In other words, the main externalities could very well lie in the real sector and not within the confines of financial markets. The foremost priority belongs to a once-and-for all reduction of the debt burden in order to stop the indirect effects on investment and growth.

(3) The real costs of adjustment in the debtor countries depend heavily on the quality of the economic policies pursued and realized. Even though efficiency in financing cannot be improved on by "gimmicks" or "tricks", the efficiency of adjustment policies could very well improve. How? Debt-equity swaps might be used as a vehicle to attract FDI, to improve the credibility of the legal framework, reduce the degree of regulation, to develop local capital markets, to induce repatriation of flight capital and last but not least to privatize state owned corporations. G.F. does raise these points but discards them lightly: because they are not important - or because they do not fit into his analytical framework? In my view, the positive externalities on the real sector of the economy as well as on the political process in the debtor country far outweigh the distributive types of externalities dominating in G.F.'s paper.

In my view, there is a lot to gain by institutional innovation for investors as well as the local economy without imposing any negative externalities on creditors and/or other countries.

(4)   A fourth controversial issue of a general nature is the concept of LCS and its rather narrow interpretation, namely that the debtor country can only gain from LCS induced by DES at the expense of creditors (by reducing the market value of a country's total debt). Now even assuming that this total value does remain constant, DES has many other consequences which, in my view, are economically (and not only in an accounting sense) highly relevant.

(i)   DES entails not only a currency substitution but also a change of the creditor. Substituting MNCs or local firms for international banks changes the structure of the debt and may well improve the quality of the debt (substitution of budget deficit/balance of payments deficit financing through banks by project financing of industrial entrepreneurs).

(ii)   A switch of the creditor is also advantageous with regard to the separation of old and new debt. This is very important as the old creditors will always try to target new credits on the market value of the existing stock of old debts. G.F. raises this point in the context of DES but overlooks the advantage of rendering bygones really bygones. Inflows of capital by completely new creditors such as MNCs or even local firms could be exclusively interested in the future returns on investment financed with their money. If a debtor country can jump on a higher growth path, then the debt problem is greatly diminished. Growth dynamics looms much larger than static efficiency of financial markets.

(iii) National sovereignty, international liquidity and a swap of creditors will also change the risk allocation between debtor and creditor nations as well as the default costs. History shows that a diversification of creditors reduces default costs for both debtors and creditors. It is hard to believe that all these long-term aspects of the debt structure are correctly reflected in the parameter p. As I see it, the observed p's in secondary markets represent rather the write-offs of the banks based on the default risks under present conditions. There is, in my opinion, an ex ante/ex post problem. The market value p of existing debt is mainly determined by the probability of default.

As long as a country does not default, its obligations are represented by the face value. If it defaults, p jumps to zero. In other words, if a country really is willing and able to pay, it must stick to the face value. Furthermore, the face value is the number appearing in the statistics, e.g. for debt/export ratios. And these do have real consequences both with respect to interest rates and to credit availability. Therefore, the market value p may be less than "true", but at the same time the face value may be more than an illusion. If one could disregard the face value, the international debt problem would be automatically contained. The more critical the situation gets, the more the market value goes down. But at what p begins bankruptcy?

Competitive Performance, Regulation and Trade in Banking Services

Anthony Saunders and Ingo Walter

I.   Introduction

A dominant feature of the global financial services industry today is intensified competition facing banks and other financial institutions. Among the important environmental forces driving this change are continued exchange-rate and interest-rate volatility, persistent financial disintermediation and securitization, progressive financial deregulation and market interpenetration, and rapid technological evolution in financial processes and products. It is an environment that is increasingly forcing a radical reassessment in strategic positioning on the part of firms in the industry, and an equally radical reassessment of public policies toward the financial services industry.

There has been considerable academic and practitioner interest regarding the regulation of banking and financial services. In part, this interest is linked to the ongoing GATT negotiations regarding the regulation of international trade in services *per se*.

Recent research by Walter (1985), (1987) and Grubel (1986), among others, has focused on whether trade in financial services is somehow different from trade in real goods. In particular, Grubel has argued that, to produce banking services abroad, one needs to transport inputs such as intermediate goods, capital and labor freely across international borders. In his view, the question of regulation or "specialness" of trade in banking services is moot, since the production function of goods contains a similar vector of inputs as the production function of bank services (although obviously in different proportions). Consequently, the question of free trade (or barriers to trade) in services is really one of free trade in the necessary inputs of service is really one of capital investment, computers, etc. Walter (1987) agrees with Grubel only in part, and identifies a range of financial

Studies in International Economics and Institutions
Vosgerau (Ed.) New Institutional Arrangements for the World Economy
© Springer-Verlag Berlin Heidelberg 1989

services that can indeed be supplied to clients in other countries without significant factor transfers.

Both views lead, as a natural progression, to analyzing international trade in bank services within a traditional international trade-theory framework such as Heckscher-Ohlin (Sagari, 1986). That is, financial services are just another output on the production possibility frontier constrained by the available supplies of inputs and marginal rates of technical substitution, and related factors.

However, from a social welfare perspective some services may have considerably different social (as opposed to private) values that are unlikely to be picked up in traditional models of trade theory (see Corrigan (1982, 1987) and Volcker (1983, 1986)). For example, a reduction in the production of some services may have significant social welfare costs and externalities extending far beyond the direct markets in which such services are traded. One such service in particular may be the provision by banks of transaction accounts which, in most developed countries, are the primary means of monetary exchange and settlement.

If one believes that major disruptions to the banking system and thus the supply of transaction accounts can have a powerful (externality) effect on the production of other goods and services in the economy, then a case can be made for treating banking transaction services as "special" and different, in a social welfare sense, than other goods and services. This question of bank transaction account specialness has generated considerable interest among academics interested in banking theory. Some academics go even further, arguing that loan services (such as monitoring, renewals, and commitments) provided by the banking system are also "special" in a social welfare sense, and thus are uniquely different from other financial services such as underwriting and casualty and life insurance services provided by securities firms and insurance companies.

Nevertheless, if specialness (however significant) can only be protected by rigid and anti-competitive barriers both among clients (or customers), arenas (or market areas) and products then the social benefits of protection may well be offset by the social costs relating to losses in efficiency and innovation.

The probability that restrictive policies will lead to *net* welfare losses seems all the more likely given the fact that the bank specialness argument tends to confuse the costs of individual bank failure (quite frequent) with the costs of systemic failure (rare). In particular, the potential "loss", in a social welfare sense, from an individual bank failure is likely to be small since customers simply switch transaction accounts and loan accounts to other banks - thereby preserving the existing level of transaction al loan services flows. At worst, asset prices - in terms of risk premiums on deposits and loans - will adjust upwards. Offsetting any losses from an *individual* bank failure would be the gains from reallocating scarce resources from the inefficient bank to the rest of the economy.

In the case of a multiple-bank or systemic banking panic, the potential social welfare loss is indeed large, however. As Schwartz (1987) and others have noted, the Central bank through the instruments of monetary policy (the discount window and open market operations) can always avoid major contractions in the supply of bank services by expanding the quality of high powered money. Such an expansionary policy was patently missing during the 1929-33 banking panic in the U.S.

If it is accepted that destruction of bank services (specialness) can be avoided (even in a worst case scenario of contagious runs) through appropriate use of monetary policy instruments, then there appears to be no valid specialness rationale for continuing regulations at the micro level that prevent interpenetration of each other's products and markets among banks, commercial firms and other financial institutions (such as investment banks and insurance companies).

In the remainder of the paper, we evaluate the trend toward an international financial services industry, and the level of barriers remaining to a system of full global competition among participating players by utilizing a taxonomy for analyzing the international market in banking and financial services suggested in Walter (1987).

II. A Taxonomy of Banking Markets

There are three core dimensions that define the international market for banking and financial services (Walter, 1987):

1. Client   (C-dimension)
2. Arena   (A-dimension)
3. Product   (P-dimension)

Figure 1 depicts these dimensions in the form of a matrix comprised of C x A x P cells. Each cell has a distinctive internal competitive structure, based on fundamental economic as well as public-policy related considerations. Technological change and deregulation have had an important influence in terms of (a) accessibility of geographic arenas, (b) accessibility of individual client groups by players originating in different sectors of the financial services business, and (c) substitutability among financial products in meeting personal, corporate or government financial needs.

Client

The following categorization of the major client groups in the C-dimension of the C-A-P grid may be appropriate: (a) Sovereign: Sovereign states and their instrumentalities. (b) Corporate: Non-financial corporations regardless of industry classification, ranging from MNCs and parastatals to middle-market and small, privately owned companies. (c) Correspondent: Other financial institutions in the same industry subcategory (e.g. correspondent banks). (d) Private: High net worth and high net income individuals. (e) Retail: Other individual clients, generally in significant volume.

These client groups can be broken down into narrower segments, each differing with respect to product-related attributes such as currency and timing requirements, liquidity and maturity needs, risk levels, industry categories, overall service-level requirements, and price sensitivity. Effective market definition and segmentation in the financial services industry involves identifying coherent client groups that embody relative uniformity with respect to each of these variables.

Figure 1:

International Financial Services Activity (C-A-P Matrix)

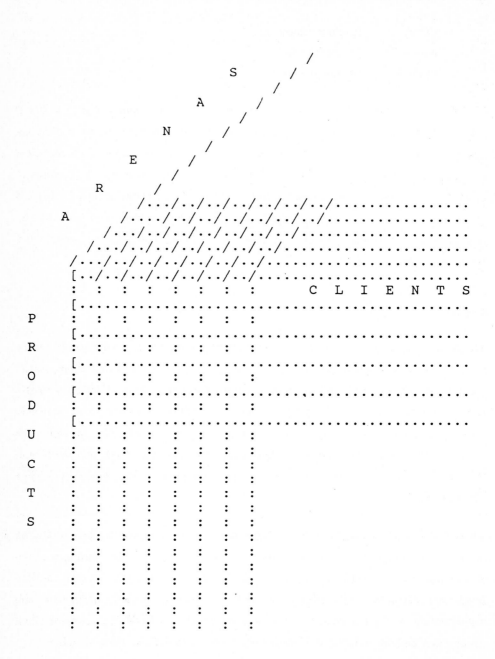

Arena

The international market for financial services can be divided into various onshore and offshore arenas with respect to geographic location. Each arena is characterized by different risk/return profiles, levels of financial efficiency, regulatory conditions, client needs, and other variables. The Arena dimension of the matrix in Figure 1 can be taken into the analysis at the global, regional, national, sub-regional and location-specific levels, although the national level is unique due to the significance of regulatory and monetary policies.

Geographic interpenetration of financial institutions with respect to various domestic and offshore arenas has become very significant indeed. For example, in 1950 only 7 American banks had activities abroad, with 95 branches. By 1970 there were 79 banks with 536 branches, and by 1984 there were about 150 banks with over 1000 branches that booked assets in excess of $337 billion. This actually understates the degree of internationalization by U.S. banks, since forms of involvement other than branches are not captured in the data. Nor do the data capture the growing involvement abroad by U.S. investment banks, brokerage houses and other types of financial services firms.

According to a study by Morgan Guaranty (1986) foreign banks had 577 branches, agencies and subsidiaries in the United States in 1986, booking $411 billion in deposits (13% of the U.S. total) and $110 billion in business loans (22% of the total U.S. market and 50% of the New York City market).

The reasons for the rapid growth in the activities of financial institutions in various onshore and offshore arenas lie primarily in the nature of the services provided. It is often imperative for a financial institution to be physically close to the client in order to do business effectively. While a certain amount of a business can certainly be done through correspondent relationships and travel, the increasingly complex nature of financial services and client needs has enhanced the importance of reliable 'direct connect' relationships involving the ability to establish a viable commercial presence in the host country.

Product

Financial services offered in the global market have expanded dramatically. With a clear requirement for product differentiation in the marketplace, firms in the industry have created new instruments and techniques tailored to the needs of their clients. Financial institutions produce five more or less distinct "primary" products that are sold to clients. All financial services that appear in the market, including the most complex innovations, can be broken down into one or more of these "primary" categories.

1. *Credit products*: Although credit products have become a less significant source of returns for many international financial institutions, they remain the core of much of the business. Credit activities range from straightforward term lending to sophisticated and specialized forms such as project finance.

2. *Financial engineering products*: These comprise the design and delivery of technology-intensive financial services specifically structured to satisfying often complex client objectives at minimum cost. In a world where borrowers, issuers, savers and investors often have distinctive and complex objectives, financial engineering is perhaps the ultimate form of product differentiation, and accounts for a great deal of the value-added creation observed in domestic and international capital markets. Financial technologies can be either "disembodied" or "embodied". Purely disembodied financial technology normally takes the form of advisory services that institutions undertake for clients, often based in part on client-specific information. Embodied financial technology combines this with one or more financial transactions sold to the client as part of a package.

3. *Risk management products*: Risk bearing has long been recognized as one of the key functions of financial institutions, and one of the reasons they tend to be heavily regulated. The main forms of exposure include credit risk, interest-rate risk, liquidity risk, foreign exchange risk, country risk, project risk, commodity risk, and technical risk in areas such as cash transmission. Risk management activities can be broken down into (a) those in which financial institutions themselves assume all or part of the exposure, and (b) those in which the institutions provide technology needed to achieve a shifting of risk or themselves take on

exposure only on a contingent basis - i.e., an off-balance sheet commitment to buy or sell, borrow or lend. Effective risk-reduction through diversification clearly depends on the independence of the various risks represented in a firm's portfolio of exposures. Financial institutions provide risk management services that range from simple standby credit lines and forward interest rate agreements (FRAs) to explicit, tightly-defined products addressed to a broad range of contingencies.

4. *Market access products*: Financial institutions can provide value-added services to clients by using their internal networks to transfer information, funds or securities from one client or arena to others. Accomplishing this requires both tangible and an intangible networks covering various clients and arenas, including state-of-the art internal operations and systems capabilities.

5. *Arbitrage and positioning*: This involves activities that financial institutions engage in for their own account, which facilitate and in many cases make possible the supply of the first four types of financial services to clients internationally.

Arbitrage opportunities occur when the same asset is priced differently in different markets (or market segments), often because of information asymmetries. "Pure" arbitrage takes place when an asset is simultaneously bought and sold. By this definition, financial institutions rarely engage in pure arbitrage. Rather, they engage in positioning - buying an asset in a particular market, holding it for a time (however short), and subsequently reselling it in the same or different market. The institution is thus exposed to "differential risk", due to the possibility that the underlying price differential may evaporate or be reversed during the time needed to complete the transaction. Exposure to differential risk depends jointly on the time necessary to complete the transaction and the underlying volatility in the price of the specific asset and the markets in which it is traded.

Positioning has become an integral part of managing international financial institutions during a time of significant exchange-rate and interest-rate volatility, and in turn drives securities, options and futures trading and dealing.

This classification of international financial services into five generic categories can be broken down still further into some 50 more or less distinct financial services that are made available to individual client segments in various market arenas (Walter, 1987).

Cell Structure and Linkages

The market cells in Figure 1 each exhibit different characteristics in terms of competitive structure. Variations may occur because of differences in the number of vendors, the presence or absence of anticompetitive behavior among them, the availability of substitutes for the services provided, monopoly power on the part of suppliers of inputs, potential competition from new entrants, and the like. These conditions, together with the cost of accessing a particular cell, define the expected excess returns that can be derived from each. At the same time, there are economies of scale to be derived from selling individual financial services to multiple clients or in multiple arenas, and economies of scope to be derived from selling multiple products to the same clients. These scope- and scale-driven linkages through the C-A-P matrix help explain the drive towards globalization of the banking and financial services industry.

Regulatory Barriers to Competition and Protectionism

The U.S. Treasury (1979), the OECD (1983) and Walter (1985, 1987) have undertaken extensive surveys of restrictions imposed on foreign-based banks and other firms in the financial services industry. There are basically two types of barriers to market-penetration in this industry, entry barriers and operating barriers.

Entry barriers range form complete embargos (including visa denial to foreign bankers) and limiting foreign presence to representative offices only (with no banking powers), to restrictions on the forms that foreign presence can take and limits on foreign equity positions in local financial institutions. In terms of Figure 1, a firm that is blocked out of a particular national market faces a restricted lateral opportunity set that excludes the relevant tranche of C-cells and P-cells. To the extent that entry barriers are the outcome of protectionist lobbying, they will create excess returns in some or all of the cells in that tranche. Windows of opportunity, created by countries relaxing entry barriers, tend to be taken advantage of by institutions envisioning potentially high returns in some of the previously inaccessible cells.

Having gained access to a particular national market, foreign-based financial institutions generally become fully subject to domestic monetary-policy, supervisory and regulatory controls. At this point there are three possibilities: (a) Domestic regulations fall less heavily on foreign players than on their domestic competitors; (b) The nominal incidence of regulation is identical for both; or (c) Foreign players are subjected to more restrictive regulation than their local competitors. The latter involves the explicit use of operating barriers to restrict competitive positioning of foreign-based institutions. These include restrictions on expatriate employment, number and location of offices, client-groups that may be served, types of business that may be handled (including trust business, lead-management in securities underwriting, and retail deposit-taking), permissible sources of funding, and tolerance of anti-competitive behavior on the part of local institutions. In such cases, foreign-based firms have achieved access to the relevant arena-tranche of the C-A-P matrix, but are constrained either in terms of the depth of service they can supply to a particular client-segment (Type-A barriers) or in terms of the set of clients they are permitted to serve (Type-B barriers).

III. Summary and Conclusion

We have argued in this paper that it is difficult to justify the micro-regulation of market arena, client and product competition among firms engaged in the financial services market internationally, unless one can put forward a strong case that a subset of these firms, namely banks, provide a special or unique set of services that would be harmed by such competition.

In the first section of the paper it was argued that the relative social welfare uniqueness of bank services tends to be exaggerated, partly due to a failure to distinguish clearly among the costs of an individual as opposed to systemic bank failures. Given that even systemic bank failure can be avoided by appropriate Central bank monetary policies, and therefore the social "costs" of such events largely mitigated, the case for restrictive micro-regulation of international financial services appears to be weakened and the case for free trade in international financial services considerably strengthened.

A short review of the existing barriers to international financial services competition revealed a pervasive and heterogeneous array of restrictions that inhibits potential competitive benefits in terms of efficiency and innovation.

It is our belief that pursuing policies to increase the level of free trade in financial services will in no way detract from the volume of transactions and loan services produced either domestically or internationally. That is, any (residual) specialness provided by banking firms is not necessarily adversely impacted by the absence of micro (as opposed to macro) regulation.

References

Aliber, Robert Z. (1984), International Banking: A Survey, *Journal of Money, Credit and Banking* (November).

Bailey, Elizabeth E. and Ann F. Friedlander (1982), Market Structure and Multi-product Industries, *Journal of Economic Literature* (September).

Bank for International Settlements (1986), *Recent Innovations in International Banking*, Bank for International Settlements, Basel.

Corrigan, E.G. (1982), Are Banks Special?, *Federal Reserve Bank of Minneapolis Annual Report*.

Corrigan, E.G. (1987), Financial Market Structure: A Larger View, *Federal Reserve Bank of New York* (January).

Crane, Dwight B. and Samuel L. Hayes, III. (1982), The New Competition in World Banking, *Harvard Business Review* (July-August).

Gray, H. Peter and Jean M. Gray (1982), The Multinational Bank: A Financial MNC?, *Journal of Banking and Finance* (March).

Grubel, Herbert G. (1977), A Theory of Multinational Banking, *Banca Nazionale del Lavoro Quarterly Review* (December).

Hayes, Samuel III, A.M. Spence and D.V.P. Marks (1983), *Competition in the Investment Banking Industry*, Harvard University Press, Cambridge, Mass.

Kaufman, G.G. (1987), The Truth About Bank Runs, paper presented at the CATO Conference on the Financial Services Revolution: Policy Directions for the Future.

Morgan Guaranty Trust Company (1986), America's Banking Market Goes International, *Morgan Economic Quarterly* (June).

Neu, C.R. (1986), International Trade in Banking Services, paper presented at a NBER/CEPS Conference on European-U.S. Trade Relations, Brussels (June), mimeo.

Office of Technology Assessment, U.S. Congress (1986), *International Competition in Banking and Financial Services*, OTA, Washington, D.C. (July), mimeographed.

Organization for Economic Cooperation and Development (1983), *Trade in Services in Banking*, OECD, Paris.

Panzar, John C. and Robert D. Willig (1981), Economies of Scope, *American Economic Review* (May).

Pastre, Olivier (1981a), *Multinationals: Banking and Firm Relationships*, JAI Press, Greenwich, Ct.

Pastre, Olivier (1981b), International Bank-Industry Relations: An Empirical Assessment, *Journal of Banking and Finance* (March).

Pecchioli, R.M. (1983), *Internationalization of Banking*, OECD, Paris.

Porter, Michael E. (1980), *Competitive Strategy*, Free Press, New York.

Sagari, Sylvia B. (1986), *The Financial Services Industry: An International Perspective*, Doctoral dissertation completed at the Graduate School of Business Administration, New York University.

Schwartz, A.J. (1987), Financial Stability and the Federal Reserve Safety Net, paper prepared for the AEI Project on Financial Services Regulation (February).

U.S. Department of the Treasury (1979), *Report to the Congress on Foreign Government Treatment of U.S. Banking Organizations*, Department of the Treasury, Washington, D.C. Updated in 1984.

U.S. Office of the Controller of the Currency (1982), *Foreign Acquisitions of U.S. Banks*, U.S. Government Printing Office, Washington, D.C.

Volcker, P.A. (1983), *Statement Before the Committee on Banking, Housing and Urban Affairs*, United States Senate (September 13).

Volcker, P.A. (1986), *Statement Before the Subcommittee on Commerce and Monetary Affairs of the Committee on Government Operations*, United States House of Representatives, (June 11).

Walter, Ingo (ed.), (1985), *Deregulating Wall Street*, John Wiley & Sons, New York.

Walter, Ingo (1987), *Barriers to Trade in Banking and Financial Services*, Trade Policy Research Centre, London.

Walter, Ingo and H. Peter Gray (1983), Protectionism in International Banking, *Journal of Banking and Finance* (December).

Yannopoulos, George N. (1983), The Growth of Transnational Banking in Mark Casson (ed.), *The Growth of International Business*, George Allen & Unwin, London.

COMMENTS

Bernd Genser

As a representative of the public economics branch, although called "Finanzwissenschaft" in the traditional German terminology, I cannot exhibit any major competence in topics dealing with financial markets or bank services especially. The paper of Saunders and Walter shows that it is becoming increasingly difficult to describe the manifold and more and more specialized services of financial institutions and their nonfinancial competitors, much less to criticize and to judge them.

Nevertheless there seems to be one major point in the paper which I want to concentrate on: the explicit, although in some statements weakened position that at least some bank services are special, in particular "transaction accounts", which E. Corrigan refers to, or "bank loans", as Eugene Fama has pointed out. This specialness is due to external benefits, associated with the production of those services. Thus they will be undersupplied in private markets, as the market equilibrium does only recognize private utility connected with those services and ignores additional social utility gains.

The first part of the Saunders/Walter paper deals with the structure of existing, non-perfect international markets for financial services. As a matter of fact, market failures are generated by these imperfections (rents to certain banks by entry barriers and operating constraints to potential competitors) which cause welfare losses like similar constraints in national or international commodity markets.

The second part tackles the specialness of bank services as the source of liquidity for the economy, following the lines of Corrigan who points out banks as transmission belts for monetary policy. Within this view the externality problem is dealt with again stressing the provision of "transaction accounts" as a special bank service as compared to other goods and services by banks and nonbanks.

Studies in International Economics and Institutions
Vosgerau (Ed.) New Institutional Arrangements for the World Economy
© Springer-Verlag Berlin Heidelberg 1989

Saunders and Walter, as I understand them, share the view of Corrigan and accept that these bank services cause positive externalities by providing a social good "confidence in the economy" as long as the banking sector works or by avoiding bank runs and economic crashes. Another positive externality, the improvement of the quality of monetary policy in an economy with a well-developed banking sector, is not considered important by the authors.

Summing up these arguments about the specialness of bank services I'd like to offer three conclusions which make me hesitate to accept the authors' recommendation in favour of deregulation.

(1) If bank services are special and generate externalities an unregulated market will bring about efficiency losses, which should be avoided by suitable policy measures. Measures might be Pigou-subsidies, making use of the price mechanism, as well as compulsory regulations which mitigate Pareto-inefficiencies.

(2) If the policy maker is faced with existing regulations, which are known to generate welfare losses, but being forced to accept them, he may still look for an optimal second best policy to reduce welfare costs of irremovable distortions. As we have learned from second best theory, policy measures in this case will be recommended not only in the distorted market, but will also comprise markets of complements and substitutes which are affected indirectly because of interdependence relations.

(3) If the welfare-oriented policy maker is free to abolish existing regulations in financial markets then he might nevertheless ask whether there don't exist superior policy measures to solve the externality problem which prevents unregulated markets from arriving at the welfare optimum. Again, suitable cost-benefit analyses should help to discriminate among competing policy measures.

Thus deregulation and liberalization of bank services will be an efficient policy only if these services do not generate externalities and do not conflict with merit wants. But then these services are not special but simple, purely private goods which can be allocated efficiently by perfect markets. Deregulation of international financial markets will be an efficient policy device if specialness of bank services can be denied.

If, on the other hand, a certain element of specialness is prevailing, deregulation might also prove beneficial, as long as welfare losses caused by government failure are reduced. But in this case the deregulation device will always be dominated by any Pareto improving regulatory measure.

References

Corrigan, E.G. (1982), Are Banks Special? Federal Reserve Bank of Minneapolis Annual Report.

Fama, Eugene (1985), What's Different About Banks? *Journal of Monetary Economics*, pp. 29-39.

III. Protectionism and the Uruguay GATT Round

Does The World Need a GATT for Services?

Herbert G. Grubel[1]

There appears to be very little controversy now among economists about the proposition that institutions do matter to the performance of market economies and the international economy generally. Unresolved is how much they do matter and what kind of institutions matter most. I congratulate the Konstanz conference organizers for providing a forum for the discussion of these issues. They deserve much more attention than they are getting from the vast establishment of North American researchers that is preoccupied with the formalization of economic knowledge.

In this study I address the question of a possible GATT for Services at two distinctly different levels of analysis. In the first I draw on knowledge about the nature of services and conclude that all internationally traded services cross borders after embodiment in people or material substances. As a result, trade in services is freed by perfectly traditional policy approaches, the removal of all obstacles to trade in goods and the freedom to establish business abroad.

The second section of the study sets out the standard argument that international institutions and laws permit the internalization of externalities and are therefore in the interest of the world as a whole. It then confronts this proposition with two arguments raising doubts about its validity. Thus I discuss the public choice theory which suggests that such institutions are inevitably made to serve special interest groups. I then turn to an argument made forcefully by Rodney Grey which suggests that the codification of certain rules of international behaviour about dumping and subsidies has resulted in the design of national legislation that is more illiberal than is the legislation it replaced.

The criticism of existing institutions is used as a background for the evaluation of two innovative proposals for policies designed to protect the public from the

---

[1]   Useful comments on the first draft were made by Tom Borcherding, Rodney Grey, Helmut Hesse and the participants at the symposium.

Studies in International Economics and Institutions
Vosgerau (Ed.) New Institutional Arrangements for the World Economy
© Springer-Verlag Berlin Heidelberg 1989

scourge of special interest legislation. The first proposal is that legislatures are required to accompany the discussion of all protective measures by statements of impact on consumers and producers. The second draws on the Buchanan-Tullock ideas on public choice and suggests the need for international agreement binding all legislatures to the use of two-thirds majority voting on all laws interfering with free trade.

I.   There is no Direct Trade in Services

In a recent paper I have presented an analysis which may be summarized as follows.[2] Fundamental to an understanding of trade in services is an adequate characterization of the activity. Thus, it is assumed that the delivery of all services requires a physical proximity between the producer of the service and the person or good being transformed by the service.[3] For this reason services produced by agents of Country A can be sold to consumers in Country B only through the following, exhaustive set of mechanisms.

People from B Move to A to *CONSUME* Services: tourists, students, medical patients, consumers of personal services and film-producers from Country B move to Country A to absorb services which require close physical contact with the producer. The services thus traded across borders involve all of the consumer and producer services that are associated with the activities of these individuals. Typically these services consist of food, housing, transportation and recreational services, as well as education, health care and film-studio services, to name just a few.

People and Firms from A Move to B to *PRODUCE* Services: lawyers, accountants, general workers, soldiers and other people with a wide range of skills who are citizens of Country A move temporarily to Country B to provide their specialized

---

[2]   See Grubel (forthcoming). A similar analysis is presented by Bhagwati (1984), Sampson and Snape (1985), Stern and Hoekman (1987) and Lee and Naya (1987).

[3]   See the influential paper by Peter Hill (1977).

services. National income accountants in most countries have made operational the central point of the temporary nature of the stay by considering it to result in service imports only if the person stays less than 6 months. Longer stays are considered to give rise to additions to domestic product and income. It is also worth noting that in principle the local consumption by the foreign producers of services gives rise to exports, some of which are services, during the initial 6-month stay.

Firms from Country A established in Country B provide the general services of financial capital but may also be the conduit of patent and technical services. The latter may be billed explicitly or they may be implicit in the reported rate of return on invested capital.[4] These types of factor services have nothing to do with the services produced by foreign firms. They exist also in the case of foreign manufacturing firms.[5]

Goods Move Across Borders Temporarily to *ABSORB* Services: ships and planes from Country B move to Country A to be repaired. This kind of service trade has been important historically for countries at the world's transportation cross-roads like Singapore and Malta. Entrepot trade consisting of minor processing of agricultural products and their commercial storage and distribution also gives to service trade in this category. The development of export processing zones for the assembly of electronic goods and textiles in recent years has resulted in the export of services by the countries hosting the zones.[6]

---

[4] This argument draws on the modern theory of direct foreign investment and especially the theory of internalization. It has recently been made by Rugman (1986) and Markusen (1986).

[5] Some of the widely cited statistics on trade in services have been compiled using a definition of US service exports which includes the gross output of US internationals abroad, such as McDonald, Avis and Hilton. This approach leads to a large overestimate of genuine trade since almost all of the value of services produced and sold by such service industries is made up of value-added produced by locally owned factors of production. See United States International Trade Commission.

[6] For a discussion of the economics of such zones see Grubel (1983).

<u>Goods Move Across Borders Temporarily to *PRODUCE* Services:</u> examples of trade in services in this category are transportation and oil-drilling equipment operated by or leased from agents in A providing these services in Country B.

<u>Services are Embodied in Material Substances:</u> the purchase of business, engineering, architectural, economic consulting, musical, film and a wide range of services by residents of Country A can be achieved only by the movement of people as noted above, or the transmission across borders of material substances in which these services are embodied.[7] These materials are paper and electronic and optical storage devices such as tapes, discs and films. They are also material substances like electronic signals carrying voice and data messages.[8]

Material substances which balance of payments accountants consider to be service trade are no different in principle from substances which they count as goods. In today's world all goods have embodied in them value-added provided by domestic service industries. US automobile producers have been reported as spending as much on medical services as on steel. The value-added due to manufacturing of a sophisticated computer chip typically is a very small fraction of its price. On the other hand, the value-added due to service inputs of material substances counted as a service export may be a small fraction of their final prices. This may be the case

---

[7] Bhagwati refers to trade in "splintered services" and Hoekman and Snape to "separated services". The basic idea of these analysts is that recording devices and books, for example, involve the splintering or separation of the service from its original production. This is clearly a valid description of the process. However, this approach misses the point that such service embodiment must always result in the production of a material substance which is the object of international exchange. The emphasis on the embodied service in value-added represents a powerful analytical simplification noted below.

[8] In many discussions about the nature of services, the communications industry is considered to be totally different in some fundamental way from the rest of the service sector. For example see Hill (1987). The taxonomy proposed here overcomes this dichotomy. The assumed equivalence of electronic and more traditional means for the transmission of information permits us to see that the communications industry in a fundamental sense is engaged in the same activity as are the publishers of books, newspapers and magazines, the producers and distributors of cultural capital on films and tapes and the writers of technical reports.

in the export of recordings of a concert, especially if the records are promoted and retailed abroad.[9]

It follows from the above that the division of international trade into categories of goods and services is an unnecessary anachronism, except when the latter is associated with the temporary movement of people and goods. The division is not only analytically confusing, it also has led unnecessarily to demands for the special treatment of services in negotiations for the liberalization of international trade when the same objective is attained by free trade in goods.

Policy Implications

If I am correct in the preceding analysis it is possible to conclude that there is no need for the establishment of a GATT for Services. Free trade in all goods assures automatically free trade in most of what conventionally are called service trade transactions. The remaining types of service trade which involve the temporary movement of people and goods concerns basically the right to establish and operate a business in a foreign country which is often referred to as the "right to establishment".

---

[9]   This is not to deny that many service exports have a very high ratio of value-added by services over value-added by the manufacture of physical substance. This is clearly true in the case of the communications industry or in the sale of a valuable patent right on a legal document. However, this does not conflict with the proposition that it is possible to calculate from input-output tables for all industries the direct and indirect service input requirements per dollar of final sale. The central proposition of my model is that such an index of embodied services does not provide a useful guide for the distinction between traded goods and services.

It needs also be noted that not all material substances crossing borders can be measured with equal ease. However, there are plenty of technical means for monitoring electronic signals, if the reports of international intelligence gathering capabilities are to be believed. There are also substantial difficulties associated with the ability of customs agents to assess the value of documents and electronic storage devices containing technical, scientific and cultural material. However, such international shipments usually are accompanied by invoices which may misrepresent value no more or less than do invoices for goods. At any rate, difficulties in the quantification of trade hardly appear to be a valid basis for the classification of international trade into goods and services.

As an economist I am convinced that world welfare would benefit from the attainment of free trade as well as unrestricted rights to establishment. The attainment of these goals has been and should remain the objective of multilateral negotiations among the nation states of the world. In my view, the establishment of a separate negotiation framework for trade in services would not raise the probability that these goals can be attained. Such an approach would only confuse issues and divert attention away from the central and traditional problems of free trade in all goods and the right to establishment.

II.   Agencies are Captured

One of the most important developments in economic science in the post-war years has been the application of models of individual welfare maximization behaviour to the explanation of the activities of politicians, bureaucrats and government agencies by James Buchanan, Gordon Tullock, George Stigler and others.[10] As a result of the work of these economists there is now great skepticism about the traditional proposition that collective organizations and policies produce increases in general welfare.

Instead, expectations are that public policies and organizations are captured by interest groups and that they are used to advance the fortunes of the politicians and bureaucrats responsible for their operation. Politicians and bureaucrats gain personal benefits in the form of re-election, power, income and status by the initiation of policies which provide concentrated benefits for grateful interest groups. The costs of these policies are diffuse and so small that the bearers of the cost have few incentives to oppose them. The traditional public interest is lost in the process.

---

[10]   The work of these economists has reached such prominence, especially after the award of Nobel prizes to Stigler and Buchanan, that it is not necessary any more to cite their works. However, it is necessary to cite here Bruno Frey (1984), who has applied the public choice models to an explanation of international economic organizations in much the same way in which I am in this study.

It should come as no surprise that international agencies like the GATT have behaved in ways that are consistent with these public choice models. My task of giving evidence on this matter has been made easy by the work of Rodney C. de Grey, who has been the leader of Canada's delegation to the Tokyo Round of Trade Negotiations 1975-79. In at least two articles (1985) (1986) he analyzed how the GATT has been turned into an instrument of illiberalism.

Welfare Maximizing GATT

Before a presentation of Grey's analysis, it is useful to review briefly the arguments in favour of collective institutions such as GATT. As is well known, GATT was created in the postwar years in an intellectual and political climate that was formed after experience with the maximum exercise of nationalism during the Great Depression. In the light of this experience politicians throughout the world had accepted the idea that restraints on nationalistic policies were in the interest of their countries and coincidentally also of the world as a whole.

Most important, they had also recognized that global trade liberalization was possible only if all countries removed the details of trade policy making from the influences of domestic interest group politics. It was for this reason that, in acts of almost unprecedented statesmanship, politicians in the United States and other countries granted to the President and similar governmental executive offices authority to seek international agreement on trade liberalization in the general public interest. These offices were sufficiently far removed from the normal political business of legislatures that they could not be influenced by special interest groups affected by trade policy changes. The politicians in the legislatures, at the same time, were able to keep the interest groups at bay by claiming that they had lost authority over the matter.

The initial success of GATT rounds of trade liberalization is almost without doubt, especially the early rounds in the 1950s. It is interesting to note that the success of these negotiations owed much to the general spirit of good will and the genuine desire of responsible politicians to avoid the pitfalls of nationalistic policies which they had experienced personally. Many of the GATT articles were legally imperfect and had to be fixed up in later rounds. Most governments interpreted operational ambiguities in the light of the basic spirit of the time. GATT rules were a living body of judgements that were interpreted by governments in ways which permitted them to keep special interest groups at bay.

Revival of Nationalism

Since the initial successes of GATT and the liberalization of world trade, the memories of the 1930s have faded. New generations of politicians have entered and become the majority in national legislatures. The last of the US leaders from the earlier period lost their positions of power as the heads of congressional committees in the 1970s. Similar changes have taken place in other countries. Increasingly, the selfish politicians and bureaucrats of the public choice models have taken over in national politics as well as international economic policy-making. In addition, the communications revolution and falling costs of travel have permitted special interest groups to form more cheaply and press more effectively their views with politicians. Precisely as the models predict, while pretending to serve the general national and world interest,[11] the politicians have embraced interest group politics and economic nationalism.

Interest Groups and International Economic Policies

There is no need for me to analyze here the many protectionist measures adopted by the US government since the 1970s and the many new ones being debated in

---

[11] I always find it amusing to read the rationale for protection provided by the US Congress. It appears to have no compunction about claiming that policies are in the interest of the world even if they are nothing more than attempts to impose on other nations US national standards of economic management through subsidies and regulation, as in agriculture and tax treatment of corporations.

Congress during the Reagan administration.[12] There are the voluntary export restraints, orderly marketing arrangements and industry-to-industry understandings that have been applied to wide ranges of industries, the best-known of which are automobiles, textiles and steel. There are anti-dumping, trigger price mechanisms and countervailing duties on steel and lumber. Countries other than the United States have similarly expanded their protectionist activities. The important point about all of these protectionist policies is that they have resulted from the politicization of the trade policy making process even though the rules of GATT were respected.[13] How was this possible?

Changes in GATT Rules

Between 1947 and the Kennedy Round of trade negotiations in 1963 the emphasis of GATT discussions and agreements was on the reduction of tariffs and their uniform, non-discriminatory application to all members of the organization. However, since the Kennedy Round the signatory parties and especially the largest and most powerful trading nations of the world have succeeded in getting two important changes in the operation of the system.

First, there were changes in articles of agreement and in the interpretation of existing articles which permitted the development of what Grey calls the "managed trade system". The most outstanding manifestations of this management are the regional free trade associations such as the European Economic Community, the European Free Trade Agreement and the Central American Free Trade Agreement. These organizations are in clear violation of the original principle of non-preferential tariffs. The management also resulted in the Multi-fibre Arrangement and a proliferation of bilateral, so-called "voluntary export quotas". Furthermore, there

---

12   Some of the new protectionist measures under discussion are exchange rate equalization tariffs and mandatory product-by-product retaliation. See Gramm and Kemp (1987) for a discussion of these and some new positive steps to stem the protectionist side.

13   Tom Borcherding has pointed out to me that the US Constitution has similarly been interpreted differently during different periods of history and in the process has been unofficially amended.

are all kinds of special laws concerning trade in agricultural products and trade with specific developing countries such as the Lome convention and the General System of Preferences.

Second, the Tokyo Round especially has resulted in the specification of conditions under which certain national protective measures can be applied legally. Examples of such so-called contingency measures are anti-dumping duties, countervailing duties, procurement regulations and safeguard actions. They have always been on the books of most countries on the grounds that some methods for escape from international obligations under national emergencies were needed. In practice, they have become complicated, highly effective, discretionary and discriminatory instruments of protection. Their codification by GATT has greatly expanded politicians' opportunities to court the favours of special interest groups by imposing restrictive trade measures.[14]

GATT - an Extension of National Interest Group Politics

Public choice theory can explain these changes in GATT rules. They represent the expression of political interest group activities at two levels.

First, within democratic countries politicians and bureaucrats are forever searching for opportunities to generate benefits for interest groups that lead to personal gains at the lowest possible costs in terms of resistance by injured interest groups. Workers and producers in industries who are provided protection from foreign competition meet the requirements of the politicians and bureaucrats almost ideally.

---

[14] "One result of negotiations designed to regulate the use of contingency measures...can be the increase in the overall capacity of governments to restrict trade....The nature of (contingency) intervention requires a large bureaucratic establishment....Even for the most highly developed modern state, it is difficult to work this apparatus responsibly and effectively." [Grey (1985), p.26.] In the traditional model of the public sector, this difficulty of working the system is an obvious disadvantage. In the light of the new theory of public choice it is exactly the characteristic desired by politicians and bureaucrats. They can make it work very effectively to serve their purpose which, however, is not typically coincident with the "responsible" public interest.

Benefits are highly concentrated, costs are diffuse and can be minimized by easy nationalistic rhetoric. It was obviously possible for the beneficiaries of the changes in GATT to get them adopted as goals in the various rounds of negotiation. There have also undoubtedly been elements of opportunism in the national legalistic interpretation of GATT codes.

Second, the nation states that make up GATT membership are themselves divided into groups that act to maximize the welfare of their own constituencies at the expense of world welfare. The most important of these groupings consists of the industrial and developing countries. Many analysts, including Grey, have presented evidence that GATT rules have favored industrial nations at the expense of developing countries, as for example in the case of rules which have permitted the Multi-fibre Agreement and the formation of the EEC.

It has always been a puzzle to economists how the restriction of access to low cost textiles and other products from the developing countries by the industrial countries can possibly be to the advantage of the latter in any sense. In the light of public choice theory, this puzzle is no more. Such restrictive trade policies serve the interest of the politicians in the industrial countries. The costs imposed on their own public and on the rest of the world are diffuse and the bearers of the cost have no instruments of retaliation.[15]

The Problem of Overall Balance

The preceding analysis of GATT's history raises an important problem of benefits and costs through time. There is little doubt that initially it was an efficient

---

[15] The demands for a New International Economic Order by UNCTAD in the 1970s was a feeble attempt to create such an instrument by a fundamental change in institutions. While such an attempt is consistent with public choice theory, it is also clear that those benefiting from the existing system can be expected to resist its reform. Moreover, the proposed alternative suffered from technical inconsistencies which in all likelihood would have resulted in large inefficiencies and lower global growth rates so that gains from income redistribution to developing countries in the longer run could easily have been less than the losses due to slower overall growth. See Grubel (1977).

instrument for reaching agreement on global and non-discriminatory trade liberalization, though the size of these benefits is not known. There also appears to be some consensus on the idea that GATT has been captured by interest groups and used for imposing on the international community costs, the magnitude of which is only now becoming apparent.

It follows, therefore, that the merit of GATT depends on the magnitude of the initial benefits minus the size of later costs, all properly discounted. If the costs will last for a long time, it is highly likely that they will outweigh initial benefits. Grey's judgement is that the institution has already resulted in more costs than benefits. Not all observers share this view and I have often been asked whether it is realistic to argue that today's world trading relationships would be more liberal if there never had been a GATT. Complicating this issue is the question what would have been the alternative arrangements for a trade regime sponsored by GATT. It is conceivable that there would have been bilateral, regional and multinational trade liberalization efforts, each with its own finite life and without lengthy codes and a permanent bureaucracy to be reinterpreted and captured by interest groups. In addition, more narrowly conceived arrangements for liberalization might have gone further and been more permanent, as for example those of the European Economic Community, than the broad, global efforts under GATT.

Given the fact that regulatory agencies are rarely returned to their initial purpose, once they have been captured by special interest groups, it is likely that Grey's assessment of the merit of GATT is correct, if not for the present, then certainly in the future.

The Same Fate for a Service GATT

If the preceding analysis is correct and national interest groups are able to use international organizations for their own benefits, it follows that the creation of a new GATT for Service Transactions in the longer run will not result in higher welfare for individual nation states or for the world as a whole. Instead, we may expect that the institution is likely to develop into an instrument of illiberalism, permitting national politicians greater freedom in the cynical use of national protective measures without literal violation of international agreements and the abuse of the institution's enforcement mechanisms for the achievement of selfish policy objectives.[16] For these reasons the world would be better off without a new GATT for Services.

III. Using Public Choice Theory

Public choice theory implies that government intervention in the domestic and international economies can be reduced only by two measures. First, the silent minority, which is the victim of legislation favouring special interest groups, must be mobilized to generate costs for the politicians and bureaucrats. A necessary condition for such a mobilization is that the victims know the size of the costs which have been imposed upon them and the undesirable income distribution and other effects which the policies have on the beneficiaries in the longer run.

It is not clear how effective the generation and distribution of such intelligence is. George Stigler (1987) is the great cynic on this matter. Milton Friedman believes that such intelligence has only a marginal influence on current politics but often is instrumental at certain times when the cumulative effects of past policies result in a crisis in policy, as they did in macro-economics in the 1970s and local government spending in California during the same decade. At such times appropriate

---

[16] This judgement is shared by Snape (1987a) page 31 in his assessment of the outcome of the next GATT round: "...it is likely that the Uruguay Round will lead to codes of behaviour and similar arrangements that major participants may insist are interpreted on a conditional most favoured nation, discriminatory basis." In another paper (1987b) he considers the likelihood that this will occur in the context of services.

economic intelligence can provide the rationale for some fundamental changes in policies.[17]

I tend to accept Friedman's judgement, even if only to sustain me during the many lonely and difficult hours I spend trying to produce such intelligence. The view certainly has persuaded Phil Gramm and Jack Kemp in the design of the "American Trade, Growth and Employment Promotion Act of 1987", which they introduced recently in the US Congress. One provision of the Act is the requirement that all trade legislation in the future must be accompanied by estimates of its costs -"or even benefits",[18] much like the requirement that now has to be met whenever Congress passes tax legislation.

Qualified Majority Voting

Second, special interest group legislation can be curbed by the use of qualified majority voting provisions. For example, the passage of legislation imposing trade restrictions may be made to require a two-thirds or 75 per cent majority. According to public choice theory, it is highly likely that such a rule would permit interest groups injured by trade restrictions to block effectively the passage of most such legislation.

---

[17]   The entire issue in the end is one of benefits in relation to costs. Milton Friedman has argued that the work of economists designed to demonstrate and measure the benefits of free trade and the costs of protection throughout history may have resulted in average global trade restrictions being only a few per cent lower than they would have been otherwise. Yet, he claims, given the low cost of producing this knowledge, the present value of the welfare gains from this lower protection is probably much higher than the present value of these costs.

Efficiency requires, of course, that all instruments for the restraint of interest group policies be used to the point where marginal costs equal marginal benefits. Friedman's judgement not withstanding the basic, unresolved question is whether the world has reached such a point in the production of economic intelligence. In interpreting evidence on this matter, we should all remember that the producers of economic intelligence are not beyond the temptation of acting like an interest group on this matter.

[18]   This phrase is verbatim from their Wall Street Journal article.

This proposal is not without difficulties. There is really no reliable evidence on how such a system would work. It is conceivable that new political coalitions and systems can overcome some of all of the restraining effects. After all, the market for votes continues to exist. Provisions are needed to permit smaller majorities to remove already existing restrictive legislation. An alternative method for dealing with this problem would be a predetermined review process of existing legislation, with its automatic expiry except when passed under the new rules.

Of course, it would not be in the interest of politicians to limit their business by the adoption of such qualified majority voting rules, unless a major crisis created the right climate, as it did in the wake of the Great Depression and the accompanying trade wars. Alternatively, pre-conditions for such a step might be created by an intellectual revolution and the opportunity for politicians to enter history books on the coat-tails of some great ideal.

Fortunately, intellectuals cannot do much, if anything, about the creation of a crisis. I am also quite sceptical that we can raise the achievement of free trade to the status of a powerful ideal around which politicians might want to rally. Nevertheless, there is some small probability attached to the chance that a significant group of politicians in a large number of countries can be made to rally behind the following operational proposal.

GATT Negotiations over Common Rules

Let there be a new GATT Agreement under which the governments of all member countries commit themselves to the adoption of legislative rules which require that passage of international trade legislation and the application of contingency rules require a two thirds majority vote. Furthermore, get the governments to commit themselves to requiring impact statements to accompany the introduction of all new legislation affecting international trade.

It requires only little thought to generate lists of difficulties that stand in the way of the adoption of such a strategy for a new round of GATT initiatives. I will resist the temptation to even get started here on such a list. However, I am convinced that such an exercise will not lead to objections that are fatal to the merit of the basic proposal, except those that have been made on the grounds of political feasibility and some others made against the basic public choice model. These objections should not deter us from thinking through the proposal made. Political objections are there to be overcome by ideas, as Buchanan and others keep reminding us. Only time will tell whether the public choice model has been a flash in a pan or a fundamental revolution in our understanding of and approach to international economic policy making.[19]

IV. Summary and Conclusions

The answer to the question raised in the title to this paper is a resounding "no". The world does not need a new international organization devoted to negotiating free international trade in services. The same objectives which such an organization would pursue can be achieved by using the institutional framework of the existing GATT in the attainment of free trade in all goods. The free movement of financial knowledge and human capital would assure that all forms of trade in services is unrestricted.

The answer is also "no" on the more fundamental grounds that international organizations such as GATT can and have been turned into instruments of illiberalism through mechanisms explained by public choice theory. It is possible to interpret recent changes in GATT regulations in the light of this theory. It is highly likely that the benefits of free trade negotiations initially have been and almost certainly

---

[19] Someone with whom I discussed my idea noted that at his university there is a rule that has to be accepted by anyone who proposes yet another application of qualified majority voting. The proposer has to stand on a scaffold with a noose around his neck and in front of an assembly of citizens. If the citizens vote, by simple majority, to reject the new proposal, the trap door is opened. This system has not yet reached my university and I am glad that I was not subjected to it during the conference at which the first draft of this study was presented. I also hope that it does not become universal because I see much intrinsic merit in the adoption of better rules to change the reward structure for democratic legislators. But I also accept the point implied by the story. Qualified majority voting is not a panacea.

will in the future result in more protection than might have been attained by alternative methods of liberalization. The analysis makes a convincing case for the proposition that a new GATT for Services is likely also to be perverted to serve the interest of politicians rather than the welfare of the world.

Public choice theory has led to the conclusion that fundamental changes in the rules governing democratic legislatures are needed to curb the power of politicians, bureaucrats and interest groups. An application of these ideas to the international scene suggests the need for a collective international agreement which binds all national legislatures to the use of qualified majority voting on legislation affecting international economic relations. It also implies the use of economic impact statements in conjunction with all trade legislation.

The call for a new GATT on the basis of such a principle has an extremely small chance of being heard and an even smaller chance of becoming the basis for policy. But the present value of the resource costs required in getting it formulated and publicized certainly is much less than the present value of the benefits from its adoption, even with the low probability of this event. At any rate, my personal interest makes me believe in the validity of this empirical judgement. I hope that other intellectuals have the same interests.

References

Bhagwati, Jagdish N. (1984), "Splintering and Disembodiment of Services and Developing Nations", *The World Economy* (June).

Frey, Bruno S. (1984), *International Political Economics*, Basil Blackwell, Oxford.

Grey, Rodney C. de (1985), "Negotiating about Trade and Investment in Services", in Stern, Robert M. (ed.), *Trade and Investment in Services: Canada/US Perspectives*, Ontario Economic Council, Toronto.

Grey, Rodney C. de (1986), "The Decay of the Trade Relations System", in Snape, Richard H., (ed.), *Issues in World Trade Policy: GATT at the Crossroads*, MacMillan, London.

Gramm, Phil and Jack Kemp (1987), "A US Pro-Trade Offensive", *The Wall Street Journal* (April 8).

Grubel, Herbert G., "All Internationally Traded Services Are Embodied in Materials or People", *The World Economy*, announced for 1987.

Grubel, Herbert G. (1983), *Free Market Zones*, Fraser Institute, Vancouver.

Grubel, Herbert G. (1982), "Towards a Theory of Free Economic Zones", *Weltwirtschaftliches Archiv*, 1.

Grubel, Herbert G. (1977), "The Case Against the New International Economic Order", *Weltwirtschaftliches Archiv*, 2.

Grubel, Herbert G. (ed.), (1987), *Concepts and Issues in Service Sector Research: A Symposium*, Fraser Institute, Vancouver.

Hill, Peter T. (1977), "On Goods and Services", *Review of Income and Wealth*, 23, 4.

Hill, Peter T. (1987), "The Service Sector: Current State of Knowledge and Research Procedures", in Grubel (1987).

Lee, Chung H. and Seiji Naya (1986), "The Internationalization of US Service Industries", Department of Economics, University of Hawaii.

Markusen, Jim, "Service Trade by the Multinational Enterprise", Fraser Institute Service Industry Study Project, forthcoming.

Rugman, Alan (1986), "A Transaction Cost Approach to Trade in Services", Dalhousie University Discussion Paper.

Sampson, Gary P. and Richard H. Snape (1985), "Identifying the Issues in Trade in Services", *The World Economy* (June).

Snape, Richard H., (ed.), (1986), *Issues in World Trade Policy: GATT at the Crossroads*, MacMillan, London.

Snape, Richard H. (1987a), *"Bilateral-Multinational Tension in Trade Policy"*, Paper presented at the Western Economic Association Meetings in Vancouver (July 7-10).

Snape, Richard H. (1987b), "Prospects for Liberalizing Services Trade", in C. Findlay and L. Castle (eds.), *Trade and Investment in Services in the Pacific*, Papers delivered at the 16th Pacific Trade and Development Conference in New Zealand (forthcoming).

Stern, Robert M. (ed.), (1985), *Trade and Investment in Services: Canada/US Perspectives*, Ontario Economic Council, Toronto.

Stern, Robert M. and Bernard M. Hoekman (1987), "Issues and Data Needs of GATT Negotiations on Services", *The World Economy*.

Stigler, George (1987), Address during the 1986 AEA meetings in New Orleans, *AEA Papers and Proceedings* (May).

US International Trade Commission (1982), *The Relationship of Exports in Selected US Service Industries to US Merchandise Exports*, USITC Publication 1920, Washington (September).

COMMENTS

Helmut Hesse

1.   Grubel's answer to the question raised in the title of his paper is a resounding "no": There is no need for a GATT for services. This conviction is based on two arguments which are thoroughly elaborated. According to the first argument "all internationally traded services are crossing borders after embodiment in people or material substances" (Introduction); therefore, liberalizing trade in goods automatically brings along liberalization of international trade in most of what conventionally are called service trade transactions. The remaining types of service trade concern the "right to establishment".

As far as the second argument is concerned, a GATT-like institution - be it for goods or be it for services - is likely to develop into an instrument of illiberalism and, therefore, is inferior to rules which bind "all national legislatures to the use of qualified majority voting" after the economic impact of legislation affecting international economic relations has been assessed. Both arguments are not entirely convincing.

There are three flaws in the first argument.

a)   Firstly and foremost, a tremendous technological progress, especially in the area of information and telematics, has taken place during the last one and a half decades. This led to what Professor Bhagwati[1] named the "splintering process": goods splinter from services and services, in turn, from goods. An important element in this process can be described as a "disembodiment phenomenon". More and more services do no longer require the physical proximity of the user and the provider and can be traded at long distances without being embodied in physical goods

---

[1]   Bhagwati, Jagdish N. (1987a).

Studies in International Economics and Institutions
Vosgerau (Ed.) New Institutional Arrangements for the World Economy
© Springer-Verlag Berlin Heidelberg 1989

when crossing national borders.[2] In such fields as finance, computer programming, data banks' services, insurance and engineering, trade has become more and more invisible and uncontrollable at national borders.

b) Secondly, it cannot be denied that there are numerous tangible outputs which serve as media for the delivery of intangible outputs, as for example software storing facilities (like floppy disks), gramophone records, cinematographic films, and so on. However, the media are rather unimportant compared with the services they deliver. Thus, the possibility to apply the rules for trade in goods to trade in services is no argument which will be accepted by those who attribute specific problems to trade in services and who call for a GATT for services.

c) Thirdly, although in a variety of services, international trade is possible without movement of providers or demanders (this is the category of "separated services" in the classification suggested by Stern and Hoekman[3]), it is difficult for a firm most of the times to sell its services effectively without a local establishment. For this reason trade in services would be noticeably facilitated if the presence of foreign commercial enterprises (be it temporary or permanent) was allowed. The "right to establish" has to be seen as an important precondition for increasing international trade in almost all services. Therefore it is not enough to just liberalize trade in all goods including the tangible media which deliver services. There also have to be negotiations concerning the 'right to establish' foreign subsidiaries, and it is exactly these negotiations which are decisive for the coming international trade order for services.[4]

2. Turning to Grubel's second argument it is tempting to linger upon his own conviction, namely that there is no chance for his qualified majority voting principle to be accepted internationally. However, there are more important objectives to his argument. To begin with, there is the diagnosis based on the argument that

---

[2] See Ewing, A. F. (1985), p. 158.

[3] Stern, Robert M. and Bernard M. Hoekman (1987), p. 40.

[4] Richardson, John B. (1987), p. 62.

"GATT has been turned into an instrument of illiberalism". Surely, protectionism has spread all over the world and deviations from the MFN treatment have "become dominant"[5] in world trade. Nevertheless, this development cannot be attributed to the failure of GATT. What has happened, in fact, was that GATT has been bypassed in numerous cases; "most major issues of global economic change are dealt with outside it"[6] and this is so because its norms and processes are a strong weapon against illiberalism. This is even true for the international regime in organized textile trade which can be described as "liberal protectionism" as Aggarwal[7] put it. The Cotton Textile Agreement "has at least served to curtail protectionism, and has helped to make world cotton textile trade much less restricted than it otherwise would have been."[8]

The sources of illiberalism can rather be found in the individual countries themselves. And Grubel wants to shift back the decision on the basic trade policy rules exactly to these countries. The major question should therefore be: can illiberalism and protectionism be tamed more easily by binding national legislatures to the use of qualified majority voting or by multilateral negotiations in the framework of GATT based on world-wide accepted rules. As Olivier Long[9] stated, "governments can find the existence of rules helpful in their efforts to resist pressure for protectionist measures, using the argument that, if they adopt them, other governments may take the retaliatory action permitted under the GATT." Moral pressure and governments' fear of losing the advantages of tariff concessions and other GATT benefits have proven to be powerful constraints against illiberal national tendencies. In this connection it should not be overlooked that all the essential provisions in the General Agreement on Tariffs and Trade can only be changed by a two-third majority or even by a consensus of the 92 contracting parties. More important than these considerations is the following argumentation. The globalization of most of

---

5   Pomfret, Richard W.T. (1985), p. 55.

6   Reich, Robert (Spring 1983) p. 783.

7   Aggarwal, Vinod K. (1985).

8   Bardan, Benyamin (1973), p. 26.

9   Long, Olivier (1985), p. 64.

the markets and the high degree of interconnectedness of the national economies call for a uniform global framework for the international trade in goods and services based on norms and basic rules that are accepted by all countries. This framework has to be reliable and stable. Stability as a public good in the world economy cannot be expected to prevail as long as all countries are free to take their own trade-regulating decisions. Binding these decisions to qualified majority voting does neither prevent national rules from differing nor - what counts more - from changing in unforeseeable ways. The world needs a GATT, for services as well as for goods.

3.   However, this statement cannot be based only on the rejection of the two arguments presented by Grubel. There are various other serious objections against the proposal to make international trade in services a special topic in international trade policy and to build up a common international framework dedicated to it.

From all these rejections those will become especially important during the Uruguay-Round which have been pronounced by the developing countries. And they strongly reject a GATT for services. In the following these concerns of the developing countries will briefly be presented. And this is done with the aim to extend the discussion of this topic to some issues, which are presently discussed world-wide.

Developing countries fear that, *first* of all, only industrialized countries have comparative advantages in services and "therefore the returns to extension of orderly trade rules to services ... will accrue to the developed rather than to the developing countries."[10] *One* argument against this statement is that the very nature of comparative advantage is dynamic and not static; "comparative advantage is changing constantly and developing countries can benefit just as much as the developed from this trend."[11] In addition, different countries have competitive advantages in different segments of the services sector. South Korea, Hongkong, Singapore, India and Pakistan already export services to a great extent. Therefore,

---

[10]   Bhagwati, Jagdish N. (1987b), p. 27.

[11]   Ewing, A.F., op. cit., p. 158.

it will be important to extend the liberalization efforts to those services from which developing countries can derive substantial advantages or from which they can acquire them soon.

Another point is that the producers and exporters of many developing countries depend upon the access to cheap and efficient banking, insurance and other services to strengthen their export performance. They would only hurt themselves by protecting their service industries.

The *second* concern of the developing countries is the limited progress in liberalizing world trade. They fear that focusing on services will weaken the efforts to keep trade in goods free. This would be detrimental to the Third World whose comparative advantage lies in trade in goods instead.

This concern is hard to understand. In all countries a continuum of dynamic comparative advantages exists, which comprises all sectors of the economy. Therefore, an efficient international division of labour cannot and should not be restricted to manufacturing industries. A country, as for instance the United States, whose traditional industries partly become senile and lose former comparative advantage, must have the chance to make use of new comparative advantages gained in service industries. Otherwise such a country would refuse to keep imports of goods free of trade restrictions. "Should reciprocity become a central theme in negotiations about services, there would almost certainly be some spillover to goods."[12] "Without the inclusion of services, the GATT formula for liberalization will remain inert."[13] Thus, negotiations on liberalization of trade in services would, unlike the fears of the developing countries, provide them with the opportunity to gain free access to the manufacturers' markets of industrialized countries. The developing countries would therefore be well advised to insist on negotiating forums and modalities that comprise trade in goods and services alike. There is no need for a GATT for services separated form a GATT for goods; but there is a need for an integral framework of international trade in agricultural products, manufactured goods and services.

---

[12] Diebold, William Jr. and Helena Stalson (1983), p. 593.

[13] Schott, Jeffrey J. and Jacqueline Mazza (1986), p. 268.

Thirdly, developing countries fear that services will expand in areas where political sensitivity, infrastructure build-ups and externalities are important.[14] These concerns have to be taken seriously. In fact, services comprise much of a nation's basic economic 'infrastructure' - banking, insurance, transport, communication, education. And it is also true that service sectors have traditionally been heavily regulated. This makes the issue of trade liberalization a very complicated one. But it does not imply that one can do without deregulation and increasing international competition in this area. Intensive competition acts as an incentive to the improvement of quality, the increase of productivity and the acceleration of innovation.[15] This argument is also true for international competition in the area of services. On the other hand, there is a real danger that negotiations on liberalizing international trade in services "will degenerate", as Waelbroek[16] put it, "into a medley of bitterly fought engagements between the bureaucrats who are responsible for the regulation of narrowly defined areas of services in the various countries". Therefore, the conclusion should be drawn that negotiations should focus on a set of general rights and principles, which will have to rule trade in all service industries alike. In view of this point it would be beneficial to start with what already exists in the GATT rather than to start from scratch. Many of the rules, principles, and procedures embodied in the General Agreement are relevant to services. The preamble to the GATT along with the provision of Article XXV could serve as the basis for negotiations within the GATT. Article I provides another important starting point: there should be strong emphasis on non-discriminatory treatment, which should be understood as meaning most-favoured-nation treatment for trade and "national treatment"[17] for investment (allowing foreigners to do no more and no less than establish comparable domestic enterprises). Presumably there will be many exceptions to these principles; the effort to codify the conditions for these exceptions should also be made within the GATT. And the same applies to the specific mechanisms which have to be established for orderly discussions of detailed issues.

---

14   Keppler, Horst (1986), pp. 87-90.

15   This point has been stressed by Richardson, John B., op. cit., p. 56.

16   Waelbroek, Jean, Comment on Bhagwati (1987), op. cit., p. 56.

17   See also: A GATT for Services, *The Economist*, Oct. 12 (1985), p. 20.

The growing importance of services is already reflected in new GATT rules adopted in the 1970's, particularly in the codes on government procurement and on subsidies.

UNCTAD, the forum preferred by developing countries, cannot boast of such experiences.

Summarizing the concerns of developing countries against the GATT for services, they prove to be unreasonable. Therefore, the result must be that the world needs a GATT for services, which has to be comprehensive in scope, and which will be settled within the GATT by means of a close co-ordination with the GATT for goods (which does not mean a pure extension of the existing rules to services). "Otherwise there is real danger ... of bilateral and regional fragmentation on the trading world in the area of services"[18] and of discrepancies between the countries resulting from the differences between the frameworks for the international trade in goods, on the one hand, and services on the other.

References

Aggarwal, Vinod K. (1985), *Liberal Protectionism. The International Politics of Organized Textile Trade*, University of California Press, Berkeley and Los Angeles.

Bardan, Benyamin (1973), The Cotton Textile Agreement, 1962-1972. *Journal of World Trade Law*, vol. 7, no. 1 , p. 26.

Bhagwati, Jagdish N. (1987a), Splintering and Disembodiment of Services and Developing Nations, *The World Economy*, vol. 7 (June).

Bhagwati, Jagdish N. (1987b), International Trade in Services and its Relevance for Economic Development, in Giarini, Orio (ed.), *The Emerging Service Economy*, Pergamon Press, Oxford, p. 27.

Diebold William Jr. and Helena Stalson (1983), Negotiating Issues in International Services Transactions, in Cline, William R. (ed.), *Trade Policy in the 1980s*, Washington, D.C., p. 593.

---

[18]   Bhagwati, Jagdish N. (1987b), p. 33.

Ewing, A. F. (1985), Why Freer Trade in Services is in the Interest of Developing Countries, *Journal of World Trade Law*, vol. 19, no. 2 (March/April), p. 158.

Keppler, Horst (1986), Die Bedeutung des Dienstleistungssektors für die Entwicklungsländer. Ansatzpunkte für die bi- und multilaterale Zusammenarbeit, *Forschungsberichte des Bundesministeriums für Wirtschaftliche Zusammenarbeit*, Band 77, Weltforum Verlag, München, Köln, London, pp. 87-90.

Long, Olivier (1985), *Law and Its Limitations in the GATT Multilateral Trade System*, Martinus Nijhoff Publishers, Dordrecht, Boston, Lancaster, p. 64.

Pomfret, Richard W.T. (1985), Discrimination in International Trade: Extent, Motivation and Implications, *Economia Internazionale*, vol. 38, p. 55.

Reich, Robert (Spring 1983), Beyond Free Trade, *Foreign Affairs*, vol. 61, p. 783.

Richardson, John B. (1987), A Sub-sectoral Approach to Services' Trade Theory, in Giarini, Orio (ed.), *The Emerging Service Economy*, Pergamon Press, Oxford et al., p. 62.

Schott, Jeffrey J. and Jacqueline Mazza (1986), Trade in Services and Developing Countries, *Journal of World Trade Law*, vol. 20, p. 268.

Stern, Robert M. and Bernard M. Hoekman (1987), Issues and Data Needs for GATT Negotiations on Services, *The World Economy*, vol. 10, no. 1 (March), p. 40.

Waelbroek, Jean, Comment on Bhagwati (1987b), op. cit., p. 56.

Policy Motives and International Trade Restrictions

Arye L. Hillman

1.   Introduction

The case for free trade is quite compelling. Certainly there are qualifications, as for example the infant-industry and optimum tariff arguments. But these qualifications are not severe. The infant-industry argument on further consideration has been shown to yield little in the way of implications for trade policy (Baldwin 1969). The optimum tariff argument which is the application of monopsony power in international trade provides no assurances that foreign retaliation will not result in an outcome inferior to free trade. Some defence-related arguments have also been suggested for departure from free trade.[1] However, as a general proposition, free trade maximizes an economy's national income and is the Pareto-efficient policy course. Yet the institutional framework governing the conduct of the developed countries' international trade policies is generally constituted in a manner which facilitates protectionist responses. As an empirical matter, departures from free trade are of course pervasive (Baldwin 1984).

My purpose in this paper is to consider why national institutional structures facilitate protectionist responses and to draw implications regarding the possible nature of institutional arrangements for the world economy, the theme of this symposium. Certainly, if the basic theorems on gains from trade as derived from international trade theory were to govern the design of institutional structures, the opportunities for protectionist responses would be more constrained. In particular, if the classical infant-industry or optimum-tariff arguments predominated in the specification of the institutional framework, one would expect this to be revealed in appropriate emphasis in the laws specifying feasible policy responses. But these classical exceptions to the case for free trade are not the prime considerations underlying the

---

[1]   For a review of these arguments, see Leonard Cheng (1987).

Studies in International Economics and Institutions
Vosgerau (Ed.) New Institutional Arrangements for the World Economy
© Springer-Verlag Berlin Heidelberg 1989

legal justification for protectionist policies. Two different hypotheses suggest themselves as underlying protectionist responses. International trade restrictions can be viewed as manifestations of social insurance objectives of governments. An alternative hypothesis is that motives of political self-interest and political support underlie the opportunities for protectionist responses. This latter hypothesis focuses on political objectives of policymakers, as distinct from the social welfare and efficiency considerations which underlie intervention motivated by social-insurance objectives.

Before proceeding to compare these two hypotheses as explanations for protectionist responses, one should consider another more preliminary question: why are protectionist policies facilitated at all, since the case for free trade persists independently of the identification of gainers and losers from trade restrictions. That is, income distribution motives alone cannot explain protectionist responses without further institutional qualification. The theorems on the gains from trade imply a free-trade outcome, whether the gainers form protection or the losers have won the right to designate the institutional structure governing policy responses. If the gainers from protection can dictate the nature of the institutionally allowable responses to protectionist pleas, they should still insist upon free trade and use their right over policy discretion to appropriate the gains from international trade. And of course if the losers form protection can designate the policy response, they choose free trade. Hence, it is impediments to domestic transfers from losers from protection to gainers which underlie an institutional framework consistent with protectionist responses. The domestic transfers, whether based on social insurance or political self-interest motives of policymakers, are for whatever reason institutionally constrained to take place with references to international considerations. Changes in *world* prices give rise to *international* trade policy responses, although the transfers could in principle be made internally to the advantage of all concerned without the deadweight losses attendant on protectionist policies.

It has been suggested that if international trade policy is the observed means of redistributing income, then this is necessarily the feasible redistributive means which incurs the *least* deadweight loss; since everybody involved, both the gainers and the losers from protection, have an incentive to effect transfers by minimizing deadweight losses.[2] This is a Pangloss interpretation of what we observe: protectionist policies have to be the most efficient means of effecting the redistributive transfers, otherwise the more efficient means of effecting the redistributive means would be employed. There is of course much to be said for this position. Ostensibly, transactions and certification costs give an advantage to a redistribution mechanism which affects domestic incomes.

A property-rights perspective is also instructive here. It has been noted that the national trade laws and the articles of GATT are formulated in a manner which implies a conception of assignment of property rights to domestic markets to domestic producers and domestic factors of production.[3] A role of GATT is the formalization of exchange of rights of market access between countries. Such market access is provided via "concessions" made to each other by the contracting GATT countries. Within this legal structure, the perception of foreign violation of domestic rights invites a foreign policy response via international trade policy rather than an explicit direct transfer from the domestic losers to the gainers from protection.

Be this as it may, let us proceed from the observation that the institutional framework allows for protectionist policies to be used to effect domestic income transfers, albeit with attendant deadweight cost. I turn to consider now the social insurance argument for such transfers.

2. The Social Insurance Policy Motive

Trade policy has been viewed as having an insurance role in protecting individuals' incomes against unforeseen changes in world markets. Thus, if "injury" to a domestic industry occurs because of trade-related change, the injured party can seek recourse via the national trade laws to protection which would preserve previous

---

[2]   For a statement of this argument, see Gary Becker (1983, 1985).

[3]   For a broad discussion of property rights and international trade regimes, see Jan Tumlir (1987).

domestic income levels. The insurance provided via trade policy thus preempts further "injury". The insurance response is not necessarily associated with an "unfair trade practice" or an appeal for antidumping or countervailing duties. It is simply the presence of randomness in world prices which is viewed as underlying the insurance motive for trade policy.

The social insurance argument has a market failure or efficiency basis. Individuals who are risk-averse and whose incomes are tied to world prices of particular goods would avail themselves of the opportunity to transact in insurance markets to eliminate or reduce the uncertainty associated with their future incomes, if insurance markets exist to facilitate such transactions. In the absence of the requisite markets, there is a role for government to correct the market failure. This is thus an efficiency argument. Social welfare is increased by policy intervention.

The important aspect of the social-insurance explanation for trade policy is that it gives rise to a *social consensus* perspective on protection.[4] In the face of the uncertainty associated with terms of trade and in the absence of insurance markets, all individuals in an economy, if sufficiently risk averse, can gain from a policy which reduces ex-post variability of prices of goods to which their incomes are tied. For by reducing variability of prices of goods protection can also reduce the variability of incomes. The consensus on a protectionist policy is ex-ante, before the realization of the random world prices which are the source of randomness into domestic incomes. However, ex-post after world prices are realized, some individuals gain and others lose from the protectionist policy. The ex-ante consensus can be viewed in terms of expected utility maximization. The expected utility of everyone can be increased by appropriate dampening of relative price variability.

In particular, consider a Ricardo-Viner or specific-factors world where individuals have undiversified claims to factor ownership. That is, an individual either derives his income from ownership of factors specific to one industry, or income is derived from claims of ownership over a mobile factor, say labor. In this setting, protection secured by one industry increases the real incomes of owners of factors specific to

---

[4] Cassing, Hillman and Long (1986) provide a detailed exposition of how the possibility of social consensus arises.

the protected industry, decreases the real incomes of all other specific factor owners, and may or may not - depending on the nature of consumption preferences and production technologies - increase the real incomes of mobile factor owners. Hence, specific factor owners are in conflict regarding protection for any industry, and the policy stance of mobile factors can only be determined after further information on preferences and technologies is introduced.

However, this is only so for realized world prices. Before world prices are known, specific factor owners do not know whether they are to be associated with an industry which will have a comparative advantage or disadvantage in international trade. Specific factor owners have no ex-post adjustment flexibility subsequent to the realization of world prices and the determination of comparative advantage. If markets allowing diversification of income sources are unavailable, the insurance which risk-averse specific factor owners might seek can be provided via trade policy guaranteeing them that there will be limitations as to the extent of "injury" which they might suffer as the consequence of trade-related change.

Mobile factor owners do have a means of exercising ex-post flexibility in adjustment subsequent to the realization of world prices. Since they are mobile, they are allocated by the competitive market mechanism to equate values of marginal product and to maximize factor incomes. A natural form of insurance is therefore provided to mobile factor owners via their intersectoral mobility. However, still, as is the case for specific factor owners, if sufficiently risk-averse, the expected utility of a mobile factor owner confronting variability in world prices can be increased by a reduction in the variability of domestic relative prices.

It is evident that protection is a means of achieving a dampening of relative price variability. Consider as an extreme case an ex-ante agreement to levy an autarkic tariff for whatever realized world price eventuates. All ex-post price variability is then eliminated. Individuals know with certainty that output prices will be those of the autarkic equilibrium, and they correspondingly know with certainty their future incomes, which are tied to autarkic output prices. But this is an extreme response which eliminates the gains from trade. One can envisage more moderate dampening protectionist responses which preserve gains from trade and reduce the uncertainty associated with future incomes.

The form of protection also affects the manner in which protection affects individuals' income in the face of randomness in world prices. An import quota in particular provides a lower bound to the domestic price which is established when the world price is realized, and thus eliminates downside risk of income falls beyond a predetermined level of income. The same lower bound to domestic prices independently of realized world prices is achieved by a system of variable levies as employed in the EEC.

Further uncertainty can be introduced by not only considering randomness in world prices but also allowing for a state where individuals have not yet committed their endowments of capital to particular industries. In that event, individuals do not know world prices and are at the same time also unaware of their prospective industry associations. Suppose that before allocations of capital to different sectors are decided, all individuals are identical in their endowments. The choice of a protectionist policy which maximizes expected utility then maximizes a Benthamite social welfare function. Ex-post transfers take place via redistribution effected by trade policy to maximize social welfare. Thus we have a social welfare formulation of the efficiency argument associated with failure of insurance markets to allow individuals to diversify income sources (Eaton and Grossman, 1985).

3.   Political Support Motives

An alternative to the social-insurance perspective on protection views restrictions on international trade is the outcome of optimization by policymakers guided by political-support motives. Of course, political-support maximization can be consistent with social-insurance protectionist responses. If the expected utilities of all individuals are increased by a commitment to an appropriate trade policy subsequent to the realization of uncertain terms of trade, the policy consensus assures maximal political support for the expected-utility maximizing protectionist policy.

The political-support perspective focuses, however, not on the possibility of consensus trade policy in the face of uncertainty but on the conflict among different self-interested groups each concerned with influencing trade policy to its advantage. Conflict is resolved via the political process. Either individuals vote on the level of protection in a system of direct democracy with single-issue voting. Or, politicians who are accountable to an electorate make trade policy decisions with a view to maximizing their probabilities of election.[5] The representative democracy case is more applicable than direct democracy, since in general individuals do not have opportunities to vote directly on particular questions concerning protection. Votes are cast for candidates for political office. The candidates are concerned with formulating trade policy proposals as parts of policy packages which will secure them political support via appeal to the voters who form their constituencies. Or candidates seek support in the form of campaign contributions which as campaign expenditures influence voters' decisions.

In a representative democracy, special interests can in particular be successful in influencing policy decisions because individual consumer/voters have little incentive to participate in the political process by acquiring information on the consequences of different policies. Individual losers from protection have an incentive to be "rationally ignorant". They have less at stake than the gainers from protection, who have the greater incentive to be organized to influence political decisions in their favor. Thus, although protectionist policies disadvantage large numbers to benefit a relatively few, protectionist outcomes are nevertheless consistent with political-support maximizing equilibria.

Whereas the social-insurance explanation for protectionist policies has an efficiency vantage, via failure of private insurance markets, the political-support perception of motives for trade restrictions is in contrast distributionally based. Trade policy is viewed as primarily a device to redistribute income from the gainers to the losers from protection. In equilibrium, the marginal gain in political support from the beneficiaries of protection is offset against the marginal loss of support from those disadvantaged from protection (Hillman, 1982).

---

[5] Peter Bernholz (1966) provides a general discussion. With particular reference to trade policy, see Robert Baldwin (1982). Wolfgang Mayer (1984) considers tariff formulation under direct democracy. A case of representative democracy is studied by Young and Magee (1986).

4.   Declining Industry Protection: Social Insurance or Political Support?

Let us now consider which of the alternatives, social insurance or political support, appears more appropriate for describing the policy motives underlying trade restrictions. We can initially approach the comparison by looking at the policy response to industry decline in the face of shifts in comparative advantage.

A declining industry is a natural candidate for protection motivated by social insurance objectives. Such an industry in confronting variability in the world price of its output has suffered an adverse price realization. Individuals whose incomes are tied to the price of the output of the declining industry because of past in-dustry-specific human capital investments find themselves correspondingly losing. The circumstances are precisely those where one might envisage a social safety net provided by government via a protectionist response. Protection transfers income from those individuals who have lost by association with the declining industry and away from others who have been more fortunate in realizations of market prices of output of industries to which their incomes are tied.

Yet observationally the declining industry is also the prime candidate for protection based on motives of political support. Since the industry is in decline, there is a natural disincentive to entry. Hence the rents due to protection which are the basis of political support will not be eroded by competitive entry. The specific factors which have been unable to exit the declining industry remain the well-defined beneficiaries of protectionist policies. Importantly, it can be shown that motives of political-support maximization give rise to protectionist responses which do not reverse industry decline (Hillman, 1982). Rather, with political-support motives underlying policy decisions, if the declining industry benefits from protection, then protection but retards the industry's decline. Industry-specific interests gain from the retardation in industry decline, but also domestic consumers and other losers from industry protection are provided with some gain via a fall in the domestic price of the declining industry's output. The potential gains made possible by a fall in the import price are therefore permitted to be realized in a manner which dis-tributes some benefits to the losers from protection. It is the political evaluation of such benefits from the fall in domestic price which in equilibrium is balanced at the margin against the benefit from the protection provided the industry. The declining industry is therefore never overcompensated for the fall in the world price of its output. The political-support equilibrium results in incomplete compensation which leaves some gain to the countervailing interests who are opposed to protection for the industry.

In terms of protectionist responses, there is thus little to distinguish the social-insurance and political-support explanations for protection. Both explanations predict a protectionist response when an industry confronts an adverse shift in international comparative advantage. Empirical studies which include industry growth as a variable explaining industry cross-section levels of protection tend to confirm an inverse relationship, but this relationship is consistent with either the social-insurance and political-support hypotheses.[6]

Of course, declining industries are not the only beneficiaries of protection in the developed economies. For example, agriculture benefits from substantial government assistance in the U.S. (and the EEC). However, it is textile and apparel, shoes, steel, automobiles, motorcycles and other manufacturing industries which have suffered adverse shifts in comparative advantage that have tended to be the principal beneficiaries of protectionist policies.[7]

5. The Institutional Structure

A different approach to an attempt to distinguish the social-insurance and political-support hypotheses for protectionist responses looks at the institutional structure which provides the framework for policy decisions. In the U.S. these decisions can be made with reference to technical prespecified requirements for protection. Or protection may be sought via appeal to political discretion exercised by the executive branch in pursuing negotiations with foreign governments, or by seeking

---

[6] See for example the empirical studies by Marvel and Ray (1983) and Godek (1985).

[7] See Hufbauer, Berliner and Elliott (1986) for a detailed study of recent instances of U.S. protectionism.

Congressional support for the formulation and passage of new trade laws or amendments to pre-existing laws.[8] Basically, the technically specified administrative track sets out the circumstances for "remedies" to be instituted to resolve difficulties confronting domestic industries. These circumstances include confirmation of dumping, subsidized imports, and other "unfair" trade and import practices, where the basis for a protectionist response is specified in some detail. More general recourse for domestic firms or industries is provided by escape-clause or safeguards cases. Here the grounds for intervention are confirmation of "injury" from imports to domestic interests. Protection would then facilitate a cessation of "injury".

The injury concept fits quite well the social-insurance motive for protection. The general purpose of insurance is the elimination or spreading of risk which is facilitated by making outcomes confronting individuals independent of realizations of the state of the world. The administrative trade laws in this sense can be perceived as embodying the social-insurance motive by addressing the problem of injury due to imports. In a manner analogous to reference to the conditions of an insurance contract, under the administrative protectionist procedures the process of ascertaining whether the circumstances of injury warrant a compensatory response is conducted at a technical level.[9] No compensatory protectionist response is provided for, unless it can be demonstrated that the cause of "injury" to domestic producers is trade-related.[10]

If circumstances are not appropriate for administratively determined protection via the confirmation of trade-related injury, the recourse is available of appeal to the political discretion of the Congress or executive. Here political-support motives are prominent. Whether the industry succeeds in securing Congressional support for

---

[8]   On the different tracks which can be taken in pursuing a protectionist response in the U.S., see Finger, Hall, and Nelson (1982). A detailed study of protectionist decision-making in the U.S. is provided by Robert Baldwin (1985).

[9]   Implementation of protectionist proposals is, however, subject to discretion at the executive level.

[10]   For a case study, see Gene Grossman (1986) who investigates the cause of injury to the U.S. steel industry.

tariff or quota protection, or whether voluntary export restraints are negotiated for an industry by the executive depends upon political cost-benefit calculations. The circumstances underlying the voluntary export restraint on Japanese automobiles are instructive. Prior to the inauguration of the restraints in 1981, the U.S. automobile industry had sought and been refused protection via the administrative protectionist track as an escape-clause case. The determination was that a domestic decline in demand rather than imports was the prime cause of any "injury" which had been suffered by the domestic industry. The executive branch negotiated the voluntary export restraints at the same time as Congressional proposals were being put forward for quota or domestic-content protection. The circumstances underlying the protection which was provided for the U.S. automobile industry are quite clearly an instance where the political support explanation for protection is appropriate.

The reason why the automobile industry in this case and other industries more generally could not qualify for protection under the technical rules was that injury was not determined to be trade-related. But if policy is guided by social insurance motives, why the particular emphasis on imports as the source of injury? The same injury is incurred if domestic demand remains stable and imports increase as when correspondingly domestic demand declines and imports remain stable.

6.   Moral Hazard and Property Rights

The reasons generally given for failure of insurance markets are moral hazard and adverse selection. Moral hazard relates to actions taken by agents which influence the probabilities of different states of the world arising. Uncertainty is thus endogeneous to individuals' actions rather than exogenous. Adverse selection refers to the incentive for individuals with low perceived probabilities of realizations of unfavorable states of the world to opt out of insurance markets, leaving participation to high perceived risk individuals. Reduced participation by low risk individuals increases the cost of insurance, in turn further driving marginal low-risk participants to self-insurance.

Consider now moral hazard in the context of social insurance when agents face trade-related risk. Exogeneous change can be associated with actions taken by foreigners which increase import penetration of domestic markets. Endogeneous change on the other hand can be related to actions taken domestically which affect the domestic industry's sales in its home market. This dichotomy of effects suggests that moral hazard can be avoided by limiting the applicability of social insurance to losses due to actions taken by foreigners, since such actions are presumed exogeneous. A moral hazard explanation can thus be proposed for the limitation of scope of social insurance to injury caused by imports.

The implicit property rights assignment is consistent. Insurance provides payment in unfavorable states of the world to compensate for losses where property rights were exercised. If the trade laws have a social-insurance basis, the associated property rights are to domestic market access. There is a legitimized (but qualified) barrier to entry against foreigners. Insurance in the form of a protectionist response is not provided against the unfavorable consequences of randomness in domestic demand. The insurance applies to injury incurred due to random or unforeseen changes in *foreign* competitors' domestic sales which compromise the domestic right of supply of the domestic market (the extent of which may be subject to change).

7.   A Justification for Social Insurance - Or Political Economy After All?

Do we then have a consistent social insurance perspective on injury-related protection provided by recourse to the national trade laws? Having presented the social insurance case in as favorable light as possible, I now wish to introduce some difficulties with this perception of the policy motive for international trade restrictions.

Theoretical problems have been raised with respect to arguments which seek to justify social insurance on moral hazard grounds. Dixit (1986) has shown that moral hazard does not preclude the provision of insurance by private markets, that the private market outcome is Pareto efficient, and that government provision of social

296

insurance consequently cannot improve upon the market outcome. As a particular case of Dixit's argument, consider two possible states of the world, high import penetration of domestic markets (a bad state for the domestic import-competing industry) and low import penetration (a good state), and let the probabilities of these states arising depend upon actions taken by the agents in the domestic import-competing industry. Individual agents' activities affecting the likelihood of the two states are not observable, but suppose that insurance purchases in a private market can be observed; in particular, let agents be constrained to purchase all their insurance from one competitive firm.[11] Each firm observes each agent's insurance purchases, and offers an insurance contract which internalizes moral hazard and achieves Pareto efficiency in a competitive equilibrium. Because of moral hazard, however, insurance is not complete. There is some self-insurance. Likewise, in the absence of exclusivity in insurance purchases, there is no justification for government intervention to provide social insurance.[12] Private insurance markets do as well as the government can do. Quite simply, the government has no information which is not available to private firms, and which private firms cannot internalize in offering insurance contracts.

Can one then envisage a private market wherein firms insure their profits against market incursions by foreigners, or where individuals deriving their incomes from ownership of industry-specific factors insure themselves against shifts in international comparative advantage which would lead them to suffer income losses? Under the same conditions as set out in the administrative trade laws, the answer would appear to be affirmative. The risk underlying insurance would be exogeneous foreign change affecting domestic incomes. Moral hazard would therefore be absent. Private insurance markets should then do just as well as the administrative procedures in ascertaining whether injury warranting compensation under an insurance contract has occurred. The case for market failure and an interventionist role for government via legal encodement of a social-insurance response thus has no support.

---

[11] This is termed an "exclusivity requirement" in the insurance literature.

[12] See Dixit (1986) for a complete exposition.

However, let us allow some moral hazard. If foreigners innovate and domestic firms do not, the source of injury to domestic firms is imports, but clearly domestic firms are subject to moral hazard in their own competitive innovative activities. Dixit's analysis suggests that domestic firms could not avail themselves of private insurance to secure given levels of profits independently of realized states of the world. However, private competitive insurance markets would still provide incomplete insurance in a Pareto efficient equilibrium which cannot be improved upon by government provision of social insurance. Thus once again there is no role for government if a private competitive insurance market is allowed to function. Firms and factor owners would simply be obliged to undertake some self-insurance, as is generally the case in other cases of risk where moral hazard is present.

If the efficiency case for protection as social insurance is compromised, we are led back to the emphasis on redistributive motives as suggested by a political-economy perspective on international trade restrictions. Uncertainty has a role in such a perspective. Producers and industry-specific interests do not know when they will need protection, insofar as shifts in comparative advantage are unforeseen. Proceeding via lobbying the Congress or the executive for protectionist intervention may be costly in consuming time and resources, and there may be considerable uncertainty associated with the outcome. Even if successful in such pursuits to influence trade policy, industry-specific interests may find themselves suffering considerable "injury" because of increased imports in the time taken to achieve changes in the trade laws. Market shares of domestic producers may be significantly eroded, and opposition to protection may be heightened by increased consumer awareness of superior import substitution possibilities for domestic goods. The administrative protection laws protect against such contingencies. The laws are in place to specify recourse and provide "remedies" when the unforeseen shifts in comparative advantage take place.

The administrative protection laws can be thus envisaged as a collective political-economy response rather than a consensus achieved in the face of insurance-related market failure. The collectivity in the political-economy response derives from the uncertainty confronting all domestic agents whose incomes are affected by trade-related change. The administrative laws in place protecting against the contingency of injury due to imports preempt the costs incurred in the lobbying and other influence-seeking activities which would have been required to secure changes in trade policy.

8.   The Efficiency Cost of Social Insurance

A final aspect of the social insurance case for trade restrictions merits emphasis. Even if the market-failure case for social insurance in the face of trade-related change were more firmly based in a justification for government intervention, one would still confront the difficulty that a protectionist response has an efficiency cost which counterbalances any efficiency gain which might be achieved. For protection influences domestic resource-allocation decisions in a manner counter to comparative advantage. Thus, incomes may be preserved in industries adversely impacted by shifts in international comparative advantage, but at the expense of more than offsetting income declines elsewhere in the economy (because of the deadweight costs of protection). This then severely qualifies the social-insurance market-failure case for protectionist responses.[13]

However, as I have argued, it does not appear that the social-insurance market-failure case has analytically very much support as a justification for government compensation via protection when domestic interests confront injury from imports. The analytics appear to favor not the efficiency-based social insurance argument but the income-distribution based political-economy explanation for government interventionist activities.

---

[13]   Other problems arise as well. For example, Hillman, Katz and Rosenberg (1987) show how the anticipation of a benevolent policy response in adverse states of the world can give rise to inefficient resource allocation. It should also be noted that industries are sometimes simply left to collapse in the face of import competition (see Cassing and Hillman, 1986). Such collapse appears inconsistent with social insurance protectionist motives.

9. The Prospect for International Institutional Arrangements

I wish now to turn to consider how social-insurance and political-support motives relate to the properties one could expect of a set of rules governing international arrangements for the conduct of trade policy.

Suppose that social insurance motives did explain trade restrictions. The efficiency motive underlying social insurance would then be consistent with cooperation among governments. Indeed, there would be mutual gains to be achieved via the broad spreading of trade-related risk. A shift in comparative advantage which were to disadvantage one country's producers of a particular good would at the same time advantage another country's producers of that good. Both countries' producers could enter into a risk-pooling arrangement to eliminate or reduce this risk. Such an arrangement would require international transfers, and hence a set of rules which institutionally specify the conditions of transfer. Just as many types of insurance currently transcend national markets, so social insurance associated with shifts in international comparative advantage could be based on international participation.

Of course, moral hazard and adverse selection difficulties suggest themselves, now writ large as producers in different countries seek to evoke transfers from foreign competitors who have been successful in making inroads into their domestic markets. One may seriously doubt whether a global social-insurance conception could be effectively institutionalized via a set of rules governing international compensatory transfers for injury suffered via trade-related change: although in principle it is evident that if the insurance market failure did underlie national compensation for trade-related industry, international cooperation would be to the advantage of all by facilitating risk-spreading among the agents bearing the risk.

To summarize then, if social insurance were the prime motive underlying national trade policy, a role (although qualified) is identified for international institutional arrangements. Such arrangements would facilitate mutual gain by international risk pooling.

But if domestic considerations of political support and income distribution determine protectionist responses, the role for international institutional arrangements becomes limited. On this view, the injury suffered by domestic interests due to imports is not the consequence of a random realization which could just as well have gone the other way. Rather, as product-cycle shifts in comparative advantage occur, some countries' industries systematically decline as others advance. The declining industries' pleas for protection are not then manifestations of risk-spreading motives which took effect before the resolution of trade-related uncertainty. The protectionist pleas for compensation for injury reflect rearguard actions in the face of structural changes in international comparative advantage.

This raises of course the question why shifts in comparative advantage are not foreseen if they are systematic, and why dynamically optimal investments in industry-specific productive assets are not made. I do not wish to suggest that there is no randomness present which can give rise to unexpected world price changes and attendant changes in domestic incomes. However, as I have proposed, with the presence of uncertainty acknowledged, the market-failure case for efficiency motives underlying social-insurance protectionist responses is not strong, either with reference to the pre-specified rules of administered protection or in terms of the response to lobbying activities directed at changing the rules as they pertain to particular industries. Rather than the social consensus associated with social insurance and risk-pooling, we confront the essential conflict inherent in distributionally based policies. Some individuals gain at the expense of others, via government income transfers secured by protection.

Of course, the political support motive for policy suggests that governments have an incentive to cooperate if the means can be found of securing mutual advantage for politically prominent sectors. This can explain the prominence of voluntary export restraints, which by imposing a collusive restriction on exports can increase producer and industry-specific rents in both exporting and import-competing industries.

References

Baldwin, Robert E. (1969), "The Case Against Infant-industry Tariff Protection", *Journal of Political Economy*, 77, pp. 195-305.

Baldwin, Robert E. (1982), "The Political Economy of Protectionism", in Jagdish Bhagwati (ed.), *Import Competition and Response*, University of Chicago Press, Chicago, pp. 263-286.

Baldwin, Robert E. (1984), "Trade Policies in Developed Countries", *Handbook of International Economics*, vol. 1, North-Holland, pp. 571-619.

Baldwin, Robert E. (1985), "*The Political Economy of U.S. Import Policy*, MIT Press.

Becker, Gary S. (1983), "A Theory of Competition Among Pressure Groups for Political Influence", *Quarterly Journal of Economics*, 98, pp. 371-400.

Becker, Gary S. (1985), "Public Policies, Pressure Groups and Deadweight Cost", *Journal of Public Economics*, 28, pp. 329-347.

Bernholz, Peter (1986), "Economic Policies in a Democracy", *Kyklos*, 19, pp. 48-80.

Cassing, James H. and Arye L. Hillman (1986), "Shifting Comparative Advantage and Senescent Industry Collapse", *American Economic Review*, 76, pp. 516-523.

Cassing, James H., Arye L. Hillman and Ngo Van Long (1986), "Risk Aversion, Terms of Trade Variability, and Social-consensus Trade Policy", *Oxford Economic Papers*, 38, pp. 234-242.

Cheng, Leonard (1987), "Economic Arguments for Self-sufficiency and Trade Reduction", *Journal of International Economics*, forthcoming.

Dixit, Avinash (1986), "Trade and Insurance with Moral Hazard", Princeton University, (August).

Eaton, Jonathan and Gene M. Grossman (1985), "Tariffs as Insurance: Optimal Commercial Policy when Domestic Markets are Incomplete", *Canadian Journal of Economics*, 18, pp. 258-272.

Finger, J. Michael, M. Keith Hall and Douglas R. Nelson (1982), "The Political Economy of Administered Protection", *American Economic Review*", 72, pp. 452-466.

Godek, Paul E. (1985), "Industry Structure and Redistribution Through Trade Restrictions", *Journal of Law and Economics*, 28, pp. 687-702.

302

Grossman, Gene M. (1986), "Imports as a Cause of Injury: The Case of the U.S. Steel Industry", *Journal of International Economics*", 20, pp. 201-223.

Hillman, Arye L. (1982), "Declining Industries and Political-support Protectionist Motives", *American Economic Review*, 72, pp. 1180-1187.

Hillman, Arye L., Eliakim Katz and Jacob Rosenberg (1987), "Workers as Insurance: Anticipated Government Assistance and Factor Demand", *Oxford Economic Papers*.

Hillman, Arye L., and Heinrich Ursprung (1987), "Foreign Interests, Domestic Politics and International Trade Policy", UCLA Department of Economics.

Hufbauer, Gary C., Diane T. Berliner and Ann Elliott Kimberly (1986), *Trade Protection in the United States: 31 Case Studies*, Institute for International Economics, Washington, D.C.

Marvel, Howard P. and Edward J. Ray (1983), "The Kennedy Round: Evidence on the Regulation of International Trade in the United States", *American Economic Review*, 73, pp. 190-197.

Mayer, Wolfgang (1984), "Endogeneous Tariff Formation", *American Economic Review*, 74, pp. 970-985.

Tumlir, Jan (1987), "International Trade Regimes and Private Property Rights", *Contemporary Policy Issues*, 5 (April), pp. 1-12.

Young, Leslie and Steven P. Magee "Endogeneous Protection, Factor Returns and Resource Allocation", *Review of Economic Studies*, 53 (1986), pp. 407-419.

COMMENTS

Thomas D. Willett

As we have come to expect from his previous work, Arye Hillman's paper offers us a stimulating contribution to the literature on the political economy of international trade policy. I agree strongly with the central theme of his paper that the standard market failure and optimum tariff arguments for trade restrictions explain only a minor portion of actual trade barriers. The major contribution of this paper in my judgment is Hillman's critique of the recently developed literature which seeks to find an efficiency basis for trade restrictions in terms of failures in the market for social insurance. While I would be inclined to see somewhat greater informational barriers to the provision of private insurance against adverse trade developments than may be suggested by Hillman's discussion, I believe that he has offered us an extremely useful and basically sound critique of the pure efficiency based social insurance arguments for trade protection.

Explaining Protectionist Policies

My major differences with Hillman involve his analysis of political support motives. Here I think that it is useful to distinguish more sharply between the narrow self-interested rent seeking motives of those who expect to directly benefit from protection and broader and more public interest motivated motives such as social insurance and foreign policy considerations which may also attract considerable political support. For the purposes of sharpening our analytical understanding of the political economy of trade policy it can be quite useful to highlight the similarities in and differences between particular alternative explanations in a quite stark manner. This is what Hillman does quite well with respect to the conflicts inherent in the political process as viewed in terms of the rent seeking

Studies in International Economics and Institutions
Vosgerau (Ed.) New Institutional Arrangements for the World Economy
© Springer-Verlag Berlin Heidelberg 1989

hypothesis in contrast to the consensual process underlying the efficient social insurance hypothesis.

It is also important, however, to undertake a broad type of political economy analysis which draws on the results of more narrowly-focused contributions such as Hillman's to consider how different explanations may fit together and interact. For example, what are the considerations which influence the relative importance of different types of explanations over time and across different institutional structures and different issue areas? For the particular purposes of Hillman's paper it was quite appropriate to abstract from considerations of bureaucratic politics. On the other hand, if, for example, one were attempting to explain why in the United States the administration of the anti-dumping statutes was switched from the Treasury to the Commerce Department such considerations would become much more important.

To explain satisfactorily the general course of U.S. trade policy developments one must go beyond the two alternative hypotheses examined by Hillman. I have no doubt that the increased international competition faced by U.S. firms over the last two decades has much to do with the increased protectionism of this period and that the rent seeking approach emphasized by Hillman has important explanatory power. In a modified form, however, so does the social insurance hypothesis. As William Niskanen and I both emphasized in our verbal remarks at the conference, political actions are frequently based on the formation of coalitions which include actors with quite different general motivations whose specific interests coincide on particular measures. As the old adage says, politics can make strange bedfellows. Indeed, even for a single actor multiple motives may be important.

It is also important for economists concerned with political economy to understand that many participants in the political process do not think like economists and that the "as if" propositions that we rely upon to justify the use of our profit maximization assumption in the theory of the firm hold much less strongly with respect to the political process. As Michael Finger emphasized, political actors often make decisions which are not based on a sound understanding of the relevant economic analysis. For example, there are many members of Congress who appear to put little if any weight on the economic proposition that trade restrictions are seldom the most efficient way to protect the incomes of domestic firms and workers from the adverse effects of foreign competition. In my experiences in government I found that many participants in the policy process just don't think that way and that such non-economic thinkers often have a decisive influence on particular policy decisions.

While most studies find that elite opinion is predominantly favorable toward liberal trade policies that of the general public in the United States is not.[1] Responses to public opinion polls on trade issues vary and depend very much on how a particular question is phrased. While quite alien to the mind sets of Ph.D. economists, there is a rather widespread belief among the public that trade restrictions will save jobs and that foreign competition can be generally damaging to the domestic economy. Although coming from quite different perceptions than those emphasized in the economics literature on social insurance arguments, such considerations contribute importantly to the formulation of public policy which appears as if the government were operating on the basis of a conservative social welfare function - conservative in the sense of tending to partially offset declines in market determined incomes.

Why this process tends to operate with a special focus on international considerations is something which is still not well understood. My hunch is that it is based far more on non-economic nationalistic views of the world than on the types of moral hazard considerations analyzed by Hillman. There are probably similar explanations for the "special" role of agricultural protection.

In any event, as Hillman emphasizes, we observe that trade protection is typically granted only when domestic industries are facing hard times. We also observe that not all industries facing hard times are equally successful in securing protection. This suggests that the rent seeking and social insurance hypotheses should be viewed in considerable part as complements rather than substitutes within a broad political support perspective. The ability to appeal to broad equity and nationalistic arguments to complement special interest considerations makes it easier to put together political coalitions strong enough to secure the adoption of protectionist

---

[1]   See, for example, Destler (1986) and Goldstein (1987).

measures. Thus to obtain major protection it appears that direct political clout by the industry in question and a plausible (to non-economists) basis for public interest appeals are both typically necessary conditions and neither by itself is typically sufficient.[2]

Alternative Benchmarks for Judging Institutional Structures

Now let me turn to the question of the role of institutional structures. Coming from the standpoint of trade theory, it seems natural to phrase trade policy questions as does Hillman in terms of "why national institutional structures facilitate protectionist responses". However, starting from a pure public choice approach which emphasizes the disproportionate political clout of small well-organized groups, the more relevant question may be why don't we see even more protectionist policies than we have.

Indeed, in the last few years several political scientists have presented cogent arguments for what they have seen as a liberal institutional bias in the American trade policy process.[3] While initially somewhat taken aback by how these political scientists phrased their questions, I have become convinced that their analysis is essentially correct in its broad outlines, and that it is quite consistent with the general thrust of public choice analysis. The question which public choice economists have tended to address is why representative democracy tends to display a bias toward protectionism relative to the benchmark of aggregate economic efficiency, while the question addressed by the political science analysis noted above

---

2   Where the administrative route is pursued the importance of the need for political clout is somewhat diminished. In my judgment this reflects fairly widespread desires to implement a type of social insurance although one whose form is not based on the first best efficiency analysis of economists. For recent discussions of the distinction between the pursuit of protection through established administrative procedures and through direct political actions, see Baldwin (1987), Goldstein (1987), and Finger, et al. (1982).

3   See Destler (1986), Goldstein (1987), and Pastor (1987). I should note, however, that in my judgment Pastor's work in particular overstates the consensual elements in U.S. trade policy formulation.

was how the importance of foreign policy considerations and reforms in the trade policy process have tended to reduce this bias relative to an unconstrained representative democracy. While the political science studies did not use this specific terminology, their benchmark for comparison was typically the process which led to the massive Smoot-Hawley tariff increases in the 1930s. That episode comes much closer to the predictions of a pure domestic interest group model than does post-war U.S. trade policy.

This suggests that the role of executive and Congressional leadership and foreign policy considerations, domestic interest groups, broad public support, and the specific institutional environment are all important elements of a satisfactory treatment of the political economy of trade policy.[4] While this is a broad list, it stops far short of throwing up one's hands and arguing that everything is important. We can in fact usefully trace the evolution of trade policy over time in terms of the changing importance of these considerations. For example, we can see both a cyclical element in protectionist pressures related to domestic business conditions and a trend toward increased protection over time brought about by the secular decline in the U.S. competitive conditions over the past two decades.[5] This is combined with the foreign policy and institutional checks considerations which have contained these pressures much more than during the Great Depression of the 1930s.[6]

In terms of the focus of this conference on international institutional structures such broader political economy analysis offers some basis for hope that international institutional agreements to limit the propensities of national governments to give in to domestic protectionist pressures have the potential for at least some modest degree of effectiveness. So does a continued emphasis on international

---

[4] On the role which ideological considerations can play within a public choice approach to political economy see the discussion and references in Marks and McArthur (1987), McArthur and Marks (forthcoming) and North (1984).

[5] For recent examples and references to earlier empirical studies on the determinants of protectionist policies see Baldwin (1985), Stern (1987) and Marks and McArthur (1987).

[6] For efforts to do so on my part see Willett (1980) and Odell and Willett (1987). See, also, Baldwin (1984).

cooperation among national leaders. Indeed, while it has become fashionable to decry the limited actions which have come out of the series of economic summits among the leaders of the major industrial countries, these meetings may have had some of their greatest importance in terms of what they helped keep from happening. While the world is far more protectionist than economists would like to see, it is still far less protectionist than during the 1930s despite all of the instabilities of the oil price shocks, stagflation, and widely-fluctuating exchange rates over the past two decades. In undertaking political economy analysis we should keep both of these benchmarks in mind.[7]

References

Baldwin, Robert E. (1984), "The Changing Nature of U.S. Trade Policy Since World War II", in Baldwin, R.E. and A.O. Krueger (eds.), *The Structure and Evolution of Recent U.S. Trade Policy*, University of Chicago Press, Chicago.

Baldwin, Robert E. (1985), *The Political Economy of U.S. Import Policy*, MIT Press, Cambridge.

Destler, I.M. (1986), *American Trade Politics: System Under Stress*, Institute for International Economics, Washington, D.C.

Goldstein, Judith (1987), "The Political Economy of Trade: Institutions of Protection", *American Political Science Review*, 80, pp. 161-184.

Finger, J.M., H.K. Hall and D.R. Nelson (1982), "The Political Economy of Administered Protection", *American Economic Review*, 72, pp. 452-466.

McArthur, John and Stephen Marks, "Constituent Interest vs. Legislator Ideology: The Role of Political Opportunity Cost", *Economic Inquiry* (forthcoming).

Marks, Stephen and John McArthur (1987), "Empirical Analyses of the Determinants of Protection: A Survey and Some New Results", paper presented at the Claremont-USC Conference on Blending Political and Economic Analysis of International Trade Policies (March), available as a Claremont Working Paper, The Claremont Center for Economic Studies, Department of Economics, Claremont Graduate School, Claremont, California.

---

[7] For further discussion and references to the literature on alternative benchmarks see Wihlborg (1987).

North, Douglas (1984), "Three Approaches to the Study of Institutions", in David C. Colander (ed.), *Neoclassical Political Economy: The Analysis of Rent-Seeking and DUP Activities*, Ballinger Publishing Co., Cambridge, Mass., pp. 33-40.

Odell, John and Thomas D. Willett (1987), "Influences on U.S. Trade Policies: Experiences and Outlook", presented at the Conference on Trade Policies and International Business Decisions, University of Southern California, April 2-4, 1987. Available as a Claremont Working Paper, The Claremont Center for Economic Studies, Department of Economics, Claremont Graduate School, Claremont, California.

Pastor, Robert (1980), *Congress and the Politics of U.S. Foreign Economic Policy: 1929 - 1976*, University of California Press, Berkeley.

Stern, Robert M. (ed.), (1987), *U.S. Trade Policies in a Changing World Economy*, MIT Press, Cambridge, Mass.

Wihlborg, Clas (1987), "Proposals for Reforming National Structures for Policy Making on International Trade", presented at the Claremont-USC Conference on Blending Political and Economic Analysis of International Trade Policy (March 1987), available as a Claremont Working Paper, The Claremont Center for Economic Studies, Department of Economics, Claremont Graduate School, Claremont, California.

Willett, Thomas D. (1980), "Some Aspects of the Public Choice Approach to International Economic Relations", Claremont Working Paper (January), The Claremont Center for Economic Studies, Department of Economics, Claremont Graduate School, Claremont, California.

Protectionist Rules and Internationalist Discretion in the Making of National Trade Policy

J. Michael Finger

The post-World War II deliberations on institutional arrangements for the world economy were successful in leading to the establishment of the International Monetary Fund and the World Bank. However, the proposed International Trade Organization which would regulate international trade was not to be. There was a general reluctance among governments to accept institutionalized restrictions on the conduct of countries' national trade policies. At the same time the ITO negotiations over the "rules" of the trading system were unsuccessful, the community of nations reached agreement on a significant package of reciprocal tariff reductions. The document or contract which gave legal effect to the agreed reduction of tariffs included three functional parts. The first of these committed each participating country to allow other participants access to its market at least as favorable as the schedule of its import restrictions it annexed to the agreement. When agreement involved reductions of tariffs, the negotiated reductions over previous rates were reflected in this schedule. Each schedule, the parties agreed, would be subject to MFN treatment within the group.[1]

The second functional part of the agreement defined the circumstances under which a country might go back on the access it had guaranteed to its trading partners in the first part, e.g., restrictions to safeguard the balance of payments, anti-dumping and countervailing duties, etc. The third functional part deals with dispute settlement or restitution - what a country can do when it senses that some benefits to it under the contract have been compromised.

---

[1] This is essentially Articles I, II, III, VII, VIII, IX and X. These articles require the posting of schedules, MFN treatment, and cut off loopholes such as inflated customs valuation, excise taxes differentially imposed on imports, etc.

Studies in International Economics and Institutions
Vosgerau (Ed.) New Institutional Arrangements for the World Economy
© Springer-Verlag Berlin Heidelberg 1989

This "contract" was, and still is, called the General Agreement on Tariffs and Trade, GATT. The GATT has, in its own language, not "members" but "contracting parties". Thus the basic institutional structure of the post-World War II international trading system is not an agreed set of rules. It is a contract through which a nation party to the contract exchanges access to its domestic market for access to the domestic markets of the other parties. This exchange of market access is subject to extensive and specific reservations as to the circumstances under which (and the procedures through which) a country may reduce this access, i.e., impose import restrictions.

The same contract, when viewed from a national rather than an international perspective, becomes a statement of the circumstances in and procedures by which a nation may impose import restrictions, subject however to the reservations it has placed upon itself in the granting of access to foreigners. Taken a step further, into national laws and regulations which provide actual legal substance to a nation's perspective on this contract, the circumstances under which a country may impose import restrictions become the rights of particular interests within the country to protection from import competition.[2] The government of a GATT contracting party is then caught between this right which national law and regulation guarantee to domestic interests and the market access it has granted to foreigners through international agreement.

Within this broad view of institutional structure, this paper will review the process in the United States of deciding and imposing trade restrictions. The focus is on the implicit property-rights conception underlying the national justification for trade intervention in the trade remedy laws of the US. The reader should note that the paper is about protection and not about trade liberalization. The "GATT system" includes two distinct mechanisms. The better known of these is the tariff negotiations process, through which trade barriers can be removed, but not imposed. This paper is about the less well-known "administered protection" process, a national one, subject to international constraints.

---

[2] The historical shift of perspective, from GATT as international agreement to maintain an open trading system to GATT as international recognition of the rights of nations to impose import restrictions, is taken up by Finger (1986).

The following section of this paper describes the formalization of the GATT contract into national law in the United States. I identify the underlying property rights conception then use this conception to explain why the VER is a popular form of import restriction. I also examine in the same context recent changes of US trade law. The argument for the validity of the model is the usual one - it helps to make sense of what we observe in the real world.

I.   The Structure of Administered Protection in the United States

Governments everywhere are subject to pressure to implement import restrictions to the benefit of particular groups. It follows that national government will have established "ways" or "tracks" to respond to or manage these pressures. Though these national tracks are, in each of the major industrial countries, more or less consistent with the GATT, their national forms tend to be quite different from one country to another. In the United States current law provides six tracks to which a domestic firm or industry may petition the US government for relief from import competition, i.e. for protection. These are:

(1)   Escape clause or safeguards (201 cases);

(2)   Antidumping;

(3)   Antisubsidy or countervailing duty;

(4)   Unfair trade practices actions (301 cases);

(5)   Unfair import practices (337 cases);

(6)   Market disruption (406 cases).

An escape clause or safeguards case is an investigation of injury to a US industry resulting from increased imports. Petitions are filed with and investigations are conducted by the International Trade Commission. The responsibility of the International Trade Commission is to determine whether or not injury is occurring to the named US industry. If the injury determination is affirmative, the ITC recommends a remedy to the President. This remedy might be imposition of tariffs, imposition of quantitative restrictions or other forms of import controls or it might be adjustment assistance without the imposition of any border measure to restrict imports. If the President chooses not to implement import relief different from that recommended by the ITC, his decision is subject to Congressional override.

Antidumping petitions are filed simultaneously with the ITC and with the International Trade Administration (ITA) of the Department of Commerce. An antidumping case entails two separate investigations: a material injury investigation (conducted by the ITC) and a sales at "less than fair value" investigation (conducted by the ITA). If both material injury and sales at less than fair value are found to exist, the Department of Commerce is required by law to impose antidumping duties in the amount of the dumping margin. The antidumping law provides specific opportunities for an agreement to be reached between the petitioning domestic party and the foreign party to terminate the case. Grounds for such agreed termination are almost always an enforceable and monitorable commitment by the foreign seller to eliminate the dumping practice, i.e. to raise the price it charges in the US market.

Countervailing duty cases, like dumping cases, are carried out under the authority of the Department of Commerce, the ITA. Cases involve an investigation of subsidy conducted by the ITA, and in most instances, an injury investigation conducted by the ITC. Injury investigations are carried out in all cases concerning duty-free goods and in those cases involving signatories to the GATT-subsidies code, against Taiwan and against all countries to whom the US has extended by treaty unconditional most-favored-nations status. In affirmatively determined cases, the Department of Commerce is required by law to impose a countervailing duty equal to the net foreign subsidy. As with the antidumping law, the countervailing duty law provides opportunities for a case to be terminated upon agreement between the petitioning party and exporter. Again, such agreement is conditioned upon an enforceable and monitorable commitment by the foreign party to eliminate the subsidy practice.

"Section 301" provides the President authority to act (1) to enforce US rights under a trade agreement; (2) to respond to a foreign government act or policy which is inconsistent with a trade agreement with the United States or which denies the benefits to the US interest under such an agreement; (3) on actions or policies of foreign government which are inconsistent with international obligations other than those arising under the GATT (for example, violations of a treaty of friendship, commerce and navigation) when those policies or actions oppress, restrict or burden US commerce. Under this section a complaint is brought by the US firm or industry to the Office of the US Trade Representative. The US Trade Representative investigates to determine if the alleged violation exists. Section 301 cases often involve the interests of United States exporters. For example, petitions by US insurance firms for access to the Korean insurance markets took the legal form of a 301 petition, based on a section of the US-Korea treaty of friendship and navigation. If the USTR formally determines that the alleged violation exists, then the President of the United States has the legal authority to take a variety of actions against the offending party, including the possibility of imposing import restrictions against the products of that country. This "retaliation" against the exports of the country to the United States may be applied on any product or service - it is not limited to product or service on which the foreign practice is applied.

Section 301 required the USTR to activate GATT dispute settlement procedures in parallel with its pursuit of the matter under US law, but the authority the section provides the President to retaliate is in no way conditioned on the outcome of the GATT process, though at a discretionary level, a GATT panel's decision as to the "GATT legality" of the accused foreign practice would carry great weight in the STR's determination. In practice, most cases are settled by bilateral negotiations between the US government and the country responsible for the violation. The "determination" part of the act functions primarily to force a negotiated settlement - to provide the President with the legal authority to impose sanctions on the violating country if the country does not reach agreement.

Section 337 of the Tariff Act of 1930 declares unlawful certain methods of competition in import trade, which might destroy or substantially injure a domestic industry, prevent the establishment of an industry or might restrain or monopolize trade and commerce in the United States. Most cases under this section involve patent infringement. Complaints are filed with and investigations are conducted by the International Trade Commission. The International Trade Commission might also investigate on its own initiative a suspected violation. If the ITC determines that the violation exists, it may recommend that the offending party not be allowed to sell that particular article in the United States. As with 301 cases, implementation of this recommendation is subject to Presidential discretion.

Section 406 causes concern market disruption resulting from imports from communist countries. They are decided by the ITC and sent to the President for a decision or final determination. The President's decision is subject to Congressional override if he rejects or modifies the ITC recommendation.

Rights to Protection

These trade remedy laws define the *rights* of particular interests within the US economy to import protection - or in the case of Article 301, to the use of import restrictions as a device for enforcing the right of a US interest to export a particular product to a particular market. There is no parallel right given to buyers of imports, no parallel right to access to imports by those interests in the US economy which benefit from this access.

The simplest illustration is the safeguards or escape clause. This clause is concerned only with injury to a domestic industry from import competition. It brings forward no question of the fairness or unfairness of the foreign trade practice which underlies these imports. The ITC investigation is aimed at and limited to whether or not there has been or likely to be injury to the "domestic industry producing an article like or directly competitive with the imported article".

The other five trade remedy figures all begin with the specification of a foreign practice which is considered "unfair". The specification of what is "unfair" is multilateral or international, in the sense that national anti-subsidy and anti-dumping practices are recognized under the General Agreement on Tariffs and Trade. In similar but not identical fashion, Section 301 takes care to deal with trade practices which are illegal under the GATT or some other international agreement (Section 301 goes beyond antisubsidy and antidumping provisions in US law in that they are more open-ended - relating to any form of inconsistent practice, not just a specified one). These matters are, however, unilateral in the sense that a national authority makes the determination of whether or not the practice in question is, in fact, dumping or some other practice proscribed by international agreement.

The conception of fair on which each of these tracks is based relates to the effects of the trading practice on competing US producers and, like the escape clause, does not take into account possible benefits to users.

Building trade policy on a conception of when a domestic interest has a right to protection has a long history in US policymaking. Schattsneider's book on the making of the Smoot-Hawley Tariff demonstrates that the "equalization tariff" idea – that the tariff should equalize the costs of producing a good outside the United States with the costs of producing it inside the United States – dominated both government and industry thinking. Indeed the equalization formula for when and how much protection an industry "should" receive stayed in the US policymaking apparatus when the reciprocal trade agreements approach was developed. In preparation for early rounds of multilateral tariff negotiations under the GATT, the ITC was required to conduct "peril points" investigations, to determine the floor below which a tariff would not be cut by the President. The cost equalization idea and the contemporary unfair trade practices idea are both "institutions" in the anthropologist's sense of the term – part of the folkways of the society, something widely enough believed within the society that it is hardly ever questioned. (When such a folkway is questioned, the raising of the question brings more suspicion to bear on the person who raises the question than on the concept itself.) Though the cost equalization idea dominated the construction of the tariff before reciprocal trade agreements days, it was not legislated into a specific legal form until later, as the "peril points" idea. In the new mechanics for making trade restrictions, the unfair trade practices concept is an institution in the anthropologist's sense, and it also has a direct expression in the law, as the rules part of the trade remedies legislation.

Overriding Discretion

The idea of injury which is basic to the escape clause and a significant part of unfair trade practices tracks to import relief is in economics the mirror image of comparative advantage. Thus the rules part of the trade remedies laws makes protection available or callable by virtually every part of the domestic economy which competes with imports. If this were the only part of the trade remedies laws, the outcome of the mechanism would be high levels of protection for all sectors of the domestic economy.

The offsetting factor is the discretionary authority the law provides the President of the United States to reject rules-based determinations and recommendations. The escape clause specifies that the President may set aside the recommendation for import relief based on the determination of injury to a domestic industry, if, in his opinion, such action would be contrary to "the national economic interest of the United States". The unfair trade practices tracks (excepting the antisubsidy and antidumping tracks) allow the President to set aside a recommendation for import-restricting actions if in his judgment such actions are not in the "policy interest" of the United States.

Excepting the antisubsidy and antidumping tracks from this legal generalization does not compromise the basic point that these rules tracks set out the rights of a domestic interest to protection and that the President has discretionary authority to set those rights aside. The tracks define the rights of domestic interests to protec-tion, but they do not define the *form* that protection will take. In practice, small matters are resolved by the rules, via a formal antisubsidy or antidumping or escape clause action. A large matter (measured by value of imports or of domestic production covered by the case), whether it begins as a dumping case or as an escape clause case, will usually lead to a negotiated settlement in which the con-straints on the President are political (he has to do something or he will lose sig-nificant support) rather than legal.[3]

In sum, domestic interests that would gain from import restrictions are given sub-stance and form in the trade remedies law. Conversely, the rights of domestic interests which bear the costs of import restrictions are given neither substance nor form. To the extent that there is a countervailing force to domestic protectionist interests, that force is not the domestic loss from protection. The discretion pro-vided the President is to allow him to implement the foreign policy interests of the United States and to respect the rights of access to the US market which the US

---

[3] See Finger, Hall and Nelson (1987) on this point.

government has surrendered, through the GATT negotiations, to foreign governments.

The meaning of the phrase "policy interest of the United States" in the unfair trade practices part of the trade remedies laws has the traditional international relations meaning - that the foreign policy interest of the United States lies in "the promotion and maintenance of stability and peace through economic means". Trade is, in this conception , not a source of mutual gain but a close parallel to foreign aid - the provision of income to foreign persons by the people of the United States, admittedly a material "cost" to the people of the United States, though one defended as necessary to achieve peace and political stability. The US executive branch, in seeking Congressional support for a US leadership role in international affairs, has usually presented its case as involving economic cost to the US.[4]

The discretion given to the President to set aside a domestic claim to protection also reflects the rights to the US market that the US government has granted to foreigners. Foreign rights to the US market are institutionalized through the trade negotiations process. In the simplest sense, the foreigners *buy* access to the US market by giving similar access to the US - by making similar "GATT concessions" to the United States. This is a straightforward application of institutionalized respect or contracts - "a deal is a deal".

The idea that the foreigner has an institutionalized right to access to the US market is reinforced by the GATT conception of "enforcement" or "dispute settlement". While it is common to think of the GATT as "the law" of international trade, the GATT as an international organization has very limited enforcement authority. Being a contracting party to the GATT implies that the standard the GATT expresses will be incorporated into the contracting party's national laws and regulations. The legal force behind these standards is then national rather than international. At an international level the dispute settlement provisions of the GATT (Article 23) do not focus on correcting a possible violation of the rules. The provisions provide that an individual country may bring a matter to the attention of the entire membership for their assistance in resolving the problem or issue if that

---

[4]   On this point, see Nelson (1987), p. 20 and references cited there.

individual country "should consider that any benefit accruing to it directly or indirectly under this agreement is being nullified or impaired". Article 23 goes on to provide that nullification or impairment of benefits might be the result of

(1) another country's action or policy in violation of the GATT;

(2) another country's action or policy which does not conflict with the GATT;

(3) The "existence of any other situation".

Thus, the dispute settlement mechanism of the GATT emphasizes a basic conception on which the agreement is built - GATT membership confers benefits to a country and the substance of these benefits is access to the markets of other countries.

The legislative history of the phrase "national economic interest of the United States" (in the escape clause) demonstrates the implicit conception that foreign access to the US market is a *cost* to the US economy. During drafting of the Trade Act of 1974, the Senate Finance Committee proposed to eliminate Presidential discretion in escape clause cases - to require the President to provide import relief when the ITC returned a positive determination of injury. (The President, in setting aside ITC findings, had often cited foreign policy interests.) The executive resisted this change, the eventual compromise being introduction of the condition that the President shall follow the ITC recommendation unless he determines that to do so is "not in the national *economic* interest of the US" (emphasis added). In directing the president toward the domestic *economic* effects of the US, the Senate Finance Committee assumed they would be directing the President toward protection - implicitly, that the national economic interest of the US was correctly defined by the escape clause, i.e. by the injury concept, and that the President should be less willing to sacrifice these interests for the interest of the world.[5]

---

5   William Ris (1977) relates the legislative history of the 1974 changes in the escape clause.

II. Applications

The institutional framework for the management of pressures for protection in the US is based on a property rights specification not readily reconcilable with freedom of international trade. The gains from trade derive from a perception of mutual advantage to trading partners, a view that gives equal weight to consumers and the expansion of their consumption opportunities as to producers and the expansion of their production opportunities. The trade remedy laws specify property rights to domestic producers. They also provide the President with the discretion to set aside these rights when, in the President's perception, they conflict with (a) obligations created through reciprocal concessions under the GATT to allow foreign producers' access to the US market, and/or (b) the foreign policy interests of the US.

The Form of Protection

Whereas the welfare propositions of international-trade theory focus on the gains from trade to consumers, the national trade laws focus on the rights of producers. The "domestic dialogue" regarding proposed import restrictions is as a consequence one-sided. Injury to producers is emphasized with no reference to the gains to consumers. Foreigners who benefit or from access of their goods to the domestic market have rights insofar as these rights have been exchanged for rights given to domestic producers, and then only subject to final national discretion regarding what constitutes a fair international trade practice.

Viewed in this setting, recent developments in the manner of conduct of inter-national trade policy are readily explicable. For example, voluntary export restraints provide relief from injury to domestic import-competing producers. At the same time, foreign profits are enhanced. The rents created by a VER provide a substantial transfer from the protected economy exporters. In this way the home government effectively repurchases the foreigners' right of access to the domestic market.

Evolution of US Trade Law

It follows from this institutional structure that domestic interests have an incentive to apply themselves to expanding the scope of the rules part of the law and to narrowing the degree of Presidential discretion to override the rules in the interest of foreigners. Robert Baldwin (1985) has tabulated changes in US trade law which specifically restrict the President's discretionary authority. In 1951 the Trade Act required that if the President rejected an ITC recommendation for import relief, he must submit to Congress an explanatory statement. In 1958 the Trade Act was changed to allow the Congress to override the President's rejection of an ITC recommendation by a two-thirds vote of the membership of each house of Congress. In 1962 the necessary vote was reduced to a simple majority to authorized membership of each house and in 1974 the overriding requirement was reduced to a simple majority of members present in voting. Bills currently before the Congress would eliminate the President's discretion to override a recommendation action which came from an unfair trade practices case. These bills would also make bilateral trade imbalances beyond a certain size "actionable" under trade remedies laws.

The GATT contract does not recognize the right to gain or maintain access to a foreign market through the use of unfair trade practices. Thus there has been through the 80s the sequential expansion of the unfair trade practices part of the trade remedies laws, an expansion which has increased *the range of foreign actions or policies which are grounds for relief from import competition.

The US-Canada Lumber Case

As a further example, sense is made of the manner whereby restrictions have recently come to be imposed on US imports of Canadian lumber.[6] Responding to a plea from US lumber producers, the US government imposed an antidumping tariff of 15 percent on Canadian softwood construction lumber in October 1986, but indicated that the tariff would be removed if the Canadian government were to impose an export tax of the same percentage. The Canadians complied on January 1, 1987. The US thereby transferred some estimated $220 (US) million of annual revenue from the US to Canada. The puzzle might be why the US insisted on the transfer. As Joseph Kalt (1987) has observed in his study of this protectionist episode, the US started a trade war which it then deliberately proceeded to lose by

---

[6]   I am indebted to Arye L. Hillman for this example.

insisting that its monopsonistic tariff be replaced by a Canadian monopolistic tariff. Again the sequence of events is consistent with the property rights concept of the national trade laws. Protection relieved domestic injury as a right of the domestic injured party, but foreigners were compensated for the loss of their right of US market access. Indeed, the final indication is that the revenue accruing to the Canadian federal government from the export tax was transferred to the injured parties, via redistribution to the provinces and allocation to forest improvement.[7]

III. Conclusions, Speculations

If the economics profession was polled on the issue "Which do you see as better, free trade or protection?", it is likely that a substantial majority would vote for free trade. If the same persons were asked "Do you prefer rules or discretion?", a large majority would likely choose "rules". Free traders might be particularly favorable to rules. For example, the *Economist* describes the agreement to hold another round of GATT negotiations as follows: "They agreed to reassert GATT's authority by strengthening the rules and enforcing them better; to halt new protectionist measures and to dismantle existing barriers to trade."[8]

While it seems intuitively proper to suggest a world trading system built on rules rather than on discretion, one must recognize that the rules built into the present system are essentially protectionist, and that the continuing openness of the system depends on the discretion the system allows to put the rules aside in order to maintain a delicate balance of agreed market access. Elaborating existing rules, e.g. the "Codes" negotiated at the Tokyo Round are not an effective way to maintain the openness of the international system. The system does not need more rules, it needs better rules - rules which give the gains (and the gainers) from trade the same legal standing now provide the losses. A user of imports whose costs are increased by restrictions his government places on access to imports should be provided a way to petition for removal of those restrictions.

---

[7] See Hillman (1987) for elaboration.

[8] *Economist*, p. 70.

References

Baldwin, R. (1985), *The Political Economy of US Import Policy*, MIT Press, Cambridge, Mass.

Clark, L.H. Jr. (1986), "GATT Needs New Morale, Not New Rules", *Wall Street Journal*, October 21.

The Economist (1987), "GATT Negotiators Under Fire", (July 16), p.70f.

Finger, J.M. (1986), "Ideas Count, Words Inform", in R.H. Snape (ed.*), Issues in World Trade Policy*, London, MacMillan.

Finger, J.M., K. Hall and D. Nelson (1982), "The Political Economy of Administered Protection", *American Economic Review*, 72, pp. 452-466.

GATT Study Group (1986), *Trade Policies for a Better World*, Geneva, GATT, 1985; reprinted in part as "The Way Forward", in R.E. Baldwin and J.D. Richardson (eds.), *International Trade and Finance*, Little Brown and Co, Boston, pp. 199-213.

Grossman, G.M. (1986), "Imports as a Cause of Injury: The Case of the US Steel Industry", *Journal of International Economics* 20 (May), pp. 201-233.

Hillman, A.L., "The Political Economy of Protection: Comment", forthcoming in Robert Baldwin (ed.), *Trade Policy Issues and Empirical Analysis*, University of Chicago Press for NBER.

Kalt, J., "The Political Economy of Protectionism: Tariffs and Retaliation in the Timber Industry", forthcoming in Robert Baldwin (ed.), *Trade Policy Issues and Empirical Analysis*, University of Chicago Press for NBER.

Nelson, Douglas H. (1987), "The Domestic Political Preconditions of US Trade Policy: Liberal Structure and Protectionist Dynamics", Paper prepared for the World Bank Conference on "Political Economy: Theory and Policy Implications", Washington, D.C., June 17-19.

Ris, William K., Jr. (1977), "Escape Clause Relief under the Trade Act of 1974: New Standards, Some Results", *Columbus Journal of Transnational Law*, 16, pp. 297-325.

Schattsneider, F.F. (1935), *Politics, Pressures and the Tariff*, New York Prentice-Hall.

Vaubel, R. (1986), "A Public Choice Approach to International Organization", *Public Choice*, No. 1, 55, pp. 39-57.

Witzke, von, H. (1986), "Endogeneous Supranational Policy Decisions: The Common Agricultural Policy of the European Community", *Public Choice*, No. 2, 48, pp. 157-174.

COMMENTS

Gary C. Hufbauer

It is well known that the General Agreement on Tariffs and Trade contains two major components:

(1)   The trade liberalization component: this includes the framework for trade negotiations and tariff bindings, the unconditional most-favored-nation rule, and the national treatment rule;

(2)   The mercantilistic component: this includes national rights to raise non-bound tariffs, to impose countervailing and antidumping duties, to exclude government procurement from national treatment, and so forth.

In surveying United States trade policy, Michael Finger concludes that the mercantilistic component of GATT has been used not so much as a framework for implementing *national* policy, but rather as a framework for exercising *producers' property rights*. The property rights in question entail closing the domestic market to foreign suppliers who, in one fashion or another, have displayed "obnoxious" behavior.

At Congressional insistence, U.S. trade laws enacted since the 1970s - the Trade Act of 1974, 1979, 1984, and now 1987 - have created a succession of new producers' property rights within (and sometimes outside) the umbrella of the mercantilistic component of GATT. In similar fashion, Presidents Nixon, Ford, Carter and Reagan granted extensive "administered" protection to powerful industries - textiles, steel, automobiles, among others - thereby encouraging the idea that the domestic market belongs to domestic producers.

Studies in International Economics and Institutions
Vosgerau (Ed.) New Institutional Arrangements for the World Economy
© Springer-Verlag Berlin Heidelberg 1989

Finger's conception of the mercantilistic component of GATT echoes the teachings of the "public choice" school (pioneered by James Buchanan and Gordon Tuloch). Public choice economists argue that, over time, statutory and administrative law will become ever more encrusted with rent-seeking practices, until finally the legal apparatus collapses from the weight of its own waste. According to this view, there is very little that academics can do to arrest the rent-seeking process. At best, they can illuminate the disease, in hopes that the victims of rent-seeking will put up a stronger and better informed fight.

However, an optimist would argue that not all legislators and bureaucrats become handmaidens of special interests. Some political leaders, in fact, retain a capacity for statesmanship. I am an optimist. Finger's paper accordingly prompts me to explore three avenues by which statesmen might alter the property rules to achieve more liberal trade results:

1. Repeal or limit the existing rights of action that enable domestic producers to claim import protection.

2. Enlarge the President's discretion to override producers' property rights in the domestic market.

3. Create offsetting property rights for those producers who have a stake in open markets.

1. Repeal Existing Producers Property Rights to Import Protection

America's trading partners would surely applaud the repeal of existing property rights that are used to restrict foreign access to the domestic market. However, any such legislation would run counter to strong tides now flowing through Washington.

The tides may be illustrated by the Trade Act of 1987. At this time (August 1987), the Conference Committee has not yet met and it is uncertain whether the Conference bill will become law. However, nestled in the Senate and House bills are numerous provisions designed to aid particular industries. Most of those provisions are disguised in the more general framework of the antidumping and countervailing duty laws. Among the domestic industries that would benefit from the creation of new property rights in the "unfair" trade statutes are titanium, ammonia, cement and aircraft.

In addition, the expanded antidumping laws would impose new burdens on "repeat offenders", on "downstream dumping", and on non-market economies. One provision in the Senate bill would significantly expand the scope of countervailable subsidies to cover virtually any form of government assistance, such as electric power supplied by a state-owned utility. The Senate bill would also create new private rights of action against foreign suppliers when the domestic producer alleges copyright violation, patent infringement, or customs fraud. All these may seem like technical provisions, but in the hands of skilled attorneys they can become weapons for chilling large amounts of trade.

For the moment, therefore, talk of curbing property rights seems altogether fanciful. Indeed, U.S. trade legislation is moving in the opposite direction. The Uruguay Round of trade negotiations, however, might make it possible to curtail private rights of action on a reciprocal basis. For example, Japan, the European Community, and the United States might give each other's producers much greater access to their markets for government procurement.

Yet even in the context of trade negotiations, reform will have to be introduced with subtlety and stealth. Consider, for example, the Canada-U.S. talks on freer trade. A major Canadian objective is to limit the pre-1987 countervailing duty and antidumping duty laws (not to mention the changes threatened in the Trade Act of 1987). Congressional reaction to this proposal has been strongly negative, even though Congressional disposition toward an agreement with Canada is quite favorable.

2. Enlarge Presidential Discretion

Present law permits the President to override property interests that would otherwise flow from domestic trade legislation. Presidential discretion is most pronounced when domestic producers seek relief under Section 201, or retaliation against "unjustifiable" or "unreasonable" foreign restrictions under Section 301. Considerable Presidential discretion also exists when novel issues arise under the countervailing duty and antidumping duty statutes, or when the industry seeks a settlement other than the statutory duty. But, as Finger points out, the pattern of trade legislation since the 1960s has been to limit the President's discretion to override producers' property rights.

The Trade Act of 1987 continues this pattern. Indeed, the major procedural theme of the 1987 Act is to reduce Presidential discretion. The bills reported out by the House and Senate would curtail Presidential discretion to deny relief in four major substantive areas:

(a) The bills would loosely "mandate" retaliation when foreign countries restrict U.S. access to foreign markets: Presidential discretion to sidetrack Section 301 petitions would be diminished, but not eliminated.

(b) The bills would make escape clause relief procedurally similar to countervailing duty and antidumping duty relief: the President could mold the *form* of relief, and to some extent its *level*, but not the *existence* of relief.

(c) The bills would circumscribe Presidential access to "fast track" Congressional procedures for passing legislation that would implement the bargains reached in the Uruguay Round negotiations.

(d) The bills would enlarge the "automatic" administrative law rights found in the countervailing duty, antidumping duty, patent infringement and other "unfair" trade laws.

Paradoxically, the first two limitations on Presidential discretion might end up servicing the interests of a liberal trading system. The trading system today might be much better off if Presidents Carter and Reagan had more frequently used their discretionary powers to grant escape clause relief and Section 301 relief; and, at the same time, had less frequently used their discretionary powers to grant "voluntary" export restraints and other quantitative limitations on imports. The flowering of quantitative restraints in the late 1970s and 1980s has been the most damaging aspect of U.S. trade policy in recent years.

The second two limitations on Presidential discretion found in the Trade Act of 1987 are more questionable. It is not helpful to hobble the President's power to enact the Uruguay Round results; nor is it useful to enlarge the scope of "automatic" trade restrictions that flow from the "unfair" trade law process.

At this juncture, however, it is politically implausible to expand Presidential discretion to *deny* property rights. But again, in the context of legislation that implements the Uruguay Round agreements, it might be possible to give the President a wider range of *forms* to meet the property rights claims of producer interests. The Uruguay Round negotiations could point to such changes as relief through the use of auctioned quotas, relief financed by general revenues, relief via uniform taxes on domestic and imported goods, and relief through low rate tariffs - all in preference to the quantitative trade restraints that have become so ubiquitous.

3. Create Offsetting Property Rights

The third major way to answer the creeping growth of property rights for producers that want controlled access to domestic markets might involve the creation of offsetting property rights for producers that want open access to both domestic and foreign markets. Market-opening creates rents for low-cost producers just as surely as market-closing creates rents for those with favored access. And the creation of new legal rights for rent-seekers interested in prying open markets is not altogether fanciful. Indeed, the broad thrust of the Trade Act of 1987 to open foreign markets for U.S. exporters represents a conceptual step in this direction. Another step in the same direction: the Senate bill provisions that would require the International Trade Commission to assess the impact of escape clause relief on industrial and household consumers.

Many other market-opening possibilities can be imagined. For example, a "clean hands" defense might be created in the antidumping and countervailing duty statutes: the petitioning firm would be precluded from seeking relief if it engaged in similar "unfair" practices. Another possibility: the Uruguay Round negotiations could create a procedure for the private enforcement of GATT rights, especially Article 23 relating to the nullification of impairment of GATT benefits. This procedure would enable affected producers to complain about "voluntary" export restraints and other measures that erode GATT benefits.

To conclude: it may be true, as Finger asserts, that U.S. domestic producers now control the use of the mercantilistic provisions in GATT. However, rent-seeking is a two-edged sword. If there are statesmen left in the American political system, there is no reason why they cannot redesign the private property aspects of trade law to place much greater emphasis on market-opening measures.

IV. Institutional Arrangements for International Production

Institutional Arrangements for Natural Resources

Horst Siebert[*]

World wide, institutional arrangements for natural resources have undergone a major redesign in the last twenty years. Property rights for reserves of oil and minerals have effectively gone over from international firms to the resource countries. For some renewable resources threatened by extinction such as endangered species new property rights have been established. The "High Sea", the "res nullius" (Hugo Grotius 1601) or a non-property up to now, has different subsets of property titles attached to it such as the 200 mile economic zones, international fishing commissions and schemes for using the minerals of the sea bottom. Environmental scarcity - another aspect of nature's resources - has forced the industrial nations to introduce major laws regulating the national use of the environment as a receptacle of waste. A series of transfrontier pollution problems like the acid rain in Europe or global issues such as the protection of the ozone layer still have to be solved. Eventually, property rights for the atmosphere or outer space will have to be developed.

Institutional arrangements and property rights are related concepts. A property right specifies the allowable use of resources and goods and it may be envisioned as a set of norms and sanctions, legal rules and procedures as well as informal ways defining the feasible set for decision making of the individual units of an economy. In contrast to such a narrowly interpreted concept of a property right institutional arrangement is a wider term including a set of property rights, for instance for an economy, as well as relationships among autonomous economic units such as contracts. More specifically, institutional arrangement suggests a broader term of norms and rules including such concepts as the incentive system of an economy, "Ordnung" and the economic constitution.

---

[*]   I appreciate comments from D. Folkerts-Landau, B. Frey, J. Keck, C. Kirchner, E. Mohr and G. Ronning.

Studies in International Economics and Institutions
Vosgerau (Ed.) New Institutional Arrangements for the World Economy
© Springer-Verlag Berlin Heidelberg 1989

Institutional arrangements for natural resources may be a matter of contractual relations between private organizations such as resource suppliers and buyers. But in many instances the government is involved as one partner in the contractual relationship, for instance by defining taxation schemes for the resource industry. Governments will come in when merit goods are at stake such as securing part of the resource rents for the country or taking into account the interest of future generations, and when public goods are involved, for instance in the case of environmental quality.

What is so specific about property rights and institutional arrangements for natural resources? Our contention is that natural resources exhibit specific characteristics that have implications for institutional arrangements. Analyzing these implications will provide additional insights into institutional economics and may permit analogies to institutional arrangements for other economic issues. In section 1, we study some specifics of natural resources and of their use. Among the many characteristics, different types of risk evolve as an important category. Risk allocation and risk management is therefore at the core of institutional arrangements for natural resources. In the case of private risks, contractual arrangements can be used to shift some of the risk from one agent to another. These contractual relationships such as extraction rights and long-term contracts and their risk shifting properties will be addressed in section 2. Contractual arrangements may not be incentive compatible. One of the agents may have an incentive to breach the contract so that the contract becomes obsolete. This contract risk is analyzed in section 3. Finally, social risks may arise in using natural resources, requiring specific institutional settings. Reduction of social risk implies to attribute the user costs of social risks. This aspect of institutional arrangements is studied in section 4.

1. Specifics of Natural Resource Allocation

The production and the use of natural resources is characterized by a set of specifics.

Long-time horizon. If we follow the Hotelling paradigm, the extraction of natural resources is determined in an intertemporal optimization framework with a time horizon extended far into the future. This is due to the fact that the stock of a non-renewable resource is finite implying the explicit consideration of user costs; in the case of a renewable resource a long-run steady-state of the resource stock has to be established. As a more practical argument, the lifetime of technical facilities in the resource industry such as mining shafts, smelters and refineries is estimated to be 20 to 30 years or more.

Vertical stages of production. Technically, natural resource products are not produced in a single process of production; they follow a vertical chain of production processes with the stages exploration, setting up the extraction facilities, financing, resource extraction, refining and distribution. As a rule, these stages of production are spatially separated. For instance, refining activities tend to be located near the market of the final product.

The vertical stages of production may be organized within a hierarchy, for instance an international oil firm with complete downstream integration, or they may involve a set of agents such as the resource countries, exploration firms, banks, contractors, extraction firms, refining firms and distributors. When different agents are involved, markets and analogous mechanisms of coordination as well as property rights, for instance the right to extract, play an important role.

Besides production, recycling and the return of unusable resource material (SO_2, other emissions) to nature is another aspect of the vertical stage of production and of use.

High set-up costs. The resource industry is characterized by high set-up costs. For instance, developing the North Slope of the Prudhoe Bay in Alaska has cost US-$ 24 billion; US-$ 6.7 billion were spent for the Ekofisk oil field in the North Sea. Other examples are given in Siebert (1986). High set-up costs do not only arise in resource development but also in transportation (port facilities, pipelines, LNG-facilities), in refining and converting (electricity plants) and on the demand side (energy saving capital).

Private risks. The characteristics of the resource industry mentioned so far, namely long-time horizon, high set-up costs and a set of autonomous players in the different vertical stages of production are already a sufficient reason why the

336

relationship between the different autonomous agents tends to be of a long-run nature. Another argument in this direction is the existence of risks which are too large to be carried by a single actor and somehow must be reduced for the single agent by shifting part of the risk to other agents.

Risk means that some of the variables relevant for an agent, for instance for the profit-maximizing mine, are random variables. The agent can assign probabilities to the occurrence of a specific value of a variable. Risk then is defined as the deviation of the value of a variable from the mathematically expected value, that is from the mean.

It is usual to distinguish technological, economic (market) and political risks (Siebert 1986). Technological risks relate to innovations in extraction procedures (Alaska), to the success of exploration (exploration risk) and to the quality and the size of a deposit (resource risk). Economic risks refer to the resource price, to quantities sold and to costs (operating costs, closing costs, completion costs). Finally, political risks address expropriation, variations in extraction rights and in taxation schemes or in permits. All these risks make up financial risk. The sums invested in a project may be lost; the present value of profit is a random variable.

The risks of the resource industry are to a large extent explained by high set-up costs and the other characteristics of the resource industry. For instance, a randomness in price becomes especially relevant when high set-up costs are involved and when the decision problem is characterized by a long time horizon.

Idiosyncratic investment. High set-up costs and high private risks create an additional problem when the investment is transaction-specific or "idiosyncratic" (Williamson 1979, 234). This case arises when the capital value of a project is at the mercy of the other agent. Consider for instance the case when the product of a mine can only be sold to one buyer or when the supply can only be provided by one seller. Expropriation of an extraction facility by the resource country, a drastic change in the taxation schemes, variations in the transport conditions by a pipeline company are other examples. In all these cases, indivisibilities are involved giving rise to the strategic position of one agent. It is not possible to undermine the strategic position of an agent by markets. For instance, as a rule there is no market for extraction rights with many partners on the supply side. Note that only part of the set-up costs are idiosyncratic because markets, if they exist, are a vehicle to destroy idiosyncracy.

The agent with the idiosyncratic investment is "locked in" in his position as soon as the investment is undertaken. Then he is exposed to the risk of strategic behavior by the other agent. The idiosyncratic character of part of the high set-up costs in the resource sector leads to the necessity of long-run contractual arrangements by which the risk of strategic behavior is reduced.

Social risk. The production and the use of natural resources may also give rise to social risk. Then, private contractual arrangements cannot allocate risk because public goods aspects are involved. Institutional arrangements have to be developed which introduce incentives to reduce the social risk.

It may be argued that all the above arguments relate to large-scale investments in general and that they are not specific to the resource industry. If this view is correct, the resource sector exhibits only a gradual variation of a more general problem. It seems to me that the resource industry shows a concentration of specific characteristics. Moreover, experience suggests the resource industry applies institutional arrangements such as project financing and long-term contracts that are not formal in other industries.

2.   Risk Allocation in Contractual Arrangements

Risk shifting is based on the phenomenon that a given variance in a variable does not have the same impact for different agents. The agents may have different attitudes towards risk, they may have different target functions and they may have a different set of constraints for their maximization behavior. A given variance in the price of a natural resource has a smaller risk for a country if the country not only exchanges the resource against consumption goods but if it has accumulated financial assets. Or assume that a resource country uses part of the resource in production at home. Then the probability of a fall in the resource price will hit the country's export earnings, but industrial activity at home may be stimulated due to lower resource prices. A distribution with weight in the tail for low prices of a natural resource represents a risk for a resource-exporting country, but a similarly skewed probability distribution is an insurance to a resource-importing country.

In order to understand risk allocation we first develop a frame of reference in which we assume only one agent being the sponsor, the operator and the supplier of capital. Consider a price risk as shown in Figure 1a with mean $\bar{p}$ and let α measure the price risk. Let the price risk α be identically and independently distributed over time so that the distribution shown in Figure 1a holds for each period.[1] The firm as a single agent cannot influence the given probability distribution of the resource price in a period.

The decision problem of the resource firm is to determine the optimal time profile of extraction for a finite resource stock, and if capacity is not fixed by technical conditions, to determine its optimal level of initial investment. Let A denote initial financial outlays, let π (t) be period profits and let δ be the discount rate. Then the resource firm maximizes the expected utility of the present value of profits

$$EU\,\Omega \; = \; -A + EU \int_0^T e^{-\delta t} \, \pi \, (t) \, dt$$

subject to the usual constraints. Due to the price risk α in each period, the present value of profit Ω of the resource firm is a random variable (Figure 1b). Although the price risk α for any period is given, the firm can influence the probability distribution of the present value of profit, i.e. its variance ρ, by adjusting the time profile of extraction (and the initial level of investment). Thus, the probability distribution for Ω in Figure 1b reflects an "optimal" time profile of extraction for the firm. Note that the risk-averse agent will not choose the mean $\bar{\Omega}$, but the certainty equivalent present value of profit $\hat{\Omega}$.

---

[1] Price risk is not affected by the business cycle so that there is no covariance structure between price and the business cycle (quantities sold). Moreover, it is assumed that the stochastic uniformation is complete, i.e. an agent does not get additional (risk reducing) information over time and does not learn. In that case, risk would have to be modeled as a stochastic process, for instance as a Wiener process.

Figure 1

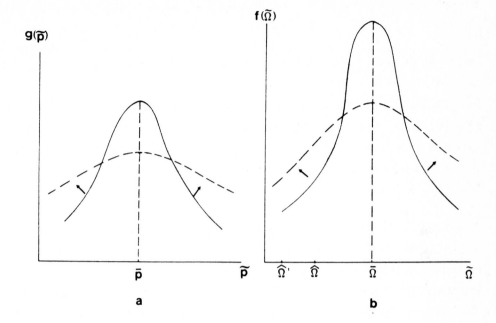

a

b

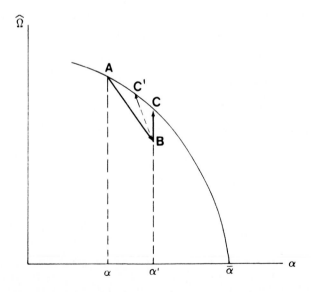

Figure 2

Assume now that there is more risk α' in the probability distribution of price in each period (Figure 1a). Assume that the increased price risk in each period implies a larger spread in the present value of profit for a constant mean $\bar{\Omega}$, that is the present value of profit $\tilde{\Omega}$ has become more risky; the variance has increased.

The firm's adjustment to the increased risk can be broken down into two effects: If the (risk-averse) firm does not adjust its control parameters to the increased risk, for instance, if it sticks to its previous extraction profile, the variance of the present value of profits ρ is increased as shown in Figure 1b. The firm will choose $\hat{\Omega}$' instead of $\hat{\Omega}$ with $\hat{\Omega}$' lying to the left of $\hat{\Omega}$. In Figure 2, the movement from $\hat{\Omega}$ to $\hat{\Omega}$' due to a higher price risk α' is shown by the movement A to B with A corresponding to $\hat{\Omega}$ and B to $\hat{\Omega}$'.

The firm will, however, adjust its expected-utility-maximizing control parameters in such a way that the variance in the resource price becomes less relevant for the present value of profit. By adjusting its control parameters, e.g. the time profile of extraction, to the increased price risk α' the firm can influence the probability distribution of the present value of profit ρ, so that a more favorable probability distribution (not shown in Figure 1b) will yield a certainty equivalent for the present value of profit somewhere between $\hat{\Omega}$' and $\hat{\Omega}$ (Figure 1b). The arrow BC in Figure 2 illustrates the increase in the certainty equivalent present value of profit due to adjustment of the internal control parameters of the firm.[2] We then define a functional relationship between the expected present value of profit and the level of risk after the firm has used all internal adjustments to risk: adjusting the time

---

[2] In the case of price risk it is reasonable to assume that the probability distribution of the resource price cannot be influenced by the firm. With respect to other risks, for instance cost risk, the firm may be in a position to influence the risk. In that case, the arrow BC' indicates that the risk per period can be reduced.

profile of extraction, adjusting the level of initial investments, etc.[3] Then we have a function $\hat{\Omega}(\alpha)$ for which we postulate the property

$$\Omega(\alpha) \text{ with } \hat{\Omega}_\alpha < 0, \quad \hat{\Omega}_{\alpha\alpha} < 0. \tag{1}$$

Equation 1 is illustrated in Figure 2. With price risk in each period increasing, the certainty equivalent present value of profits is reduced.

2.1 Risk Allocation

If we now introduce a second agent, the firm may be able to vary the density function of the present value of profit Ω, or reduce the price risk α. For instance, the firm may be able to sell the resource stock to a second agent for a lump sum payment Ω_{LL} thus eliminating the price risk completely. The difference $\Omega - \Omega_{LL}$ is the risk premium that the firm is willing to give up in order to obtain its "certainty equivalent profit". Another example is a long-run sales contract. For instance Ω_L may be the result of a long-run sales contract with a lower (and upper) bound on the resource price. Institutional arrangements for risk allocation will affect the probability distribution of the present value of profit for one agent by truncating it or by directly altering the density function. In the case of truncating, the unfavorable tail is partly cut off, thus increasing the mean and reducing the variance.

---

3   We can define a function describing the relationship between the variance of the present value of profit and the price risk

$$\rho = \rho[\alpha, m], \quad \partial\rho / \partial\alpha > 0, \quad \partial^2\rho / \partial\alpha^2 < 0$$

where m denotes the control instruments such as the time profile of extraction. Then

$$\hat{\Omega}(\rho), \quad \hat{\Omega}_\rho < 0, \quad \hat{\Omega}_{\rho\rho} > 0$$

and equation 1 can be written as

$$\hat{\Omega} = \hat{\Omega}(\alpha), \quad \hat{\Omega}_\alpha = \hat{\Omega}_\rho \quad \partial\rho / \partial\alpha < 0, \quad \hat{\Omega}_{\alpha\alpha} = \hat{\Omega}_{\rho\rho} \quad \partial^2\rho / \partial\alpha^2 < 0$$

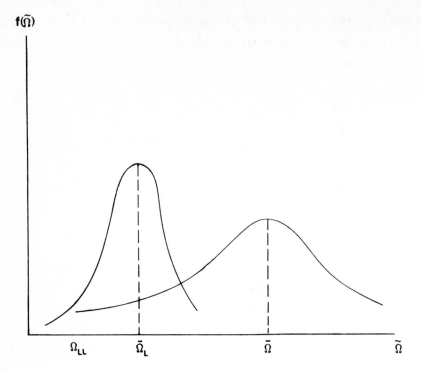

Figure 3

Assume that a continuum of risk reducing institutional arrangements Γ exists, so that we have a relationship describing the remaining risk α as a function of Γ

$$\alpha(\Gamma) \quad , \quad \alpha_\Gamma < 0, \quad \alpha_{\Gamma\Gamma} > 0 \ . \tag{2}$$

With a price v for using the institutional arrangement Γ, we have for the present value of profit of the resource firm

$$G = \Omega\left[\alpha(\Gamma)\right] - v\,\Gamma \tag{3}$$

with

$$\frac{dG}{d\Gamma} = \Omega_\alpha \alpha_\Gamma - v = 0 \ . \tag{3a}$$

The term $\Omega_\alpha{}^\alpha{}_\Gamma$ in equation 3a denotes the willingness to pay for a marginal variation of the institutional arrangement Γ; it can be interpreted as the demand function for shifting risk as shown in Figure 4 .

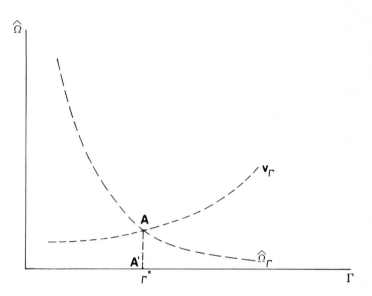

Figure 4

Assuming that v increases with the level of risk shifted, Figure 4 illustrates the shifting of risk. The institutional arrangement Γ allows benefits for the demand side to shift risk (demand side rent) and for the supply side taking over the risk (supply side rent).

In reality, the institutional arrangement can take a variety of forms and risk allocation will vary with the institutional arrangement. In the following, we study the risk allocation properties of extraction rights.

2.2 Extraction Rights

An important institutional arrangement for natural resources is the right to extract. In defining this right, the government may have quite a few different objectives in mind. It may want to develop its resource base, it may want to recuperate some of the resource rents and it may want to prevent a too early depletion of the resource stock. But at the same time, the institutional arrangement must be attractive enough for firms to explore, to provide capital, technology and access to markets. These aspects may weigh especially heavy in the case of developing countries. The allocation of risks associated with the development of the resource base varies with the institutional arrangement.

Traditional concessions. Prior to the oil crisis, the traditional concessions gave the firm the right to explore and to extract. As a rule, this extraction right referred to all the resources of the country,[4] including reserves not yet discovered (Kobrin 1984). The firm had to pay a royalty, and it carried all the economic risks (except for the proportion of revenue risk carried by the country in form of royalty income). The concessions had a duration of up to seventy years, so that the extraction rights used to be rather stable. With the property rights of resources going over to the resource countries, the contracts became less stable.

Production sharing. In this form of contract, a state resource firm and a foreign firm cooperate (Blitzer et al. 1982). The foreign firm undertakes the exploration, puts up the capital for the development of the resource deposit and also carries the operating costs. A certain percentage of output is used to cover the firm's cost ("cost oil"), the remaining part of output is split between the state firm or country and the private firm ("profit oil"). The private firm carries the political risk, the exploration risk and the cost risk. Revenue risk is split between the country and the firm.

Toll-per-barrel. The toll per barrel contract is a specific type of a production sharing arrangement. The country pays a fixed toll per barrel to the foreign firm. Both the price risk and the quantity risk are taken over by the country.

---

[4] Talking of a country is an abbreviation. Country here means the set of agents in a nation including the government, sectors of the economy etc. Risk taken over by the country will be allocated to the different agents within a country. Risk allocation among the agents within a country may have an impact on the risk allocation between the country and the firm. This was pointed out by B. Frey.

Service contracts. In the case of service contracts, the country pays the firm for a specific service such as exploration, the delivery of extraction facilities (turn key contract), the operation of facilities, refining or distribution. By a set of such service contracts and by bringing in foreign capital through borrowing (instead of equity capital), the country attempts to unpackage the services provided by the multinationals. The country takes over all the risks, the firm being exposed to the political risk only.

A specific form of the service contract is the "net-back" contract used by Iran and Saudi Arabia in 1985 and 1986. The country sells the crude receiving the net of the refined product after transportation and refining costs have been subtracted. The crude is sold today, and the net will only be determined after a lapse of two months when the refined product has reached the market. The country thus takes over all the economic risk, and specifically the price risk for the period between the sale of the crude and the sale of the final product.

Nationalization. As an extreme case, the country may extract the resource via a state company thus taking over all the economic risks.

Bidding schemes. Contractual arrangements grant a right to extract. Under a set of conditions, the value of these extraction rights can be determined in auctions. If the auction requires an initial lump sum fee and no period payments, the up front financial exposure of the resource firm is increased. Such an arrangement is only conceivable where the political risk is negligible. It is therefore no surprise to find auctions applied in industrial countries, for instance for off-shore licences in the U.S. Even then, an initial lump sum payment may tilt the time profile of extraction too much in favor of present generations, and a tax per unit extracted, a royalty or a profit related payment may be necessary to generate an extraction profile with longer run orientation. Instead of initial lump sum payments, bidding arrangements can relate to payments in each period, to quantities, revenues or profits. Apparently, a developing country could reduce the political risk for the firm by making an initial lump sum payment to the firm and then requiring a higher tax per unit of output or a higher royalty later. However, this is unrealistic because the developing country is short of financial capital.

A specific problem arises if bidding schemes establish a monopoly for the successful bidder in future periods, for instance if the country has only one resource base. Then care must be taken that the monopoly is checked by other institutional devices.

The existing contractual arrangements produce different allocations of risk to the resource country and to the firm. In Table 1 risks are shown vertically and contractual arrangements horizontally. In the case of concession, the firm takes over all the risks, whereas in the case of nationalization all the risks go over to the country. Production sharing and toll per barrel contracts partition the risk among country and firm.

Table 1: Risk Allocation and Extraction Rights

Contractual Relations Risks		Concession	Production sharing	Toll-per-barrel	Service contract	National-ization
Political Risk		Firm	Firm	Firm	Firm	–
Exploration Risk		Firm	Firm	Firm	Country	Country
Economic Risk	Cost Risk	Firm	Firm	Firm	Country	Country
	Quantity Risk	Firm	Firm	Country	Country	Country	Country
	Price Risk	Firm	Firm	Country	Country	Country	Country

2.3   Taxation

The taxation of natural resources can be considered to be a specific institutional arrangement for the development of natural resources. The purpose of resource taxation may consist in participating in the resource rents or in influencing the time profile of extraction, but taxation schemes also have an impact on the allocation of risks associated with a resource project. Write-offs for capital allow to recuperate financial outlays quickly; depletion allowances may have a similar role. Hotelling-type severance taxes represent an incentive to shift extraction into the future and to take over some future price risk.

An interesting taxation scheme is the resource rent tax (Garnaut and Clunies Ross 1975; 1983; Meyer 1984). The resource rent tax is a profit tax; investment can be written off immediately (100 per cent). A negative profit can be carried forward to the next periods. An interest rate agreed upon in the contractual arrangement between resource country and the mining firm is applied to the loss being carried forward. The firm starts paying taxes with a percentage rate in the cash flow in each period as soon as the current value of the accumulated cash flow in a period becomes positive.

The resource rent tax is intended to prevent a too early depletion of the resource stock and to reduce the incentive for contract risk (obsolescence bargaining). Carrying forward the loss with a discount rate reduces the period cash flow relevant for taxation; thus the political appetite for changing the taxation scheme is weakened.

2.4   Long-term Sales Contracts

Long-term sales contracts are another example of a contractual relationship prevailing in the resource industry. Such contracts are universal in the natural gas industry, they dominate in the world coal trade (80 per cent of the total trade) and they are also used in petroleum (around 40 per cent, 1983) and in the uranium and in the steel industry. The basic reason for these long-run sales contracts is that buyer or seller may be locked in by their initial investment which is transaction specific. A randomness in some variables like the resource price or in quantities supplied or bought will reduce the profitability of the investment and may make it (partly) obsolete. A long-term sales contract will reduce part of the risk (Siebert 1987), for instance by cutting off part of the unfavorable tail in the probability distribution of the present value of profit.

To what extent risk, for instance financial risk of a mine, can be shifted depends on the specifics of the contract. We here order the contractual arrangements along a continuum with backward and forward integration as extreme cases.

Backward integration. The buyer integrates extraction, transportation, refining and similar activities into his organization, and he takes over all the risks. Assuming that the buyer has paid a lump sum initially, the seller of the resource stock has shifted all his risks.

Plus cost. The contract specifies an initial price and allows for a cost increase, possibly a mark-up. Adjustment clauses can relate to different cost categories such as transportation, mining equipment etc. (Pollard 1985, Vogelsang 1986). The seller of the resource is protected against revenue risk and also against cost risk. As a rule, the take is fixed. The disadvantage of cost plus arrangements is a hazard problem because the buyer cannot control the costs of the seller.

Fixed price. Fixed price contracts can come in various forms. A floor price protects the seller in truncating the unfavorable part of the density function of the resource price and consequently of the present value of profit; the price risk is shifted to the buyer. A fixed price ceiling protects the buyer and shifts all the risks to the seller. If instead of an upper and a lower bound on the price the contract specifies a single price, both parties are protected against unfavorable cases. If low prices materialize, the seller is protected; with high prices, the buyer receives the advantage.

Take or pay. In this arrangement the buyer can reduce quantities to a certain limit without financial consequences. When this limit is reached, payments have to be made even if delivery of the take had occurred. The sums paid can be used for the payment of deliveries in the future. Thus, the supplier is exposed to minor fluctuations in demand, but he is protected against major variations. The take or pay provision guarantees a minimal level of revenue; it cuts off part of the unfavorable tail in the probability distribution of the present value of profits.

Price adjustment clauses. Price adjustment provisions allow for changes in the contract. The "most-favored-nation" clause ties contract prices to prices paid in other contracts, for instance in the same geological basin, or links them to the price of a dominating energy (oil in the case of coal). A specific form of price adjustment is brick pricing. Prices are adjusted for part of the quantity every other year.

Take or pay with price clauses. In reality we observe a mixture between take or pay contracts and price adjustment clauses. A pure take contract without specifying the price shifts the quantity risk away from the seller, but the financial risk arising from the randomness in price still remains. Similarly, fixing a price without specifying quantities does not protect against the financial risk sufficiently. A combination of quantity and price rules can exclude unfavorable cases for the profit of buyer and seller. Specific risk aspects for one agent, for instance, when the buyer is too severely committed, can be accommodated through special provisions such as "market out". As a rule, a more precise agreement on one variable, e.g. quantity, allows more leeway with the other variable, e.g. price, and vice versa.

Vertical forward integration. In this case, the seller takes control of the downstream activities, and the long-run contract is substituted by a vertical hierarchy. The seller takes over all risk.

Bidding. Long-run sales contracts can be auctioned off among the suppliers (Vogelsang 1986) with the successful bidder paying a lump sum for the right of delivery. This lump sum payment is supposed to capture the resource rent of the supplier. The problem is that a monopoly may be established and that moral hazard problems may be involved (see above).

Table 2 shows how the allocation of risk shifts with different types of long-term sales contracts.

Table 2: Risk Allocation and Long-run Sales Contracts

Risks \ Contract Forms		Backward Integration	Plus-Cost*	Floor Price*	Take or Pay		Fixed Price Ceiling	Forward Integration
Financial Risk		Buyer	Buyer	Buyer	Buyer	Seller	Seller	Seller
Revenue Risk	Price Risk	Buyer	Buyer	Buyer	Buyer	Seller	Seller	Seller
Risk	Quantity Risk	Buyer	Buyer*	Buyer	Buyer	Seller	Seller	Seller
Cost Risk		Buyer	Buyer	Seller	Seller		Seller	Seller
Contract Risk		Seller	Seller	Seller	Seller/Buyer		–	Buyer

* with guaranteed take

2.5 Large-scale Ventures

Large-scale resource ventures represent an interesting example of an institutional arrangement of risk allocation. In contrast to extraction rights and long-run contracts, large-scale ventures do not represent a bilateral relationship of risk allocation. Many agents are involved in large-scale ventures: the project operator making the investment and operational decisions, sponsors providing some of the capital, know-how and access to market, contractors responsible for construction, suppliers of input, banks and other financial institutions, the government defining the right to extract, granting permits of operation and specifying taxes, as well as international organizations and the customer (Siebert 1987d).

The different types of risk are allocated to the different agents in a complex net of contractual arrangements.The financial risk is split up into a set of risks which are taken over by different agents. Here are some of the most important instruments of risk shifting:

Limits on financial exposure. Financial risk can be reduced by putting a limit on financial exposure. This can be achieved by establishing a vehicle company separating the risk of the large-scale venture from the sponsor's balance sheet (Walter 1986). The financial risk can be further reduced by bringing in additional sponsors thus spreading the risk on many shoulders.

Shifting financial risk to banks. The project operator can reduce his financial risk through project finance. Banks provide part of the capital taking over some of the financial risk. If in some future periods the price will fall and if principal and interest cannot be paid, the banks may loose part of their investment. Cofinancing from international organizations is another way to reduce financial risk.

Supplier and customer credit. The supplier of an input may provide a credit in order to stimulate his sales, either in the case of machinery or when a large-scale venture uses a permanent stream of the input (coal in electricity generation). The customer may be willing to provide a credit to be paid off by future deliveries. In this case, customer credit is likely to be linked to a long-run sales contract.

Shifting set-up cost to the resource country. Price risk and the financial risk can be shifted by reducing initial outlays for the right to extract and then receiving only a portion of the price which is random. In theory, the price risk could be shifted by moving away from a concession with a large initial lump sum payment to production sharing, a toll per barrel contract or even a service contract. In the real world, this option of risk shifting, however, increases the political risk of a change in taxation schemes or in the contract (obsolescence bargaining, contract risk). It is therefore rather unlikely as a risk management policy. Moreover, the historical change from concession of the 1960s to the more recent forms of contracts such as the toll-per-barrel arrangement reflects a change in the property rights and in the bargaining position vis-à-vis risk assignment.

Completion guarantees. Completion risk can be reduced by completion guarantees from the leading contractor and by stand-by-letters of credit from banks (Walter 1986).

Long-run sales contract. Price risk can be reduced by using long-run sales contracts (see above).

Downstream integration. Under specific conditions, a firm may be able to reduce price risk by vertical integration. Such an approach can be followed if downstream products are less volatile in price, or more specifically, if downstream activities open up a secure line of production (chemical products in the case of an oil producing firm) whose price has a negative correlation with the oil price. Note, however, that this policy requires additional financial outlays, and although the price risk may be reduced, the risk of financial loss may rise. Of course, vertical integration may be spread over time thus allowing the reduction in the risk of financial loss.

Integrated risk management. Although the different types of separate risks mentioned above partly overlap, they may arise simultaneously thus increasing the variance in the present value of profit. The increase in the price risk, in environmental and technological risk eventually augment the variance of expected profits. Therefore, different policies of risk management may be called for simultaneously. Institutional arrangements are required that reduce several risks such as the risk of financial loss, the risk of technological failure and price risk at the same time. A case in point is the Russian-German gas deal where German banks provided the financing, a German and other international steel producers delivered the pipes and other technological equipment and where a long-run sales contract reduced Russia's price risk.

Risk allocation can be interpreted as a system of contractual arrangements or a set of risk markets for the different types of risk and among different participants. The different contracts are interlinked in the sense of a general equilibrium model. Successfully shifting completion risk to the leading contractor implies a reduction in financial risk and may have an impact on financing. Allocating the price risk to the customer or to a government also reduces financial risk and requires lower risk premiums to be paid to banks.

2.6   Contractual Arrangements and other Forms of Coordination

Contracts and arrangements must be compared to other arrangements for coordination such as spot markets, future markets and coordination through hierarchies. The problem is under what conditions which "governance structure" (Williamson 1979, 235) does a better job than other mechanisms of coordination.

The relative advantage of a contractual arrangement varies with the existence and efficiency of markets. Contracts for extraction rights are not needed if a market for extraction rights can be established. Project finance is not necessary if the capital market is perfectly efficient with respect to large-scale ventures. And long-run sales contracts are not needed when the time depth of future markets in the resource area is sufficiently large. Apparently, contractual arrangements loose their advantage with the efficiency of markets. The relative advantage of contractual arrangements also varies with the amount of risk that agents on different sides of a market perceive. Consider the world oil market with its "anxiety gap" in the seventies. When the excess supply on the spot market dropped to 2 mbd, the price was expected to rise. In such a situation, long-term contracts play an important role. When market conditions and the perceived risk of disruption change such as in the eighties, spot-markets become more interesting (see "net-back contracts").

3.   Stability of Contractual Arrangements

Contracts represent an institutional arrangement by which risks of the resource industry are allocated *ex ante* to the different agents involved. These contractual arrangements attempt to alleviate the risky position of one of the agents or of both.

3.1. Classical and Relational Contracts

Due to the very nature of the risk allocation contractual arrangements have a specific quality distinguishing them from the classical contract. The classical contract is characterized by discreteness and presentation. The transaction is discrete and "entirely separate not only from all other present relations but from all past and future relations as well" (Macneil 1978, 856). The "presentation of transaction involves restricting its expected future effects to those defined in the present" (Macneil 1978, 862). According to Williamson (1979, 236), the identity of the parties can be treated as irrelevant, the nature of the agreement is delimited and remedies for non-performance are clearly defined.

A classical contract cannot fulfill the risk allocation needed in the resource industry. Presentation in the strict sense is not possible because risk must be accommodated and contractual claims are contingent on the states of nature materializing in the future. Moreover, a specific transaction is not separated from other transactions; a long-run relationship exists between the parties involved. Different "governance structures" (Williamson 1979) such as a neoclassical contract and a relational contract are needed.

The neoclassical contract is characterized by making discreteness and presentation more "blurred", allowing adjustment of the contract and devising mechanisms such as arbitration to ensure the stability of the contract. Whereas the neoclassical contract still is a contract, the relational contract is a brother concept of relationships including relations within a firm. The relational contract can be interpreted as a social relationship, it is "a minisociety with a vast array of norms beyond those centered on the exchange and its immediate processes" (Macneil 1978, 901).

3.2 Causes of Contract Risk

There are two underlying reasons for the instability of contractual arrangements: a change in market conditions and the idiosyncrasy of investment.

Ex post versus ex ante. The contract is supposed to protect the single agent against a too unfavorable state of the world. Risk is allocated ex ante, and each partner expects a benefit from the contract. When the states of the world emerge, the expected benefits may not show up, and an agent may evaluate the contract as a serious disadvantage. Market processes may have undermined the advantages of a contract to a specific agent. An example is a pay-or-take contract in a situation with extremely low resource prices (for instance the iron ore contracts between Japan and Venezuela altered in 1986).

Idiosyncrasy. Another cause for the instability of a contract consists in the idiosyncrasy of investment and the locked-in position[5] of one partner which gives a strategic position to the other partner, once investment is undertaken. This phenomenon is a systematic cause of contract risk even if market processes do not undermine the expected contract benefits for a specific agent. The attitude towards the contract changes systematically with the change in the bargaining position, that is with the investment being undertaken. Then, the contractual arrangement can become obsolete (obsolescence bargaining, Vernon 1971).

3.3   Reducing Contract Risk

Both causes of contract risk represent a hazard problem. A partner may show opportunistic behavior and walk away from the contract. This attempt is partly checked by the more permanent nature of the relationship since an agent having a disadvantage today can expect a benefit tomorrow. The hazard problem is also affected by attitudes towards contracts and by the dichotomy between private advantages and moral sentiments. For a merchant of the Hanse in the "good old days" a word given was binding even if conditions became unfavorable. This behavior was possibly motivated with an eye to his followers in the firm. Today, the world may have a shorter memory, at the same time being more complex. Moreover, there may be something specifically American in the hazard aspect.

---

[5]   The idiosyncrasy problem is also at the core of the borrowing problem. As soon as the credit is granted, the creditor is locked in and the sovereign borrower can behave strategically.

Since the contractual arrangement cannot be enforced as in a classical contract due to the contingent-claims aspect, other mechanisms must be developed to prevent a partner from walking away from a contract. An important approach is to keep the contractual arrangement flexible and to allow adjustment to new conditions. Price adjustment clauses, cost escalators and other mechanisms such as the "most-favored nation clause" provide some type of formal flexibility. Standards, direct third-party determination of performance (arbitration) and to some extent one-party control of terms are more complicated institutional mechanisms to accommodate changing economic conditions. A much broader approach is to specify modalities of a renegotiation (Harries 1980) or an "agreement to agree" (Macneil 1978, 870). Finally, a contract may be more stable if conditions are clearly specified under which an agent may discontinue the contract. For instance, the "market out" provision allows the buyer to discontinue his take if prices are too unfavorable. "Force majeure" or hardship clauses relate to situations in which it has become impossible for a partner to continue a contract.

The more systematic contract risk due to the idiosyncracy of investment requires a different remedy. Adjustment clauses cannot solve idiosyncracy problems. Strategic behavior of one partner made possible by the locked-in position of the other agent must be prevented by the contractual arrangements. More specifically, the incentive for strategic behavior must be eliminated in the contractual arrangements or must be checked by appropriate opportunity costs. A case in point is the resource rent tax which attempts to prevent "obsolescence bargaining". Explicitly carrying forward the capital cost or past losses to the future by an agreed discount rate reduces the political demand in the resource country to change the contract because period profits are expressed correctly. Moreover, excessive period profits are subject to a profit tax. Another example is project financing which can be interpreted as a complex net of contractual arrangements where the relational contract refers to a set of many agents partly checking each other. Finally, the idiosyncratic nature of investment may be offset by the control of technology so that there may be a countervailing asset specificity with respect to technology in favor of the foreign firm.[6] Asset specification on both sides of a contract is a precondition for equilibrating hazards (Masten 1987, Williamson 1985).

4. Attributing the User Costs of Social Risks

In the analysis so far, we have studied the problem how risks in the resource sector can be allocated to different agents through contractual arrangements. This problem only refers to so-called private risks being defined as the variance in variables relating to resources as private goods, for instance to the price of oil, to quantities sold or to the present value of period profits. In these cases, the risk is carried by the autonomous subsystems of the economy. Private risk may be reduced by shifting it to another agent. Private risk is not correlated across persons and can be interpreted as independent risk (Dasgupta 1982, 81).

4.1 Social Risk

In contrast to private risk, the use of natural resources may also be connected with social risks relating to the randomness in some public goods aspect of natural resources. The public goods aspect implies that the resource in question "must be used in equal amounts by all" (Samuelson 1954). Examples are the risk of extinction, the risk of too early depletion if markets are short-sighted and the risk of environmental degradation, for instance through the accumulation of pollutants. In the case of social risk, all agents are exposed to the same randomness. Risk is correlated across persons, and, by definition, risk cannot be shifted.

Pure social risks cannot be handled by private contractual arrangements. However, under a set of conditions the public good aspect may be changed into a private good if private parties can develop property rights and thus transform the social risk into private risk. We then would have a Coase scenario for risks (Siebert 1987a).

---

[6] I owe this comment to C. Kirchner.

Another approach is to interpret the management of social risk as a special aspect of the more general problem of expressing opportunity costs, or in an intertemporal interpretation, user costs through appropriate institutional arrangements.

Property rights, or more specifically their transferability, can be interpreted as a vehicle which makes sure that the opportunity costs of private decisions are taken into account. Consider the normal static allocation problem of using a resource in a specific activity. Then the transferability of the property right, together with a set of other conditions such as working markets, guarantees that the opportunity cost of using the resource in a specific activity, that is the utility foregone from using it in another opportunity, is taken into account in the decisions of the autonomous subsystem of an economy.

As a rule this also holds for intertemporal decisions. User costs, that is the opportunity costs of not using the resource in the future, are expressed by a set of institutional arrangements such as future markets, selling the capital value of a resource stock to the next generation, selling land, a resource firm, evaluating a resource firm in the stock market etc. If it is judged that these mechanisms are not sufficiently oriented towards the future and that user costs are underestimated by markets, i.e. that too high a discount rate is applied, the government can introduce additional institutional aspects such as steering the permits for the quantity to be extracted or using appropriate taxation (severance taxes) that shift the time profile of extraction into the future. In this case, a public goods aspect of caring for the future has been brought in by a new institutional reasoning.

4.2 Signalling the User Costs of Social Risks

How can user costs of social risks in using natural resources be signalled to the subsystems of the economy? As an example consider the risk of extinction or the risk of environmental degradation (Siebert 1987) where environmental quality is a random variable. Two issues arise: First, how much risk is society willing to tolerate? Second, by which institutional arrangement can we ensure that the tolerable level of risk is not surpassed?

The target problem of determining the tolerable or optimal level of social risk exhibits all the problems of public goods: the aggregation of individual preferences for public goods may not be consistent (Arrow Paradoxon); the individual may behave as a free rider and the institutional mechanisms for aggregating individual preferences may not satisfy the usual optimality criteria of economics (for instance voting). Nevertheless, the political process has to determine the tolerable level of social risk.[7] Practical decision rules such as benefit-cost analysis as well as practical institutional mechanisms (voting systems, constitutional restraints, log rolling, etc.) come into play.

Once the tolerable level of social risk is specified as the target, the problem is to devise institutional arrangements in such a way that the user costs are signalled to the autonomous subsystems and that the user costs are taken into consideration by the decentralized units. Since we are dealing with social risks, the institutional arrangement cannot aim to shift the risk. The appropriate policy therefore is risk reduction. This can be obtained by new property rights for resources and for environmental use.

In the real world we see a broad spectrum of new property titles in the area of natural and environmental resources ranging from direct controls to price incentives. Extending government control in space (200 miles zone) and other dimensions (emissions; extinction of species), using permits for extraction or for emissions, introducing the transferability of permits including markets for permits, relying on price mechanisms via taxation (severance taxes, emission taxes) and defining product norms can be interpreted as institutional arrangements to reduce social risk. In this problem of developing new incentives for the use of natural resources, the public good problem overlaps with the common property issue. In the past, quite a few natural resources have been used as a common property with free access (fish of the ocean, the environment as a receptacle of wastes).

The costs of risk reduction play a role in determining the tolerable level of risk. An important aspect of the management of social risk therefore is how the costs of

---

[7] All the problems known from determining the optimal environmental quality also arise in the case of social risk. Compare Siebert (1987).

risk reduction are allocated to the agents causing the risks. For instance, in contrast to natural hazards such as earthquakes a significant ingredient of environmental risks is man-made, namely pollutants. Thus, one strategy of risk reduction is to attribute the costs of reducing social risks to the decentralized units of the economy. By efficiently allocating the costs of risk reduction to those decentralized units that cause the social risk in the first place, an incentive is installed to reduce the social risk. If the environment can be used free of charge as a receptacle of waste, no incentive is installed to reduce emissions. If emission taxes, other pricing instruments for emissions and other policy instruments are applied, in a rather general way some of the social risk of environmental degradation is reduced.

5.   Conclusions

The production and the use of natural resources is characterized by a long-time horizon, a multitude of agents in different stages on the vertical scale of production, high set-up costs, private and social risks as well as idiosyncratic investment. The existence of private risks has led to institutional arrangements by which part of the risks can be reduced for the individual agent and shifted to another agent. Such arrangements are extraction rights, taxation schemes, long-run scales contracts and project finance. Contractual relations may involve only two parties, but they can also be a complex net of contractual arrangements between many agents as in large-scale ventures.

Contractual arrangements in the resource industry for the reduction of private risk are exposed to contract risk. In contrast to the classical contract, the contractual arrangements lack discreteness and presentation, and the relational contract may not be stable. Market processes may induce a partner to behave opportunistically, and the idiosyncracy of investment may imply "obsolescence bargaining". Therefore, long-run contracts representing contingent claims must be flexible to accommodate new developments.

Resource production and resource use also involve social risk which cannot be shifted because they have a public good aspect. Here risk management requires institutional arrangements by which the user costs of social risk and the opportunity costs of reducing the risk are transmitted to the decentralized units of an economy.

References

Blitzer, C.R., D.R. Lessard, and J.L. Paddock (1984), Risk Bearing and the Choice of Contract Forms for Oil Exploration and Development, *Energy Journal*, 5, pp. 1-28.

Broadman, H.G. (1986), Elements of Market Power in the Natural Gas Industry and the Rule of Private Carriage, *The Energy Journal*, 7, pp. 119-138.

Broadman, H.G. and D.A. Toman (1986), Non-Price Provisions in Long-Term Natural Gas Contracts, *Land Economics*, 62, pp. 111-118.

Canes, M.E. and D.A. Norman (1985), Long-Term Contracts and Market Forces in Natural Gas Market, *The Journal of Energy and Development*, 10, pp. 73-96.

Carney, E.M. (1978), Pricing Provisions in Coal Contracts, Rocky Mountain Mineral Institute, Matthew Bender, New York, pp. 197-230.

Charlton, D.W. (1979), Contracts, Price Rigidity and Market Equilibrium, *Journal of Political Economy*, 87, pp. 1036-1062.

Charlton, D.W. (1986), The Rigidity of Prices, *American Economic Review*, 76, pp. 637-658.

Christy, F.T. (1975), Property Rights in the World Ocean, *Natural Resources Journal*, pp. 695-712.

Coase, R.H. (1937), The Nature of the Firm, *Economica* 4, pp. 386-405.

Coase, R.H. (1960), The Problem of Social Costs, *Journal of Law and Economics*, Vol. 3, pp. 1-44.

Daintith, T.C. (1982), Energy Information Administration, Natural Gas Producer/Purchase Contracts and Their Potential Impacts on Natural Gas Markets, *Document DOE-EIA-0330* (June).

Daintith, T.C. (1985), The Design and Performance of Long-Term Contracts San Domenico (FJ), *Italian E.U.I. Working Paper* Law Department, European University Institute.

Daintith, T.C. (1987), Contract Design and Practice in the Natural Resources Sector, in F. Nicklisch (ed.), *Heidelberger Kolloqium Technologie und Recht* 1986, forthcoming.

Dasgupta, P. (1982), *The Control of Resources*. Oxford.

Diamond P. and E. Maskin (1979), An Equilibrium Analysis of Research and Breach of Contracts : I: Steady States, *Bell Journal of Economics*, 10, pp. 282-318.

Furubotn, E.G. and S. Pejovic (1972), Property Rights and Economic Theory: A Survey of Recent Literature, *Journal of Economic Literature* 10, pp. 1137-1162.

Garnaut, R. and A. Clunies Ross (1975), Uncertainty, Risk Aversion and the Taxing of Natural Resources Projects, *Economic Journal* 85, pp. 272-287.

Garnaut, R. and Clunies Ross, A. (1983), *Taxation of Mineral Rents*, Clarendon Press, Oxford.

Grotius, H. (1601), *De Mare Liberum sive de Jure quod Batavis Competit ad Indicana Commercio*, Dissertation, reprinted as *Freedom of the Seas*, Oxford 1916.

Harries, H. (1980), "Adaptation of Long-Term Contracts, in Pearce, D.W., Siebert, H., Walter, I., (eds.), *Risk and Political Economy of Resource Development*, Macmillan, London, pp. 165-169.

Hartje, V.J. (1983), *Theorie und Politik der Meeresnutzung. Eine ökonomisch-institutionelle Analyse*, Campus, Frankfurt.

Henry, C. (1974), Option Values in the Economics of Irreplacable Assets, *The Review of Economic Studies*, 41, pp. 89-104.

Hubbard, R.G. and R.J. Weiner (1985), Nominal Contracting and Price Flexibility in Product Markets, *NBER Working Paper* no. 1738.

Jeckel, H. (1985), Ölterminmärkte - Nutzungsmöglichkeiten und Risiken, *Zeitschrift für Energiewirtschaft*, pp. 220-234.

Jones, R.A. and J.M. Ostoy (1984), Flexibility and Uncertainty, *Review of Economic Studies*, 51, pp. 13-32.

Joskow, P. (1985), Vertical Integration and Long-Term Contracts: The Case of Coal-Burning Electric Generating Plants, *Journal of Law, Economics and Organization*, I, pp. 33-80.

Joskow, P. (1987), Contract Duration and Relationship-Specific Investments: Empirical Evidence from Coal-Markets. *American Economic Review* 77, pp. 168-185.

Kirchner et. al. (1979), *Mining Ventures in Developing Countries, Interests, Bargaining Processes and Legal Concepts*, Deventer and Frankfurt.

Kobrin, S.J. (1984), The Nationalization of Oil Production, 1918-1980, in: Pearce, D.W., Siebert, H. and Walter, I. (eds.), *Risk and the Economics of Resource Development*, MacMillan, London, pp. 137-164.

Lampert, R.A. (1983), Long-Term Contracts and Moral Hazard, *Bell Journal of Economics*, 14, pp. 441-452.

Long, N.V. and N. Vousden (1977), Optimal Control Theorems, in Pitchford, J.D. and S.J. Turnowsky (eds.), *Applications of Control Theory to Economic Analysis*, North Holland, Amsterdam, pp. 11-34.

Macneil, I.R. (1985), Relational Contract - What We Do and Do Not Know, *Wisconsin Law Review*, pp. 483.

Macneil, I.R. (1987), Contracts: Adjustment of Long-Term Economic Relations under Classical, Neoclassical and Relational Contract Law, *Northwestern University Law Review*, 72, pp. 854-905.

Masten, S. R. (1987), Equity, Opportunism and the Design of Contractual Relations, *Zeitschrift für die gesamte Staatswissenschaft*, forthcoming.

Masten, S.E. and K.J. Crocker (1984), Regulation and Non-Price Competition in Long-Term Contracts for Natural Gas, University of Virginia, *Working Paper* (December).

Masten, S.E. and K.J. Crocker (1985), Efficient Adaption in Long-Term Contracts: Take-or-Pay Provisions for Natural Gas, *American Economic Review*, 75, pp. 1083-1093.

Meder, H. (1984), *Die intertemporale Allokation erschöpfbarer Naturressourcen bei fehlenden Zukunftsmärkten und institutionalisierter Marktsubstitution*, Peter Lang Verlag, Frankfurt am Main.

Meyer, A. (1984), Besteuerung von erschöpfbaren Ressourcen: Die Rohstoffrentensteuer, in: Siebert, H. (ed.), *Intertemporale Allokation*, Frankfurt, pp. 367-394.

Mikesell, R.F. (Ed.), (1971), *Foreign Investment in the Petroleum and Mineral Industries: Case Studies of Investor-Host Country Relations*, Johns Hopkins University Press, Baltimore.

Norman, D. (1984), Indefinite Pricing Provisions in Natural Gas Contracts, American Petroleum Institute, *Discussion Paper* no. 34, Washington.

Palmer, K.F. (1980), Mineral Taxation Policies in Developing Countries: An Application of Resource Rent Tax, *IMF Staff Papers*, 27, pp. 517-542.

Pierce, R.J. (1982), Natural Gas Regulation, Deregulation and Contracts, *Virginia Law Review*, 68, pp. 63-115.

Polinski, A.M. (1983), Risk Sharing through Breach of Contract Remedies, *Journal of Legal Studies*, 12, pp. 427-444.

Polinski, A.M. (1986), Fix Price versus Spot Price Contracts: A Study in Risk Allocation, *NBER Working Paper* no. 1817.

Pollard, D.E. (1985), Long-Term Bauxit Sales Contracts, *Natural Resource Forum*, 9, pp. 25-32.

Radetzki, M. (1982), Has Political Risk Scared Mineral Investment Away from the Deposits in Developing Countries? *World Development* 39-48.

Roberts, B. (1980), The Effects of Supply Contracts on the Output and Price of an Exhaustible Resource, *Quarterly Journal of Economics*, 95, pp. 245-260.

Rosen, S. (1985), Implicit Contracts: A Survey, *Journal of Economic Literature*, 23, pp. 1144-1175.

Schanze, E. (1981), *Mining Ventures in Developing Countries*, Deventer and Frankfurt.

Scott, R.E. (1987), Risk Distribution and Cooperation in Long-Term Contracts, in F. Nicklisch (ed.), *Heidelberger Kolloqium Technologie und Recht*, forthcoming.

Shavell, S. (1985), The Design of Contracts and Remedies for Breach, *Quarterly Journal of Economics*, 100, pp. 121-148.

Siebert, H. (1983), *Ökonomische Theorie natürlicher Ressourcen*, Mohr, Tübingen.

Siebert, H. (1985), *Economics of the Resource-Exporting Country. Intertemporal Theory of Supply and Trade*, Greenwich, Conn.

Siebert, H. (1987), *Economics of the Environment. Theory and Policy*, 2nd ed., Heidelberg.

Siebert, H. (1987a), Environmental Pollution and Uncertainty - Prevention and Risk Allocation, in: F. Holzheu, *Society and Uncertainty*, forthcoming.

Siebert, H. (1987b), Langfristige Lieferverträge im internationalen Ressourcenhandel, *SFB 178, Diskussionbeiträge*, forthcoming.

Siebert, H. (1987c), Nutzungsrechte und internationale Rohstoffversorgung, *Ifo-Studien*, forthcoming.

Siebert, H. (1987d), *Risk Allocation in Large-Scale Ventures*, Kyklos, forthcoming.

Siebert, H. and M. Rauscher (1985), Vertical Integration by Oil-Exporting Countries, *Intereconomics*, 20, pp. 211-216.

Tirole, J. (1986), Procurement and Renegotiation, *Journal of Political Economy*, 94, pp. 235-259.

Townsend, R.M. (1982), Optimal Multiperiod Contracts and the Gain from Enduring Relationships Under Private Information, *Journal of Political Economy*, 90, pp. 1166-1180.

Townsend, R.M. (1984), Theories of Contract Design and Market Organization: Conceptual Bases for Understanding Future Markets, in Anderson, R.W. (ed.), *The Industrial Organization of Future Markets*, Heath, Lexington.

Vernon, R. (1971), *Sovereignty at Bay: The Multinational Spread of US Enterprises*, Basic Books, New York.

Vogelsang, I. (1986), *The Role of Contract in International Coal Trade*, mimeo, Boston.

Walter, I. (1986), *Financing Natural Resource Projects*, mimeo, Fontainebleau, New York.

Williamson, O.E. (1979), Transaction-Cost Economics: The Governance of Contractual Relations, *The Journal of Law and Economics*, 22, pp. 233-261.

Williamson, O.E. (1985), *The Economic Institutions of Capitalism*, Free Press, New York.

SUMMARY OF THE DISCUSSION

Jonathan P. Thomas

The paper identifies six specific features of natural resource industries, namely a long-time horizon, vertical stages of production, high set-up costs, private risks, idiosyncratic investment, and social risk. It is argued that these features have implications for the institutional arrangements. These features are perhaps largely characteristic of national resource markets, but there are other features which are important in international markets. Firstly, property rights tend to be much less well defined, consider for example orbital slots for satellites. At a national level, common property problems are being sorted out, but not at the international level. In the absence of transaction costs, it is true that it does not matter a great deal who gets the original property rights. But with transaction costs it is important to have institutional arrangements which allocate the rights to those who can best use them. Secondly, exchange rate risks should be mentioned, although these of course are not specific to resource markets. Finally, political risks need to be taken into account in international markets, although it is not clear that companies take more political risks in international markets than they do in the domestic market. For example, Chevron at the moment has probably got more political power in communist governed Angola than in the U.S. - it is quite possible that property rights in Angola are less exposed to political risks.

Legal research into hard-mineral projects suggests that host governments are often willing to agree to adjustment in arrangements in favour of the investing company, in response to changed market conditions. Moreover, while there certainly exists the problem of locked-in agents with little or no bargaining strength, as discussed in the paper, empirical research suggests that the involvement of third parties, especially international organizations like the World Bank, can alleviate the problem. The reason is clear: the host government may have an interest in prolonging relations with the third party, if not with the investing company. Another

Studies in International Economics and Institutions
Vosgerau (Ed.) New Institutional Arrangements for the World Economy
© Springer-Verlag Berlin Heidelberg 1989

interesting development, which can help to resolve some of the problems mentioned in the paper arising from idiosyncratic investment, is the possibility of breaking up the overall investment into smaller parts, thus involving more parties than just the host government and investor. In this case, it is very difficult for the host government to proceed effectively with projects that have been expropriated. This may explain the dwindling in recent years in the number of expropriations.

A further empirical issue, which is of great importance from the point of view of the paper, is whether institutional arrangements are industry specific or country specific. Evidence from contracts in the areas of oil, hard minerals, and forest projects, suggests that there is an industry specific pattern to such contracts. On the other hand, as host countries have become more experienced in dealing with transnational corporations, country specific rules have developed, and it is probably correct to say that current contracts reflect both industry and country specific rules.

Property Rights in Information and the Multinational Firm: The Case of Technical Learning in a Multiplant System

Eirik G. Furubotn

1. Introduction

The growing literature on the multinational enterprise (Buckley 1981), (Dunning 1971), (Kindleberger 1969), (Vernon 1977) indicates that, at the simplest level, the MNE can be understood as a firm that owns income generating assets in more than one country. Accepting this definition, certain questions follow. We should like to know, inter alia, why this type of structural arrangement comes into existence, and why foreign direct investment may seem attractive to a firm. Current explanations of these matters differ somewhat but tend to emphasize the role of organizational economics and, thus, suggest that the MNE emerges as the solution to the problem of deciding whether firms or markets should be used for allocating resources.[1] Characteristically, it is argued that, even when other factors are favorable, the appearance of the MNE depends on the condition that: ...the *internalization* of international transactions must be preferable to the arm's length use of markets (Ethier 1986, p. 805).

Since there is evidence that firms undertaking multinational operations tend to be those that are engaged in technological research and innovation (Mansfield 1979), the international transactions required often involve the transmission of information. This fact is significant. In practice, there are special difficulties associated with technology transfers that make the choice of organizational means, or institutional structure, particularly important. While contracts and markets cannot be completely ruled out as possible devices for facilitating the exchange of knowledge, market transactions between independent firms become less desirable options when

---

[1]   See, for example: Buckley and Casson (1976), Casson (1979), Dunning (1981), Kindleberger (1969), McCulloch (1984), Rugman (1980), Williamson (1975), (1981).

Studies in International Economics and Institutions
Vosgerau (Ed.) New Institutional Arrangements for the World Economy
© Springer-Verlag Berlin Heidelberg 1989

complex and continuing transfers of information must take place. Generally speaking, as contracts have to become more complicated, transaction costs rise and other problems appear (Alchian and Demsetz 1972), (Klein, Crawford and Alchian 1978), (Williamson 1975). It is, of course, the growth of these unfavorable trends that can lead ultimately to direct foreign investment, the internalization of trans-actions and the formation of a MNE (Magee 1977).

Consistent with this general approach, the present paper is also interested in infor-mation transfers. But the activities considered involve more than the simple trans-fer of proprietary technical knowledge from one producer to another.

What is stressed is the idea that, in many cases, production experience brings about learning and improvement of technology. Firms must be concerned, then, with the utilization of the "messages" that come to them over time through learning. Given a multiplant system, efficiency demands that institutional arrangements permit the consolidation of systemwide learning so that technology can advance at the most rapid pace possible. Such consolidation depends, in turn, on a particular ownership structure and a relatively low-cost exchange of messages among units in the inter-national system. Under the conditions assumed in the model presented below, many transactions are involved each period, and the transmission process must go on over time until the potential of the learning curve is exhausted. The collection, treat-ment and dissemination of large amounts of technical information implies signifi-cant costs. However, if the argument of the paper is correct, internalization of transactions via a MNE is likely to yield advantages. Specifically, the costs of transferring technical information under the MNE are almost certain to be lower than they would be under different organization of the required activities.

When a group of plants producing a common commodity is able to cooperate effectively and speed up the learning process, welfare gains can emerge. As long as the social rate of discount is positive, improved technology available at an earlier date is worth more than the same technology available at a later date. Moreover, by accelerating the development of technology, the time shape of a firm's profit stream can be changed and its net present value increased. This condition is important because it implies that each firm has incentives to seek out an organiz-ational structure that will promote the acceleration of learning. But, insofar as organizational economics indicates that the most rapid advance of learning (and technology) is brought about by the *internalization* of interplant transactions, the total situation suggests the need for multinational firms. In other words, if conditions are generally favorable to direct foreign investment, technical learning may assume importance. It appears that, whenever the learning phenomenon is significant empirically, another basis exists for the formation of multinational firms. The remainder of the paper will attempt to develop this argument more systematically.

2. Cumulative Output and Technical Change

Conventional microeconomic theory places major emphasis on the relation between a firm's output rate and its corresponding cost of production. As Alchian (1959) has emphasized, however, productive operations have other dimensions or characteristics, and it is important to take cognizance of these relatively neglected features. That is, if a more complete and satisfactory model of production is to be established, certain modifications must be made in orthodox neoclassical analysis. The firm's total cost at any moment should be understood to depend not only on the rate of output but also on the total contemplated volume of output, the time period at which the first unit of output is to be forthcoming, and the length of the interval over which the output is to be made available. These variables are, of course, interrelated; when the values of any three are specified, the value of the fourth is automatically determined. For purposes of the present paper, the key variable of the group is *cumulative output*. What has to be considered is how variations in the firm's total contemplated output affect costs and, hence, economic behavior.

According to the literature, an increase in the firm's planned cumulative output (V) can affect cost in *two* general ways. First, there is evidence that a larger planned V is produced in a different fashion from that of a smaller planned V and, inter alia, involves *qualitatively different* capital inputs.[2] Alchian asserts that: ..."the method

---

[2] The situation described can be interpreted as one in which the firm shifts from one production subfunction to another. See: Furubotn (1964), (1965), (1970).

of production is a function of the volume of output, especially when output is
produced from basic dies - and there are few, if any, methods of production that
do not involve 'dies'" (1959, p. 29). Moreover, given physical principles, durable
equipment intended for long production runs tends to be available on relatively
favorable terms so that increased expenditure on more durable inputs results in a
more than proportionate increase of output potential.[3] For any given rate of output, then, the relation between the firm's total cost of production (C) and planned
cumulative output (V) can be summarized as follows:

$$\partial C/\partial V > 0, \qquad \partial^2 C/\partial V^2 < 0 \quad .$$

The second connection linking cumulative output to cost arises from the fact that
longer production runs permit substantial on-the-job experience to be gained and
learning to take place. In short, knowledge increases as V becomes larger; *technological advance* occurs and the firm's cost function is permanently lowered.[4] This
means that, after learning has come about, any volume of output can be produced
more cheaply. It is true, however, that there is an upper limit on the improvement
in technical efficiency that can be attained via learning no matter how much
cumulative output is produced. As Arrow has indicated:

> A ...generalization that can be gleaned from many of the classic
> learning experiments is that learning associated with repetition of
> essentially the same problem is subject to sharply diminishing returns.
> There is an equilibrium response pattern for any given stimulus,
> towards which the behavior of the learner tends with repetition (1962,
> pp. 155-56).

The ideas here are familiar and, in industrial engineering circles, the significance
of the "learning curve" or "progress curve" for technology seems to be well understood. Moreover, it is possible to explain the basis of self-induced technical change
plausibly by pointing to such factors as: progressive improvement of job skills and

---

3   Alchian notes that: "Different methods of tooling, parts design, and assembly
is the usual explanation given in the production engineering literature" (1959
p. 29).

4   Effectively, the set of production subfunctions in existence changes as technical knowledge is improved.

372

labor effectiveness, general advances in coordination, shop organization and engineering liaison, more efficient subassembly production, and more efficient tools. There is also substantial empirical information testifying to the reality of the effects discussed in the theoretical literature.[5] Alchian, for example, mentions that production experience in the airframe industry falls into a definite pattern such that the cost of the 2n-th item is 80 per cent of the cost of the n-th item. Similarly, Arrow (1962) cites a number of studies that illustrate the learning effect. The case of the Horndal iron works in Sweden is of particular interest. At Horndal, even though there was no new capital investment in the plant over a long period of time, it was found that output per man-hour rose on the average of 2 per cent per annum. Given this evidence, Arrow concludes that the increased performance can only be imputed to learning from experience.

Writings on the learning curve suggest that output-induced changes in technical efficiency can be expected to appear in many different industries, and to exert significant impact on the cost of producing output. It would seem, therefore, that learning phenomena should be accounted for in the theory of the firm and, as will be argued, especially in the theory of the *multinational* firm. To simplify discussion, it will be convenient to construct an elementary model of technological evolution that explains how the productive efficiency of an oligopolistic firm can increase as the firm's cumulative output grows over time and it gains on-the-job experience. Assume that the firm in question operates subject to a stock-flow production function of the general form:

$$q_t = f_t(x_t, K_o, \alpha_t), \qquad t = 1, 2, ..., T \quad . \tag{1}$$

Output per period (q_t) depends on a current input flow (x_t), a capital stock (K_o), and contemporaneous technology as represented by the parameter α_t. The capital goods employed are of a particular type and have a given durability of T periods.[6] An output flow (q_t) appears at the end of each period (1, 2, ..., T) after the

---

5 Alchian cites a number of references (1959, p. 36), including: Hirsch (1952).

6 Physical depreciation of the capital stock is assumed to occur only at the end of the T-th period but, then, to 100%.

durable capital goods have been put in place at the end of period t = 0 to co-operate with the current input (x_t). Capital goods are assumed to be malleable ex ante but not ex post. At each cross section of time, (1) is taken to be strictly concave and to possess the mathematical properties conventionally ascribed to production functions.

What is special about the model being developed is the idea that the firm's production experience leads to progressive technical improvement. For simplicity, we say that this improvement always takes the form of *neutral* technological change and that it is revealed as a change in the magnitude of the shift parameter α_t. Ceteris paribus, enterprise productivity can be said to depend on the history of the firm's past outputs. It is true, of course, that the interrelations among cumulative output, learning and technological improvement can be complex, and not easily captured in a simple mathematical formula. For example, technical change may be linked to a series of lagged relations, to rates of output, or rates of increase in output, etc. Moreover, learning can result from deliberate attempts to change production processes via "value engineering." These latter activities are based in part on production experience and are carried on while output continues to flow from the firm. Nevertheless, despite these problems, the purposes of the model will be served adequately if the technical learning equation is reduced to:

$$\alpha_t = u_o + g(Z_{t-1}; \varepsilon_t) \quad , \qquad t = 1, 2, ..., T \quad . \tag{2}$$

Here, the symbol u_o represents the value of the technical efficiency parameter (α_1) before any production experience has been obtained (i.e., at t = 1 when Z_o = 0). In general, of course, past outputs count and the firm's cumulative output is important. But the technological outcome at any round is also influenced by chance factors. Thus, at the beginning of any period t = τ parameter α_τ depends on the initial value u_o, the firm's total volume of output summed from period t = 1 through period t = τ - 1 (or $Z_{\tau-1}$), and a random variable ε_t. More concretely, ε_t can be understood as a normally distributed random variable with a zero mean and finite variance. The cumulative output at $t = \tau$ is by definition:

$$Z_{\tau-1} = \sum_{t=1}^{\tau-1} q_t \quad .$$

(3)

As indicated earlier, the central idea is that the value of the parameter α_t will vary systematically with the firm's cumulative output and follow a generally rising path until some critical output total $\hat{Z}$ is reached. From that point onward, technological efficiency is effectively unchanging and the parameter remains at the upper limit $\hat{\alpha}$.[7]

Since oligopolistic markets are often characterized by stable prices, it is not unreasonable to assume, for simplicity, that the oligopolist being considered in the model maintains his price *unchanged* over time even though moderate demand shifts occur and even though his costs of production fall progressively with cumulative output.[8] Given this special price behavior, the quantity of product sold each period will depend on the succession of demand curves faced by the firm over its planning interval 1, 2, ..., T. By assumption, the planning interval is established by the durability of the initial capital stock (i.e., T). The firm's output solution ($q_\tau{}^*$) in any period $t = \tau$ is important because the value of the technological parameter in the next period ($\alpha_{\tau+1}$) is determined, in part, by $q_\tau{}^*$ and the additional production experience it implies. If the equilibrium outputs of the oligopolistic

---

[7] It is conceivable, of course, that some new development, such as the installation of complementary capital equipment, could enhance productivity.

[8] This assumption is essentially one of convenience; the intent of the paper is not to consider oligopolistic pricing policy. It is necessary, however, to have some indication of the firm's planned outputs over time so that cumulative output and technical learning can be estimated. In defense of the "fixed-price" assumption, it can be argued that price changes tend to be difficult and costly to make if illegal collusion exists in the industry, if contracts with buyers have to be renegotiated, etc. In short, given existing constraints, frequent price changes can be responsible for greater losses than gains. See: Stigler (1947). For a more sophisticated theory relating the learning curve and oligopolistic behavior, see: Fudenberg and Tirole (1983), (1986, pp. 17-30).

enterprise are estimated as $q_1{}^*$, $q_2{}^*$, ..., $q_T{}^*$, it follows that a particular timepath of technical improvement will be revealed.[9]

In general, it is apparent that no matter what specific price-output policy is pursued by the oligopolist, some definite output stream will emerge and some definite timepath of technical improvement can be estimated for the enterprise. Consider an oligopolistic firm that has a history of operation in an industry but that is now contemplating investment in a new plant designed to replace its existing facility.[10] We assume that the firm accepts the price-output policy established in the industry and plans to adjust to this policy over time. Then, given the data of the system, the firm's optimal investment and production program can be determined. Under the projected conditions in the oligopolistic industry, the development of the firm can be traced from period t = 0 when the new plant is put in place. The results obtained are sensitive to the assumptions made about a variety of matters - oligopolistic pricing policy, market demand, learning rates, etc. Any firm, however, must make initial choices and formulate an operating plan so that it has some conception of where it is going over time. The decision taken with respect to the capital stock ($K_o{}^*$) is especially important because, once committed to a particular type of durable capital equipment, the firm tends to be locked in and, characteristically, will face substantial costs if it attempts to change the original stock $K_o{}^*$ before its normal replacement date. Limited flexibility can, of course, be secured by varying the current input stream (x_t) as more information becomes available over time, and by following appropriate inventory policy, but the basic decision on capital structure still looms large as a factor affecting the long-term profitability of the firm.

---

[9] No consideration is given to inventory policy and its possible effects on the development of technology.

[10] The problem is set up in this way to secure a simple point of departure for subsequent discussion.

3. Technical Information and the Motivation for Direct Investment

The firm discussed in section 2 was assumed to be operating wholly within one country and to have no foreign branches. A question arises, therefore, as to what circumstances may induce this firm to undertake direct investment abroad and transform itself into a multinational enterprise. Certainly, a shift to multinational organization is not automatic. According to current thinking, the transition comes about only if certain special conditions are met.[11] First, it is obvious that a firm must be able to *compete* abroad; but there may be considerable difficulty in penetrating a foreign market. Indigenous firms possess advantages by virtue of their superior knowledge of the local environment, their understanding of domestic business activities, etc. Thus, if a foreign company is to be successful in overcoming local competition, it must have some "compensating advantage." Various possibilities exist here but, in the case of the firm being considered in the model, it is sufficient to say that, as an oligopolistic producer, it has ownership advantages in the area of proprietary technical information so that it can compete. However, even granting that the oligopolistic producer is able to sell output in foreign markets, it does not necessarily follow that the firm will set up manufacturing subsidiaries abroad. Quite conceivably, the oligopolist could carry on all production in the domestic economy and export to foreign countries. For direct investment to be regarded as a serious alternative, then, two additional conditions must hold.

The literature suggests that locational considerations must dominate and render concentrated production unattractive. This would be the case if, e.g., tariff and transport cost barriers were so high as to make exportation of the product from a central location unprofitable. In other words, the situation envisioned is one where foreign sales are feasible but are most profitable only when actual production is *undertaken in the foreign country*. Then, from the standpoint of a firm contemplating entrance into a foreign market, the effective question is whether it should use "markets" or "organization" to accomplish its objectives. Clearly, a choice can exist for the oligopolist described above; the firm may have to decide between initiating market transactions and licensing foreign firms to produce the commod-

---

[11] The argument is stated clearly and succinctly in: Buckley (1981), Ethier (1986).

ity, or establishing plants abroad via direct investment and producing the commodity itself. Insofar as analysis of the costs and benefits associated with the respective approaches reveals that the internalization of international transactions promises greater profit than the use of contracts and markets, a shift to multinational organization is indicated.

If this logic is accepted, the existence of the multinational enterprise is explained by three basic factors - imperfect competition or ownership advantages, locational influences, and internalization. It appears, however, that theoretical discussions of the multinational enterprise increasingly emphasize the organizational basis of direct foreign investment as the area deserving study. Concern is with the circumstances under which internalization of transactions is likely to take place. Thus, Ethier argues:

> ...internalization should be the focus of theories of direct investment. Internalization is the only one of the three key elements not already incorporated into trade theory. Locational considerations are basic to the pure theory of international trade,and ownership advantages figure prominently in our recent theories of trade and imperfect competition. Internalization, by contrast, is one of our critical "black boxes," always appealed to but never explained. The central task of any general equilibrium theory of the multinational corporation must be to elucidate the role of the internalization issue (1986, pp. 805-06).

Given this perspective, key problems of the multinational firm are subsumed within the economics of organization. It becomes important to consider the forces that determine the boundaries of the firm and decide its internal structure. Property-rights arrangements and transaction costs take on crucial significance. Analysis of these matters is not entirely straightforward, however, because, as noted, markets and organizations represent alternative means for coordinating productive activity. A priori, there can be no presumption that internalization will always be the best solution. Rather, each case must be decided on the basis of the economic and technical conditions present.

When cumulative output affects technical efficiency, production experience, however achieved, has significance for the firm. Ceteris paribus, any information gained over time through production contributes to the lowering of the firm's costs and an increase in its profits. Relative to the oligopolistic producer described earlier, this situation means that technological considerations and the need for information exchange may push the firm toward multinational organization.[12] In effect, manufacturing units are worth more when operating within some integrated, multiplant structure than they are when operating independently. The integration requirement does not imply, of itself, that a multinational enterprise must emerge but, as will be shown below, contractual agreements capable of generating the same results as the MNE would be difficult to bring about for a set of independent firms.

In any event, once we conceive of the possibility of a network of plants (or firms) cooperating in the exchange of technical information, equation (3) must be re-written in a new form:

$$Z_{t-1} = \sum_{t=1}^{\tau-1} q_t + \beta_{\tau-1} \left[\sum_{i=1}^{n} \sum_{t=b}^{\tau-1} Q_{it} \right] \quad , \quad 0 \leq \beta_{\tau+1} \leq 1 \quad . \quad (3')$$

What this expression suggests is that the oligopolist's *effective* cumulative output at t= τ- 1 is the sum of two components - viz., the cumulative output produced domestically over the interval t=1 through t= τ -1 plus some fraction ($\beta_{\tau-1}$) of the cumulative output produced by the n foreign plants in the network from t=b through t= τ -1. For simplicity, we assume that all of the n plants operating abroad were established at the same time. The founding date of these plants, t=b, represents a period after t=1, the date the original (domestic) plant began production. Note that each foreign plant manufacturing the product (Q_{it}) adds something to the group's cumulative output and, hence, can be expected to contribute to the learning process through which improved understanding of technology (α_t) is obtained. It seems plausible to assume that, in general, each plant in the network will follow a somewhat different learning path over time. That is, as production experience is extended, period by period, each of the n+1 plants is not likely to discover pre-

---

[12]   This case is to be distinguished from one based on scale effects. Multiplant economies can arise from a more intensive utilization of some fixed factor available in the oligopolist's home plant, but this situation is distinct from trade in information.

cisely the same information about technology at precisely the same time as its fellow members in the group. "Messages" come to each plant as a result of the productive activities undertaken but, at any round, the actual message to be secured is not known in advance. The elements of knowledge received per period are, in effect, random variables. Thus, at any cross section of time, there is advantage to be gained from the *unification* of the information collected by the n+1 members of the system.

Given the conditions described, it is true, nevertheless, that a certain amount of *duplication* of experience will take place in the system. In addition, there will always be some *losses in the transmission* of information to the central headquarters. When the operation of a network of similar plants is considered, then, a unit of the commodity produced by a foreign plant is not fully equivalent to a unit of the commodity produced by the domestic plant in advancing learning. This condition is reflected in the model by using the parameter $\beta_{\tau-1}$ in (3') to "reduce" the cumulative output term associated with the production of the foreign subsidiaries. In general, the parameter β_t will tend to vary with circumstances; its value at any point depends, in a complex way, on the number of foreign plants in the system (n), the cumulative volume of output turned out by these plants (V_{t-1}), and on a random variable η_t. For purposes of the model, the following simplified expression can be used to suggest the relations extant.

$$\beta_t = h(n, V_{t-1}; \eta_t) \tag{4}$$

A reasonable conjecture might be that, ceteris paribus, increasing cumulative output (V_{t-1}) has the effect of diminishing the magnitude of β_t. Similarly, there is reason to believe that, beyond some point, an increasing number of firms (n) will cause β_t to decline, ceteris paribus. At base, these results appear because of the increasing potential for transmission losses and duplication of findings as V_{t-1} and n increase in magnitude. Chance factors also intervene here; and the random variable η_t, which is normally distributed and characterized by finite variance and a mean of zero, is intended to reflect such forces. At any round, conditions may make the given production increment more or less significant for progress. In any event, once the value of parameter β_t is established, it is possible to register the system's cumulative output (Z_{t-1}) in *standardized* units. Equations (4) and (3') yield the cumulative output level that actually counts in the oligopolist's learning process. In other words, it is the "corrected" value of output, Z_{t-1}, that is employed in (2) to secure the magnitude of the technological parameter (α_t) for any period.

While the output of foreign plants may have to be discounted somewhat in calculating the effect their operations have on learning, this does not mean that foreign plants are inconsequential. Moreover, their contribution to technical progress can be made greater if action is taken at the individual plants to enhance the normal discovery process based on experience. Programs such as value engineering are also related to cumulative output, and these may be used to increase learning through deliberate experimentation and research (Miles 1961). Insofar as the n+1 plants are integrated within one firm and are controlled by a central technology office, the ancillary engineering programs can be coordinated and made more effective. Such positive practices are clearly helpful. In general, it seems likely that the magnitude of β_t will vary from industry to industry. But as long as β_t is greater than zero, the existence of foreign plants will have some effect in *accelerating* technical progress for the parent firm (and for the system). Conceivably, the value of β_t can be relatively large. Consolidating the increments of knowledge gained per period by the n+1 plants not only concentrates experience but can occasionally lead to unexpected breakthroughs. Certain combinations of information may open the way for sudden, substantial advances in understanding (Hess 1983, pp. 131-49). Such forward leaps are more likely to appear earlier in time when the learning of the full system can be drawn upon at each period.

Acting alone, each individual plant can assess, and gradually fit together, the succession of "messages" it receives over time. In this way a unit, facing given demand conditions, is able to increase its understanding of technology. Indeed, given sufficient time, a plant (or firm) operating in isolation may be capable of capturing <u>all</u> of the information that is to be obtained from production experience. But the "full understanding" position ($\hat{\alpha}$) will, in general, be reached much later in time by the isolated plant than by the integrated network of plants. Another point deserves mention here. At each cross section of time, the production of an increment of output by an isolated plant can bring about greater or lesser learning depending on the message the plant receives. There is a random process at work that determines the elements of technical information thrown up at each period; and a single plant can experience significant variation in outcome. Conditions are different, however, when a network of cooperating plants exists. As the number of plants in the integrated system increases, variance in terms of effective learning per period will tend to be reduced for the system.[13] This means, in turn, that technical progress will unfold more smoothly over time and that the net present value of the integrated firm will be enlarged. Again, consolidation shows its advantage over isolation.

The model of section 2 was able, given certain simplifying assumptions, to project the values of the technological parameters that would hold at different cross sections of time as the firm added to its production experience: i.e., $\alpha_1{}^*$, $\alpha_2{}^*$, ..., $\alpha_T{}^*$. The firm here was said to operate solely within the domestic market and to have only one plant. Next, we assume that this firm transforms itself into a *multinational enterprise* and operates manufacturing plants in both the domestic economy and in foreign countries. Using the same basic assumptions about domestic demand, price policy, etc., but including now the impact of the foreign subsidiaries on learning, a new set of technological parameters will emerge: i.e., α'_{b+1}, α'_{b+2}, ..., α'_T. This series begins at period t=b+1, reflecting the fact that the foreign plants were established in period t=b. Each of the technological parameters here will be *larger* than its counterpart ($\alpha_t{}^*$) in the first set from period t = b+1 to t = H. At t = H, we have $\alpha_H{}^* = \hat{\alpha}$; the technological parameter at this time is as large as it can be because, by assumption, the possibilities for further learning (via production) have been exhausted. Of course, from t = H onwards, the neutral technological parameters are the same whether the oligopolist operates with or without foreign plants. Given the assumptions of the analysis, the outcome is clear. What production abroad can accomplish, apart from disseminating the oligopolist's special technical knowledge as of period t=b, is to *speed up* the arrival and utilization of new technical information. But such a change in the timing of knowledge is important! Production experience is compressed and the learning process is accel-

---

[13] In the model, all foreign plants were founded at the same time and were made aware of the most advanced technology of the period. If these conditions did not hold, some plants would be further along the learning curve than others, and much subsequent production experience in the system would be redundant.

erated. In short, the foreign subsidiaries, by pushing the oligopolistic firm to the critical $\hat{\alpha}$ value more quickly (say at t = M), enable the firm to enlarge its net present value.[14]

What should be emphasized at this point is that the oligopolistic firm of our illustration has limited opportunities for increasing its profits other than by arranging for production to take place in foreign countries. According to the assumptions made, greater domestic production, and acceleration of technology, cannot be achieved through greater exports. Similarly, major increases in output destined for the domestic market are ruled out by the tacit agreements that permit the firms within the oligopolistic industry to find a modus vivendi and a more or less stable equilibrium. It is true that the firm can move in completely new directions and undertake domestic product diversification or the development of totally new technologies. But such strategies can tend to be both costly and risky. Thus, assuming that there is comparatively easy investment access to foreign markets, this option must appear attractive.

Equation (3') indicates that production of the commodity at any given plant has the effect of generating valuable technical information as a type of by-product. What is important, therefore, is to establish an organizational scheme that will permit effective use to be made of the knowledge by-product. Since pooling of the information secured at each production locus can multiply the value of the separate strands of information discovered, *exchange of the elements learned among members of the producing group* has to be viewed as advantageous. Such consolidation of knowledge creates value by making improved technology available sooner rather than later. It is also clear that the multinational enterprise will represent the appropriate organizational means to obtain the benefits promised here if information exchange can be accomplished with lower transaction costs through the internalization of transactions than through the use of markets. Which approach is superior will depend upon circumstances, but a priori reasoning suggests that when the home office and the outlying plants are required to exchange a large volume of

---

[14] The critical cumulative output volume associated with $\hat{\alpha}$ is $\hat{Z}$. Obviously, this level can be achieved more quickly if greater total production takes place per period in the system (and b > o). Instead of reaching $\hat{\alpha}$ at t = H, $\hat{\alpha}$ can be attained at, e.g., t = M.

complex information on a recurring basis, direct foreign investment (and internalization) is likely to be the least-cost solution (Williamson 1981, p. 1563).

Assuming that general economic conditions are favorable and that the oligopolistic
producer does, in fact, establish a series of wholly-owned subsidiaries abroad, certain conditions follow. First, when setting up the subsidiaries (at period t=b), the
oligopolist has to make a significant investment, and has reason to see that each
foreign plant is provided with equipment comparable to that used in the domestic
plant and is given the benefit of the oligopolist's production experience up to that
point. Second, the oligopolist's domestic headquarters must undertake the task of
coordinating the exchange of technical information within the network. Then,
subsequent to t=b, <u>multilateral</u> information exchange goes forward. Each period,
newly learned technical data flow into headquarters from the n plants in the field.
This input together with the information gleaned in the domestic plant over the
same period are combined to yield improved technical understanding. In symbolic
terms, a revised technological parameter α'_{t+1} emerges for use in the next period.
It follows that the more efficient technology implied by α'_{t+1} will bring about
change in the production function used by the oligopolist's domestic plant and,
also, in the production function used by the n foreign plants. In other words, the
benefits derived from the pooled information will be dispersed by central headquarters to all of the units participating in the integrated organization. Each sector
gains from the collective experience of the group; and no special sharing rules are
necessary because the equity holders of the MNE are the ultimate beneficiaries of
improved technical efficiency in the system. That is, since all of the knowledge
by-products are owned by the same group of stockholders, no costly market
exchange of rights in information is necessary.[15] Moreover, under this scheme,
the process of technological acceleration will continue over time from period t =
b+1 to t = M. At the latter date, progress ceases because all plants will enjoy a
situation in which the technological parameter is at its maximum value $\hat{\alpha}$.

According to the earlier model of section 2, the oligopolist made a decision concerning investment in domestic production capacity without considering the effect

---

[15] It is true, of course, that agency problems may arise within the multinational
enterprise.

multiplant operation could have on the evolution of technology. As a consequence, the solution values found for the durable capital input $(K_0{}^*)$ and the current input stream $(x_1{}^*, x_2{}^*, ..., x_T{}^*)$ are not optimal in the new situation, at period $t = b$, after direct foreign investment has been made. Profits, of course, must suffer relatively unless some corrective action is taken. But alteration of the originally chosen capital stock $(K_0{}^*)$ tends to be costly to effect before period $t=T$. Thus, the more likely approach is to change the variable input (x_t), period by period, as more information on technology becomes available over time. Since the commodity price $(\bar{p})$ is fixed by tacit or explicit agreement among the firms in the industry, and since any attempt to readjust this price unilaterally must be viewed as risky, the oligopolist is, in effect, forced to maximize profit subject to a series of constraints. Nevertheless, the presumption here is that profit, and not other possible objectives such as growth, does represent the main focus of the oligopolist's policy actions.

The use of a multidivisional form of business organization by the oligopolist is consistent with this interpretation (Williamson 1981, p. 1561). In general, the M-form tends to have some advantages in limiting the pursuit of nonprofit managerial objectives and in ensuring that resources are allocated among the divisions of a firm in accordance with their profitability. As has been observed by Buck:

> ...Williamson's theory of the firm is heavily dependent upon profit. Instead of organizing a unitary (or 'U-form') control structure, where a central management team needs wide expert knowledge to control functional divisions of specialists (such as finance, sales, personnel and production functions), he adopts the compound hierarchy or multi-divisional form ('M-form') to monitor profitability. The advantage of this form is that the central controllers are less uncertain about the effectiveness of individual divisions as they need little expert knowledge to compare the aggregate performances of, say, European and U.S. divisions of a multinational company producing and selling similar commodities. It must be noted, however, that the M-form suffers from communication problems and the duplication of specialist staff across divisions (1982, p. 26).

In the case being considered, the MNE is organized as an M-form structure (Stopford and Wells 1972), with strategic planning, major policy decision making, and technical coordination all taking place within its central office. Various conditions must hold if the foreign investments undertaken by the firm are to be profitable but, on the technical side, a prime requirement is that learning for the system be facilitated. Thus, headquarters can be expected to handle the task of coordinating and processing the data flows, while managers at the foreign plants deal with the problem of applying the improved technology (α'_t) effectively as it arrives. Insofar as technical learning is accelerated, the potential for greater profits is enhanced. Moreover, the potential is likely to be realized because the extent of technical improvement is known by the central office and, thus, it is relatively difficult for local managers to dissipate the advantage by diverting company resources to their own ends.

4. Choice of the Optimal Institutional Structure for Technology Transfer

It is widely recognized in the literature that the exchange of information between agents represents an important activity in the international economy (Helpman 1984), (Teece 1977). Conditions often arise that make it desirable to transfer technology and organizational skills from one country to another; and, then, the problem is to decide whether such international transactions should be carried out internally through a firm or externally across markets. Insofar as a market approach is used for technology transfer, corresponding reliance must be placed on the contracting process (D'Aspremont and Gerrard-Varet 1979). But, depending on the nature and extent of the technical information to be conveyed, difficulties may be encountered here. Simple contracts may not be feasible while more complex agreements can be too costly to write and to monitor and enforce. In short, even though it might, at first, seem advantageous for an oligopolist to transfer proprietary knowledge concerning his product abroad and have independent foreign firms produce the commodity for their domestic markets, it is not clear that a suitable agreement for this purpose can always be concluded.

According to organizational economics, there are some cogent reasons why markets may prove to be inefficient means for the international exchange of information. Buckley summarizes one of the major difficulties as follows:

The arguments that firms will often prefer foreign direct investment to licensing are more subtle. Hymer (1976) argued that the advantage possessor cannot appropriate the full return (or rent) from its utilization because of imperfections in the market for knowledge. Such imperfections arising from "buyer uncertainty" (the buyer being unable to assess the worth of the knowledge to him until he is in possession of it), lack of an institutionalized market for knowledge and the dependence of the value of knowledge on its secrecy. The seller thus cannot induce competitive bids in order to appropriate the full returns (1981, p. 72).

In terms of our earlier example, this means that the oligopolist possessing proprietary technical knowledge may not be able to make a convincing disclosure of his "asset" to potential buyers (Williamson 1981), (Arrow 1971). Technology transfer by contract is jeopardized because informational asymmetry exists - the potential buyer, having only limited understanding of what is being offered, has to be wary of opportunistic representations by the seller. By its nature, information is hard to sell, but the difficulties are compounded when *international* exchange is contemplated. As has been pointed out, differences in language, business practices, law, etc. tend to militate against mutual trust and make necessary more elaborate and costly procedures for implementing agreements than would be required for exchange within a single country. Nevertheless, despite the obstacles that may exist, contracts and markets cannot be ruled out completely as possible means for the transfer of technology. Under some circumstances, at least, it is feasible to write and enforce incentive-compatible contracts that will dispel the fear of opportunism and allow both contractual parties to secure benefits. In principle, the latter can be relatively simple to formulate (Ethier 1986, pp. 819-21); but even if contracts must be more elaborate, possibilities for market transactions still exist. As Williamson has explained:

> ...The complex contractual alternative is to negotiate a tie-in sale whereby the technology and associated know-how are transferred as a package. Since the know-how is concentrated in the human assets who are already familiar with the technology, this entails the creation of a "consulting team" by the seller to accompany the physical technology transfer - the object being to overcome start up difficulties and to familiarize the employees of the foreign firm, through teaching and demonstration, with the idiosyncrasies of the operation (1981, p. 1563).

To the extent that impacted information is a significant factor in the international transfer process, the need for a "tie-in" approach is clear. It is also true, however, that the movement of consulting teams et al between firms can pose additional problems at both the contractual and practical levels.

In general, what is suggested here is that contracts tend to become unmanageable when the firm transferring technology must make repeated exchanges with foreign contractual partners and must, at each round, convey a large volume of diverse information. Given uncertainty, any lengthy, ongoing relationship will require periodic adjustment. But not all contingencies can be provided for in advance. Ceteris paribus, the more complex the original contract the greater the transaction costs - which can become prohibitive. Moreover, although attempts may be made initially to establish terms so as to allow for possible changes in economic and technical circumstances, no specification can be sufficiently prescient to provide protection against all alterations in the state of nature. While it may be feasible to write contracts that account for a limited number of contingencies, it is impossible to do so when the number of contingencies is very large. Incomplete initial information, the possibility that new information relevant to the agreement will emerge asymmetrically over time, and opportunistic behavior on the part of the contracting agents create severe difficulties for long-term contracts and for contract adjustment rules (Hart 1983). The implication of this situation is, of course, that a point can be reached where a different form of business organization is required to transfer knowledge efficiently. Contracts may have to be replaced by direct foreign investment and internalization.

> ...complex contracting is apt to give way to direct foreign investment. A more harmonious and efficient exchange relation - better disclosure, easier reconciliation of differences, more complete cross-cultural adaptation, more effective team organization and reconfiguration - all predictably result from the substitution of an internal governance relation for bilateral trading under these recurrent trading circumstances for assets, of which complex technology transfer is an example, that have a highly specific character (Williamson 1981, p. 1563).

The points made in the current literature about the conditions that limit the use of markets have direct relevance for the technological case being studied in the present paper. What is obvious, however, is that, in our model, the information transfer problem is substantially more complex than those normally considered. And the complexity factor is important because it suggests that under the assumptions of the model, the appropriate form of business organization for undertaking foreign production of the commodity will almost inevitably be the *multinational enterprise*. In other words, given the structure of transaction costs, the oligopolist will have incentive to internalize international transactions and proceed with direct investment in foreign countries - provided other factors permit such investment. Moreover, since relatively close coordination and cooperation among the units in the integrated system are required to accelerate technical learning, the foreign plants should have divisional status within an M-form organizational arrangement (Williamson 1981, p. 1561).

From what has been indicated earlier (section 3), it is clear that the oligopolist and its n foreign divisions engage in two distinct types of information exchange. First, there is the movement of knowledge, in period t=b, from the headquarters of the oligopolist to each of the overseas plants. This is a once-and-for-all transfer relating to the shift of the oligopolist's existing proprietary technology (as of t=b) to production locations abroad. Second, there is a continuing exchange of "messages" based on the learning achieved, period by period, as production experience is gained at each location. With the integrated MNE structure, information flows into headquarters from the field and is consolidated. After an assessment of the various messages is made and the fruits of collective learning are reaped, the result, in the form of improved technology, is sent back to the n divisions of the integrated firm. It is apparent that insofar as n is large, many transactions are involved each period; and the transmission process goes on over time until the limiting value for the technological parameter ($\hat{a}$) is reached. The collection, treatment and dissemination of large amounts of technical information must lead to significant costs for the firm, but internalization means that these costs are likely to be <u>lower</u> than they would be under different organization of the activities. Of course, if the information-exchange process is to be undertaken at all, the benefits from the program must exceed its costs so that a profit increase is possible for the firm.

In this connection it should be pointed out that the estimation of how profits will be affected by the consolidation and utilization of the information learned at the n+1 plants can go forward more confidently under internalization of transactions. For one thing, common ownership of the information in the system, as occurs with the MNE, limits uncertainty and serves to reduce the problems of information disclosure and exchange. While managers at the individual plants must be held accountable for the local costs incurred in securing and relaying information to headquarters, and for their efficiency in extracting information from production experience, the pricing and sale of discrete elements of knowledge can be avoided. Further, authority, or the centralization of technological decision-making and co-ordination activities, tends to economize on the transmission and handling of information (Hess 1983, chapt. 11). One important aspect of centralization relates to the use of business "codes." Normally, internal communication channels are de-signed with a view to cost minimization, and as Arrow has noted:

> The role of coding has two economic implications: (a) it weakens but does not eliminate the tendency to increasing costs with scale of operations; (b) it creates an intrinsic irreversible capital commitment of the organization (1974, p. 55).

Even though costs will rise with scale, coding does permit a greater number of individual information sources to be pooled efficiently. This is obviously desirable but there is a down side.

> The need for codes mutually understandable within the organization imposes a uniformity requirement on the behavior of the participants. They are specialized in the information capable of being transmitted by the codes, so that, in a process already described, they learn more in the direction of their activity and become less efficient in acquiring and transmitting information not easily fitted into the code. Hence, the organization itself serves to mold the behavior of its members (1974, pp. 56-57).

There may be some bias or distortion in the information transmitted within an integrated organization such as an MNE but, on balance, it would seem that communication will be accomplished more efficiently and cheaply through internal channels than through interfirm contracts.

One reason for difficulty in interfirm communication lies in the fact that firms tend to adopt different codes, and "translation" can be imperfect. At the same time, since the costs of changing codes are high, there can be no presumption that firms, even those in the same industry, will converge rapidly to a uniform code. Domestic-foreign communication can, of course, be correspondingly more troublesome. From this standpoint, then, it appears that the internalization of international transactions is likely to yield benefits. While consulting teams may still be needed to facilitate the transfer of complex technical information among units in the system, the transfer process should be accomplished more cheaply and speedily and with less loss of data, when all of the interacting parties share a common corporate culture. Similarly, the existence of easy communication together with central co-ordination of the technological program promises advantages. Within limits, the learning process at each plant can be influenced by rational management so that there is less duplication of findings. There can also be more scope for experimentation with efficiency enhancing activities such as value engineering. The MNE organization seems inevitable because to achieve comparable results through market transactions and a set of multilateral contracts would almost certainly involve greater use of resources.

5. Alternative Contractual Schemes

The superiority of the MNE for carrying out repetitive technological transfers within a large network of plants can be understood even more readily if close consideration is given to alternative ways of organizing the transfer process (Casson 1979). What has to be recognized first, however, is that when direct investment is rejected and production is carried out at each location by an independent firm, continuing information transfers need not occur. In the limit, simple licensing agreements could be used merely to transfer the oligopolist's basic proprietary knowledge to the licensees. There would be no necessity to contract for the transfer of the new knowledge being secured over time through the learning going on at each plant. Then, each firm, operating independently, would be forced to accumulate the lessons of production experience slowly. While the limiting technological parameter $\hat{\alpha}$ would ultimately be reached at each location, opportunity for larger gain would be lost. Technology would advance less rapidly than would be feasible under an integrated MNE; and, in financial terms, the losses would be greater the greater the rate of interest.

In principle, the things learned at each firm are private property and are subject to trade. But the transfer of knowledge from one firm to another is by no means automatic.[16] Unlike the case of the MNE described in section 3, when n+1 *independent* firms are considered, there can be no assurance that all of the "messages" from the respective production facilities will be gathered together and utilized to advance technology. In short, equation (3') does not necessarily hold for the oligopolist or for any other independent foreign firm in the system. Insofar as a possessor of information is able to sell his rights in it to others, a motive for exchange exists. The trouble is, however, that the would-be seller may not be able to appropriate the value of the information he possesses. Brushing aside this problem for the moment, there is still another difficulty to be faced. Assume that each firm operates independently and *attempts to contract with each other firm* in order to gain access to all of the elements learned per period at the different production locations in the system. But, then, even if all of the required information transfers were actually made at appropriate prices, and even if the implications of the new knowledge for technical improvement were assessed correctly by each firm, it is obvious that this procedure is inefficient. Unwarranted repetition of effort is involved in the transmission and processing of data.

> Since transmission of information is costly, in the sense of using resources, especially the time of the individuals, it is cheaper and more efficient to transmit all the pieces of information once to a central place than to disseminate each of them to every one (Arrow 1974, p. 68).

Granting this logic, a different contractual plan might be devised that would economize somewhat on communication and processing. For example, the oligopolistic firm could attempt to secure current technical information from the n

---

16 While a firm's production experience may not be strictly proprietary (Liberman 1982), the assumption of the paper is that the uncontrolled diffusion of experience is very modest. In other words, the case considered is not that of a production externality. Markets are not bypassed and direct interaction between units does not take place to any significant extent.

foreign licensees via *market transactions*. Then, having assembled all of the technical results learned in any period τ, the oligopolist's central office could establish the improved technology $(\alpha_{\tau+1})$ for use next period. The oligopolist's objective, of course, would be to benefit from the new technology itself and to sell the new information to the n firms abroad. Fewer market transactions would be required under this organizational structure, and there would be less duplication of activity. Yet, despite such advantages, the plan has serious limitations.

The basic problems of information disclosure and contract complexity assert themselves strongly here. Since the material learned by a firm in any round of its productive operations is determined, in part, by a stochastic process, the outcome, in terms of useful knowledge gained, is always uncertain ex ante. Moreover, the ultimate value of any "message" received by a firm may not be known until all contemporaneous messages from all n+1 firms are brought together and interpreted. Even with the best will, then, a firm cannot know what it will "produce" at any period. In effect, the normal difficulties of information disclosure are compounded, and a firm attempting to sell a claim on its "technical discoveries" is offering a highly uncertain product. Thus, if the oligopolist of our example is to buy technical information from the n foreign firms, it would seem likely that the contracts for any period would specify a uniform payment to each firm based on the expected value of the probability distribution of learning events. That is, since the content of any given contribution is uncertain, the oligopolist must consider the full distribution of knowledge increments that is generated by the production experience of all firms in the network. This approach to contracting may not function too well, however, because strategic behavior on the part of the sellers cannot be ruled out; and, in any event, not all learning results from the operation of a random process. Any firm may use resources and make deliberate efforts to increase learning as production goes forward. But if reward for such positive behavior cannot be captured easily through markets, the incentive to undertake exploratory actions, or to coordinate them with the actions of other firms, is weak.

The other side of the transfer problem poses difficulties too. Specifically, we find that even if the oligopolist can make suitable market arrangements and bring in all of the technological data from the field,[17] troubles are not over. The new technology ($\alpha_{\tau+1}$), once it is produced at the oligopolist's headquarters, must be sold to the n foreign firms if maximum efficiency of the system is to be sustained under a contractual regime. Yet, such sales by the oligopolist need not be accomplished easily. Ideally, each of the n firms would be willing to pay some positive price to gain access to the improved technology ($\alpha_{\tau+1}$) for producing the licensed commodity. Any given foreign firm, however, may choose to follow a more devious strategy. That is, any firm j can assume that, if one of the other n-1 firms in the network purchases the new technical information, it (i.e., j) can then secure the information from that firm more cheaply. Since the same information ($\alpha_{\tau+1}$) is being offered to all n firms, an incentive for *resale* transactions exists; and it is also true that the original developer of the new knowledge (the oligopolist) faces real difficulty in trying to prevent resale transactions.[18] The general result is that, regardless of the true worth of $\alpha_{\tau+1}$ to the various firms (and to society), the oligopolist may not be able to realize more than a fraction of this value.[19] The fact that a free-rider problem obtains here means, of course, that no firm may have much interest in producing information for market. Nevertheless, all is not lost. The inappropriability problem discussed can be circumvented through different business organization. The oligopolist can undertake direct foreign investment and, through internalization, be assured of reaping the rewards from learning in the n+1 system. In short, the generator of information need not have to sell his information in order to be able to appropriate its value (Hirschleifer 1971).

---

[17] Parties to the transactions may be able to use subjectively determined probabilities to make decisions about the prices at which to buy or sell information.

[18] Any customer for information becomes a potential competitor in the marketing of information. Moreover, the costs of policing and enforcing rights in transferred informational property are high. In the case being considered, patent laws do not apply. What is at issue are knowledge increments that can improve the efficiency of an existing technical process. But clear-cut ownership rights in these discoveries may be hard to establish, and violations of rights may be hard to prove.

[19] The oligopolist can, of course, use the $\alpha_{\tau+1}$ knowledge to improve his own plant's productive efficiency.

One more form of organization deserves attention. Assuming there is a desire to secure the advantages of internalization while still preserving the independent status of the n firms operating abroad, all firms in the system could act collectively and set up a special technical bureau to deal with information transfers. This bureau would be financed by contributions from all n+1 firms and would be responsible to the "industry" rather than to any one firm. The scheme would avoid a shift to MNE organization and single-firm control but has other difficulties. In general, it seems unlikely to achieve the level of efficiency that would be realizable with the MNE.

If an independent technical bureau is to be established to serve the n+1 firms using the same production technology, the first problem that arises concerns the way in which the bureau is to come into existence. Presumably, representatives of the various firms would have to get together and agree on the details of the project. Such action, however, does not come about costlessly. Some individuals would have to take on the burdens of initiating the plan and, even when the project was finally in motion, substantial transaction costs would be incurred by the participants. On balance, the initiation and implementation costs faced by a group of disparate firms operating in different countries would almost certainly be larger than the costs falling on a MNE that was taking similar action and setting up a technical bureau in its headquarters.

Perhaps a group-supported bureau relate to the difficulties in deciding how the organization's operating costs and benefits are to be apportioned among the n+1 participating firms. Since the individual firms are likely to differ in respect to size, the market conditions they face, etc., it cannot be assumed that they will reach easy agreement on a "sharing" rule. Conflict can emerge if the perception is that certain firms stand to gain advantages that are out of keeping with their sacrifices. Thus, both at the outset and subsequently, internal political struggles by firms for influence and control may lead to less than efficient operation of the bureau. Moreover, even when agreement exists concerning the bureau's structure and its proper mode of functioning, there are additional problems to be dealt with. The supporting firms must find some effective way to monitor the ongoing activities of the bureau and make sure that their rights in this independent agency are being respected.

Under ideal conditions, the n+1 firms in the cooperative network will send technical data to the bureau and receive continually updated information on the most efficient technology available $(\alpha_{\tau+1})$. Since market transactions and information pricing problems are avoided, there is gain here. As explained earlier, technical advance is accelerated and the profits of each participating firm should rise relatively. Nevertheless, it is not clear that the "productivity" of the groupsupported bureau will be as great as that of the corresponding unit operating within a MNE. For one thing, the existence of many independent firms, and different business codes, suggests that communication will not be as efficient as in a MNE. Further, while the independent technical bureau may be able to coordinate the research activities of the n+1 firms to some extent, there is less incentive for any given firm to extend itself in new undertakings. Presumably, no firm wishes to provide more information to the group if other firms are not making equivalent efforts, and if no additional reward accrues to its actions. In principle, of course, contracts could be written that would generate efficient incentives for technical experimentation, but such agreements would be costly to reach and adjust. Thus, de facto, the main impulse for technological improvement would have to come from the learning provided by production experience. Even here, however, a moral hazard problem could arise. Since the collection of technical information and its transmission to the center is costly, a firm would have some interest in becoming a free rider. Despite its contractual agreements with the group, the firm could find it advantageous to act less zealously than warranted in securing and relaying the benefits of production experience. Generalized, this process could become seriously damaging.

The preceding discussion indicates that institutional arrangements different from those of the MNE are not particularly well adapted to deal with the special case in which technology advances through group learning. One way of interpreting this result is to say that dispersed ownership of certain technical information leads to an unfavorable situation that is not easily corrected through market transactions. Each separate production unit acquires technical information as its cumulative output increases and learning takes place. But to make the most effective use of the data collected each period, all of the strands of information in the system must be consolidated. Consolidation of knowledge acts to speed up understanding, to accelerate technological progress, and to create economic value. It follows, then, that business organization has to be adjusted to facilitate consolidation. Insofar as market exchange of technical information is costly and beset with difficulties, the best plan of action is to obviate such exchange. What is required is an organizational structure in which common ownership of system-wide information obtains. This is, of course, found in the MNE.

6.   Conclusions

In the case considered by the present paper, it was assumed that production units operating in different countries are required to exchange relatively large volumes of complex, technical information on a continuing basis. Given this situation, a major concern must be to find the most efficient organizational means to accomplish the information transfers. Property-rights arrangements and transaction costs become important; and it is evident that organizational economics must play a central role in explaining the emergence of the multinational firm. Indeed, ceteris paribus, the effective problem reduces to one of deciding whether the desired international transactions in information can best be carried out through the internal channels of a MNE, or through market relations among a number of independent firms. In general, there can be no presumption that the MNE will always represent the ideal solution. If, however, substantial technological learning is likely to occur in a multiplant system and if significantly decreased costs are in prospect, internalization must appear as a good option. Ultimately, the disadvantages that may be associated with investment in and operations of foreign subsidiaries have to be weighed against the advantages that learning promises. Integration of n+1, geographically separated, production units within a single business enterprise can lead to certain special benefits. With integrated organization, the gains appropriable from the ownership of information will be higher, and transaction costs in the system will tend to be lower. As long as learning is important, then, the MNE promises greater efficiency than any alternative arrangement based on independent firms trading across markets.

If the preceding argument is correct, the improvement of technology that comes about with production experience can constitute a significant force in encouraging the formation of multinational firms. In theory, there will be greater or lesser incentive for movement to MNE organization depending on the extent of the value that can be created by speeding up technological advance and changing the time stream of profits. The prospect of large gains via learning means that institutional structure should be designed to facilitate learning, and this condition means, in turn, that internalization of international transactions must take place. For the case considered, then, the MNE is indicated as the preferred form of business organization when technical and economic factors in the system make learning a crucial element for profitability. More concretely, it seems possible to say that, ceteris paribus, the push toward MNE organization will be greater when conditions are such that:

(i)   The learning curve, or experience curve, promises major changes in technological efficiency as an organization's cumulative output grows.

(ii)   The technical discoveries at each plant in the system are sufficiently varied, period by period, so that excessive duplication of learning is avoided.

(iii)   Internal transmission of information within an integrated multiplant system can be accomplished with little loss of data and at relatively low transaction cost.

(iv)   The gains from learning can be enhanced by centrally coordinated programs in value engineering and in other research activities related to production experience.

(v)   The interest rate, or social discount rate, is comparatively high.

(vi)   New products, based on newly developed technologies, are introduced frequently so that the multiplant firm has continuing opportunities for learning.

What the analysis suggests is that a large, multiplant system, seeking to benefit from group learning, will inevitably need to conduct extensive and continuing transfers of information. But this is precisely the type of system that is ill adapted to use market transaction and, thus, must shift to internalization and MNE status.

References

Alchian, A.A. (1959),"Costs and Outputs", in M. Abramovitz et al., *The Allocation of Economic Resources*, Stanford University Press, Stanford, pp. 23-40.

Alchian, A.A. and H. Demsetz (1972), "Production, Information Costs, and Economic Organization", *American Economic Review*, 62 (December), pp. 777-795.

Arrow, K.J. (1962), "The Economic Implications of Learning by Doing", *Review of Economic Studies*, 29 (June), pp. 155-173.

Arrow, K.J. (1974), *The Limits of Organization*, W.W. Norton, New York .

Buck, T. (1982), *Comparative Industrial Systems*, Macmillan, London.

Buckley, P.J. (1981), "A Critical Review of Theories of the Multinational Enterprise", *Aussenwirtschaft*, 36 (March), pp.70-87.

Buckley, P.J. and M. Casson (1976), *The Future of the Multinational Enterprise*, Macmillan, London.

Casson, M. (1979), *Alternatives to the Multinational Enterprise*, Macmillan, London.

D'Aspremont, C. and L. Gerard-Varet (1979), "Incentives and Incomplete Information", *Journal of Public Economics*, 11, pp. 25-45.

Dunning, J.H., (ed.) (1971), *The Multinational Corporation*, Allen and Unwin, London.

Dunning, J.H. (1973), "The Determinants of International Production", *Oxford Economic Papers*, 25 (November), pp. 289-335.

Dunning, J.H. (1981), "Explaining the International Direct Investment Position of Countries: Towards a Dynamic or Developmental Approach", *Weltwirtschaftliches Archiv*, 117, pp. 30-64.

Ethier, W.J. (1986), "The Multinational Firm", *Quarterly Journal of Economics*, 101 (November), pp. 805-833.

Fudenberg, D. and J. Tirole (1983), "Learning by Doing and Market Performance", *Bell Journal of Economics*, 14, pp. 522-530.

Fudenberg, D. and J. Tirole (1986), *Dynamic Models of Oligopoly*, Harwood, Chur, Switzerland.

Furubotn, E.G. (1964), "Investment Alternatives and the Supply Schedule of the Firm", *Southern Economic Journal*, 31 (July), pp. 21-37.

399

Furubotn, E.G. (1965), "The Orthodox Production Function and the Adaptability of Capital", *Western Economic Journal*, 3 (Summer), pp. 288-300.

Furubotn, E.G. (1970), "Long-Run Analysis and the Form of the Production Function", *Economia Internazionale*, 23 (February), pp. 3-35.

Hart, O.D., (1983), "Optimal Labour Contracts under Asymmetric Information: An Introduction", *Review of Economic Studies*, 50, pp. 3-35.

Helpman, E.(1984), "A Simple Theory of International Trade with Multinational Corporations", *Journal of Political Economy*, 42, pp. 451-471.

Hess, J.D (1983), *The Economics of Organization*, North-Holland, Amsterdam.

Hirsch, W.(1952), "Manufacturing Progress Functions", *Review of Economics and Statistics*, 34 (May), pp. 143-155.

Hirschleifer, J. (1971), "The Private and Social Value of Information and the Reward to Innovative Activity", *American Economic Review*, 61 (September), pp. 561-574.

Hymer, S. (1970), "The Efficiency (Contradictions) of Multinational Corporations", *American Economic Review*, 60 (May), pp. 441-448.

Hymer, S. (1976), *The International Operations of National Firms: A Study of Direct Investment*, MIT Press, Cambridge.

Kindleberger, C.P. (1969), *American Business Abroad: Six Lectures on Direct Investment*, Yale University Press, New Haven.

Klein, B., R. Crawford and A.A. Alchian (1978), "Vertical Integration, Appropriable Rents, and the Competitive Contracting Process", *Journal of Law and Economics*, 21 (October), pp. 297-326.

Leiberman, M. (1982), "The Learning Curve, Pricing, and Market Structure in the Chemical Processing Industries", Ph.D. thesis, Harvard University.

Magee, S.P. (1977), "Information and the Multinational Corporation: An Appropriability Theory of Direct Foreign Investment", in J.N. Bhagwati, (ed), *The New International Economic Order: The North-South Debate*, MIT Press, Cambridge.

Mansfield, E., A. Romeo and S. Wagner (1979), "Foreign Trade and U.S. Research and Development", *Review of Economics and Statistics*, 61 (February), pp. 49-57.

Markusen, J.P. (1984), "Multinationals, Multi-Plant Economies and the Gains from Trade", *Journal of International Economics*, 16, pp. 205-226.

McCulloch, R. (1984), "U.S. Direct Foreign Investment and Trade: Theories, Trends, and Public Policy Issues" in A. Erdilek, (ed.), *Multinationals as Mutual Invaders: Intraindustry Direct Foreign Investment*, Croom Helm, Beckenham, England.

Miles, L.D. (1961), *Techniques of Value Analysis and Engineering*, McGraw-Hill, New York.

Rugman, A.M. (1980), "Internalization as a General Theory of Foreign Direct Investment: A Re-Appraisal of the Literature", *Weltwirtschaftliches Archiv*, 116, pp. 365-379.

Stigler, G.J. (1947), "The Kinky Oligopoly Demand Curve and Rigid Prices", *Journal of Political Economy*, 55 (October), pp. 432-449.

Stopford, J. and L.T. Wells (1972), *Managing the Multinational Enterprise; Organization of the Firm and Ownership of the Subsidiaries.* Basic Books, New York.

Teece, D.J. (1977), "Technology Transfer by Multinational Firms", *Economic Journal*, 87 (June), pp. 242-261.

Vernon, R. (1977), *Storm Over the Multinationals: The Real Issues*, Macmillan, London.

Williamson, O.E. (1975), *Markets and Hierarchies: Analysis and Antitrust Implications: A Study in the Economics of Internal Organization*, Free Press, New York.

Williamson, O.E. (1981), "The Modern Corporation: Origins, Evolution, Attributes", *Journal of Economic Literature*, 19 (December), pp. 1537-1568.

COMMENTS

Heinz Hauser

Professor Furubotn argues that learning curve effects provide an additional argument for the growing emergence of multinational enterprise (MNE). He first develops a model which includes technical learning as a cost reducing shift parameter in an oligopolistic optimization calculus. The specification of the model is such that augmenting cumulative output over any given period of time leads to greater profits. Because exporting to foreign markets is excluded explicitly, adding foreign production to domestic output follows straightforwardly. He then evaluates alternative modes of exchanging information across markets or within internal organizations. The exchange of information leading to higher efficiency in production (learning) has high costs in arm's length market transactions and internal governance structures are more efficient in transmitting the required information. Thus: technical learning is an additional driving force for MNE.

Ownership Advantage, Locational Factors and Internalization
for a Theory of MNE

I fully agree with Professor Furubotn's starting point and with his main conclusion. He maintains first that the existence and the growing importance of MNE presuppose three conditions:

a) First, the company must command a firm specific asset which can be exploited on world markets (ownership advantage).

b) Second, there must be locational factors which make foreign production more profitable than exporting.

Studies in International Economics and Institutions
Vosgerau (Ed.) New Institutional Arrangements for the World Economy
© Springer-Verlag Berlin Heidelberg 1989

c) Third, there must be some organizational advantage in coordinating the activities of domestic and foreign production internally rather than across markets.

For MNE to be a sustainable organizational mode, all three conditions must be met. Ownership and locational advantages are assumed to be given; the paper then concentrates on organizational analysis.

I also agree with the main conclusion of Professor Furubotn's paper. Strong learning effects, combined with locational factors which make foreign production profitable, provide a strong impetus for the emergence of MNE. Within the model of the paper, MNE is almost inevitable. MNE not only allows for exploiting ownership advantage on a broader scale, it also adds a second source to the profit stream: greater efficiency for domestic and foreign production through advanced learning.

Learning and Institutional Choice

The main difficulty I have with the paper centers on the question of whether learning effects are a good candidate for an analysis of institutional choice. Paragraphs 2 and 3 build on the learning curve effects and lead to the conclusion that adding foreign production to an integrated information network is a profitable strategy. Paragraphs 4 and 5 then discuss the relative merits of alternative governance structures for processing and transmitting technical and economic information.

My point is that the very existence of learning curve effects cannot be discussed independently of transaction costs. Oliver Williamson has made a strong case in his book "Markets and Hierarchies" (pp. 16-19) that learning curve effects are the result, I stress the result, of high transaction costs of acquiring this information across markets. If relevant technical and economic information can be bought on the market, there is no need for costly experience and for sliding down the learning curve over time. If market transactions were a viable solution, a firm need not wait but could directly aim for full efficiency by buying available information.

The first part of Professor Furubotn's paper lends strength to this argument. Learning is modelled as a shift parameter, dependent on effective cumulative output only. If learning information were potentially transferable across markets, it would have to be included in the input flow x_t with a price r_t. The question would then be whether experience should be gained through production over time, or bought on a market, a typical make or buy decision. Within Professor Furubotn's model there is no contractual or organizational choice. Exchanging new information internally is, within the structure of the model, defined as being superior to market transactions.

If the governance structure for the exchange of learning experience were really a choice, as is argued in paragraphs 4 and 5, for the integration of foreign plants, there would be no good reason to start with the concept of a single firm's cumulative output. Profits could be enhanced by drawing on the cumulative production experience of the industry in question.

I do not question the importance of transaction cost arguments for the choice of the contractual structure governing the exchange of information. But I would suggest reversing the argument. High transaction costs for exchanging technical and economic information across markets are responsible for the phenomenon of learning effects based on a single firm's cumulative output. Organizational economics is prior to modelling learning curve effects. Given learning curve effects, the choice of the governance structure cannot be discussed sensibly.

Organizational Failure

The inappropriate application of institutional choice to learning curve effects may also be responsible for the fact that paragraphs 4 and 5 provide not really an institutional choice analysis but more a market failure discussion. Problems of organizational failure are not addressed adequately. Footnote 15 ("It is true, of course, that agency problems may arise within the multinational enterprise") is surely an inadequate reference to co-ordination and incentive problems within firms. The α's and β's in equations 2, 3, and 3' are positive, or 0 in the limiting case that all potentially available information is exploited, but never negative. But size, approximated by cumulative output, can have negative efficiency impacts. An institutional choice analysis has to deal with the boundaries of both the market and the organizational mode for coordinating economic activities.

To provide a corollary: Within the model structure of the paper, there would be a strong case for worldwide monopoly. Even leaving price effects aside, bringing world output under the control of a single firm would be the most efficient way of organizing production. Learning effects would be strongest in this case. I know that models are defined with a view to a specific explanatory objective, and that my interpretation stresses the point to the limits of being unfair. But it sheds light on the one-sided discussion and on the fact that organizational failures are not dealt with in the paper adequately. Institutional choice analysis is neither market failure nor organizational failure in isolation; its distinctive feature is that it deals with a choice between imperfect institutional arrangements, each one having its boundaries at the relative merits of alternative modes for organizing production and exchange.

An institutional choice approach must start with the assumption that all contractual and/or organizational arrangements deal with the same behavioral characteristics. Informational asymmetries, asset specificity which gives rise to appropriation risks, opportunistic behaviour, and the pursuit of individual objectives to the detriment of the group's values endanger not only market transactions but are also common features within organizations. Otherwise, the vast literature on bureaucratic inefficiencies would be obsolete. This symmetry in transactional assumptions is not always found in Professor Furubotn's discussion. To take just a few examples: why should a foreign plant, which is run as a profit centre, have an incentive to share profit enhancing information with the entire group? A single unit within a large organization has as much a free-rider incentive as an independent partner within a contractual arrangement not to share learning experience. How can organizational slack be overcome, if the controlling central unit does not have good external control information (e.g. shadow market prices) on whether best knowledge and effort have been applied? In sum, the discussion in paragraphs 4 and 5 seems to me too lenient with respect to organizational failures.

Information and MNE

The foregoing comments have been confined to a discussion of the arguments developed in Professor Furubotn's paper. I would like to conclude with two remarks which go beyond the topics dealt with in the paper and which are not a critique of Professor Furubotn's exposition (a paper has to limit its reach and cannot deal with all possible aspects of an issue). In this section I shall elaborate the point about the importance of information for the emergence of MNE; in the concluding section I will comment on the basic problem of circularity in the institutional choice debate.

Information flows are of crucial importance for explaining MNE, and learning effects as developed in Professor Furubotn's paper may be part of it. They will be especially important in industries with steep learning curves and short product life cycles. There are industries where individual firms have not reached the bottom of the learning curve by a sizable margin at the time when the product life cycle ends. The chips industry or the airframe industry may be cases in point. In instances like these, multinational production to accumulate experience and to accelerate learning is a strong cost reducing device.

Nevertheless, I doubt whether the learning curve model can explain the most important factors which drive the observable internationalization process of industry. If I had to explain the emergence of MNE on informational grounds, I would stress factors like the following: knowledge of markets and building up of reputation capital which both are facilitated by direct commercial representation; efforts to plug into regionally separated pools of knowledge for product development and design; international recruitment of staff in research, production, marketing and finance, which is extremely difficult for firms operating under only one jurisdiction, but which is of essential importance for firms competing on world markets. Strengthening and extending a firm's core skills, which are the essence of its competitive position, very often necessitate international operation. Information is a central argument for MNE, but it goes beyond learning curve effects in the sense of more efficient production of given products.

406

Institutional Choice and Efficiency

Let me close with a general remark on the growing body of institutional choice literature which has produced useful taxonomies and classification schemes. There is some convergence regarding the relevant transaction characteristics (informational asymmetries or impactedness, asset specificity, ambiguities in monitoring and evaluating outcome, opportunistic behaviour) which must be addressed in designing contractual arrangements. There is growing consent on the relative effectiveness of different contractual and/or organizational arrangements (governance structures), and one can find numerous applications of institutional choice analysis to contractual designs which can be placed somewhere between an arm's length market transaction and integrated hierarchical control. A certain consolidation of the discussion is observable.

Nevertheless, there remains a crucial problem of circularity in the argumentation. Because we have no good criteria for measuring transaction costs independently, there is always a temptation to postulate that efficient institutional arrangements will survive and to conclude that an observable institutional arrangement is efficient because it has survived.

This circularity would not be so severe a problem if we could be assured that markets are competitive in products and in organizational design. But then we have to confront the difficult issues of potential competition and entry barriers. Evaluating competitive impact of potential entry is already difficult if we stay within well defined organizational structures; the literature on strategic entry deterrence gives ample proof of this. The evaluation of potential competition is even more difficult if we deal with alternative institutional designs and with transaction cost arguments.

The argument shows up most clearly if we go back to the very essence of transaction analysis.[1] The transactional assumptions of neoclassical price theory make it possible that all opportunities for mutually beneficial exchange or cooperation are

---

[1] The following argumentation is developed more extensively with respect to cooperative R & D in Boscheck, Ralf (1988).

fully exploited. If one allows for more realistic behavioral and transactional assumptions, e.g. information asymmetries, transaction specific assets, opportunistic behaviour, very costly external monitoring, it is by no means clear that all mutually beneficial exchange takes place. Partners to the cooperation have to design contractual or institutional arrangements which are apt to make the exchange transaction economically viable. It is partly misleading to think of institutional choice as selecting the most efficient transaction mode for a given transaction. The first task is to design arrangements which make it possible that an exchange which is potentially beneficial to both partners can be accomplished at all.

The most fundamental transaction risk is the exposure to an appropriation risk of quasi-rents. If partners to an exchange earn a quasi-rent in the transaction which means that their resources are redeployable only at a significantly lower return, they run the risk that their more mobile partner(s) appropriate part of this quasi-rent. Very often, ongoing business relations involve a high degree of immobility of resources. Assets are designed to be partner-specific. Partner-specific know-how has to be built up at a cost. Partner-specific information codes make communication within the transaction more efficient than outside the transaction. Partial immobilization of resources in a given exchange relation (idiosyncratic exchange in the terminology of Oliver Williamson) is a very common feature of business life. It is prevalent if information is an important part or the main object of an exchange.

Transactions in which partners enjoy different degrees of mobility are most vulnerable to appropriation risk and therefore have high transaction costs. They will not be stable, or not come through in the first place. In situations like these it is necessary to equalize mobility, either by coming close to conditions of spot exchange for both partners, or by deliberately immobilizing the more mobile partner. Many institutional arrangements create exit barriers for all partners to an exchange, as a means of introducing and securing cooperative behaviour by a shared profit position. But, as the strategic deterrence literature has shown, exit barriers are at the same time entry barriers. Exit barriers in the form of sunk costs are the most credible instrument for signalling post entry behaviour which is not profitable to the potential entrant. Contractual arrangements which reduce appropriation risk and transaction costs by creating conditions favourable to cooperative behaviour very often give good opportunities for collusion and create barriers for potential entrants.

To return to the starting point of this section: as long as we have no good analysis of the impact of potential competition on the institutional choice of economic agents, and as long as we have no good criteria for measuring transaction costs independently, institutional choice analysis will have to face the Panglossian dilemma: institutions will survive if they are efficient and they are deemed efficient because they have survived.

References

Boscheck, Ralf, Cooperative R & D, Competition and Efficiency: An Efficiency Assessment for Antitrust, *Aussenwirtschaft*, vol. I/II, 1988.

Williamson, Oliver, *Markets and Hierarchies: Analysis and Antitrust Implications*, New York, The Free Press, 1975.

New Institutional Arrangements in International Economic Law: The Working of Codes of Conduct

Christian Kirchner

I.   Introduction

New institutional arrangements for the world economy are in many instances *legal institutions* like the International Monetary Fund (IMF), the General Agreement on Tariffs and Trade (GATT), bank regulations, long-term contracts in resource economics and so on. These legal institutions are of interest for economists because they affect the functioning of the international economic system; institutional changes may lead to more efficiency of the world economy or reduce it. These institutions are of interest for lawyers as well, because they are part of the overall *legal framework* of the world economy. They are centre-pieces of what is called *international economic law*[1]. International economic law poses various difficult and complex problems to lawyers: the lawmaking process differs from national legislation, the binding force of legal or semi-legal rules of international economic law often is different from that of national law. And the relationship between lawmaker and addressee may be quite different on the international level as compared to the level of the nation state. The problems mentioned are not too difficult to deal with, if there is an international treaty between nations establishing an international organization like the IMF or the GATT. The problem is still manageable if private actors, on the basis of consensus, create their own contract law as in inter-

---

[1]   The term "international economic law" itself is highly controversial; for different definitions see: Fikentscher (1983); Meesen (1985); Mertens, Kirchner and Schanze (1982), pp. 280-306; Schanze (1986), pp. 17-49, with a detailed discussion of the various approaches.

Studies in International Economics and Institutions
Vosgerau (Ed.) New Institutional Arrangements for the World Economy
© Springer-Verlag Berlin Heidelberg 1989

national investment contracts.[2] The complexity of the problem situation fully comes into play when the lawmaker is an international organization without law-making powers established by an international treaty, and if the output of this law-making process is a legally not binding code of conduct, and if the addressees are not only nation states but private enterprises as well. Such is the case if codes of conduct adopted by the General Assembly of the United Nations or by its subsidiary organs are at stake. The phenomenon of such kind of "law", called "soft law", is puzzling lawyers working in the field of international economic law.[3] It may be too early at this stage of uncertainty and lack of practical experience with the real functioning of codes of conduct to start an institutional analysis of these new institutional arrangements of international economic law. But such analysis which could provide us with better knowledge about the functioning of codes of conduct is urgently needed because such codes are used as legal tools in order to reach a number of economic policy goals. Despite this broad application of international "soft law" the real economic impact of codes of conduct is not very intensive.[4] And this discussion finds only weak assistance in economic theory.[5]

It would be hypocritical to try here to fill that gap. But it seems worthwhile to develop a concept for an institutional analysis of codes of conduct. In order to clarify such a type of analysis the concept should be exemplified by the analysis of a code of conduct already in force showing all the characteristics mentioned above: international "soft law" which addresses not only nation states but internationally

---

[2]   Empirical research on such international investment contracts in the field of resource economics is the subject of the Frankfurt research project on the transnational law of natural resources: the research is documented in a series, "Studies in Transnational Law of Natural Resources", published for the Institut für Ausländisches und Internationales Wirtschaftsrecht, Frankfurt am Main, Deventer, Frankfurt am Main, 1979-1987; see especially Kirchner et al. (1979); Schanze et al. (1981); Schanze (1986).

[3]   Baade (1980a), pp. 6, 7; Ebenroth and Karl (1987), p. 75; Bryde (1981), p. 4; Fikentscher (1983), pp. 67-70; Hailbronner (1981); Horn (1980a), pp. 447, 448; Wengler (1976).

[4]   See for example Wang (1981), pp. 14, 15; Kartte and Hölzler (1981), pp. 390-392.

[5]   Abbot (1985); Caves (1982); Kirchner (1975), pp. 13-80.

active enterprises (private ones, state-owned ones, or para-statals) called, in the terminology of the United Nations, "multinational enterprises" and "transnational corporations" respectively. "The Set of Multilaterally Agreed Equitable Principles and Rules for the Control of Restrictive Business Practices" - more easily called the "Restrictive Business Practices Code" (RBP-Code) - was adopted by the General Assembly of the United Nations on December 5 1980.[6] The RBP Code is used as an example here, but not in order to show its desirability or undesirability; the kind of analysis to be applied here is a positive one, aimed at improving our knowledge about the foreseeable real impact of the code of conduct concerned. This kind of knowledge may be helpful for promoting the adoption of further codes of conduct or - depending on the outcome of the analysis - may serve as a warning not to engage in this kind of lawmaking in the future. The lack of practical experience with the application of the RBP Code is a handicap for the analysis but it does not interfere with the goal of this paper to develop a concept of institutional analysis of institutions of international economic law. If the concept is well-construed, the prognosis derived from the exemplary application of the concept may later be tested by empirical evidence.

II.   An Institutional Economic Approach to International Economic Law

An institutional economic analysis of *national economic law* has to deal with given legal rules from a national lawmaker - either a representative political body or law courts - and their impact on the behaviour of given addressees. A pure economic

---

[6]   UN GA Res. 35/63, Doc. TD/RBP/Conf. 10 (1980); International Legal Materials 19 (1980) 813; reprinted in: Ebenroth and Karl (1987), pp. 545 - 554, and in: Gewerblicher Rechtsschutz und Urheberrecht, Internationaler Teil 1982, pp. 642-646, and in Simmonds (1979-1986), p. 1. The literature on the Code today is extremely broad; see as examples: Atkeson and Gill (1981); Baade (1980b); Czako (1981); Davidow (1980); Davidow (1984); Ebenroth and Karl (1987), pp. 224-236; Fikentscher (1982); Fikentscher (1983) pp. 212-234; Fikentscher and Straub (1982); Greenhill (1978); Guertin (1980); von Hahn (1982): Hailbronner (1981); Hailbronner (1982); Joelson (1976): Kather (1986): Kolvenbach (1982); Petersmann (1984); Steeg (1985): Syquia (1980); Wang (1981).

analysis of law[7] will then compare different legal rules as to their differing welfare implications measured in efficiency gains or losses and transaction costs consequences respectively.[8] An institutional analysis should add an analysis of the lawmaking process trying to understand the economics of political decision making as well as include an analysis of the administrative process which is essential for the implementation of legal rules. The (legal) rules for the lawmaking process itself can be taken as given; the same is true for the binding force of such legal rules which are the output of the official lawmaking process.

An institutional economic analysis of *international economic law* is confronted with additional problems: because of the lack of a world state lawmaking becomes a multi-actor play. So far the legal doctrine has stuck to the assumption that only nation states and such international institutions upon which nation states have conferred the lawmaking powers were authorized to create international law. Private actors are mere addressees of the national law applicable to their activities. But empirical research in the field of international economic law has shattered these assumptions. Private actors play an important part in the international lawmaking process.[9] Nation states are active in a variety of divergent methods of creating international law or rules and principles which are not legally binding but which nevertheless possess certain characteristics of law.[10] If an institutional economic analysis of international economic law shall explain the working of such international economic law it has to take into account these new developments.

An institutional economic analysis of international economic law should, therefore, start with studying the lawmaking process and the rationales of the various actors concerned. One of the central issues is the question why *international* economic law has been created in the matter of concern and why this matter has not been dealt

---

7   See for instance Behrens (1987); Assmann, Kirchner and Schanze (1978); Gäfgen (1983); Polinsky (1983); Posner (1977); Schäfer and Ott (1986).

8   Williamson (1979); Picot (1982); as an example of a transaction cost analysis of legal institutions see Kirchner, Picot (1987).

9   Empirical evidence in the field of resource economics has been collected by the Frankfurt research group; see footnote 2.

10 See footnote 3.

with by nation states on the national level. This type of analysis should illuminate the intended functions of the part of international economic law which is to be analyzed. Those functions may but do not necessarily have to be the same as the objectives stated in the legal provisions under review.

An economic analysis of international economic law is not bound to decide the issue whether or not the legal provisions under review are international law, international "soft law" or just rules and principles carrying some moral power. But economic analysis has to answer the question of how those "legal provisions" actually influence the behaviour of their addressees. If the *sanctions* for not complying with these "legal rules" are not legal ones, e.g. publication of detailed cases of "misbehaviour", they can, nevertheless, be effective. In international economic law the problem of how economic actors are influenced by legal rules has to take into account the various levels of *implementation*. The behaviour of the economic actors may be affected by the rules themselves, by activities of nation states which implement such rules and by international organizations which either implement such rules or are able to sanction the non-compliance with such rules. The interrelation between these three main groups of actors may be more complicated if there are *feedbacks*: thus multinational enterprises may have some influence on the activities of either their home states or of host states. These nation states may have more or less influence on the working of international organizations.

If the economic impact of legal rules of international economic law is analyzed by these methods, the final stage of analysis has to deal with the delicate issue of welfare implications of such rules on a world level.

III. Historical Background

After World War II the United States and her western allies made an attempt to create new institutional arrangements for the world economy. The two centre-pieces were the Bretton Woods Agreement establishing the International Monetary Fund[11] and the envisaged International Trade Organization (ITO) created by the

---

[11] Fikentscher (1983), pp. 344–353; Jackson (1977), pp. 352–395.

Havana Charter of 1948.[12] The Havana Charter was only partly successful because only very few countries ratified this international treaty; The United States never adopted it.[13] Only the part of the Havana Charter dealing with the elimination of trade barriers became effective as the General Agreement on Tariffs and Trade (GATT) in 1951.[14] Those provisions of the Charter which aimed at eliminating private trade barriers erected by international cartels by means of restrictive business practices never came into force. Article 46 section 1 of the Charter was to read:

> "Each Member shall take appropriate measures and shall co-operate with the Organization to prevent, on the part of private or public commercial enterprises, business practices affecting international trade which restrain competition, limit access to markets, or foster monopolistic control, whenever such practices have harmful effects on the expansion of production or trade and interfere with the achievement of any of the other objectives set forth in Article 1."

After the failure of the Havana Charter several international organizations started activities in the field of dealing with restrictive business practices in international economic relations.[15] The United Nations Conference on Trade and Development (UNCTAD) took up the issue of regulating restrictive business practices in 1968.[16] The developing countries had realized that private trade barriers erected by restrictive business practices would harm their efforts to export to the industrialized countries.[17] It was that connection between restrictive business practices and the economic development and trade perspectives of Third World countries which made

---

12 Fikentscher (1983), pp. 96, 180; Joelson (1976), pp. 841-843; Kather (1986), pp. 18-21; Kirchner (1975), pp. 87-89; Petersmann (1979/80), pp. 24, 25.

13 Kather (1986), p. 21: Kirchner (1975), p. 89.

14 Jackson (1977), pp. 396-399; Joelson (1976), p. 844; Fikentscher (1983), p. 96; Kather (1986), p. 22.

15 Organizations involved were: GATT, ECOSOC, UNCTAD and OECD; Joelson (1976), pp. 843-847; Kather (1986), pp. 22-29; Kirchner (1975), pp. 89-92; Steeg (1985), pp. 2-6.

16 Kather (1986), p. 30; Kirchner (1975), p. 90.

17 UNCTAD Resolution 25 (II) March 27, 1968, § 1: UN Doc. TD/97 Vol. I, p. 38.

the dealing with restrictive business practices one of the cornerstones of the envisaged New International Economic Order (NIEO).[18] The breakthrough took place in the mid-seventies when various groups of experts were set up to work out a code of conduct on restrictive business practices.[19] An agreement on such a code of conduct was reached after two sessions of a diplomatic conference held under UNCTAD's auspices in 1979 and 1980. The United Nations Conference on Restrictive Business Practices concluded its negotiations and approved a "Set of Multilaterally Agreed Equitable Principles and Rules for the Control of Restrictive Business Practices" on April 22 1980.[20] The General Assembly adopted the Set of Principles and Rules as a consensus resolution on December 5 1980.[21]

IV. Goals, Contents, and Legal Character of the RBP Code

1. Goals

In its preamble the RBP Code combines several objectives. The old objectives of the Havana Charter are reflected in the statement that restrictive business practices can adversely affect international trade and that a code of conduct for the control of such practices can contribute to the development and improvement of international economic relations. The connection between the system of international free trade - the main tasks of the GATT - and international competition law is

---

[18]   See Fikentscher (1983), pp. 116, 117; Joelson (1976), pp. 848, 849; Kather (1986), pp. 41-44; Petersmann (1979/80), pp. 28-44; the fundament of the envisaged New International Economic Order (NIEO) was Resolution 3281, the "Charter of Economic Rights and Duties of States" (UN Doc. A/9631 [1974]); German version reprinted in: Mertens, Kirchner and Schanze (1982), pp. 330, 331; as far as the role of controlling restrictive business practices as part of the New International Economic Order is concerned, Resolution 3362 (UN Doc. A/10301 [1975]) urged that "restrictive business practices adversely affecting international trade, particularly that of developing countries, should be eliminated ...".

[19]   See Joelson (1976), p. 858; Kather (1986), pp. 44-59.

[20]   Kather (1986), p. 64; Kolvenbach (1982), p. 390; Czako (1981), p. 313.

[21]   Kather (1986), p. 64; Kolvenbach (1982), p. 390.

seen in the expressed desire that restrictive business practices should not impede or negate the realization of benefits that would arise from the liberalization of tariff and non-tariff barriers affecting international trade. Besides these well-known "classical" objectives there are two new goals: "to contribute to attaining the objective in the establishment of a *new international economic order*", and "harmful effects on international trade have to be particularly controlled as far as developing countries and their economic development is concerned."

Part A ("Objectives") of the RBP Code adds some further goals to that catalogue, namely "greater efficiency in international trade and development, particularly that of developing countries", the "creation, encouragement and protection of competition", the "control of the concentration of capital and/or economic power", the "protection of the interests of consumers in both developed and developing countries". Taken together, this set of objectives tries to combine an international competition law with consumer protection law and development law for the countries of the Third World. It has to be kept in mind that, due to the lawmaking process of the RBP Code, divergent interests of industrialized and developing countries had to be harmonized. Therefore, the original *main goal* of preventing restrictive business practices, exercised by international cartels and internationally active business enterprises, to impede or negate the effects of liberalization of tariff and non-tariff barriers has been combined with a specific protection of developing countries against adverse effects of such restrictive business practices. It has correctly been stated that in any control of international cartels and multinational enterprises by international organizations emphasis is on the trade barrier aspect[22]. The heterogeneous character of the set of objectives of the RBP code may diffuse this importance of the main goal; but it should be evident that for a real international competition law there is no basis for consensus on a world level. And the protection of developing countries against activities of so-called transnational corporations - as multinational enterprises are called in the UN-terminology - is the main objective of the planned Code of Conduct on Transnational Corporations;[23]

---

[22] VerLoren von Themaat (1981), p. 92.

[23] Böckstiegel, Catranis (1980); Ebenroth and Karl (1987); Fatouros (1980); Fatouros (1984); Hossain (1980), pp. 9-15; the 1983 draft is reprinted in: Ebenroth and Karl (1987), pp. 583-600.

the RBP Code regulates just some of the activities of those enterprises, i.e. restrictive business practices which may be used as substitutes for tariff and non-tariff barriers.

2. Contents

The RBP Code defines "restrictive business practices"[24] very broadly: "acts or behaviour of enterprises which, through an abuse or acquisition and abuse of a dominant position of market power, limit access to markets or otherwise unduly restrain competition, having or being likely to have adverse effects on international trade, particularly that of developing countries, and on the economic development of these countries, or which through formal, informal, written or unwritten agreements or arrangements among enterprises, have the same impact".

In Part C (Multilaterally agreed equitable principles for the control of restrictive business practices) it is stated that appropriate action should be taken in a mutually reinforcing manner at national, regional and international levels to eliminate, or effectively deal with, restrictive business practices, including those of transnational corporations, adversely affecting international trade, particularly that of developing countries and the economic development of these countries. Furthermore, the Code asks for collaboration between governments at bilateral and multilateral levels.

In Part D (Principles and rules for *enterprises*, including transnational corporations) the Code asks enterprises to conform to the restrictive business practices laws, and the provisions concerning restrictive business practices in other laws, of the countries in which they operate. These companies "should refrain" from certain restrictive business practices which are then enumerated. The most important ones seem to be

- agreements fixing prices, including exports and imports;
- collusive tendering;
- market or customer allocation arrangements;
- allocation by quota as to sales and production.

---

24   Part B (i).

In Part E (Principles and rules for *states* at national, regional and subregional level) the Code asks the member states to adopt, improve and effectively enforce appropriate legislation and to implement judicial and administrative procedures for the control of restrictive business practices. Furthermore, the member states should establish appropriate mechanisms at the regional and subregional levels to promote exchange of information on restrictive business practices. International collaboration is also called for in Part F (International measures) which defines the role *UNCTAD* is to play in the further development of international control of restrictive business practices. The three main issues are the information of UNCTAD by the member states on their activities in this field, an annual report of UNCTAD on developments in restrictive business practices legislation and on restrictive business practices, and continued work within UNCTAD on the elaboration of a model law or laws on restrictive business practices in order to assist developing countries in devising appropriate legislation.

The *institutional machinery* for the implementation of the RBP Code is provided for in Part G (International institutional machinery): an Intergovernmental Group of Experts on Restrictive Business Practices operating within the framework of a Committee on UNCTAD. The main tasks of this body are to provide a forum and modalities for multilateral consultations, discussions and exchange of views, to undertake and disseminate periodically studies and research on restrictive business practices, to invite and consider relevant studies, documentation and reports from relevant organizations of the United Nations system, to study matters relating to the Set of Principles and Rules, to collect and disseminate information on matters relating to the Set of Principles and Rules, to make appropriate reports and recommendations to States on matters within its competence, and finally to submit reports on its work. Besides this, the Intergovernmental Group of Experts has to make proposals to a United Nations Conference which has to review all the aspects of the Set of Principles and Rules and which is to be convened by the Secretary-General of the United Nations under the auspices of UNCTAD for the improvement and further development of the Set of Principles and Rules.

3.   Legal Character of the RBP Code

The RBP Code is a so-called "voluntary code".[25] The rules and principles of the Code are not legally enforceable.[26] But lawyers are engaged in a lively discussion of whether such voluntary codes, despite their wording which expressively does not bind the addressees[26], create a sort of international law called "soft law" which has to be taken into account by national law makers, national and international law courts and tribunals and which can over time acquire the quality of international customary law.[27] It is not the right place here to line out the various arguments in detail. But it should be noted that the RBP Code was adopted by the General Assembly of the United Nations as a *consensus resolution* and that the divergent interests of the three main groups of countries negotiating the code - the developing countries (Group A), the western industrialized countries (Group B) and the socialist countries (Group C) - have been carefully harmonized by the two diplomatic conferences in 1979 and 1980. It has been pointed to the fact that the legal character of a voluntary code of conduct may change over time due to the implementation of the code and further developments.[28]

One characteristic feature of the RBP Code is that it addresses enterprises directly and thus creates (legally non-binding) obligations for such corporations.[29] The problem in international law then is whether multinational enterprises become subjects of international law.[30] The question may be left open here; but the discussion itself clearly shows that multinational enterprises are viewed as independent actors within the institutional framework of the world economy and that the

---

[25]   Czako (1981), p. 330; Fikentscher and Straub (1982), p. 639; von Hahn (1982), p. 367; Petersmann (1984), p. 30.

[26]   The relevant sections of the Code use the word "should" instead of "shall".

[27]   Baade (1980a); Bryde (1981), pp. 21-35; Hailbronner (1981), pp. 335-342, 352-362; Hailbronner (1983), p. 21-30; Horn (1980a), pp. 447, 448.

[28]   Bryde (1981), pp. 23-27; Petersmann (1984), p. 31.

[29]   Baade (1980a), pp. 7, 8; Bryde (1981), p. 19-21; Hailbronner (1981), p. 335.

[30]   See Hailbronner (1983), p. 16; Baade (1980a), p.8; Bryde (1981), p. 20; Wildhaber (1978), p. 37 with a detailed discussion.

notion that they may take part in international disputes only if diplomatic protection is provided for them by their home state is no longer valid.[31] But due to the fact that the RBP Code does not create its own tribunal for disputes arising from the application of the General Principles and Rules the problem of whether multinational enterprises become subjects of international law has not to be decided in practice.

V.   Institutional Analysis

Up to now there has been no economic analysis of the impact of internationally regulating certain restrictive business practices of multinational enterprises.[32] Economic analysis has excessively dealt with the question whether international trade and investment activities of multinational enterprises add to the welfare of their host states.[33] This host country perspective has been one of the driving forces in creating the RBP Code as has been mentioned. But if one assumes that there are positive welfare effects from restricting certain activities of multinational enterprises by host countries, the question has to be answered why then *international regulation* is sought by such states. This issue has been studied as far as the GATT system is concerned;[34] the author of that study, Kenneth W. Abbott, has found out that national governments find themselves in a *dilemma situation* when they have to decide on either to grant protection to national industries or to liberalize international trade and thus diminish tariff and non-tariff-barriers. Multilateral negotiations as being provided by the GATT system are a given way to avoid this dilemma.[35] Unfortunately, this line of arguments does not fit to solve the problem

---

[31]   Wildhaber (1978), p. 37; Hailbronner (1983), p. 16.

[32]   An economic analysis of the restrictive business practices section of the Havana Charter is to be found in Kirchner (1975), pp. 173-179.

[33]   From the vast literature on this subject see Hymer and Rowthorn (1970); Kartte and Hölzler (1981); and Caves (1982) with a Bibliographical Essay (pp. 300-305).

[34]   Abbott (1985).

[35]   Abbott (1985), pp. 504-532.

of why an international regulation of restrictive business practices could be sought by the member states of the United Nations. Another proposal has been mentioned by Richard Caves: if host states engage in a national regulation of the activities of multinational enterprises they must fear that other countries undercut their endeavours by offering better terms to those companies.[36] *International* regulation thus may be viewed as a *cartel-like activity* of those nation states which assume that their national welfare is positively affected by a regulation of certain restrictive business practices. This argument certainly holds if applied to the regulation of investment of multinational enterprises in developing countries and may, therefore, be of help in explaining the interest of these countries in the planned Code of Conduct on Transnational Corporations.[37] But as far as the control of restrictive business practices is concerned, there is another issue which has to be taken into account: up to now there has been an *asymmetry of competition laws* in the world. Whereas most western industrialized countries today have a more or less effective antitrust law which applies not only to activities of their nationals but to activities of foreign enterprises in case their market is affected,[38] many countries of the Third World either do not possess such a law or are not able to apply it effectively to activities of foreign enterprises. If a single state tries to undertake steps in the direction of creating an effective antitrust law it must be aware of its competitors in the Third World who offer antitrust havens for multinational enterprises. International regulation thus may be viewed as an endeavour of developing countries to set off their regulatory set-back vis-a-vis industrialized western countries. But such consideration cannot explain why the RBP Code has been adopted by a *consensus resolution*, i.e. with the consent of the western industrialized countries and the socialist countries as well. *Socialist countries* are confronted with similar problems as developing countries because they have no extraterritorially applicable antitrust laws. But on the other side they apply central co-ordination of their export and import activities. They make use of national monopolies which act on international markets as single units. Nevertheless, cartel-like activities of multi-

---

[36] Caves (1982), p. 297.

[37] See footnote 23.

[38] Rehbinder (1965); Rehbinder (1981); Ebenroth and Karl (1987), pp. 212-220.

national enterprises would adversely affect their welfare situation. And the import and export monopolies show many deficiencies, so that decentralization even in this sector is pending in a number of socialist states. International regulation of restrictive business practices would, therefore, be beneficial to socialist countries. The only remaining problem is that international regulation of restrictive business practices may affect the activities of *state enterprises* of these countries as well as diminish economic rents which could be earned from the exercise of monopoly power. The group of socialist countries has been aware of this problem and - unsuccessfully - tried to exempt state enterprises from the application of the RBP Code.[39] The fact that in the second diplomatic conference which then approved the Set of Equitable Principles and Rules the socialist countries no longer tried to add an explicit exemption for state enterprises[40] shows that the probability of application of such equitable principles and rules on the activities of state enterprises must have been seen as rather small. This may be due to the fact that international trade between socialist countries and developing countries often takes place within a well defined framework of a bilateral arrangement between the two participating states.[41]

But if the group of developing countries and that of socialist countries expect some welfare gains from the international regulation of certain restrictive business practices it remains to explain why the group of *western industrialized states* approved this Code. If the provisions contained in the Code are effective they will restrict certain activities of multinational enterprises from industrialized countries and cut some economic rents. It would be cynical to assume that the group of western industrialized countries approved the Code because they expected it to be absolutely ineffective and thus worthless. It is true that the voluntary character of the Code's provisions makes it a rather weak weapon but - as has been mentioned - the implementation of such a voluntary code may over time lead to legally binding principles and rules. The next assumption could lead into the direction that the group of western industrialized countries had already in the past created a code of

---

[39]   Fikentscher and Straub (1982), p. 638; Atkeson and Gill (1981), p. 3.

[40]   Atkeson and Gill (1981), p. 3.

[41]   Jackson (1977), p. 1065.

conduct on such restrictive business practices which proved to be of some importance, the OECD Guidelines on Multinational Enterprises.[42] The new provisions of
the RBP Code would not add anything really new to existing national antitrust law
and this OECD Code. There are some hints in the history of the creation of the
RBP Code which assumingly strengthen this hypothesis: the western industrialized
countries tried to avoid three developments:[43]

- establishment of an UNCTAD implementation machinery which could
  develop into another forum for attacking the activities of multinational
  enterprises;

- application of the Code to intra-company activities as these activities are
  not regulated by most existing antitrust laws;

- misuse of regulatory powers of developing countries in applying the new
  equitable principles and rules without proper defense of multinational
  enterprises.

But even with all these arguments which could explain that the group of western
industrialized countries would not fight a protracted war against international
regulation of restrictive business practices it is not clear why these countries actively participated in the adoption of the RBP Code . Here the connection between
the GATT case and the RBP Code case comes into play again. If the RBP Code
actually cuts some economic rents of multinational enterprises by outlawing certain
practices which adversely affect developing countries - which do not possess
extraterritorially applicable antitrust laws - the overall effect of the code could be
to strengthen the economic welfare of those countries. It has been mentioned

---

[42] The OECD Declaration on international investment and multinational enterprises of June 21 1976, contained as annex the "Guidelines for Multinational
Enterprises"; International Legal Material 15 (1976), 976; the text of the 1984
revision is reprinted in: Ebenroth and Karl (1987), pp. 632-639; for a
discussion of these guidelines see: Baade (1980b), pp. 429-431; Bryde (1981),
pp. 12-15; Hailbronner (1981), p. 351; Kartte and Hölzler (1981), p. 391;
Kolvenbach (1982), pp. 395-396; Petersmann (1984), p. 29; Steeg (1985), pp.
3-6.

[43] The background of the negotiations is discussed in: Benson (1980), pp. 451-
453; Czako (1981), pp. 319-320; Kolvenbach (1982), p. 390.

already that certain restrictive business practices have similar effects as trade barriers on the basis of tariff and non-tariff barriers. In lowering these barriers the governments of industrialized countries would reduce protection for their national enterprises in a joint effort and simultaneously lower the burden of the state to provide development aid to the countries concerned and to mitigate the pressure of these countries for more concessions within the GATT system. The RBP Code may thus be viewed as a concession of industrialized countries granted to developing countries within a worldwide network of negotiations on different levels. For governments of industrialized countries this concession would even then be a rational policy if their national enterprises would loose some economic rents.

An institutional analysis should not end here. There are two other groups of actors which have played an important part in creating the RBP Code, the UNCTAD and the multinational enterprises.

It should be evident that UNCTAD - as every international organization - must not be simply identified with its official goals but has an interest in stabilizing and expanding its own activities. Codes of conduct seem to be an ideal tool in order to prove that an organization is indispensable. The negotiating process of the RBP Code was in the hands of UNCTAD which appointed the experts for the various ad hoc groups of experts[44] and which organized the diplomatic conferences held under its auspices.[45] But such activities automatically end with the adoption of the UN resolution approving the code of conduct. New tasks are conferred upon the international organization concerned if the implementation of the code is laid into its hands. As has been seen from Part G of the RBP Code, UNCTAD was only partly successful in making the implementation of the code its own task. This is due to the opposing interests of the group of industrialized countries as mentioned above. Nevertheless, UNCTAD has some role to play in the implementation and further development of the Code, especially in the elaboration of a model law on restrictive business practices for developing countries. Thus the overall impact from its activities concerning the RBP Code is quite satisfactory for the UNCTAD. It

---

[44]   Atkeson and Gill (1981), p. 2; Czako (1981), pp. 318, 319; Kather (1986), pp. 30-59.

[45]   Czako (1981), p. 320; Fikentscher and Straub (1982), p. 638.

should be mentioned that UNCTAD acts as a competitor to the Center on Transnational Corporations (CTC) which is in charge of creating the Code of Conduct on Transnational Corporations covering similar grounds to the RBP Code. UNCTAD was able to reach a consolidation period of the RBP Code before the CTC was able to accomplish the adoption of the UN Code on TNCs.

Multinational Enterprises had no access to the negotiations of the RBP Code. But they were able to indirectly influence some formulations of the Code, especially as far as the voluntary character of the Code and the catalogue of restrictive business practices covered by the Code are concerned.[46] Nevertheless, the actual Code poses a number of serious problems to these enterprises,[47] mainly in the field of new and more stringent national regulation of business practices by developing countries. But certain central issues for such enterprises have not been included into the Code:

- intra-company transactions;

- market allocations by means of licensing patents and trademarks;

- parallel behaviour.

But the fact remains that certain economic rents stemming from restrictive business practices not covered by the extraterritorial application of national antitrust laws will be diminished if the Code ought to be effective.

The institutional analysis of the creation of the RBP Code may thus be concluded with the hypothesis that the coalition formed by developing countries, industrialized countries (western and socialist ones) and the UNCTAD has overruled the multinational enterprises but granted considerable concessions to them which may have an impact on the effectiveness of the Code.

---

[46]   Guertin (1980); and the literature found in footnote 44.

[47]   A detailed criticism is found in: Guertin (1980); von Hahn (1982).

VI. Economic Analysis

If the institutional analysis can illuminate some activities of those actors who created the RBP Code it can - on the other hand - say little about the real economic impact of the Code and its welfare effects on a world level. The institutional analysis has to make assumptions about the interests of the actors and their knowledge (at the time of negotiating the Code).

The economic impact of the RBP Code depends on the way it influences the activities of the economic actors. Addressees of the Code are multinational enterprises and nation states in charge of regulating the activities of such enterprises. Before trying to evaluate the welfare implications of such influences two questions have to be answered:

- What does the voluntary character of the RBP Code mean for its real impact on the activities of multinational enterprises?

- Which practices covered by the Code can be substituted by practices not covered?

As has been mentioned, the issue of whether the provisions of the RBP Code would be legally binding or not has only been decided in the final stage of the creation of the Code and may be regarded as the price the group of developing countries was willing to pay for the *consensus* resolution by which the Code eventually was adopted. But on the other hand, Part G (International institutional machinery) provides for a United Nations Conference to be convened under the auspices of UNCTAD for the purpose of reviewing *all* the aspects of the Set of Principles and Rules. This means that in future pressure may be exerted to make the provisions of the RBP Code legally binding.[48] Non-compliance with the provisions of the code, therefore, may have the effect that in future legal sanctions may be applied. This may be viewed as a pending threat which has to be taken into account by multinational enterprises. If there should be a larger number of open cases of non-compliance this threat might well be real. One may state that the impact of the legally non-binding provisions of the code is rising over the time with

---

[48] For the position of the group of developing countries see Syquia (1980.

growing numbers of cases of non-compliance. This type of mechanism should be expected to have a real impact on the activities of multinational enterprises. Furthermore, the open discussion of a case of non-compliance could impair the goodwill of the enterprise concerned. It is noteworthy that the group of industrialized western countries were not willing to accept special investigation powers of UNCTAD into potential cases of non-compliance. Such investigations could be viewed as a pre-stage to official litigation procedures with the UNCTAD serving as tribunal.

In evaluating the real impact of legally non-binding provisions of the RBP Code one has to take into account the various levels of the implementation process: nation states are asked to take appropriate actions and to collaborate.[49] In practice that could mean that national antitrust laws have to be interpreted in the light of the RBP Code.[50] The violation of provisions of the Code could thus be sanctioned by national antitrust authorities or law courts. And, finally, the obligation to exchange information between states[51] could strengthen the position of affected developing countries which then may apply not only legal but political measures as well.

Altogether it has to be expected that despite the voluntary character of the RBP Code the probability of a real impact of its provisions on multinational enterprises is pretty strong. Therefore, one may expect that cases of open violation of the main types of restrictive business practices (agreements fixing prices, collusive tendering, market or customer allocation agreements, allocation by quota as to sales and production) will be very rare in the future.

But it has been mentioned that there is the possibility of multinational enterprises reaching the same ends - as being sought by the application of the said restrictive business practices - by other means. The most important issue in evaluating the real impact of the RBP Code, therefore, is the possibility of circumventing its

---

[49] Part C (i) 1, 2; for a critical analysis see: von Hahn (1982), p. 377.

[50] Fikentscher and Straub (1982), p. 642; Meessen (1981), pp. 1131, 1132; Hailbronner (1981), pp. 352-362.

[51] Part E 7; critical analysis: von Hahn (1982), p. 377.

428

provisions. Here the typical problems of antitrust law arise, namely the issue of parallel behaviour in tight-knit oligopolies and the control of misuse of market power. It cannot be expected that international competition law will be more effective than national antitrust laws are. But there is one specific trait of *international* competition law which differs considerably from national antitrust law: the market allocation problem. The example of European Community Law clearly shows that market allocations by means of industrial property rights can be successfully handled only if it is outlawed that industrial property rights - like patents, trademarks, copyrights - may be used for these purposes.[52] The RBP Code does not contain such provisions as being applied in EC competition law. It has been proposed that in order to deal with this problem on an international level a revision of the Paris Convention is necessary which redefines the territoriality of patents and trademarks. The RBP Code has left open this issue which may or may not be solved by the planned Transfer of Technology Code.[53]

Coming back to the catalogue of restrictive business practices to be outlawed by the RBP Code one may come to the conclusion that *price fixing agreements, collusive tendering, and allocation by quota* will be effectively outlawed by the Code. Multinational enterprises engaging in such activities must be aware of non-legal sanctions impairing their goodwill, by sanctions of their home states, by sanctions of host states concerned and by the threat of strengthening the binding force of the provisions of the RBP Code in the future. But it is not to be expected that cases of market allocation by means of industrial property rights, parallel behaviour and misuse of market power will be affected by the RBP Code.

In evaluating the welfare effects of the RBP Code one has to compare two situations: (1) application of national antitrust laws and the OECD Code; (2) application of national antitrust laws, the OECD Code and the RBP Code. As has been stated above, the main effect of the RBP Code will be in the field of price fixing

---

[52] Kronstein (1973), pp. 276-371; Kirchner (1974), pp. 182-209; Ebenroth and Karl (1987), pp. 265-267, 274, 275, 278-283, 291-292.

[53] Ebenroth and Karl (1987), pp. 291, 292; the draft international code of conduct on the transfer of technology is reprinted (1985 version) in: Ebenroth and Karl (1987), pp. 601-630; the relevant clause, chapter 4, no. 10 (export restrictions) is still under consideration.

agreements, collusive tendering, and allocation by quota. Such business practices
are typical cases of exerted monopoly power connected with respective monopoly
rents. Such monopoly rents do not reflect superior economic efficiency of those
who earn these rents. Therefore, the welfare analysis is not too difficult. In such
cases adherents of different schools of thought on antitrust are on common ground
in the call for banning such business practices.[54] Seen on the world level the RBP
Code is expected to cut some economics rents earned from monopoly power,
thereby enhancing the overall welfare level. But it is not yet clear today whether
such positive effects of the Code will be outweighed by some negative effects
stemming from over-regulation of multinational enterprises in developing countries,
thus eliminating certain activities of such enterprises which might be adding to the
overall welfare level. But the RBP Code avoided an overly expanded and vague
catalogue of restrictive business practices.[55] Furthermore, the main effect on the
level of developing countries will be the enactment of competition laws on the
basis of the model law to be worked out by a group of experts under the auspices
of UNCTAD.[56] What is to be expected in this field is that more and more developing countries will adopt competition laws comparable to those of many
western industrialized countries. The asymmetry in international antitrust will, over
the time, be diminished and eventually abolished. The welfare implication of such
development should be viewed positively. But here is where controversy between
different schools of thought in antitrust starts. The alleged disadvantages of antitrust - as being stated by the Chicago School[57] - are mainly in the field of control
of concentration of economic power and of control of misuse of that power.[58]

---

54 Wang (1981), p. 4; for a critical analysis of the different antitrust approaches see: Kirchner (1980).

55 Part D 3.a); the discussion about this catalogue was highly controversial; see the literature cited in footnotes 44, 46, 47.

56 Fikentscher and Straub (1982), p. 738; the "considerations of the revised draft of a model law or laws on restrictive busess practices" as of Nov. 7, 1984, is reprinted in: Ebenroth and Karl (1987), pp. 640-646; UNCTAD doc. TD/B/RBP/15/Rev.

57 Kirchner (1980), pp. 572-579.

58 Kirchner (1980), pp. 574-579.

Both aspects should not be of major importance in applying new competition laws of developing countries because even with the co-ordination of antitrust policies by means of a model law the competition between developing countries is expected to be strong enough to restrain a too rigid antitrust policy in the field of control of economic power.

To sum up, the overall welfare effect of the RBP Code on a world level is expected to be positive. But the real impact will be confined to few areas of restrictive business practices.

VI.   Conclusion and Outlook

The analysis has shown that new institutions in international economic law like codes of conduct have a real impact on the international economic systems and that statements about their welfare implications are possible if enough assumptions - which should be tested empirically - are introduced. The voluntary character of such codes is no major obstacle in creating effective rules in international economic law. In the case of the RBP Code the analysis of of the economic impact was implied by the fact that only a few of its provisions are effective and that the welfare implications of the restrictive business practices at stake are not too controversial. If such analysis is to be applied to the proposed Code of Conduct on Transnational Corporations the evaluation of the welfare implications will be much more difficult and will have to make use of modern theories of deregulation.

An analysis of this type could be useful in assisting lawyers in evaluating the economic impact of the legal rules they create, implement and interpret. For economists this type of analysis could serve as an incentive to expand international economic theory further into institutional analysis and to base such theory not on global models but on an analysis of economic activities of the various actors. Such actors are not only producers and consumers but the various institutions which create and implement legal rules for the institutional setting of the world economy as well.

References

Abbott, Kenneth W. (1985), The Trading Nation's Dilemma: The Functions of the Law of International Trade, *Harvard International Law Journal*, 26, p. 501.

Assmann, Heinz-Dieter, Christian Kirchner and Erich Schanze (1978), *Ökonomische Analyse des Rechts*, Kronberg/Taunus.

Atkeson, Timothy B. and David G. Gill (1981), The UNCTAD Restrictive Business Practices Code: A Step in the North-South Dialogue, *International Lawyer*, 15, p. 1.

Baade, Hans W. (1980a), The Legal Effects of Codes of Conduct for MNEs, in: Norbert Horn (ed.), *Legal Problems of Codes of Conduct for Multinational Enterprises*, Deventer and others, 3.

Baade, Hans W. (1980b), Codes of Conduct for Multinational Enterprises: An Introductory Survey, in: Norbert Horn (ed.), *Legal Problems of Codes of Conduct for Multinational Enterprises*, Deventer and others, 407.

Behrens, Peter (1987), *Die ökonomischen Grundlagen des Rechts*, Tübingen.

Benson, Stuart E. (1980), UN Conference on Restrictive Business Practices, *American Journal of International Law*, 74, p. 451.

Böckstiegel, Karl-Heinz and Alexander Catranis (1980), Verhaltenskodex der Vereinten Nationen für multinationale Unternehmen: Illusion oder absehbare Realität? *Neue Juristische Wochenschrift*, 33, p. 1823.

Bryde, Brun-Otto (1981), *Internationale Verhaltensregeln für Private - Völkerrechtliche und Verfassungsrechtliche Aspekte*, Frankfurt am Main.

Caves, Richard E. (1982), *Multinational Enterprises and Economic Analysis*, Cambridge, Mass. and others.

Czako, Judith M. (1981), The Set of Multilaterally Equitable Principles and Rules for the Control of Restrictive Business Practices, *Law and Policy in International Business*, 13, p. 312.

Davidow, Joel (1980), The UNCTAD Restrictive Business Practices Code, in: Norbert Horn (ed.), *Legal Problems of Codes of Conduct for Multinational Enterprises*, Deventer and others, p. 193.

Davidow, Joel (1984), The Implementation of International Antitrust Principles, in: Seymour J. Rubin and Gary Clyde Hufbauer (eds.), *Emerging Standards of International Trade and Investment, Multinational Codes and Corporate Conduct*, Totowa, N.J., 119.

Ebenroth, Carsten-Thomas and Joachim Karl (1987), *Code of Conduct - Ansätze zur vertraglichen Gestaltung internationaler Investitionen*, Konstanz.

Fatouros, Arghyrios A. (1980), The UN Code of Conduct on Transnational Corporations: A Critical Discussion of the First Drafting Phase, in: Norbert Horn (ed.), *Legal Problems of Codes of Conduct for Multinational Enterprises*, Deventer and others, 103.

Fatouros, Arghyrios A. (1984), The UN Code of Conduct on Transnational Corporations: Problems of Interpretation and Implementation, in: Seymour J. Rubin and Gary Clyde Hufbauer (eds.), *Emerging Standards of International Trade and Investment*, Totowa, N.J., 101.

Fikentscher, Wolfgang (1982), United Nations Codes of Conduct: New Paths in International Law, *American Journal of Comparative Law*, 30, p. 577.

Fikentscher, Wolfgang (1983), *Wirtschaftsrecht, Band I. Weltwirtschaft, Europäisches Wirtschaftsrecht*, München.

Fikentscher, Wolfgang and Wolfgang Straub (1982), *Der RBP-Kodex der Vereinten Nationen: Weltkartellrichtlinien*, Part I and II, Gewerblicher Rechtsschutz und Urheberrecht, Internationaler Teil, 637, p. 727.

Gäfgen, Gerard (1983), Entwicklung und Stand der Theory der Property Rights. Eine kritische Bestandsaufnahme, in: Manfred Neumann (ed.), *Ansprüche, Eigentums- und Verfügungsrechte, Schriften des Vereins für Socialpolitik*, Berlin, 43.

Greenhill, Colin R. (1978), UNCTAD: Control of Restrictive Business Practices, *Journal of World Trade Law*, 12, p. 67.

Guertin, Don L. (1980), A Business View on the Implementation of Codes of Conduct, in: Norbert Horn (ed.), *Legal Problems of Codes of Conduct for Multinational Enterprises*, Deventer and others, 295.

Hahn, Helmuth von (1982), Kodex der Vereinten Nationen gegen Wettbewerbsbeschränkungen im internationalen Handel - Chancen und Risiken, in: Clemens-August Andreae and Werner Benisch (eds.), *Wettbewerbsordnung und Wettbewerbsrealität*, Festschrift für Arno Sölter, Köln and others, 367.

Hailbronner, Kay (1981), Völkerrechtliche und staatsrechtliche Überlegungen zu Verhaltenskodizes für transnationale Unternehmen, in: Ingo von Münch (ed.), *Staatsrecht - Völkerrecht - Europarecht*. Festschrift für Hans-Jürgen Schlochauer zum 75. Geburtstag zum 28. März 1981, Berlin, New York, 329.

Hailbronner, Kay (1983), *Entwicklungstendenzen des Wirtschaftsvölkerrechts*, Konstanz.

Horn, Norbert (1980a), Die Entwicklung des internationalen Wirtschaftsrechts durch Verhaltensrichtlinien, *RabelsZ*, 44, p. 423.

Horn, Norbert (ed.), (1980b), *Legal Problems of Codes of Conduct for Multinational Enterprises*, Deventer and others.

Hossain, Kamal (1980), Introduction, in: Kamal Hossain (ed.), *Legal Aspects of the New International Economic Order*, London, New York, 1.

Hymer, Stephen and Robert Rowthorn (1970), Multinational Corporations and International Oligopoly; The Non-American Challenge, in: Charles P. Kindleberger (ed.), *The International Corporation*, Cambridge, Mass., London, 57.

Jackson, John H. (1977), *Legal Problems of International Economic Relations*, St. Paul, Minn.

Joelson, Mark J. (1976), The Proposed International Codes of Conduct as Related to Restrictive Business Practices, *Law and Policy in International Business*, 8, p. 837.

Kartte, Wolfgang and Heinrich Hölzler (1981), Internationale Unternehmen und Wettbewerb, in: Wilhelm H. Wacker, Helmut Hausmann and Brij Kumar (eds.), *Internationale Unternehmensführung. Managementprobleme international tätiger Unternehmen.* Festschrift zum 80. Geburtstag von Eugen Hermann Sieber, Berlin, 379.

Kather, Peter (1986), *Der Kodex der Vereinten Nationen über wettbewerbsbeschränkende Geschäftspraktiken*, München.

Kirchner, Christian (1975), *Internationale Marktaufteilungen. Möglichkeiten ihrer Beseitigung mit einer Fallstudie über den internationalen Arzneimittelmarkt*, Frankfurt am Main.

Kirchner, Christian (1980), Ökonomische Analyse des Rechts und Recht der Wettbewerbsbeschränkungen (Antitrust Law and Economics), *Zeitschrift für das gesamte Handelsrecht und Wirtschaftsrecht* 144, p. 563.

Kirchner, Christian and Arnold Picot (1987), Transaction Cost Analysis of Structural Changes in the Distribution System: Reflections on Institutional Developments in the Federal Republic of Germany, *Journal of Institutional and Theoretical Economics*, 143, p. 62.

Kirchner, Christian, Erich Schanze, Fabian G. von Schlabrendorff, Albrecht Stockmayer, Thomas W. Wälde, Michael Fritzsche, Reinhard Patzine, (1979), *Mining Ventures in Developing Countries. Interests, Bargaining Process and Legal Concepts*, Deventer, Frankfurt am Main.

Kolvenbach, Walter (1982), Verhaltenskodizes für Multinationale Unternehmen: Problem oder Hoffnung? in: Clemens-August Andreae and Werner Benisch (eds.), *Wettbewerbsordnung und Wettbewerbsrealität*, Festschrift für Arno Sölter zum 70. Geburtstag, Köln and others, 381.

Kronstein, Heinrich (1973), *The Law of International Cartels*, Ithaca, London.

Meesen, Karl Matthias (1981), Internationale Verhaltenskodizes und Sittenwidrig-keitsklauseln, *Neue Juristische Wochenschrift*, 34, p. 1131.

Meesen, Karl Matthias (1985), Zu den Grundlagen des internationalen Wirtschafts-rechts, *Archiv für Öffentliches Recht* 110, p. 398.

Mertens, Hans-Joachim, Christian Kirchner and Erich Schanze (1982), *Wirt-schaftsrecht*, 2nd ed., Opladen.

Petersmann, Ernst-Ulrich (1979/80), Internationales Recht und Neue Internationale Wirtschftsordnung, *Archiv für Völkerrecht*, 18.

Petersmann, Ernst-Ulrich (1984), Codes of Conduct, in: *Encyclopedia of Public International Law*, published under the auspices of the Max Planck Institute for Comparative Public Law and International Law under the direction of Rudolf Bernhardt, Vol. 7, Amsterdam, New York, Oxford, 28.

Picot, Arnold (1982), Transaktionskostenansatz in der Organisationstheorie: Stand der Diskussion und Aussagewert, *Die Betriebswirtschaft* 42, p. 267.

Polinsky, A. Mitchell (1983), *An Introduction to Law and Economics*, Boston, Toronto.

Posner, Richard A. (1977), *Economic Analysis of Law*, 2nd ed., Boston, Toronto.

Rehbinder, Eckard (1965), *Extraterritoriale Wirkungen des deutschen Kartellrechts*, Baden-Baden.

Rehbinder, Eckard (1981), Abs. 2 § 98, in: Ulrich Immenga and Ernst-Joachim Mestmäcker (eds.), *GWB. Gesetz gegen Wettbewerbsbeschränkungen. Kommen-tar*, München, 1871.

Schäfer, Hans-Bernd and Claus Ott (1986), *Lehrbuch der ökonomischen Analyse des Zivilrechts*, Berlin and others.

Schanze, Erich, Michael Fritzsche, Christian Krichner, Fabian G. von Schlabren-dorff, Albrecht Stockmayer, Wolfgang Hauser, Martin Bartels and William Mahoney (1981), *Mining Ventures in Developing Countries*, Part 2: Analysis of Project Agreements, Deventer, Frankfurt am Main.

Simmonds, Kenneth R. (ed.), (1979-1986), *Multinational Corporations Law. The U.N. and Transnational Corporations*, Dobbs Ferry, N.Y.

Steeg, Helga (1985), Internationale Verhaltensregeln für internationale Investitionen und multinationale Unternehmen, *Zeitschrift für Unternehmens- und Gesellschftsrecht*, 15, p. 1.

Syquia, Enrique (1980), The UNCTAD Code and Problems of Transfer of Technol-ogy and Restrictive Business Practices: The Viewpoint of Developing Coun-tries, in: Norbert Horn (ed.), *Legal Problems of Codes of Conduct for Multi-national Enterprises*, Deventer and others, 210.

VerLoren van Themaat, Pieter (1981), *The Changing Structures of International Economic Law*, The Hague, Boston, London.

Wang, N.T. (1981), Analysis of Restrictive Business Practices by Transnational Corporations and Their Impact on Trade and Development, in: Oscar Schachter and Robert Helawell (eds.), *Competition in International Business, Law and Policy on Restrictive Business Practices*, New York, 3.

Wengler, Wilhelm (1976), Rechtsvertrag, Konsensus und Absichtserklärung im Völkerrecht, *Juristenzeitung*, 31, p. 193.

Wildhaber, Luzius (1978), Multinationale Unternehmen und Völkerrecht, in: Luzius Wildhaber, Bernhard Großfeld, Otto Sandrock and Rolf Birk, *Internationalrechtliche Probleme multinatinaler Korporationen (International Law Problems of Multinational Corporations)*, Heidelberg, Karlsruhe, 7.

Williamson, Oliver E. (1979), Transaction Cost Economics: The Governance of Contractual Relations, *Journal of Law and Economics*, 22, p. 233.

COMMENTS

William A. Niskanen

This is a strange paper.

Although the restrictive business practices (RBP) code was approved nearly seven years ago, Prof. Kirchner has not identified one change in national legislation, one court case, or one change in business practices that would testify to either the effectiveness or desirability of this code.

For the moment, I will accept his primary assertion that an international code of conduct, even if formally voluntary, may have some effect on government and business practices in individual nations. All the more reason to examine whether the specific code is likely to be desirable.

Prof. Kirchner, like Adam Smith, is correctly suspicious when businessmen in the same industry gather for even the most innocent activities. He should be even more suspicious when lawyers and politicians convene in international meetings, if the results of their deliberations have any prospect of having the force of law.

If the final vote on the RBP code had been delayed for several months, the Reagan administration, with my full support, would probably have voted against approving this code. Let me give you a number of reasons for this position.

1.　　It is increasingly unclear whether most national antitrust laws are desirable. In the United States, most of the academic debate has narrowed to the question of whether to maintain Section 1 of the Sherman Act or to abolish all the antitrust laws.

2.　　Even if some national legislation may be desirable, a common international code may not be desirable. Let me use the example of environmental law. In most cases, where pollutants have no significant external effects beyond one nation, it is best to leave the choice of environmental policy to national or subnational governments; this permits recognition of differences in preferences for environmental benefits and differences in the means to achieve these benefits. In other cases, such as acid rain and ozone depletion, where each nation uses a common global pool, some international coordination may be desirable, depending on the specific policy selected.

The general issue is whether to let the international Tiebout process work. For business practices, the issue is whether such practices have significant external costs beyond national borders. My judgment is that most business practices do not meet this test.

3.   The RBP code contributes to the general illusion of the "New International Economic Order" that the problems of the poor countries are due primarily to the business practices of multinational corporations or the government policies of the developed countries. All of us have a responsibility not to reenforce this dangerous illusion.

4.   Most important, the RBP code does not address the major source of restrictive practices. Section E of this code commits governments to enforce this code against businesses, but not to refrain from such practices themselves. The governments of the developing countries, for example, are primarily responsible for the producer cartels in coffee, oil, tin, and rubber. The governments of the developed countries are primarily responsible for the buyer cartels affecting semiconductors, steel, and textiles and apparel. Few, if any, restrictive business practices are sustainable without government enforcement. The RBP code is directed at the wrong target.

In summary, there may be a case for an international RBP code. Prof. Kirchner, however, has not made this case.

Competing Institutional Arrangements and Internationalization

Carsten-Thomas Ebenroth*

I.   Introduction

In the past couple of decades, the relevance of national markets in determining economic policies has largely disappeared; a globalization of markets has taken place. Several factors made this internationalization possible:

(1)   The "technological revolution" in transport and communication;[1] transport of both goods and information became easier and national markets became interdependent.

(2)   The economic advances of the newly industrializing countries such as the South-East Asian countries, Brazil and Argentina, created a new international division of labour. The strong influence of this shift on the growth of the world trade volume was witnessed in the 1970s[2], when world trade grew at an annual average of 6.7%. During the recession at the beginning of the '80s, growth in world trade volume decreased considerably, but picked up strongly from 1983 again.[3]

(3)   Increased foreign direct investment contributed to an integration of markets, too. Foreign direct investment makes markets more homogeneous, broadens the perspective of firms operating in different markets at the same time,

---

*   The author thanks Jesko Hentschel, M.A., and Jörg Wulfken, attorney at law, research fellows at the Centre on International Economics, University of Konstanz, for their contribution.

1   *Ebenroth, C.T.* (1987a), pp. 46-47.

2   IMF (1987), p. 138.

3   Average 1983-1986 growth rate 5%; IMF, ibid. (fn. 2), p. 138.

Studies in International Economics and Institutions
Vosgerau (Ed.) New Institutional Arrangements for the World Economy
© Springer-Verlag Berlin Heidelberg 1989

induces the division of labour along vertical lines in the production process and thereby creates trade flows.

(4) Cross-border financial claims not only increased with foreign direct and portfolio investments, but also with increased international borrowing and lending. The expansion of the Euromarkets facilitated a tremendous expansion of the lending to developing countries, which reached an estimated $1,200 billion in 1987.[4]

These moves towards the global integration of national markets were eased by international institutional arrangements that were formed after World War II in the aftermath of nationalistic policy responses in the wake of the Great Depression. It was recognized that the protectionist policies of the 1930s - that led to a sharp decline in the world trade volume and only increased the strains on the national economies - should be eliminated in the future. Institutions like the International Monetary Fund, the GATT, the United Nations, and the OECD were formed to take away from national policy makers decisions which could influence the international economic environments. But these institutional arrangements are far from being able to regulate and co-ordinate national economic policies in a desirable way:

- Non-tariff barriers such as voluntary export restraints or quality standards undermine the free-trade spirit of GATT. The "Generalized System of Preferences" as well as the safeguard-clauses of the General Agreement on Tariffs and Trade further weaken this institution.

  - The international monetary system is characterized by no agreed-on rule relating countries' currencies since the breakdown of the Bretton-Woods System of fixed exchange rates at the beginning of the '70s. The large fluctuation of the exchange rates of the major currencies has produced an intense discussion over possible reforms. The increased importance of international versus national financial markets due to the growth of Euromarkets

---

[4]   IMF, ibid. (fn. 2), p. 180.

and the variety of financial innovations demands new international institutional arrangements.

- With the increase in cross-border direct investment, the need to harmonize existing regulations arises in order to reduce the risk of these investments and to facilitate further growth. Countries are in an intensive global competition to attract foreign direct investment (FDI). It is important to distinguish factor markets from institutional markets when looking at foreign direct investment. Factor markets contain the economic conditions, while institutional markets entail the legal framework of the host country.[5] It is difficult to influence factor markets in the short run; institutional markets, on the other hand, are quite sensitive to policy changes.

But making proposals for how international institutions should be reformed cannot be the only task facing economists and lawyers. Economic theory has for a long time stressed the importance of free trade and factor flows for world economic growth. In reality, one finds the opposite happening - protectionist policies are a fact of international economic relations. To explain why the potential gainers of free trade cannot gather as much support as the losers, we need political economy and property rights analysis to grasp the institutional structures both on a national and international level.

II.   International Trade

1.   Economic Theory and International Trade

Before dealing with the institutional setting under which international trade takes place today, a brief reference should be made as to what economic theory tells us in this respect.

Mainstream economists have stressed for a long time that the free movement of goods and factors maximizes both world and - unless the country is large enough

---

[5]   See *Ebenroth, C.T.*, ibid. (fn. 1), p. 68.

to influence its terms of trade by restricting it[6] - also national welfare.[7] These proposals for the international regulation of trade are therefore straightforward: Governments or other institutions should not interfere in trade, since if each country specializes in the production of those goods which its comparative advantages entail (either in the Ricardian sense of production techniques or in the Heckscher-Ohlin sense of relative factor endowments) all countries will benefit. Criticism of the "free trade doctrine" has been mainly concerned with

- *the static nature* of the theory:

  for countries to undertake structural adjustments along lines of comparative advantage is welfare-improving in the long run, but introduces adjustment costs reducing welfare in the short run. Thus the decision to liberalize depends highly on the rate of time preference of society and often the politicians themselves.

- the inability of the theory to take account of the *changing patterns* of comparative advantage:

  thus an often heard argument is that the specific industries need protection (especially at the beginning of the development process) in order to enable them to achieve the most efficient production method (either through economies of scale or "learning by doing"). This "infant industry argument" for protection has shown to be only of a second best nature: instead of a tariff, a subsidy for this specific industry should be used which gives the desired incentive for production, but does not force consumers to pay a higher price for the commodity.[8]

- the abstraction from the *level of economic* activity of the trading partners:

  the Dependency-School, prominent in the 1950s and 1960s, asserted that trade will increase the gap between developed and developing nations,

---

[6] See *Johnson, H.G.* (1950-51), pp. 28-35, for the original analysis. Whether the tariff in this case really improves welfare depends heavily on whether retaliation measures are levied or not.

[7] Compare here *Samuelson, P.A.* (1962), pp. 820-829.

[8] *Baldwin, R.E.* (1969), pp. 295-305.

because the terms-of-trade of the LDCs will have to decline and their exports will be met by protection by the developed countries.

In a world characterized by direct (tariffs, quotas) and "indirect" trade impediments (non-tariff barriers such as quality standards, administrative barriers) economic analysis implies that, on an aggregate level, lifting trade barriers should enable the gainers of this liberalization to fully compensate the losers. But it is obvious that the "non-traders", those that gain from protection, are often more powerful than the "traders" in the political process.[9]

Hillman[10] argues in this volume that the existence of protectionist trade policies could be due to either the social insurance motive or the power of interest groups. The social insurance motive implies that the government protects the income and jobs of risk-averse economic agents, since high transaction costs make internal compensation of the losers by the gainers of freer trade impossible. If this were the motive for protection, it could well be that government intervention increases social welfare by maximizing the expected utility of the society. But the social insurance motive is not very likely to be the incentive for trade intervention, since private insurance firms could perform this function as well as the government without interfering in the international flow of goods. Thus the well-known economic analysis of protectionism[11] seems to still be the most valuable approach to explain the appearance and persistence of impediments to trade. The rational behaviour of sector-specific groups that can gain a lot from protectionist measures (import-competing industries) is to pressure politicians, who have short time horizons, to introduce trade barriers.

---

[9] *Curzon* (1986) recently used these terms to describe the motives of different GATT members. See *Curzon, G. and V.* (1986), pp. 19-35.

[10] *Hillman, A.L.* (1987), Policy Motives and International Trade Restrictions, Konstanz Symposium Paper, July.

[11] See e.g. *Baldwin, R.E.* (1982), pp. 263-286.

The "property-rights" literature[12] adds another factor which explains the persistence of protectionism. Examining the making of national trade policy in the U.S., Michael Finger notes in his contribution to this symposium that for a GATT contracting country, "the circumstances under which a country may impose import restrictions become the rights of particular interest within the country to protection from import competition".[13] The national market thus becomes the property of the national firms operating in it. The government is obliged to intervene on behalf of these firms if foreign firms try to enlarge their market share, as long as such intervention does not contradict the legal provisions accepted. In this respect, free trade is regarded as foreign aid, involving economic costs to the domestic economy.

2.   Shortcomings of the GATT from the Free Trade Perspective

The General Agreement on Tariffs and Trade (GATT) was signed in 1947, and, since the "Havana-Charta" of 1949 was never ratified (and the International Trade Organization never formally established), it remains the most important body regulating international trade (reference to other international organizations such as UNCTAD or OECD will be made below). 93 countries are members of GATT, over 30 others have applied for membership. Important trading nations such as the USSR and East Germany are non-members. The USSR's application was turned down in the Uruguay-Round because the problem of assessing comparative advantage and effectiveness of tariffs in a large non-market economy was felt to be too difficult.

The GATT is often thought of as an organization to "establish free trade", although it is much better described as one that tries to reduce uncertainty about future markets and promotes trade. Member countries have contractional obligations and face retaliatory measures if they violate the rules and agreements of the contract

---

12   See *Furubotn, E.G. and S. Pejovich* (1974), for the economic analysis and review of the earlier literature.

13   *Finger, M.J.* (1987), Protectionist Rules and International Discretion in the Making of National Trade Policy, Konstanz Symposium Paper, July.

(e.g. Article VI). The usefulness to member governments rests mainly in their ability to have a foothold against national special interest groups.

As is well-known, the GATT is based on the principles of non-discrimination (most-favoured nation clause of Article I) and the adherence to agreed-on tariff levels to reduce uncertainty in the system. But there do exist major loopholes and exceptions:

(1) The general agreement tried to limit trade impediments to price measures and explicitly prohibited quantitative restrictions and export and import licences (Article XI).[14] But the rise of non-tariff barriers to restrict trade could not be countered: qualitative requirements, administrative procedures, and especially so-called "voluntary export restraints" undermine the spirit of GATT.[15] Voluntary export restraints were mainly used by the industrial countries to protect their labour-intensive industries (such as textiles) against the competition from the newly industrializing countries. Producing countries have an incentive to agree to such self-restraints, because they can internalize the higher price in the protected market; they receive a quota rent. But it is obvious that there are severe strains on the developing economies, since the restriction distorts production and consumption.[16] Additionally, as comparative advantage shifts, restricted countries will benefit from the guaranteed market access sooner or later.[17] The GATT was only able to regain control over these non-tariff barriers by tolerating the establishment of the Multi-Fibre Agreement in 1974. This agreement, covering the most threatened industry in the industrialized countries (textiles), fixes export and import quotas for the participating nations. It is administered by GATT officials and constitutes the major departure from GATT rules.

---

[14] See e.g. *Dam, K. W.* (1977), for the original text and an analysis.

[15] On voluntary export restraints and their implications see *Hamilton, C.* (1984).

[16] See *Eggerstedt, H., Hentschel, J. and Noh, T.J.* (1987), for an economic analysis of VER's on developing countries.

[17] *Eggerstedt et al.*, ibid. (fn. 16), p. 13.

(2) Article XXIV explicitly excludes customs unions and free-trade areas from obedience to the non-discriminatory principle. The draft of the General Agreement viewed such free-trade zones as being helpful to stimulate trade, so long as a global reduction of trade impediments could not be achieved. But it is entirely possible that customs unions or free trade areas complying with Article XXIV may be strongly protectionist in effect, due to their internal policies (e.g. agricultural subsidization in the EEC) and their "trade diversion" effect.[18]

(3) Articles XII (restrictions to safeguard the balance of payments) and XIX ("escape clause") are major loopholes of the general agreement and are often applied to increase protectionist measures. Article XIX, referring to "conditions as to cause or threaten serious injuries to domestic producers", as necessary for giving a country the right to restrict imports, often leads to higher tariff levels when applied. This leaves the GATT-members with a mechanism that enables them not to stick to negotiated tariff levels.

(4) Quite a few economists argue that the special treatment of developing countries in the General Agreement hinders not only free trade and the efficient allocation of resources along lines of comparative advantage, but also the development perspectives of these countries[19].

The special status of developing countries manifests itself in:

a) Article XVIII, which allows the use of quantitative restrictions, if the country is in balance of payments difficulties (Section B). Section C provides for the protection of infant industries.

---

[18] The discussion about the trade-diversion effect of customs unions and free-trade zones was touched off by *Viner, J.* (1950), pp. 41-56. If a country imports a commodity from two supplier countries and it leaves the previously equal tariffs only against *one*, the import structure will change (= trade diversion) in favour of the preferentially treated supplier.

[19] See *Langhammer, R.* (1987).

b) Part IV of the GATT (amendment in 1964), which gave the developing countries a group status as in UNCTAD and provided the possibility for them not to participate in multilateral tariff reductions, if this is felt to counter their development needs.

c) The Generalized System of Preferences (GSP) formed at the Tokyo Round in 1979. The "Enabling Clause" exempted countries from the non-discriminatory principle concerning preferential treatment of the developing countries (tariffs, preferential trade agreements among the developing countries).

It is argued that these preferential treatments are not in the interest of developing countries, since they enable the latter to pursue "inward-oriented" development policies. Although this term is never defined and agreed on in the literature, the general conception is that inward-looking policies are those favouring production and investment in the home market versus production and investment for exports. The World Bank Report 1987[20] and several recent studies[21] all stress the importance of exports for economic growth and the success of "outward-looking policies" (those that do not bias their incentive structures against exports) in promoting exports and growth.

One should not neglect though that the development success of the often cited East-Asian countries cannot be simply copied by other countries. Dependence on primary exports of a large number of developing countries is met by severe protectionism, especially of the agricultural sector, by the industrialized countries. Fluctuating commodity prices and export earnings, combined with the unwillingness of the developed countries to undertake necessary structural adjustments, leave a lot of developing countries even today with a strong pessimistic view concerning trade.

---

[20] *World Bank Report* (1987).

[21] See here *Heitger, B.* (1987), pp. 249-261; or *Balassa, B.* (1985), pp. 23-35; *Chow* (1987, pp. 55-63), on the other hand, stresses that causality between exports and growth runs both ways, so that a simple correlation between the two variables does not yield the (desired) outcome that exports are important for growth.

3. Competing Institutions Affecting Trade

The previous section focused on the GATT and its shortcomings, but a brief look should also be taken at the other, competing institutions affecting international trade[22].

The United Nations Conference on Trade and Development (UNCTAD) was established in 1964 due to the action and ideas of *Raul Prebisch*. His economic thinking[23] (Dependency-School) shaped the proposals and proceedings of the UNCTAD (which was established, after its first meeting, as a permanent body of the United Nations Assembly). The developing countries were disillusioned with the GATT because the bargaining procedure in the GATT rounds (principal supplier rule)[24] excluded them to a large extent from the decision-making process. In their view, the GATT also did not address issues of economic development and was therefore not an institution likely to actively help the status of the developing world in the world economy. UNCTAD's proposals which were broadly described as the New International Economic Order after the 1976 conference in Nairobi are concerned with

- stabilizing and raising raw material prices through international commodity agreements

- providing increased tariff preferences to the less developed countries (LDCs)

- expanding aid and waiving debt payments

- making more technology available at lower prices

- improving the inter-LDC trade relations.

---

[22] See *Dam, K.W.*, ibid. (fn. 14), pp. 378-389.

[23] These are outlined in *Prebisch, R.* (1965).

[24] In GATT negotiations, the usual bargaining procedure is that the largest importer of a commodity negotiates mutual tariff reductions with the largest supplier ("principal supplier rule"). Other countries then often accept the negotiated terms.

Although UNCTAD lacks an effective enforcement structure, its influence in shaping the international economic environment should not be underestimated. The joint action of the developing countries ("Group of 77") gave rise to a re-thinking of GATT's provisions for developing countries. Both Part IV of the GATT (1964) and the Generalized System of Preferences (which represents a violation of the GATT principle of non-discrimination) have to be viewed as concessions to developing countries.

The dependency theorists, having shaped UNCTAD's view of the world trading system, stress that important differences have to be made concerning the level of economic development of the trading nations. Free trade between industrialized and developing countries need not be beneficial for the latter.[25]

UNCTAD therefore stresses the necessity of managed markets and discriminatory trade arrangements in favour of LDCs. The UNCTAD conference of 1987 made a major contribution in this respect. After the failure of UNCTAD to sponsor specific commodity agreements (Cocoa-Conferences 1966 and 1967), the Integrated Commodity Program was formulated in Nairobi (1976). With the signing of the USSR at the 1987 Conference in Geneva, the agreement finally became effective to sponsor a variety of commodity buffer-stocks and make compensatory payments for low export earnings possible.

The GATT, based on the liberalization doctrine of the neo-classical trade theory, had other aims. That the two institutions can co-exist is mainly due to

(a)   the narrow spectrum of GATT-activity, namely to reduce tariff levels and avoid certain non-discriminatory trade practices

(b)   the unenforceable nature of UNCTAD-decisions

(c)   the acceptance of UNCTAD proposals in the General Agreement (Part IV, generalized system of preferences, tolerance of commodity agreements in Articles XX (H) and XXV of GATT).

---

[25]   See *Prebisch, R.* (1950).

But if the GATT is not going to serve the desire of the industrialized countries to be a forum for the discussion of mutually better trade conditions, there might well be a shift of negotiating trade issues among developed countries only to the Organization for Economic Cooperation and Development (OECD). Up to now, the latter has been concerned with co-ordinating governmental activities affecting trade (quality standards, harmonization of technical laws and regulations) rather than with discouraging governmental activities like the GATT.

The members of all the international institutions mentioned are obviously unwilling to give up their trade-policy sovereignty. This is due to opposing theories about the benefits of world trade and the stronghold which interest groups have in the shaping of national policies. It manifests itself in safety-clauses in the GATT, allowing members not to adhere to the basic principles of the agreement. It also manifests itself in competing institutions discussing and making reform proposals in the international trade spectrum. Both UNCTAD and the OECD ("rich man's club") are concerned with pursuing and advancing special interests. The GATT can only exist because it is narrow in scope and willing to make concessions (Multi-Fibre Agreement, Generalized System of Preferences), even if these violate the non-discrimination principle.

Most of the reform proposals made for GATT today are only "wishful thinking" if one takes these constraints into consideration. Nevertheless, a first step to broaden the General Agreement would be consultations between the IMF and GATT. Most of the trade restrictions brought before the GATT Council are based on Articles VII and XVIII b, both applying to balance of payments imbalances. The cause of payments difficulties is never analyzed and there seems to be a task for the IMF to survey policy adjustments if GATT members use these provisions.

III. Markets

1.   The Current International Monetary System and Its Problems

The international monetary system is a major determinant of international factor and good flows.

The International Monetary Fund (IMF) is the central organization of the international monetary system, due to the broad support of industrialized and developing countries membership, its powers, and the size of its resources.[26] Since the IMF came into existence in 1944, the number of organizations and less formal bodies concerned with matters of international monetary policy has grown steadily (e.g. OECD, GATT, and the European Monetary System). Thus the international monetary law is not confined to the IMF Agreement, but also includes the statutes and other legal instruments of these other organizations and bodies, as well as customary international law concerned with monetary matters[27].

The IMF can exercise surveillance over the international exchange rate system, while the member countries have to provide the needed information to the IMF (Art. IV (3) IMF Agreement). From the legal point of view this is a rather nominal function.[28] Since the breakdown of the Bretton-Woods system of adjustable pegs at the beginning of the '70s, member countries can choose their own exchange rate regime. Today, freely floating exchange rates (among the world's major currencies) exist as well as regional fixed exchange rate regimes (European Monetary System), while most of the developing countries have pegged their rates to one or a basket of major currencies. In the Second Amendment to the IMF Agreement, member states have agreed on a general obligation to pursue a policy of international economic stabilization (Art. IV (1) IMF Agreement), although legally the IMF has no right to directly influence the national economic policy of its members.

This international monetary environment has been characterized by an *"excessive"* volatility of the exchange rates, although it has not been agreed on how "excessive" could be defined. But in the minds of economists and politicians, exchange rates have certain "normal" equilibrium levels. Both large deviations from this equilibrium level as well as large fluctuations are extremely undesirable because there has been a strong negative impact on economic performance and trade. Additionally,

---

[26]   *Gold, J.* (1984), p. 38.

[27]   See *Gold, J.*, ibid. (fn. 26); *Mann, F.A.* (1985), pp. 396-403 (397/398).

[28]   *Mann, F.A.*, ibid. (fn. 27), p. 397.

some authors claim that the real exchange rate instability in the developing countries is, to a large extent, caused by the high degree of variability of the industrialized nations' currency values.[29]

The debt crisis is another threat to the stability of the international monetary environment. Excessive bank lending in the '70s and the beginning of the '80s was due to the expansion of Euro-markets and the availability of large amounts of funds for commercial bank lending created thereby (because no reserve requirements exist), as well as the recycling of the Petro-dollars. That overlending took place was recognized when Mexico admitted in 1982 that it could not service its debt. Not only did this influence the willingness of commercial banks to make new loans, but at the same time all economic indicators turned against the heavily indebted nations: U.S. interest rates rose due to the tremendous budget deficit (and since a large part of the debt was on a variable interest rate basis this directly influences the debt service volume), the world economy went into a recession, and a lot of industrialized nations used protectionist measures to avoid structural changes. Quite a few debtor nations were not able to service their debt and had to enter into rescheduling arrangements.

The volume of private bank lending to LDCs and the vulnerability of banks (especially U.S. ones) threatens the international monetary and world economic system; if the debt is not serviced, the consequent write-offs would cut deeply into the equity capital of banks, causing a lot of them to go bankrupt. The current interbank lending volume would spread this bankruptcy around the world. Thus time had and still has to be gained in order for banks to build up loss-reserves and partly write off their debts. The necessary funds needed to gain this time have been made available by a unique co-operation between private banks, governments, and international institutions.

---

[29]   *Edwards, S.* (1987).

2. Competing Institutional Arrangements in International Monetary Policy

When the Bretton Woods system of pegged exchange rates came under severe pressure at the beginning of the '70s, most economists and politicians argued for a system of freely floating exchange rates. The latter offered the possibility to regain
effective control over monetary policy, which was assigned under the system of
pegged rates to stabilize the value of one's currency vs. the dollar. Additionally,
politicians hesitated to further accept the dominant role of the U.S. monetary
policy, since the U.S. was the only country not bound to use its monetary policy in
order to peg its currency value. The expansionary monetary policy of the Federal
Reserve at the beginning of the '70s raised doubts of whether the U.S. would
pursue a non-inflationary monetary policy in the future. The gains outweighed the
partial loss of the effectiveness of fiscal policy under a flexible exchange rate
regime, since the induced depreciation or appreciation of the currency would
partially offset the intent of the fiscal policy through its destimulating or
stimulating effect on the export sector.

But, as already mentioned above, the flexible rate system has been characterized by
wide swings in the exchange rates. Different proposals for a more stable international monetary system can be made depending on what triggers the instability of
the present system.

One view is that the instabilities are inherent to the flexible rate system itself,
which would mean that the international monetary system should move to a different institutional arrangement once again: fixed exchange rates, target zones, or even
a return to the gold standard, as it is sometimes proposed. This is the position of
France, Italy, and a majority of the Third World countries.[30] The arguments for
managed exchange rate systems have been debated for decades. In favour of
managed exchange rates it is argued that foreign exchange markets are subject to
speculative bubbles and runs that make a purely floating rate a poor guide for
resource allocation. Managed rates are alleged to keep exchange rates closer to
fundamentals. Managed exchange rates provide necessary "rules of the game" to

---

[30]   See *Novel, P.* (1985), pp. 8/9.

limit the discretion of national policy authorities. Finally, reduced exchange rate volatility is an important end by itself, moving the world closer to the norm of a world currency, with efficiency gains that are judged to be analogous to a unified currency on the national level.[31]

Opponents of this view hold that the volatility is due to the underlying unstable conditions on the national level. Thus, one should think about institutional reforms that bind national economic policies, and monetary policies in particular. A public choice approach to this problem tries to create a decision-making process of national economic policies which cannot be easily captured by national interest groups. Domestic monetary policies should aim at target variables like the rate of inflation, or/and growth of GNP. Reduced variability of monetary and fiscal policies and thus national discretion would be a major step towards improving international monetary stability.[32]

Current theoretical and empirical knowledge does not permit a decision as to what the true underlying causes of the exchange rate variability are. The European Monetary System is an example of a rather well-functioning managed exchange rate system with respect to adjustments.[33]

Currently, nevertheless, there is not much scope for a change if one takes the political elements[34] into account. The European Monetary System is part of a broader process of economic and political integration within the European Community. An institutional arrangement based on fixed exchange rates or target zones requires a particular degree of political and economic consensus among participating states; presently a consensus among IMF members on this point is lacking.

---

[31] For further discussion on this point, see *Sachs, J.* (1986).

[32] *Willett, T.D.* (1987).

[33] See the judgement of *Wegner, M.* (1987).

[34] See here *Issing, O.* (1980), pp. 522-542 (541).

3. New Developments in International Financial Markets and Some Major Problems

Closely related to the evolution of the world monetary order is the internationalization of financial markets which has taken place in the past couple of decades. There has been a rapid transformation of financial techniques and products as well as of institutions and regulations.

Reasons for the current financial transformations are:

- the "technological revolution" in the computer and communication industries which lowered the costs of financial transactions and now permits world-wide, 24-hour stock trading;

- excessive government financial requirements (e.g. the U.S. budget deficit) and the indebtedness of the LDC's, which led to an enormous increase in cross-border claims;

- the change in the direction of capital net flows in the 1980s, when the sharp decrease of OPEC investible surpluses led to a reduced supply of bank deposits and a reduction in syndicated bank credits;

- the rise in inflation and the increased volatility of interest rates and exchange rates;

- growing competition in international financial markets, stimulating innovation and structural change.[35]

Capital flows are not only influenced by the economic conditions (rates of return on capital) but also by the legal and political environment of the host country; in international finance the institutional markets are of tremendous significance compared with factor markets, because each country is able to quickly adopt the necessary legal framework independently of other countries' regulations.

---

[35] An analysis of the underlying conditions for financial innovations can be found in: *Bank for International Settlements*, (1986), p. 169; see also *Deutsche Bundesbank*, (1986a), pp. 25-35.

Due to these factors financial markets changed radically, although the unprecedented wave of change and innovation makes it very difficult to distinguish "ends
from means, causes from effects, and actions from reactions".[36] First of all,
national markets which originated in the 1960s when Euromarkets expanded
drastically, moved together (*globalization*). Later on, an integration of the Euro-
Currency Market and individual national markets occurred. Increasing activities of
foreign bank entities in national financial markets contributed to the process of
globalization.[37]

Closely related to the globalization of international financial markets, the process of
liberalization and *deregulation* of domestic capital markets occurred.[38] Beginning
in 1974, when the United States and some other major oil-importing countries
relaxed their controls on capital inflows, a second wave of deregulation came in
1979 with the scrapping of the British and Japanese exchange controls on capital
outflows.[39] Perhaps the most dramatic event in the continuing evolution of securities trading is the so-called Big Bang, the "sweeping deregulation" of the London
Stock Exchange that took place on October 27, 1986, with its abolishment of fixed
commissions in favour of negotiated rates and the abolishment of the distinction
between brokers (who execute trades for investors) and jobbers (who buy and sell
on their own account to make a market in one or more stocks).[40] In Germany, the
deregulation of financial markets was introduced by a liberalization of capital
inflows, a lifting of restrictions on purchases by non-residents of domestic bonds
and money market instruments, the abolition of the coupon tax and a modification
of the minimum reserve requirements. Currently, the abolishment of the German

---

[36] *Corrigan, E.G.* (1987), pp. 1-5 (1).

[37] See *BIS* ibid. (fn. 35), p. 149; *Schaad, E.F.* (1987) pp. 45-51. See, e.g., for
West Germany *Deutsche Bundesbank* (1987), pp. 32-37.

[38] The process of deregulation is decribed in *Denning, U.,* (1987); *Franke, G.*
(1987), pp. 429-444 (436).

[39] For further details, also in other western countries, see *BIS*, ibid. (fn. 35),
p. 149.

[40] For a description of "Big Bang" see *Palmer, J.D.* (1986), pp. 38-43 (40);
Schaad, E.F., ibid. (Fn. 37), p. 47.

transfer duty stamp tax ('Börsenumsatzsteuer') and a reform of the German Stock Exchange is discussed.[41] The worldwide wave of deregulation and liberalization was a strong impetus for the integration of international and domestic financial markets.

A third trend in international banking has been the shift towards *securitization* which covers the replacement of traditional bank loans in favour of marketable debt instruments (securities).[42] Commercial banks have become major managers of securities while their role as borrowers has been reduced. Bond financing in international markets has grown steadily, surpassing the volume of bank loans in 1983 for the first time. Today they account for 80% of the whole credit volume in international financial markets.[43] In the context of securitization a lot of new financial instruments have been developed, such as Note Issuance Facilities (NIF's), Revolving Underwriting Facilities (RUF's), Euronote Facilities, as well as currency and interest rate swaps.[44] Banks are no longer borrowers of money, thus the new financial instruments mentioned are all off-balance-sheet activities; but banks principally take the same risks as a borrower if they underwrite the sale of securities.

Securitization led to rapid growth in the volume of market transactions and to increasing concentration of the banking business in a few main financial centres such as London, New York and Tokyo. The concentration of the banking centres has shown that probably the Anglo-American lawyers have kept the specific strategic opportunities with more flexibility than their continental European counterparts. Central banks supervisory power, banking supervisory laws, accounting principles for business and taxation, and a specific spread of risk evaluation have

---

[41] A survey over the legal framework of recent liberalizations on West German capital markets gives *Schwarck, E.* (1987), pp. 2041-2048.

[42] See *BIS* ibid. (fn. 35), p. 129; *Dombret, A.,*1987, pp. 326-330 (326); *Deutsche Bundesbank* (1986a), p. 25; *Schatzmann, H.* (1987), pp. 178-182.

[43] For further details see *Stevenson, M.* (1987), p. 4.

[44] For a detailed description of major new financial instruments see *BIS* ibid. (fn. 35), pp. 17-126; *Schatzmann, H.,* ibid. (fn. 42); *Deutsche Bundesbank,* (fn. 35) p. 27; *Bauer, H.P.* (1987), pp. 183-189.

offered for the international law firms based in New York and London many opportunities to create new business. A country or a capital market with territorial sovereignty which wishes to attract foreign direct investment must create the right legal environment. In that respect, the United Kingdom law, having grown to serve the needs of the colonial empire, is more flexible and adaptive to changing circumstances.

But these innovations in international financial markets also create problems.

- Most of the new financial instruments are off-balance-sheet transactions - although the risks of these new instruments do not differ from traditional on-balance-sheet activities to a large extent - so that national banking supervision cannot fully cover these new instruments. Consequently, market transparency has diminished. Additionally, it is questionable whether the amount of equity capital is still adequate.

- As a result of an increasing globalization, shocks and disruptions can be more quickly transmitted to markets, institutions, and geographic locations far away from the initial source of the shock.[45]

- Settlement risk became a top issue among international bankers, describing the danger that the counterpart of a trade in securities or foreign exchange will not perform either due to illiquidity or due to technical or operational difficulties which interrupt delivery of funds. The problems can be horrific, as in the case of the Bank of New York's computer failure in 1985 which forced the New York Federal Reserve to lend $23 billion to the banking system to stave off disaster.[46]

- Another danger arising from recent financial market developments is that the increased level of competition led to a sharp cut of profit margins. Currently, large parts of international capital market business are unprofitable, eventually

---

[45]   *Corrigan, E.G.*, ibid. (fn. 36), p. 2

[46]   See *Lascelles, D.* (1987), p. 21.

forcing many participants to drop out. But the drop-out of major market participants may cause serious crises of the international financial system.

- The expansion of international financial markets has taken place during a time
  of falling interest rates, economic growth, decreasing inflation, and a stock
  market booming around the world. The durability of globalization, liberalization, deregulation, and securitization will be tested in a reversed situation.

4.   Competing Institutional Arrangements for International Financial Markets

Several proposals for institutional arrangements in international financial markets
are made:

- To counter increasing protectionist pressure in banking and finance, a GATT
  for services is proposed. The liberalization of services has become a major
  issue in recent GATT negotiations, although it is argued that a GATT for
  services is not needed, because the division of international trade into categories of goods and services is artificial.[47]

- A policy of "national treatment", whereby foreign banks and security organizations have the same privileges and responsibilities as domestic institutions,[48]
  would be a major step towards free capital flows. Another important point to
  prevent protectionism in international banking and finance is the international
  harmonization of banking supervision regulations, which have to include
  capital adequacy standards as well as security market regulations. Harmonization may be reached under bilateral or multilateral agreements. A recent
  example of a bilateral contract is an agreement between the Bank of England
  and the banking authorities in the U.S. regarding a comprehensive and consistent approach to capital adequacy standards for U.S. and U.K. transnational

---

[47]   *Grubel, H.* (1987).

[48]   *Corrigan, E.J.*, ibid. (fn. 36), p.3.

banking organizations. Multilateral agreements may be reached under the auspices of GATT. Multilateral agreements achieve a wide spread of harmonization, but generally it takes a long time to reach consensus under the GATT legal framework.

- In order for regulatory authorities to regain control over national banking activities, two major approaches are possible. One is to create a functioning deposit insurance system with capital requirements, market value accounting, and closure rules, as well as variable insurance premiums. The other possibility is to create "riskless" banks through a separation of their payments and investment functions so that the deposit insurance system becomes largely superfluous.[49] But how should the national banking system be organized? Is it more preferable to allow large universal banks as in Germany and in Switzerland or to separate commercial and investment banking as under the Glass-Steagall Act? It is alleged that the separation of activities has fostered product innovations and shows a superior record in providing financial instruments with market determined yields.[50] But it seems that the monopolistic structures of a separated system lead to productivity losses, which caused its partial breakdown.[51]

Finally, it should be noted that innovation in financial instruments is a market response to unstable economic circumstances. An international monetary policy providing stable economic conditions would reduce many of these incentives for new financial instruments.

---

[49] *Scott, K.,* (1987).

[50] *Folkerts-Landau, D.* (1987).

[51] *Schaad, E.F.,* ibid. (Fn. 37), p. 47.

IV. Investments

1. Competing Economic Arrangements for the Transfer of Resources

It has been pointed out above that proposals for reform of the international trade
and monetary system depend crucially on the underlying economic assumption
about the functioning of the system. With respect to international investment (at
least in developing countries) the same picture arises, since the benefits of foreign
direct investment are not universally accepted. Singer[52] stresses that foreign direct
investment in the export sector of developing countries creates a dualistic economic
structure characterized by a high-productivity sector producing for primary exports
and a low-productivity sector producing for the domestic market. A continuous
productivity gap observed between the two sectors indicates that foreign investment
does not become an integral part of the LDCs and that the often claimed spread of
technology does not take place. Thus protection of the domestic industries should
occur, biasing the incentive structure against export-orientated industries.

His argument is much weaker today than in the 1950's, because the generalization
that developing countries export primary products cannot be made, nor is it
obvious that the export sector hampers technological progress. On the other hand,
every foreign investment need not be beneficial for the home country either. Investments in consumption industries and supply of consumer goods that create
demand through vigorous marketing without supplying positive externalities
(employment, technology) for the domestic economy, are an example.

a) The Concept of Foreign Direct Investment

The international transfer of resources is characterized as being external, if the
contracting parties are legally and economically independent. Trade is the most
important means of external resource flows, whereas internal flows of resources are

---

[52] *Singer, H.,* (1950), pp. 473-485.

carried out as direct investment.[53] Direct investments have to be distinguished from portfolio investments; in the latter case the investor does not seek managerial control. A direct investment may take the form of new ventures or of the acquisition of existing enterprises with substantial voting power, usually over 25%.[54]

Foreign Direct Investment has been booming in the past decade, reaching more than 57 billions of Special Drawing Rights (SDRs) in 1985.[55] No other major country outdoes the U.S. as a "multinational". U.S. investments abroad reached 18 billions of SDRs in 1985, whereas U.K. foreign investments amounted to 8 billions of SDRs; but Japanese and German companies are catching up rapidly, reaching 6.3 billions of SDRs (Japan) and 4 billions of SDRs (Germany). 98% of funds invested abroad are of industrial countries' origin and 70% of total FDI are investments in industrial countries as well. 30% (14 billions of SDRs in 1985) of foreign direct investment are made in developing countries, of which only a few, such as Saudi-Arabia (2.7 billions of SDRs), the People's Republic of China (1.6 billions of SDRs), Brazil (1.3 billions of SDRs), Singapore (1.1 billions of SDRs), Malaysia (0.675 billions of SDRs), and Mexico (0.5 billions of SDRs) attract the major share.

Increasing FDI is responsible for the current situation in which approximately one third of the world trade in manufactured goods is intra-company trade.

b) Incentives for Foreign Direct Investment

Why do enterprises invest abroad instead of exporting or licensing?[56]

One motivation for FDI is "*tariff jumping*": if a country has levied import tariffs, firms might choose not to export, but to undertake local production instead.[57] But

---

[53]   *Ebenroth, C.T.*, ibid. (fn. 1), p. 54; *Karl, J* (1987), pp. 17-18.

[54]   See *Deutsche Bundesbank* (1965), p. 19.

[55]   Data, regarding FDI, are taken from *IMF* (1986), pp. 64-69.

[56]   For a survey on this question see *Buckley, P.J.* (1981), pp. 70-81.

[57]   For a recent analysis of tariff jumping see *Bradner, J.A./Spencer, B.J.* (1987), pp. 257-279; see also *Caves, E.R.* (1982).

the multinational expansion of American enterprises to Europe began shortly after the 2nd World War, long before there was any threat of protectionism. And it was most vigorous in the two countries with the least danger of protectionism: Great Britain and West Germany. Similarly, the multinational investment of the Japanese in manufacturing plants in the U.S. began long before there was any threat of protectionism.

Another important factor of investment abroad are *marketing pressures*. It is simply not possible to maintain substantial market standing in an important area unless one has a physical presence as a producer.

Further, FDI is used as a *hedging instrument* against exchange rate insecurity, because income and costs are in the same currency. Sales can be kept at a constant level even in periods of appreciated currency in the country of the parent company, which usually leads to export losses due to increased prices in foreign markets.

A property rights approach to FDI offers an explanation why and under which circumstances investments abroad (internal transactions) lead to a reduction of transaction costs compared with other forms of resource flows, such as licensing or exporting (market transactions). This *internalization theory* as the modern theory of multinational enterprises (MNEs)[58] stresses international market imperfections as creating advantages of internalization.[59] Those are:

- the increased ability to control and plan production;

- exploitation of market power by discriminatory pricing;

- avoidance of potential government intervention by devices such as transfer prices;

- avoidance of uncertainties in the transfer of knowledge.[60]

---

[58]   *Rugman, A.M.* (1982), pp. 9-23 (11).

[59]   See *Buckley, P.J.*, ibid. (fn. 56), p. 77; *Ebenroth, C.T.*, ibid. (fn. 1), pp. 52, 248-251.

[60]   *Furubotn, E.G.* (1987).

2.   Competing Legal Arrangements for FDI

The legal framework of FDI is created on different levels:

The *national level* with regulations of the host country as well as regulations of the capital exporting country; *bilateral* agreements between both countries; contracts between the private investor and the host country; or *multilateral* agreements.

a)   Legal Framework of the Host Country

It is important for the host country to create a stable legal framework for FDI. Host countries are in competition with each other to attract foreign investment. The possibilities of a host country to influence its factor market are rather limited. But it can influence its institutional market in order to attract FDI even if factor markets do not offer the same attractive conditions to investors as other countries do.[61]

No country permits totally unrestricted foreign investment. Main legal instruments of host countries to influence FDI are regulations and restrictions of foreign trade and payments ("Aussenwirtschaftsgesetze"). Most of the developing countries, a lot of socialist countries, as well as "traditional" host countries such as Canada and Australia supervise and direct FDI by special *Investment Codes* which differ from each other according to the policy objectives of the host country's government.[62] In recent years a lot of countries, such as China, the USSR, Hungary, Yugoslavia, Mexico, Canada, etc., have deregulated their national investment codes in order to attract further foreign investment.[63] Some states have provided special investment

---

[61]   *Ebenroth, C.T.*, ibid. (fn. 1), p. 54.

[62]   *Ebenroth, C.T.*, ibid. (fn. 1), pp. 71-74.

[63]   In the recent German literature see *Ban, C.* (1986), pp. 429-433; *Bergmann, W.* (1986), pp. 695-697; *Berkemeier, A.* (1986), pp. 433-439; *Frisch-Philipp, W./Offergeld, K.* (1987), pp. 507-512; *Heuser, R.* (1986), pp. 423-426; *Kochinke, J.M.* (1986), pp. 520-525; *Kovac, J.* (1986), pp. 607-611; *Loitz, K.M.* (1986), pp. 870-871; *Münzel, F.* (1986), pp. 945-949; *Schweisfurth, T.* (1987), pp. 489-499.

areas ("Wirtschaftssonderzonen") to foreign investors where they offer investment incentives such as tax advantages or free repatriation of profits. Other investment codes require a so-called "local equity participation"; consequently FDI has to be organized as joint ventures, e.g. in Poland. China, as another example, has different investment regulations on FDI without Chinese participation, on equity joint ventures and on contractual joint ventures. Some countries "protect" special sectors of the economy; foreign investors are then illegal. Such "closed areas" are the electronic industry in Brazil and some branches in Poland such as the assurance industry. All investment codes require the information of national authorities, and generally a permission of the host country; though in the U.S. and in West Germany foreign investments are usually permitted.

It should be noted, however, that the change of national legislation has always been left to the host country due to the "lex posterior rule". Thus, national legislation of the host country cannot create a stable legal framework which protects the investor against disadvantages, e.g. against expropriation. From the investor's point of view other legal arrangements are required.

b)   Regulations of Capital Exporting Countries

A lot of capital exporting countries encourage national enterprises to invest in other countries, particularly in developing countries. These national regulations are generally intended to reduce the investors' political risks and to improve the conditions of an investment flow.[64]

The Federal Republic of Germany, as an example, has a broad legal program to encourage German investment abroad:

It assumes guarantees to insure political risks of German investments in developing countries.[65] The insured risks are:

---

[64]   *Ebenroth, C.T.*, ibid. (fn. 1), p. 74.

[65]   See § 9 Bundeshaushaltsgesetz 1986, BGBl. 1985 I, pp. 2338 ff.; amount insured 1986: DM 15 bn.

- expropriation, nationalization and similar measures of the host country;

- war, revolution and other armed conflicts;

- unilateral moratoriums of the host country;

- impossibility of capital transfers and repatriation.

Prerequisites for such a government guarantee are: 1. appropriate legal protection for the investment in the host country, and 2. social desirability of the investment for both countries.[66]

The German government further assumes guarantees for investments in the petrol industry due to service contracts, as well as guarantees for the cooperation of German firms in other foreign commodity projects,[67] and offers tax advantages for German investments abroad.[68]

It also offers loans up to DM 2.5 millions to small and middle-sized German enterprises to support the establishment of branches in developing countries,[69] and the "Deutsche Finanzierungsgesellschaft für Beteiligungen in Entwicklungsländern GmbH" (DEG), - a state-owned German financing and advice centre - offers financial aid for German joint ventures in developing countries as well.[70] Additionally, the "Deutsche Gesellschaft für Technische Zusammenarbeit" (GTZ) gives legal and technical advice for company cooperation.

---

[66] For further details see *Bundesanzeiger* Nr. 137 (30. 7. 1986), p. 10141.

[67] Survey in: *Bundesminister für Wirtschaftliche Zusammenarbeit (BMZ)*, (1987), pp. 55-57.

[68] Auslandsinvestitionsgesetz, in: *BGBl.* 1969, I, pp. 1211 ff.; zuletzt geändert durch das 22. Haushaltsstrukturgesetz, BGBl. 1981, I, p. 1523; Entwicklungsländer-Steuergesetz, BGBl. 1979, I, p. 558; see further the Double Taxation Agreements between West Germany and 55 foreign countries, a list is in: BStBl. 1987, I, p. 164.

[69] See *Bundesanzeiger* Nr. 133 (20.7.1979).

[70] For details see *BMZ*, ibid. (fn. 67), pp. 62-66.

466

c) Bilateral Investment Treaties

In order to improve the investor's legal protection in the host country, a lot of states have reached bilateral investment treaties (worldwide more than 200). Most of them involve West Germany (51 on 1st October, 1986),[71] followed by the U.S. and Switzerland. The United States, relying until recently on investment guarantee clauses in her "Treaties of Friendship, Commerce and Navigation" with other nations, has now developed a "Model Bilateral Investment Treaty", and negotiates treaties of that type with several developing countries.[72] West German treaties follow a model draft treaty as well.[73] Generally, all bilateral investment treaties contain the following rules:

- a definition of "expropriation", the prerequisites of an expropriation in the host country, and regulations on the compensation; generally, the compensation has to be "prompt, adequate and effective";

- a guarantee for free flows of capital and gains;

- a most-favoured nation treatment; companies of the contracting party have to be treated in the same way as own nationals, or companies of any third state; exemption: companies of third countries on account of their membership in, or association with, a customs or economic union, a common market of a free trade area.

But bilateral investment treaties only entitle the "home country" of the investor to perform legal protection in the case of illegal treatment by the host country. The

---

[71] See the list of West Germany's bilateral investment treaties in: *BMZ*, ibid. (fn. 67), pp. 140-142.

[72] *Riesenfeld, St.A.* (1985), pp. 246-250 (249).

[73] See, as an example, the "Treaty between Somaly Democratic Republic and the Federal Republic of Germany Concerning the Encouragement and Reciprocal Treatment of Investments", in: *Ebenroth, C.T.*, ibid. (fn. 1), pp. 647-659 (Annexe IX).

"home country" is the country with which the investor has a "genuine link". A genuine link requires 1. the legal competence of the home country over the investment, and 2. the principal domicile of the business head-quarter to be in the home country. The investor faces two disadvantages of such a legal construction: firstly, it is open whether the home country takes the dispute into arbitration or to the International Court of Justice, secondly - concerning the increasing internationalization of enterprises -, it will not be sure if the arbitration tribunal or the International Court of Justice acknowledges a country as a "home country" of the investor, as in the well known Barcelona Traction Case.[74]

d)   Investment Contracts Between the Investor and the Host Country

In order to protect foreign investment against subsequent legal changes and to avoid the investor's dependence on diplomatic protection by its home country, investment contracts between the investor and the host country evolved after World War II. These contracts intend to create a specific legal framework for one single investment and they are considered a supplement to national regulations as well as to bilateral agreements between the capital exporting country and the host country.

Investment contracts generally contain an *"arbitration clause"* entitling the private investor to sue the host country in the case of legal dissent about investments, e.g. the amount of compensation due to an expropriation by the host country.

Further, investment contracts often contain so-called *"stabilization clauses"* which try to avoid modifications of the investment conditions. The validity of these clauses is generally acknowledged; nevertheless, there have been international arbitration awards on liability for breach of contract, such as the Kuwait-

---

[74]   *ICJ* Reports (1970), pp. 3-357 ff.; see also *Wallace, D.C.* (1981), pp. 30-33.

AMINOIL Arbitration,[75] the Lybia-Oil Companies Arbitration,[76] and the Congo-AGIP Arbitration.[77]

Using a "*choice of law clause*", the investor tries to reach agreements with the host country on the application of a third country's law, or on public international law, thus preventing the host country from subsequently changing the law governing the contract. Notwithstanding the ruling of the Court of International Justice in the Serbian Loan Case,[78] it is now acknowledged that contracts between a state and a private law person are either subject to the law explicitly chosen by the parties, or if this did not take place, to the rules of the law closest to the contract.[79] Whereas Anglo-American lawyers are pragmatic (only asking what parties have agreed on), there is still some discussion about the legal character of such contracts (as in Germany).

e) Multilateral Agreements on Foreign Direct Investment

Up to now, only a few multilateral agreements on FDI have been negotiated.

(1) International Centre on Settlement of Investment Disputes (ICSID)

The convention on the ICSID from March 1965[80] created an international forum for investment litigations. The convention does not contain regulations relating to substantive law, but only establishes an organizational framework for the settlement of litigations.

---

[75]   *ILM*, Vol. XXI (1982), pp. 976-1053.

[76]   *ILM*, Vol. XVII (1978), pp. 1-37.

[77]   *Yearbook of Commercial Arbitration* (1983), p. 133.

[78]   Judgement No. 14, PCIJ Series C, No. 16 (III).

[79]   See *van Hecke, G.* (1984), pp. 54-59 (54).

[80]   Text in *ILM* (1965), p. 432.

(2)   Guaranteed Recovery of Investment Principle (GRIP)

Since summer 1986, the International Finance Corporation (IFC)[81] - a World Bank subsidiary - offers within the GRIP a new service to promote and to protect foreign investments as joint ventures in developing countries. It is intended to shift the investment risk from the private investor to the IFC. Therefore, the investor transfers his investment capital to the IFC, which participates in the joint venture on its own account. Profit will be shared between the investor and IFC, but the IFC bears the full risk of losses. Thus, the World Bank hopes to augment investment flows from industrialized countries to developing countries.

(3)   Multilateral Investment Guarantee Agency (MIGA)

The MIGA, a world bank foundation, pursues similar aims. According to Article 2 of the MIGA Convention from October 11th 1985, its objective is to encourage the flow of investment for productive purposes among member countries, particularly to developing countries (Article 14). To serve this objective, MIGA will issue guarantees against non-commercial risks. The Agency is entitled to carry out complementary activities, as well as to exercise incidental powers as "shall be necessary to the furtherance of its objective" (Article 2). The covered non-commercial risks are:

- currency transfer restrictions by the host governments (Article 11 a(i));

- expropriation and similar measures due to any legislative or administrative action or omission attributable to the host governments, with the exception of non-discriminatory measures which governments normally take to regulate economic activities in their territories (Article 11 a(ii));

- breach of contract if the investor does not have recourse to a judicial or arbitral forum, or such a decision is not rendered in a reasonable period of time (Article 11 (iii));

- war and civil disturbance (Article 11 (iv)).

---

[81]   See *Deutsche Bundesbank* (1986b), p. 48.

Disputes between the Agency and any member, or among members shall be submitted to the Board of Directors for a decision (Article 56 a). The Board will consist of a minimum of twelve directors (Article 32). But any member may refer to the Council of Governors - composed of one Governor appointed by each member country (Article 1 b) - for final decision (Article 56 b). Thus it can be foreseen that the attempts to specify a compensation to be paid when expropriating a foreign investment would be channeled into the settlement system which would create in an iterative way a multilaterally accepted definition of what property is.

The Convention, which is open to all World Bank member countries and Switzerland, will assume its activity if a minimum of five industrialized and fifteen developing countries deposit their ratification instruments, and the amount of not less than one third of the authorized capital (1 billion of SDRs) will be provided (Article 61 b).[82]

(4)   Code of Conduct

A further attempt to control FDI on a multilateral level are Codes of Conduct. Since 1977, several codes have been worked out by the UN. It is the "Tripartite Declaration Concerning Multilateral Enterprises and Social Policy" from November 16th 1977, adopted by the International Labour Organization (ILO),[83] the "Set of Multilaterally Agreed Equitable Principles and Rules for the Control of Restrictive Business Practices",[84] better known as "Restrictive Business Practice Code", adopted on April 22nd 1980, the "International Code of Marketing of Breastmilk Substitutes", dated May 21st 1981,[85] and the "International Code of Conduct on the Distribution and Use of Pesticides",[86] dated November 22nd 1985, as well as the "Draft International Code of Conduct on the Transfer of Technology" from

---

[82]   For further information see *Ebenroth, C.T.* (1987b), pp. 641-649.

[83]   Text in: *Ebenroth, C.T.*, ibid. (fn. 1), pp. 533-544 (Annexe I).

[84]   Text in: *Ebenroth, C.T.*, ibid. (fn. 1), pp. 545-554 (Annexe II).

[85]   Text in: *Ebenroth, C.T.*, ibid. (fn. 1), pp. 555-564 (Annexe III).

[86]   Text in: *Ebenroth, C.T.*, ibid. (fn. 1), pp. 565-582 (Annexe IV).

June 5th 1985.[87] Of particular significance for the flow of FDI is the "Draft United Nations Code of Conduct on Transnational Corporations",[88] dated June 2nd 1983. This Code comprises two main parts: one "Activity Part" (§§ 6-46) which contains duties for MNE's with respect to national sovereignty and observance of domestic laws, and secondly, a "Treatment Part" (§§ 47-58) containing the corresponding rights of MNE's. The Code of Conduct on Transnational Corporations intends to enhance the integration of MNE's into the economy of the host country. To fulfil this function it must be able to attract foreign investors.[89]

It is not contradictory that the Code is not legally binding; UN legal norms are not regarded as an integral part of public international law according to Article 38 of the ICJ Agreements. Thus, Codes of Conduct are often considered as international "soft law"; nevertheless, they may influence current law on different levels: on the international level, the Code might lead to a customary international law in the long run, creating legally binding norms according to Article 38 I lit. b ICJ Agreement. On the national level, the existence of the Code should influence domestic jurisdiction as well as domestic legislation. Even if a code will not be adopted - just as the Code of Conduct on Transnational Corporations and the Code on Technology Transfer which have not yet been agreed on fully - it serves as a negotiating scheme for the contracts between the investor and the host country.[90]

The above-described different legal arrangements for FDI could create a complete legal framework for international capital flows. It would not be a unified legal framework as, for example, the "Hague Uniform Law on the International Sales of Goods", or the "UNCITRAL Convention on the International Sales of Goods", but it might be adaptable to each foreign investment. And this seems to be an important aspect concerning the worldwide dispersal of FDI. Countries can then offset for low factor endowments by creating a liberal legal environment and thereby attract FDI.

---

[87]   Text in: *Ebenroth, C.T.*, ibid. (fn. 1), pp. 601-630 (Annexe VI).

[88]   Text in: *Ebenroth, C.T.*, ibid. (fn. 1), pp. 583-600 (Annexe V).

[89]   *Ebenroth, C.T.*, ibid. (fn. 1), pp. 67.

[90]   See *Ebenroth, C.T.*, ibid. (fn. 1), pp. 78-81.

472

V. Summary and Outlook

The above discussion has shown that internationalization has been proceeding rapidly in capital and direct investment markets as well as in international trade. This also holds for the service sector, which has not been analysed specifically. This continuing internationalization is still met by short-sighted, egoistic national economic policies. International cooperation, such as the 'Louvre Agreement' in the international monetary field, is not effective enough, as has been seen in recent months. The tension arising from the internationalization of the world economy and from an economic regulatory framework on the national level creates major economic and political problems. These differ, though, according to the nature of the economic transaction.

Mainstream economists have pointed out for decades that unrestricted trade is beneficial to world economic welfare. But since individual groups (with different degrees of influence in forming national policy perspectives) will be affected differently by free trade, national policies towards trade are not the same. Protectionism (in favour of import-competing industries), fierce supply competition (subsidizing exports), and differing policy objectives of international institutions influencing the international goods flows are a result of these differing national attitudes. As outlined above, institutional arrangements by UNCTAD, GATT, or the OECD are not able to regulate and to coordinate national policies affecting trade.

Different problems are encountered when one focuses on international investment and financial markets, which are characterized by 'demand competition', that is, countries try to supply a regulatory framework which attracts investors as well as financial transactions. The internationalization of the world economy creates fierce competition in both the factor and institutional markets, but since the former are not easily influenced, competition takes place mainly in institutional markets. The deregulation of national financial markets and the liberalization of numerous national investment codes in order to attract foreign investment are examples of such competition among countries. Particularly in the field of international capital transactions, national factor endowments are of minor significance; due to the rapid technical progress they can be carried out everywhere. States compete with each other in a 'race of laxity'.

A well-functioning world economy depends on coordination and cooperation between countries. Several recent crises emphasize this. Weak pollution regulations in order to attract foreign investments led to the export of pollution from industrialized to a large number of Third World countries. Countries with high environmental protection standards are disadvantaged. Even leading businessmen attribute the recent stock market disturbances to the uncontrolled liberalization of financial markets.[91] Necessary regulation of the institutional markets can only be reached by international cooperation. The internationalization of the world economy has to be accompanied by an internationalization of the regulatory authorities!

Two options exist to achieve such international cooperation: either the creation of uniform laws or the strengthening of international organizations. The former has proved to be difficult to achieve and lags behind the rapid pace of internationalization, as intended reforms, e.g. the uniform code of the sale of goods, have shown. The second alternative builds on restriction of national sovereignty, which countries are unwilling to give up (GATT). Furthermore, strategies are likely to achieve the smallest possible international consensus.

Are prospects for international institutional arrangements in the world economy quite small?

---

[91]   See *H. Kaufmann* (1987).

References

Albers, W. et al. (eds.) *Handwörterbuch der Wirtschafts-Wissenschaften*, Instalment 8, Tübingen, pp. 522 ff. (541).

Balassa, B. (1985), Exports, Policy Choices, and Economic Growth in Developing Countries after the 1973 Oil Shock, *Journal of Development Economics*, Vol. 18, pp. 23-35.

Baldwin, R.E. (1969), The Case Against Infant-Industry Protection, *Journal of Political Economy* 77, pp. 295-305.

Baldwin, R.E. (1982), The Political Economy of Protectionism, in: Bhagwati, J. (ed.), *Import Competition and Response*, Chicago, University of Chicago Press, pp. 263-286.

Ban, C. (1986), Erweiterte Möglichkeiten für ausländische Investitionen in Ungarn: Gemischte Gesellschaften in zollfreien Zonen, in: *RIW*, pp. 429-433.

Bauer, H.P. (1987), Kapitalmarkt-Swaps und Swap Markt, in: *Der Schweizer Treuhänder* 5/87, p. 183-189.

Bergmann, W. (1986), Neue Joint Venture-Gesetzgebung in Polen, in: *RIW*, pp. 695-697.

Berkemeier, A. (1986), Technolgietransfer-Verträge nach Brasilien im Spannungsfeld zwischen Privatautonomie und staatlicher Wirtschaftsintervention, in: *RIW*, pp. 433-439.

Bernhardt, R. (ed.): *Encyclopedia of Public International Law*, Instalment 8, pp. 397/398.

Bhagwati, J. (ed.), (1982), *Import Competition and Response*, University of Chicago Press, Chicago.

Bradner, J.A./Spencer, B.J. (1987), Foreign Direct Investment With Unemployment and Endogenous Taxes and Tariffs, in: *Journal of International Economics* 22, pp. 257-279.

Buckley, P.J. (1981), A Critical Review of the Multinational Enterprise, in: *Aussenwirtschaft*, pp. 70-81.

Bundesanzeiger (20.7.1979), Nr. 133, "Förderrichtlinien".

Bundesanzeiger (30. 7. 1986), Nr. 137, p. 10141, "Richtlinie für die Übernahme von Garantien für Kapitalanlagen im Ausland vom 21. 7. 1986"; "Allgemeine Bedingungen für die Übernahme von Garantien für Kapitalanlagen im Ausland", September 1986.

Bundesminister für Wirtschaftliche Zusammenarbeit (BMZ), (1987), *Deutsche Unternehmen in Entwicklungsländern*, 3rd ed., pp. 55-57.

Caves, E.R. (1982), *Multinational Enterprise and Economic Analysis.*

Chow, P.C.Y. (1987), Export Growth and Industrial Development, *Journal of Development Economics* 26, pp. 55-63.

Corrigan, E.G. (1987), Coping with Globally Integrated Markets, *FRBNY Quarterly Review*/Winter 1987, p. 1.

Curzon, G. and V. (1986), Defusing Conflict Between Traders and Non-Traders, *The World Economy*, Vol. 9, pp. 19-35.

Dam, Kenneth W. (1977), *The GATT: Law and International Economic Organization*, University of Chicago Press.

Denning, U. (1987), Die Deregulierung des internationalen Finanzsystems seit 1975, forthcoming in *Hamburger Jahrbuch für Wirtschafts- und Gesellschaftspolitik*, 32. Jahr.

Deutsche Bundesbank (1965), Die deutschen Direktinvestitionen im Ausland, in: *Monatsberichte der Deutschen Bundesbank*, December, p. 19.

Deutsche Bundesbank (1986a), Innovationen im internationalen Bankgeschäft, in: *Monatsberichte der Deutschen Bundesbank*, April, p. 25.

Deutsche Bundesbank (1986b), Internationale Organisationen und Abkommen im Bereich von Währung und Wirtschaft, Sonderdruck Nr. 3, 3rd ed., p. 48.

Deutsche Bundesbank (1987), Die Auslandsbanken - eine neue Untergruppe der Bankenstatistik, in: *Monatsberichte der Deutschen Bundesbank* (January), pp. 32-37.

Dombret, A. (1987), Securitization, in: *Zeitschrift für das gesamte Kreditwesen* 8/1987, p. 326.

Ebenroth, C.T. (1987a), Code of Conduct - Ansätze zur vertraglichen Gestaltung internationaler Investitionen, pp. 46-47.

Ebenroth, C.T. (1987b), Zur Bedeutung der Multilateral Investment Guarantee Agency für den internationalen Ressourcentransfer, in: *JZ*, pp. 641-649.

Edwards, S. (1987), Implications of Alternative International Exchange Rate Arrangements for the Developing Countries, Konstanz Symposium Paper, July.

Eggerstedt, H., Hentschel, J. and Noh, T.J. (1987), Quantitative Trade Restrictions Against Developing Countries, *Asian Economies* 62, pp. 5-23.

Finger, M.J. (1987), Protectionist Rules and International Discretion in the Making of National Trade Policy, Konstanz Symposium Paper, July.

Folkerts-Landau, D. (1987), The Process of Innovation, Institutional Change and Regulatory Response in the International Financial Markets, Konstanz Symposium Paper, July.

Franke, G. (1987), Organisation und Regulierung internationaler Finanzmärkte, in: Schneider, D. (ed.), *Kapitalmarkt und Finanzierung*, Schriften des Vereins für Socialpolitik, Gesellschaft für Wirtschafts- und Sozialwissenschaften, Instalment 165, Berlin, pp. 429-444 (436).

Frisch-Philipp, W./Offergeld, K. (1987), Neuerungen für ausländische Investitionen in Mexiko, in: *RIW*, pp. 507-512.

Furubotn, E.G. and Pejovich, S. (1974), *The Economics of Property Rights*, Cambridge, Mass.

Furubotn, E.G. (1987), Property Rights in Information and the Multinational Firm: The Case of Technical Learning in a Multiplant System, Konstanz Symposium Paper, July.

Gold, J. (1984), Legal and Institutional Aspects of the International Monetary System: Selected Essays (Vol. II), IMF, Washington D.C., p. 38.

Grubel, H. (1987), Does the World Need a GATT for Services?, Konstanz Symposium Paper, July.

Hamilton, C. (1984), Economic Aspects of "Voluntary Export Restraints", Institute for International Economic Studies, Seminar Paper No. 290, Stockholm.

Hecke, G. van (1984), Contracts Between States and Foreign Private Law Persons, in: Bernhardt, R. (ed.), *Encyclopedia of Public International Law*, Instalment 7, pp. 54-59 (54).

Heitger, B. (1987), Import Protection and Economic Performance - Their Impact on Economic Growth, *Weltwirtschaftliches Archiv*, 123, pp. 249-261.

Heuser, R. (1986), Das Recht ausländisch kapitalisierter Unternehmen in der Volksrepublik China, in: *RIW*, pp. 423-426.

Hillman, A.L. (1987), Policy Motives and International Trade Restrictions, Konstanz Symposium Paper, July.

ILM, (1965), Vol. IV , p. 432.

ILM, (1978) Vol. XVII, pp. 1-37.

ILM, (1982) Vol. XXI, pp. 976-1053.

IMF (1986), Balance of Payments Statistics, pp. 64-69.

IMF (1987), World Economic Outlook.

Issing, O. (1980), Währungspolitik, internationale, in: *Handwörterbuch der Wirt-schafts-Wissenschaften*, Albers, W. et al. (eds.), Instalment 8, Tübingen, pp. 522 ff. (541).

Johnson, H.G. (1950-51), Optimum Welfare and Tax Revenue Tariffs, *Review of Economic Studies* XIX, pp. 28-35.

Karl, J. (1987), *Die Potentialorientierung beim internationalen Ressourcentransfer*, pp. 17-18.

H. Kaufmann, Chief Economist of Salomon Bros. Inc. (1987), cited in *Süddeutsche Zeitung* of October 29, 1987, "'Zinspapst' fördert straffere Zügel".

Kochinke, J.M. (1986), Das rechtliche Umfeld von Investitionen in Belize, in: *RIW*, pp. 520-525.

Kovac, J. (1986), Gründung und Geschäftsführung von Wertungen ausländischer Unternehmen in Jugoslawien, in: *RIW*, pp. 607-611.

Langhammer, R. (1987), Die Sonderbehandlung der Entwicklungsländer im GATT - Eine Kosten- und Nutzenbilanz, manuscript paper for 50th membership meeting of Association of Economic Research Institutes, Bonn, April.

Lascelles, D. (1987), Settlement Risk Becomes a Top Issue, in: *Financial Times*, July 3, p. 21.

Loitz, K.M. (1986), Neues Investitionsgesetz in Kanada, in: *RIW*, pp. 870-871.

Mann, F.A. (1985), Monetary Law, International, in: Bernhardt, R. (ed.), *Encyclopedia of Public International Law*, Instalment 8, pp. 397/398.

Münzel, F. (1986), Neue Regeln zur Investitionsförderung in China, in: *RIW*, pp. 945-949.

Novel, P. (1985), A Quoi Bon Réformer le Système Monétaire International, in: *Le Monde Diplomatique* 11/1985, pp. 8/9.

Palmer, J.D. (1986), "Big Bang goes the Market", in: *Time*, Oct. 27, 1986, pp. 38-43 (40).

Prebisch, R. (1950), The Economic Development of Latin America and its Principal Problems, United Nations Commission for Latin America.

Prebisch, R. (1965), Towards a New Trade Policy, Proceedings of the United Nations Conference on Trade and Development.

Riesenfeld, St.A. (1985), Foreign Investments, in: Bernhardt, R. (ed.), *Encyclopedia of Public International Law*, Instalment 8, pp. 246-250 (249).

Rugman, A.M. (1982), Internalization and Non-Equity Forms of International Involvement, in: Rugman (ed.), *New Theories of the Multinational Enterprise*, pp. 9-23 (11).

Sachs, J. (1986), The Uneasy Case for Greater Exchange Rate Coordination, in: *American Economics Association Papers*, May.

Samuelson, P.A. (1962), The Gains from Trade Once Again, *Economic Journal* 12, pp. 820-829.

Schaad, E.F. (1987), Tendenzen im internationalen Banking, in: *Der Schweizer Treuhänder* 2/87, p. 45-51.

Schatzmann, H. (1987), Neue Kapitalmarktformen: Eine Folge der "Securitization", in: *Der Schweizer Treuhänder* 5/87, p. 178.

Schwarck, E. (1987), Das neue Kapitalmarktrecht, in: *NJW*.

Schweisfurth, T. (1987), Die Rechtsgrundlagen für Gemeinschaftsunternehmen in der Sowjetunion, in: *RIW*, pp. 489-499.

Scott, K. (1987), Domestic Bank Regulations in a World of International Banking, Konstanz Symposium Paper.

Singer, H. (1950), The Distribution of Gains between Investing and Borrowing Countries, in: *American Economic Review* 40, pp. 473-485.

Stevenson, M. (1987), "Survey: International Banking", in: *The Economist*, March 21, p. 4.

Viner, J. (1950), The Customs Union Issue, Carnegie Endowment for International Peace, New York.

Wallace, D.C. (1981), Barcelona Traction Case, in: Bernhardt, R. (ed.), *Encyclopedia of Public International Law*, Instalment 2, pp. 30-35.

Wegner, M. (1987), The European Monetary System: A Regional Bretton Woods or an Institutional Innovation?, Konstanz Symposium Paper, July.

Willett, T.D. (1987), A Public Choice Analysis of Strategies for Restoring International Economic Stability, Konstanz Symposium Paper, July

World Bank Report (1987), World Bank, Washington, D.C.

Yearbook of Commercial Arbitration (1983), Vol. 8, pp. 133.

Participants

Bernholz, Peter
(Discussion of Paper 2)

Professor der Volkswirtschaftslehre
Institut für Sozialwissenschaften
der Universität Basel, Schweiz

Borner, Silvio
(Discussion of Paper 6)

Professor der Volkswirtschaftslehre
Institut für Angewandte Wirtschaftsforschung
Universität Basel, Schweiz

Chipman, John S.
(Discussion of Paper 1)

Professor of Economics
Department of Economics
University of Minnesota
Minneapolis, U.S.A.
and Permanent Guest Professor
Universität Konstanz
Bundesrepublik Deutschland

Ebenroth, Carsten Thomas
(Author of Paper 14)

Professor der Rechtswissenschaft
Juristische Fakultät
Universität Konstanz
Bundesrepublik Deutschland

Edwards, Sebastian
(Author of Paper 2)

Professor of Economics
National Bureau of Economic
Research, and
Department of Economics
University of California
Los Angeles, U.S.A

Finger, J. Michael
(Author of Paper 10)

Chief
International Economic Research Division
Development Research Dept.
The World Bank
Washington, D.C., U.S.A.

Folkerts-Landau, David F.I.
(Author of Paper 5)

Research Department
International Monetary Fund
Washington, D.C., U.S.A.

Franke, Günter
(Author of Paper 6)

Professor der Betriebswirtschaftslehre
Fakultät für Wirtschaftswissenschaften
Universität Konstanz
Bundesrepublik Deutschland

Furubotn, Eirik G.
(Author of Paper 12)

Professor of Economics
Department of Economics
College of Business Administration
The University of Texas at Arlington
U.S.A.

Genser, Bernd
(Discussion of Paper 7)

Professor der Volkswirtschaftslehre
Fakultät für Wirtschaftswissenschaften
Universität Konstanz
Bundesrepublik Deutschland

Grubel, Herbert G.
(Author of Paper 8)

Professor of Economics and Director,
Services Industries Study Project
The Fraser Institute
Vancouver, B.C., Canada

Hauser, Heinz
(Discussion of Paper 12)

Professor der Volkswirtschaftslehre
Institut für Aussenwirtschaft
der Universität St. Gallen, Schweiz

Hesse, Helmut
(Discussion of Paper 8)

Professor der Volkswirtschaftslehre
Volkswirtschaftliches Seminar
Universität Göttingen
Bundesrepublik Deutschland

Hillman, Arye L.
(Author of Paper 9)

Professor of Economics
Bar-Ilan University
Ramat Gan, Israel

Hufbauer, Gary C.
(Discussion of Paper 10,
 Session Chairman)

Professor of Economics
Karl F. Landegger Program
in International Business Diplomacy
School of Foreign Service
Georgetown University
Washington, D.C., U.S.A.

Kirchner, Christian
(Author of Paper 13)

Professor der Rechtswissenschaft
Fachbereich Rechtswissenschaften
Universität Hannover
Bundesrepublik Deutschland

Kreuzer, Karl
(Discussion of Paper 4)

Professor der Rechtswissenschaft
Juristische Fakultät
Universität Konstanz
Bundesrepublik Deutschland

Läufer, Nikolaus K.A.
(Discussion of Paper 5)

Professor der Volkswirtschaftslehre
Fakultät für Wirtschaftswissenschaften
Universität Konstanz
Bundesrepublik Deutschland

McCall, John
(Session Chairman)

Professor of Economics
Department of Economics
University of California
Los Angeles, U.S.A.

Molsberger, Josef
(Session Chairman)

Professor der Volkswirtschaftslehre
Fakultät für Wirtschaftswissenschaften
der Universität Tübingen
Bundesrepublik Deutschland

Niskanen, William A.
(Discussion of Paper 13)

Chairman
Cato Institute
Washington, D.C., U.S.A.

Ronning, Gerd
(Session Chairman)

Professor für Statistik und Ökonometrie
Fakultät für Wirtschaftswissenschaften
Universität Konstanz
Bundesrepublik Deutschland

Saunders, Anthony
(Co-author of Paper 7)

Professor of Economics
Graduate School of Business Administration
New York University
New York, N.Y., U.S.A.

Scott, Kenneth E.
(Author of Paper 4)

Parsons Professor of Law and Business
Stanford Law School
Stanford, California, U.S.A.

Siebert, Horst
(Author of Paper 11)

Professor der Volkswirtschaftslehre
Fakultät für Wirtschaftswissenschaften
Universität Konstanz
Bundesrepublik Deutschland

Thomas, Jonathan P.
(Discussion Summary
of Paper 11)

Sonderforschungsbereich 178
Universität Konstanz
Bundesrepublik Deutschland

Vaubel, Roland
(Discussion of Paper 3)

Professor der Volkswirtschaftslehre
Fakultät für Volkswirtschaftslehre
Universität Mannheim
Bundesrepublik Deutschland

Vosgerau, Hans-Jürgen
(Editor - Introduction,
Session Chairman)

Professor der Volkswirtschaftslehre
Fakultät für Wirtschaftswissenschaften
Universität Konstanz
Bundesrepublik Deutschland

Walter, Ingo
(Co-author of Paper 7)

Professor of Economics
Graduate School of Business Administration
New York University
New York, N.Y., U.S.A.

Wegner, Manfred
(Author of Paper 3)

Vorstandsmitglied
Ifo-Institut für Wirtschaftsforschung
München, Bundesrepublik Deutschland

Willett, Thomas D.
(Author of Paper 1,
 discussion of Paper 9)

Professor of Economics
The Claremont Center for
Economic Policy Studies
Claremont Graduate School
Claremont, California, U.S.A.

G. Gandolfo

International Economics

International Economics I

The Pure Theory of International Trade

1987. 83 figures. XVIII, 319 pages.
ISBN 3-540-17971-2

International Economics II

**International Monetary Theory
and Open-Economy Macroeconomics**

1987. 50 figures. XX, 507 pages.
ISBN 3-540-17978-X

These textbooks deal with a broad range of aspects in
international economics, including new topics, topics
usually omitted from textbooks and new research
results. The books are therefore also useful as reference books. They are designed for use at both undergraduate and graduate levels. This is possible
because of their two-tier structure: the text speaks
directly to the undergraduate reader in extremely
clear verbal and graphic terms, while the appendices,
which form the second tier, are addressed to the
graduate student and the researcher. They are self-
contained treatments, in mathematical terms, of the
topics examined in the text and include generaliza-
tions and/or additional topics not dealt with there.
Each chapter contains an exhaustive and up-to-date
bibliography, which lecturers will find especially
useful in preparing selected reading lists. The ample
and balanced treatment of the various approaches to
international economics, the undogmatic and eclectic
presentation, and the clarity of exposition ensure that
the reader gains a thorough grasp of theories, facts,
and policies.

Springer-Verlag
Berlin Heidelberg New York
London Paris Tokyo Hong Kong

Springer

Yoshihiko Otani, Mohamed El-Hodiri

Microeconomic Theory

1987. Approx. 320 pages. ISBN 3-540-17994-1

This text presents a rigorous and reasonably complete statement of microeconomic theory as it exists today. It starts with a unified treatment of consumers' demand, followed by an exposition of the theory of production as well as costs and profit functions of competitive firms. Market structures are then studied in detail and finally a brief introduction to general equilibrium and welfare economics is presented.

The book contains many examples, exercises and illustrations. The method of exposition unifies several approaches to the subject. The treatment of market structure is unique and more detailed than any other book on microeconomic theory. Several parts of the book reflect the original research of the authors that has not appeared in book form before. The text attempts to give rigorous foundations to the material presented in intermediate microeconomics textbooks.

B. Felderer, S. Homburg

Macroeconomics and New Macroeconomics

1987. 97 figures. XIII, 329 pages. ISBN 3-540-18004-4

This book gives a comprehensive account of traditional and more recent developments in macroeconomic theory. It is primarily written for students at the intermediate level. The book differs from the customary expositions in that the authors do not discuss topic by topic but doctrine by doctrine. Thus, the main approaches, such as classical theory, Keynesian theory, theory of portfolio selection, monetarism, rational expectations theory, and Neokeynesian disequilibrium theory, are presented in historical order. Each of these approaches is substantiated and criticized in a self-contained chapter, and the authors have taken great efforts to bring out the relations and differences between them. A mathematical appendix contains reviews of those mathematical facts which are especially important to macroeconomic models and makes the text easy to read.

Springer-Verlag
Berlin Heidelberg New York
London Paris Tokyo Hong Kong

Springer